ECOHOUSE:
A DESIGN GUIDE

KU-015-697

ECOHOUSE:
A DESIGN GUIDE

Third edition

Sue Roaf, Manuel Fuentes and Stephanie Thomas

AMSTERDAM • BOSTON • HEIDELBERG • LONDON • NEW YORK • OXFORD
PARIS • SAN DIEGO • SAN FRANCISCO • SINGAPORE • SYDNEY • TOKYO
Architectural Press is an imprint of Elsevier

Architectural
Press

Architectural Press is an imprint of Elsevier
Linacre House, Jordan Hill, Oxford OX2 8DP, UK
30 Corporate Drive, Suite 400, Burlington, MA 01803, USA

First published 2001
Reprinted 2001, 2002
Second edition 2003
Reprinted 2004, 2005, 2006
Third edition 2007

Copyright © 2001, 2003, 2007 Sue Roaf. Published by Elsevier Ltd. All rights reserved.

The right of Sue Roaf to be identified as the author of this work has been asserted in accordance with the
Copyright, Designs and Patents Act 1988

No part of this publication may be reproduced, stored in a retrieval system or transmitted in any form or by
any means electronic, mechanical, photocopying, recording or otherwise without the prior written
permission of the publisher

Permissions may be sought directly from Elsevier's Science & Technology Rights Department in Oxford, UK:
phone (+44) (0)1865 843830; fax (+44) (0)1865 853333; email: permissions@elsevier.com. Alternatively
you can submit your request online by visiting the Elsevier website at http://elsevier.com/locate/permissions,
and selecting *Obtaining permission to use Elsevier material*

Notice
No responsibility is assumed by the publisher for any injury and/or damage to persons or property as a
matter of products liability, negligence or otherwise, or from any use or operation of any methods, products,
instructions or ideas contained in the material herein

British Library Cataloguing-in-Publication Data
A catalogue record for this title is available from the British Library

Library of Congress Cataloging-in-Publication Data
A catalog record for this title is available from the Library of Congress

ISBN: 978-0-7506-6903-0

For information on all Architectural Press publications
visit our website at www.architecturalpress.com

Typeset by Charon Tec Ltd (a macmillan company), Chennai, India
Printed and bound in Slovenia

07 08 09 10 11   10 9 8 7 6 5 4 3 2 1

Working together to grow
libraries in developing countries

www.elsevier.com | www.bookaid.org | www.sabre.org

ELSEVIER   BOOK AID International   Sabre Foundation

CONTENTS

ACKNOWLEDGEMENTS

The authors would like to thank the following people for their help in building this third edition of *Ecohouse* into an invaluable companion for the ecohouse warrior:

For chapters: Christopher Day, Andre Viljoen, Matthew Rhodes, Ian Pritchett, John Peapell, Craig Simmons, Jair Harder, Nick Grant, John Willoughby and Fergus Nicol.

For contributions to chapters: Paul Jennings, Peter Warm, Chris Kendrick, Dave Anderson, Eddie Matthews, Jeremy Dain, Chiheb Bouden, Julian Bishop, Susan Dean, and Robert and Brenda Vale.

For the maps of climate: Cherry Bonaria and drawings: Michael Howlett.

For case studies: Bjorn Berge, Krister Wiberg, Prashant Kapoor, Misawa Homes, Toshio Ota, Pablo La Roche, Mike Draper, Mike Wnek, Mike Mullins, Johan Vorster, Jimmy Lim, Puteri SC Cempaka, Felix Riedweg, Graham Duncan, Ashok Lall, Isaac Meir, Martin Evans and Silvia Schiller, David Morrison, Jose Roberto Garcia-Chavez, Charles Middleton, Christopher Day, Chiheb Bouden and the Canada Mortgage & Housing Corporation.

For support during the writing of the book: Ana Lopez and Lucas, Pedro, Paula and Lara Fuentes, Ryan Rees and Coral Rees Stephanie's beautiful new daughter; Christopher, Richard and Christina Roaf for their kindness and, for his continued help, Nigel Aust who built the new Oxford Ecokitchen (and much of the Oxford Ecohouse too).

For our publishers: thank you particularly to Soo Hamilton without whom the third edition would never have appeared, and to Alex who saw the value of making this happen. Also to Margaret Denley for her continued oversee-ing of the edition and to Neil Boon who has done so much to help promote the book.

For all our readers: thank you for your continued interest and please send in your ideas for the fourth edition as well, because we know there will be one. Ecohouses are now an established part of our vision for a sustainable future and a welcome reality for all those of us who are already lucky enough to be living in one.

Porpoise Point Ecohouse, designed by Stephanie Thomas.

INTRODUCTION TO THIRD EDITION

PASSIVE SURVIVAL HOUSING

Six years after writing the introduction to the first edition of *Ecohouse*, I sit in my Oxford study, looking out over the trees, and wonder that some still have their leaves on in early December. I am wearing a T-shirt in an unheated room and thinking, 'Oh my God, we were so right. It is all happening just as we said it would!' But the world is changing faster than I ever envisaged that handful of years ago.

We first published *Ecohouse* in 2001 and in that introduction we covered theoretical concerns over climate change and fossil fuel depletion. By the second edition of *Ecohouse*, published in 2003, these concerns were firming up with the emerging reality of more extreme climate events and growing publicity over the issue of 'Peak Oil'.

But even in the three years since 2003 so many alarming events and trends have been written on the faces of cities like New Orleans or the landscapes outside our own windows that we are all beginning to get an inkling that there is much worse to come. Even in America the cosy talk amongst the educated architects of 'Sustainable Buildings' has turned to discussions of how we design for 'Passive Survival' in our own homes, when the power fails and the storms menace[1]. People are beginning to take heed of the growing clarion calls for action in the face of the irrefutable evidence of a rapidly changing climate[2].

Four events in particular have penetrated through to the 'conventional wisdom' of the thinking public. The first was the effect of the European heatwave of the summer of 2003 that killed over 35 000 people, of whom some 15 000 alone lived in France. Many were the vulnerable elderly, living on the top floors of blocks with the traditional French, un-insinuated metal, roofs. So even traditional vernacular buildings were beginning to need adaptation to provide adequate shelter for their occupants in extreme weather[3], let alone the 'modern buildings' that typically rely on using large amounts of energy to stay comfortably cool or warm, even in temperate climates.

A heatwave also triggered the second event, the power failure that affected over 50 million people in the Eastern Seaboard of the United States of America in August 2003. In New York people had to evacuate most of the buildings in the city, because they had non-opening windows and air-conditioning systems in which the air for breathing ran out in under an hour, and internal temperatures surged within minutes. Again these buildings had failed to provide adequate shelter in extreme conditions. What was a unique 'New York' experience on a hot summer evening with people safely sleeping on the streets may, if that had happened during a snow storm in winter, have resulted in untold loss of human life.

1.
The lights go out in New York in August 2003. How many would die if this happened in a blizzard? (Source: AP/Empics).

The third event that shocked the world was the flooding of New Orleans by Hurricane Katrina in September 2005. It was not only the scale of the destruction that occurred to the buildings and the city that made the world hold its breath in horror, but the failure of the social support systems of the United States of America, supposedly the richest country on earth, to deal with the human tragedy that unfolded before our eyes.

The fourth factor has been the inexorable rise of oil and gas prices around the world, heralding the fact that we are beginning to run out of secure supplies of oil and gas[4]. In the last two years alone our gas and electricity bills have doubled in the UK, and over 1.2 million households of the 20 million in England alone have fallen into fuel poverty during that time (namely the old, the young and the poor). At the Conference on Oil Depletion at the UK Energy Institute[5] on 7 November 2006 Chris Skrebowski, a globally recognised expert, concluded that oil supplies will peak round 2010–2011 at around 92–94 million barrels per day. Speakers also voiced their alarm at the prospect of both oil and gas shortages in the UK, Europe and the rest of the world in the near future due to a range of supply problems[6].

A least we now have politicians around the world waking up to the need to act in the face of the growing economic impacts of climate change. On 30 October 2006 Sir Nicholas Stern published his *Review on the Economics of Climate Change*[7]. This was the first comprehensive UK review of the subject and clearly demonstrated that all countries will be affected by climate change, but Stern stressed that the poorest countries will suffer earliest and most. The review's major conclusions were that average temperatures could rise by 5°C from pre-industrial levels if climate change goes unchecked. Stern shows that warming of 3°C or 4°C will result in many millions more people being flooded. By the middle of the century 200 million may be permanently displaced due to rising sea levels, heavier floods and drought. Warming of 4°C or more is likely to seriously affect global food production, but by then growing areas of the world will be simply too hot to inhabit.

Warming of 2°C could leave 15–40% of the world's species facing extinction. The review reiterates that before the industrial revolution the level of greenhouse gases in the atmosphere was 280 parts per million (ppm) of CO_2 (equivalent); the current level is 383 ppm CO_2 and the level must be limited (by means, we maintain, of Contraction and Conversion policies and mechanisms[8]) to not exceed 450–550 ppm CO_2. Anything higher would substantially increase risks of very harmful impacts. But Stern claims that anything lower would impose very high adjustment costs in the near term and might not even be feasible. He states very clearly that climate change is the greatest and widest-ranging market failure ever seen.

Stern states that what we do now can have only a limited effect on the climate over the next 40 or 50 years, but what we do in the next 10–20 years can have a profound effect on the climate in the second half of this century[9]. What he does not deal with is the significance of buildings as generators of climate change. Buildings use over half of all the energy consumed globally and are responsible for over half of all the climate change emissions, yet year on year 'modern' fashionable buildings become more energy profligate.

The damage this is doing to our cities and businesses is dealt with in another London report, *Faulty Towers*[10], published in July 2006 by the international architectural group 'Gensler'. The authors issue a stark warning to commercial property investors that 75% of property developers believe that impending legislation to grade the energy efficiency of buildings (in response to the EPBD, the European 'Energy Performance of Buildings Directive'[11]) will have a negative impact on the value and transferability of inefficient buildings when certification is imposed from 2007. The report claims that 'Property fund managers are effectively sitting on an investment time bomb. The introduction of energy performance certificates will shorten the lifespan of commercial buildings constructed before the new regulations, and we expect the capital value of inefficient buildings to fall as a result.'

This will happen with homes as well when the requirement for an Energy Certificate – to be produced on the point of sale of every house in Europe – kicks in during 2007[12]. This means that anyone trying to sell a house that is expensive to run will find it increasingly difficult to dispose of. Another potential blight on housing sales relates to homes on the flood plains that may no longer be eligible for flood insurance after 2007[13].

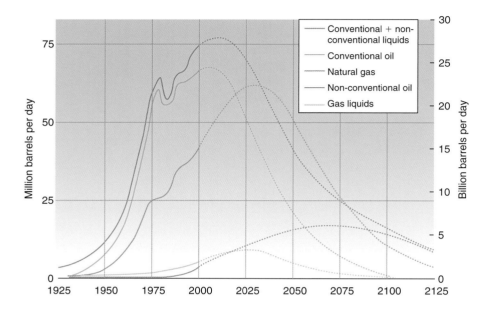

2.

Historical data to 2000, and projections thereafter, on when various fossil fuel reserve outputs will peak. Based on studies by a range of authors including Campbell and Lahererrere.[4] (Source: Boyle, G., Everett, B. and Ramage, J. (eds). (2004). *Energy Systems and Sustainability*. Oxford University Press, p. 289).

This book deals with the design and building of actual houses. Since it was published we have produced *Closing the Loop: Benchmarks for Sustainable Buildings*, in which we have tried to help people understand a wider range of the 'sustainability' issues relating to buildings including how to define and measure quality of life, community, transport, waste, air, land and water pollution, etc. If you are interested in these subjects it is a useful reference book[14].

In 2005 we produced a further, more shocking book, *Adapting Buildings and Cities for Climate Change*, in which were described, in detail, the ways in which the climate is changing, and how these changes will affect the design and performance of buildings and cities in an era of rising fossil fuel prices[3]. Writing this book made me thank God for my own safe secure ecohouse. I have just paid my quarterly gas bill, double what it was last year, but then again it is only £17.50! My bills will double in the next few years then double again and again. That is what the future will be like. Even then I will only pay around £150 for the quarter. What if you pay £300 a quarter for gas now? A quarterly bill for you in the future would be £2400. It would be impossible to pay. This is why everyone in the UK, indeed in the world, has to wake up now to the challenge of surviving in the coming years and decades in a world with more extreme weather and spiralling fossil fuel energy prices.

This is why we have included in the third edition of *Ecohouse* many more ways to exploit the clean, free, infinitely renewable energy around us to power our buildings, with new chapters on wind, hydro, ground source heat pumps, biomass and more on water conservation. We introduce more information on low embodied energy building materials and construction approaches and some fascinating new case studies.

What has become clear in the past three years of rapid change since the second edition was published is that we have the technology to survive – in fact we all had the necessary technology in the local shops in Oxford in 1995. What we desperately need now is the 'Eco-society' that will enable the necessary changes to happen in time to ensure that everyone, especially the vulnerable, can 'future-proof' themselves against what lies ahead. We urgently need to:

1 Adapt to mitigate our emissions until each of us only produces their fair earth share of greenhouse gasses, in every country, in line with the method of 'Contraction and Convergence', as set out by the Global Commons Institute[8].
2 Adapt our buildings so that we are able to survive in them through the worst that the climate can throw at us, even when the lights go out.
3 Adapt to increase the resilience of our communities to ensure that the fabric of our 'civilised' societies remains in tact through the changes ahead.

At the heart of all these 'adaptations' is the robust, resilient and safely located ecohouse, powered by renewable energy and embedded in a strong community. If you think that someone else is going to make all that happen for you, you are almost certainly wrong. It is up to you now to ensure that you, your family, your community your business, your society, your economy are all safe, because without all of them in tact it just may not be worth surviving through the coming decades of the twenty-first century.

And the time to start work on all of this is NOW, because we have around ten years before our actions cease to be important in the battle against climate change.

Sue Roaf
July 2007

The Moving Finger writes; and, having writ,
Moves on:
nor all your Piety nor Wit
Shall lure it back to cancel half a Line,
Nor all your Tears wash out a Word of it.

Omar Khayyam
Born: May 31, 1048 in Nishapur, Iran : Died: December 4, 1131

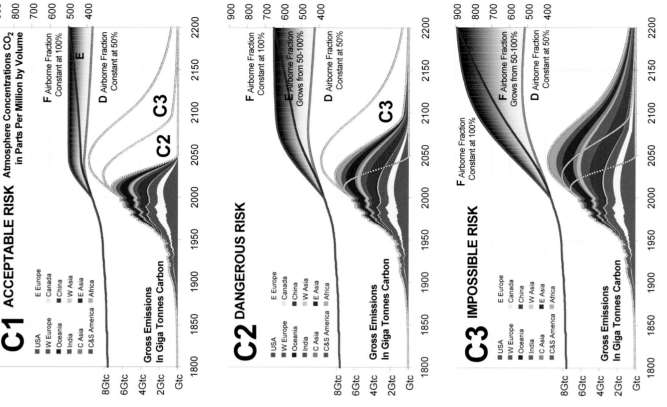

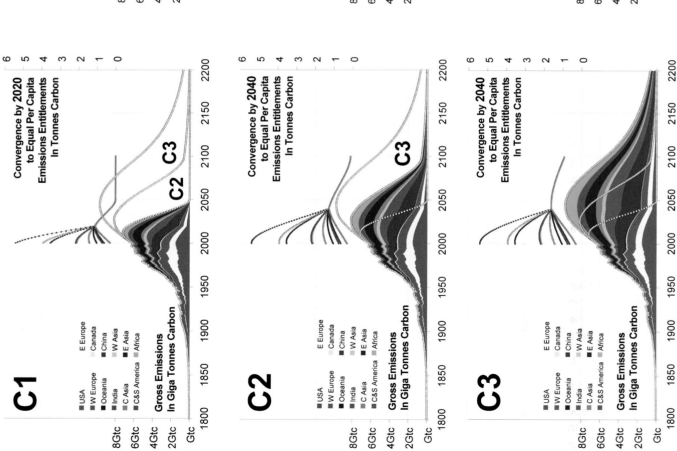

Future CO$_2$ 'path-integrals' – projecting 'aggravated rates of accumulation' of atmospheric CO$_2$ or accelerated rates of contraction and convergence (C&C) to avoid this (Source: Aubrey Meyer).

3.

CONTRACTION AND CONVERGENCE: A QUESTION OF SURVIVAL

If we are to reduce our global emissions of CO_2, humanity will have to devise a way to work together towards a common understanding of what constitutes a Fair Earth Share of emissions per capita for everyone on this planet. 'The only game in town' to do that is currently C&C – the theory of 'contraction and convergence' (for a definition statement of C&C and support please go to http://www.gci.org.uk/briefings/ICE.pdf).

The six graphs shown in Figure 3 project scenarios for future rates of CO_2 stabilisation in the atmosphere. These are 'path-integrals', in other words carbon transferred to the atmosphere added up over time, in much the same way as water accumulates in the bath as water flows through the tap into the bath and, as the plughole gradually blocks it, progressively stops draining away.

These path-integrals have the underlying carbon consumption – as 'contraction and convergence' budgets – for carbon emissions shown as well. Chart four shows convergence accelerated relative to the rate of contraction for reasons of international reconciliation.

These follow the carbon-cycle modelling published by the IPCC since the Second (1995) and Third Assessments (2000), for

1 350 parts per million by volume (ppmv),
2 450 ppmv, and
3 550 ppmv.

These IPCC reference curves are shown by line D in each case against the emissions contraction budgets also quoted by IPCC.

In each of these four reference cases, the curves for atmospheric accumulation are projected using the C&C model to show the aggravated path-integrals of rates of CO_2 accumulation in the atmosphere into the future at:

a a Constant Airborne Fraction (CAF) at 50 per cent as given with the IPCC determined rates of emissions contraction budgets and path-integrals for atmospheric accumulation – this is path 'D' in Figure 3.
b 100 per cent CAF, in other words the theoretical maximum rate of atmospheric retention of ghg emissions from human sources – this is path 'F' in Figure 3 shown, and
c a rate of ghg retention in the atmosphere that gradually increases from 50 per cent to 100 per cent over the next two centuries – this is path 'E' in Figure 3.

In other words the scenarios shown are 'pairs' of emissions budgets and atmospheric concentrations where the latter should have been stable (following IPCC given values), but can rise faster along paths 'E' due to sink increasing sink-failure and the consequent aggravated rate of concentration build-up.

C1 An emissions budget for 350 ppmv as determined by IPCC, may well rise through 500 ppmv [here called 'acceptable risk']
C2 An emissions budget for 450 ppmv as determined by IPCC, may well rise through 650 ppmv [here called a 'very dangerous risk']
C3 An emissions budget for 550 ppmv as determined by IPCC, 550 may well rise through 900 ppmv [here called an 'impossible risk'].

The justification for doing this relies on the data returned between 2000 and 2006 showing that the aggravated rate of emissions accumulation in the atmosphere is already occurring intermittently. The purpose of doing this is to highlight the much greater extent of risk with which we are already confronted, as the likelihood of aggravated rates of accumulation persisting into the future is real. The point of concern is that conditions of a runaway rise in climate change will take hold much sooner than previously foreseen, if preventive action is not urgently taken.

These 'aggravated rates of accumulation' are a fundamental strategic consideration as we try and determine a stable future over the many following decades when it:

a   hasn't yet occurred
b   is still caught in poor understanding and indecision about 'policy' to modify human fossil fuel consumption beyond 2012 when the irresolute Kyoto Protocol to the UNFCCC expires, and
c   operates under the increasingly challengeable assumption that there is still time to avert dangerous rates of climate change from taking hold when some already take the position that it is all too late; in the analogy, the bath is inevitably now going to overflow.

The priority test to keep in mind for policy to this purpose is comparing path-integrals for:

a   the rate at which we cause the problem with our global emissions total where this rate is understood as the possible and likely rates of atmospheric accumulation and therefore
b   these rates against the rates at which we are organising globally to stop triggering dangerous rates of climate change (as for example with the Kyoto Protocol) by contracting our global emissions total fast enough to avoid this.

All this shows is that we can reasonably measure the rate at which we presently still continue to cause the problem much faster than we act to avoid it with the wholly ineffectual Kyoto Protocol. In its given time period of 2008–2012, the Kyoto Protocol will theoretically and at best have avoided emitting a few hundred million tonnes of CO_2 (measured as carbon) into the atmosphere. During the same period we will have added several billion tonnes of carbon to the atmosphere from emissions virtually business-as-usual.

As soon as we factor aggravated accumulation into this it is clear that the end result will be that by 2012 we will be more, not less, deeply committed to the accelerating rate at which we are causing the problem than the response rates of C&C that are necessary to avoid it.

NOTES

1   Environmental Building News Vol. 14, No. 12: http://www.buildinggreen.com/articles/IssueTOC.cfm?Volume=14&Issue=12 or http://www.building-green.com/press/passive-survivability.cfm

2 There have been a number of media exposes of the problems – perhaps the most influential has been the Al Gore film *An Inconvenient Truth*. This included a number of images from Mark Lynas's excellent book *High Tide: news from a warming world*, 2004, Flamingo Press, London. The science behind such works has also moved on rapidly and become more accessible. For instance on climate change and its impacts see: www.ukcip.org.uk and www.ipcc.ch You do have to be careful using the internet though as there are many sites in cyberspace that are have their own agendas and some that are downright misleading. For the view of one who thinks it is already too late to act see: Lovelock, J. (2006). *The revenge of Gaia*. Penguin Publications.

3 Roaf, S., Crichton, D. and Nicol, F. (2005). *Adapting Buildings and Cities for Climate Change*. Architectural Press, Oxford.

4 For excellent discussions on the issues of Peak Oil see: www.peakoil.net, www.odac-info.org and www.energycrisis.com. For more insights into how Peak Oil estimates are arrived at see for instance: http://www.hubbertpeak.com/laherrere and Campbell, C.J. and Laherrère (1998). The End of Cheap Oil, *Scientific American*, March (http://dieoff.org/page140.htmn).

5 http://europe.theoildrum.com/story/2006/11/10/17234/128#more and http://www.odac-info.org

6 Sixth Report of the Joint Energy Security of Supply Working Group (JESS), April 2006, p.14. http://www.dti.gov.uk/files/file28800.pdf

7 www.sternreview.org.uk

8 For a full account of the theory of Contraction and Convergence see the website of the Global Commons Institute: http://www.gci.org.uk

9 http://environment.guardian.co.uk/climatechange/story/0,,1935211,00.html

10 www.gensler.com/faultytowers

11 See: www.epbd-ca.org/Medias/Pdf/15_CO_UK.pdf and http://www.eeph.org.uk/energy
www.epbd-ca.org/Medias/Pdf/15_CO_UK.pdf and http://www.eeph.org.uk/energy

12 http://en.wikipedia.org/wiki/Energy_efficiency_in_British_housing#Home_Energy_labelling

13 See: the Association of British Insurers website for more information on this: http://www.abi.org.uk/flooding and if you want to check if your house is at risk of flooding see: http://www.environment-agency.gov.uk/subjects/flood/?lang=_e and fill in your postcode.

14 Roaf, S., Horsley, A. and Gupta, R. (2004). *Closing the Loop: Benchmarks for Sustainable Buildings*. RIBA Enterprises, London.

INTRODUCTION TO SECOND EDITION

Since we deposited the manuscript for the first edition of *Ecohouse* with Architectural Press in late 2000 a surprising amount has happened. For one thing, at a global level, the rain has changed! Countries around the world are suffering the worst floods in living memory, and it is not just the poor of Bangladesh and Vietnam whose homes and lives have been devastated by these unprecedented deluges. Britain, Europe and the United States have suffered catastrophic inundations and, frighteningly, the world is beginning to realise that it simply can no longer afford to undo the increasingly devastating impacts of climate change. Germany has recently admitted that it cannot now cover the true costs of the August 2002 floods. In December 2002 the UK insurance industry began withdrawing insurance cover from homeowners around Britain located in areas prone to flooding. Also in Britain, warnings have gone out that no development should now occur on flood plains, but the proposals for housing schemes below maximum flood heights still appear in planning offices around the country almost every day. This is madness – and the person who pays will be the unsuspecting homeowner!

One of the reviewers of *Ecohouse 1* questioned why we had included sections on wind-proofing buildings from storm damage. It seems only prudent in the twenty-first century to take every precaution one can against the power of the climate because we are just beginning to get a taste of what climate change may begin to do to our buildings, and our lives, over the ensuing decades. From now on, every building should be built to withstand strong winds and those in exposed areas should be hurricane-proof!

At the level of the building, growing concern is being expressed over problems associated with the 'modern' fully air-conditioned (AC) building, even by the Doyens of the AC industry. I predict that this type of building will turn out to be a late twentieth-century phenomenon. They will, sooner rather than later, be replaced, even in the hottest climates, with buildings that can be naturally ventilated either all year, or for as much of the year as possible. There are many reasons that will drive this change, apart from the rapidly rising cost of power-energy hungry AC systems. These include the fact that the heat the AC systems produce is making cities grow increasingly warmer, becoming 'urban heat islands' (something like the heat effect caused by freezers in the local shop), and that the CO_2 emissions from AC systems have become one of the largest driving forces for climate change around the

Floodwaters from Hurricane Katrina cover a portion of New Orleans, Louisiana, illustrating the growing power of the climate to devastate ordinary lives (Source: Associated Press/EMPICS).

world. This change is strongly resisted by the related industries, services engineers and architects who simply do not know how to design passive buildings and/or get paid for doing so. It is only through major changes, such as climatic conditions, and more expensive fuel that these doubters will be shocked into evolving into the twenty-first century, but such shocks are already on the horizon and driving rapid changes in the built environment.

Perhaps the real driving force for the end of the great air-conditioning age is that of the health of building occupants. Worryingly, researchers are finding that the filters, ducts and plants for AC systems often produce much dirtier air than if one simply opened the window, even in the city (Clausen, G., Olm O. and Fanger, P.O., 2002, *The Impact of Air Pollution from Used Ventilation Filters on Human Comfort and Health*, Proceedings of the 9th International Conference on Indoor Air Quality and Climate, Monterey, vol. 1, pp. 338–343, www. indoorair2002.org). Air-condition systems can harbour potentially killer chemicals and bugs such as Legionella, moulds and particulates that are released back into the ducts from the filter, particularly when the weather changes; for instance, on getting warmer and wetter conditions in a warm front (Mauderly, J., 2002, *Linkages Between Outdoor and Indoor Air Quality Issues: Pollutants and Research Problems Crossing the Threshold*. Proceedings of the

9th International Conference on Indoor Air Quality and Climate, Monterey, vol. 1, pp. 12–13). Many internal ducts are not only seldom cleaned but also impossible to get at to clean, and to make matters worse actually give out toxic fumes from the plant, seals and ductwork itself. In addition, dirty duct air is then mixed with a cocktail of Volatile Organic Compounds: formaldehydes, moulds, fungi, dust mites and potentially toxic cleaning materials already inside rooms. This may explain why, in air-conditioned buildings, many more people succumb to Sick Building Syndrome (Bjorkroth, M., Asikainen, V., Seppanen, O. and Sateri, J., 2002, *Cleanliness Criteria and Test Procedures for Cleanliness Labelling of HVAC Components*. Proceedings of the 9th International Conference on Indoor Air Quality and Climate, Monterey, vol. 1, pp. 670–674). AC and ventilation systems that incorporate filters and long duct runs should be avoided at all costs, and of course furnishings and finishes in houses should be made of natural materials wherever possible. It is pretty easy to do once you know how.

Even in the hot humid tropics ingenious systems for using cold water pipe systems and night cooling systems could be a much more comfortable and healthier solution (see Case Studies 9 and 10 on the Lim and Surabaya houses) than subjecting yourself to the toxic soups of room air and cold shock so often experienced in overcooled and over-expensive to run buildings. The average American worker is absent from work on average for one day a month because of sick building syndrome! A figure that sounds incredible to us in the UK. Let us not forget that from here on energy, and particularly electricity, will only get more expensive, so that when you are building your new house, this is the time to future-proof yourself against not only the changing climate but also the inevitable rise and rise in the cost of powering that home and the health aspects that should, at no extra cost, be built into it. A good time to invest in opening window firms?

So what is the good news? Well, people's attitudes, as well as the market place, are actually changing fast; evidenced, for instance, by the surge of people investing in solar technologies for their homes. Nowadays, because of the very high demand for them, you wait some time to get a PV panel delivered to site in the UK! Ultimately, the driving force for such necessary changes will be shifting attitudes and mindsets of this generation. It is hard to believe that, in the face of all this growing evidence, we still succumb to the 'Easter Island Effect' and continue on a 'business as usual' approach towards the future. One good sign is that so many people have bought copies of *Ecohouse 1* and we would like to thank them for providing us with the opportunity to develop it into *Ecohouse 2*. They are the reason why Manuel, Stephanie and I have elicited the help of friends to revise many of the chapters for this edition and include new sections.

Manuel returned from his beautiful ecohouse perched on a mountain overlooking the lakes in Bariloche, Argentina, to help complete *Ecohouse 2*. Stephanie worked with us, from Florida, where she is at the Florida Solar Energy Centre and completing her own hurricane-proof ecohouse (see Case Study) on the Florida Keys, based on her Caribbean experience. This house is a great example of a pragmatic design that manages to incorporate not only the values of an ordinary American lifestyle, but also to minimise the environmental impacts of doing so while optimising the comfort and well-being of its occupants. It demonstrates that ecohouse principles can be incorporated into the mainstream of the housing market, even in the United States.

What is new in *Ecohouse 2?* Well, Mike Humphreys deliberates on life in a Hobbit Hole! Fergus Nicol helps us to estimate the design challenges of making houses comfortable in different climates with his Nicol graph. Craig Simmons explains how ecological footprints work demonstrating too that it is the lifestyle of the building occupants that matters as much as getting the design right – a good lesson. Peter Warm tells us more about, well, keeping warm, with insulation. Chris Kendrick informs us with additions to the section on cold bridges and Paul Jennings tells us how to stop buildings from leaking. The famous Dr Dave Anderson, Washington toxicologist, explains how to turn yourself into a mould detective!

Manuel has updated the Passive solar chapter using the results of a Pilkington funded study completed with Chiheb Bouden of the Tunisian Solar Energy Centre. Chiheb modelled the thermal performance of the Oxford Ecohouse under a range of 'what if' scenarios to see how wrong or right we got the initial design. Chris Laughton, of the UK Solar Trade Association, has contributed his wisdom to solar hot water system design and Bruce Cross, who designed the Oxford PV roof, tweaked the Photovoltaic chapter. Nick Grant has also added his help to our chapter on using water wisely. Stephanie has added Porpoise Point Ecohouse (Case Study 20) which she designed herself while in Oxford, and a new one in the hot Mediterranean climate of Tunis (Case Study 22) was contributed by Chiheb. We also include the new cold climate healthy house in Vancouver (Case Study 21). In addition, I am exceedingly glad that, in the recent strong deluges, I had wide Dales storm-proof gutters which rapidly dealt with even the most torrential downpours.

You can see that developing *Ecohouse 2* has been an opportunity to meet old and make new friends alike. We have built on what we always knew was going to be an important book when we first started it, quite simply because we wrote it in answer to your questions, asked when so many of you first visited us here in Oxford.

Please contact us to let us know if there are subjects we have omitted and you would like covered, and if we have got anything wrong.

I hope that young students of architecture and engineering will also read this book, as well as designers and home builders. Encapsulated in the following rationale for ecohouse design are many of the lessons they will need to build any building, however large or small, in the twenty-first century. A project to design an ecohouse, even in the architecture or engineering school studio, is a good way to learn the basic lessons of twenty-first century design, and develop an individual approach to successful eco-design, for there never is one answer.

Do check the Architectural Press website to browse for details of our ongoing Student Ecohouse Design Competition at www.architecturalpress.com.

What is sure is that the buildings of this century will not be like those of the last century. The times, and the climate for design, are changing, and the dream of endless fossil fuel is coming to an end. A new design age is upon us.

Good luck with your own ecohouse designs!

Sue Roaf
September 2002

INTRODUCTION TO FIRST EDITION

The first question to answer should be: what is an ecohouse? Eco-architecture sees buildings as part of the larger ecology of the planet and the building as part of a living habitat. This contrasts with the more common notions of many architects, who see a building as a work of art, perhaps on exhibition in a settlement or as 'frozen music' in the people-less pictures of glossy magazines. Some architects see the process of design as a production line with the building as a product to be deposited on a site, regardless of its particular environment or qualities. You will see from the case studies at the end of the book that ecohouses are closely connected to their site, society, climate, region and the planet.

Why bother making buildings connect in this way? Because the alternative is not acceptable and 'modern buildings' are literally destroying the planet. It does not help that the number of people on the planet is growing so rapidly (5.3 billion in 1990; 8.1 billion by 2020; 10.7 billion in the 2080s) or that we have increasingly sophisticated technologies to exploit the Earth's natural resources. But it should be widely known that buildings are the single most damaging polluters on the planet, consuming over half of all the energy used in developed countries and producing over half of all climate-change gases.

The shift towards green design began in the 1970s and was a pragmatic response to higher oil prices. It was then that the first of the oil shocks, in 1973, sent fossil fuel prices sky high and the 'futurologists' began to look at the life history of fossil fuels on the planet and make claims about how much oil and

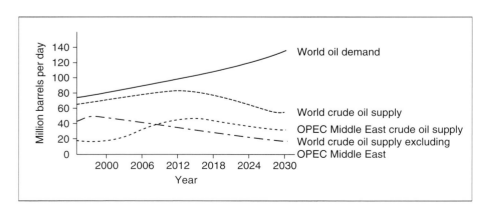

1.

World oil demand and conventional oil supply in millions of barrels per day (*Guardian*, 17 June 2000, p. 30).

gas were left. Their predictions were alarming and, 30 years on, we appear still to have abundant oil. However, their calculations on total reserves were fairly accurate and many of their predictions have yet to be proved wrong. From the features on gas, oil and coal below you can see that it is now estimated that we have left around 40 years of conventional oil reserves and 65 years of gas, at current rates of extraction. Recent studies (see Bartsh and Muller, 2000) point to 2012 as being when the oil shortages will really begin to bite hard and to start changing the face of society.

OIL: the estimates of total oil reserves have changed little in 20 years and the last big oil field discovered was in the North Sea in the 1960s. The output from the southern 48 States of America began to decline in the 1940s. The output from oil fields typically follows a form of bell-shaped curve, rising steeply to a plateau then falling sharply. Every day the world consumes around 70 million barrels of crude oil. To date, we have used around half of the total estimated oil reserves globally and it is thought that within a few years we will reach the peak of global oil production, after which time conventional oil production will decline.

The capacity for exploiting those reserves can be increased by technologies that allow more of the reserves to be extracted, for example by using pumped gas and water. Thus in the USA, UK and Norway, for instance, reserves are intensively exploited while in other areas, such as Saudi Arabia, Kuwait and Iraq, they are not. The term 'reserves' indicates the long-term potential of an oil field while 'capacity' describes what can be pumped from that field taking into consideration constraints such as the technical efficiency of the extraction process. An increase in the rate of recovery of oil from a field from 30 per cent to 60 per cent is the equivalent of doubling the proven recoverable resource.

Perhaps worst hit by the decline in oil reserves will be the fields in the USA and the North Sea, which will be badly affected by 2020. Issues of how to sustain current lifestyles in these regions, with declining oil reserves, unpredictable global oil prices and geopolitical conditions, should prove very interesting.

There is capacity for considerable expansion in oil production over the next few years to meet increased global demands from the various oil-producing countries. However, the capacity to increase supplies may well not actually meet the increasing demands. The cost of oil will depend on the match between demand and supply, the 'time lag' between synchronising these and the size of 'buffer' supplies that are currently largely held in the Gulf. Prices will rise when governments perceive a reduction in the size of the buffer, or anticipate that demands for oil are growing faster than investment in capacity expansion. The oil crises of 1973 and 1979 were caused by such a mismatch of demand and consumption. Recently the oil price on the global market has fluctuated from under US$10 a barrel to over US$30 a barrel. Our societies are highly dependent on oil, the price of which has not proven particularly predictable in the past.

The world does hold huge reserves of non-conventional oil that will be exploited when the scarcity of conventional reserves pushes the price of a barrel above $30 for long periods.

When making long-term predictions, analysts have to balance the capacity, or production, of a field against the size of its reserves and the onset of 'oil field

OIL: decline'. If, as some maintain, global production will plateau in around 2005 and we continue to increase our global demand as predicted, there is a strong likelihood of considerable volatility in oil prices in the future, as happened in the 1970s. No one is brave enough to stake their reputations on what oil will cost in 5, 10, 15 or 20 years but pundits suggest that by around 2015 global natural decline in conventional oil production will be noticeable, and may be considerable after around 2020. These declines can be compensated for by developments in non-conventional oil production but at a high cost to the consumer. One worry is that old oil fields in areas such as the Middle East and Venezuela are already showing signs of fatigue and may not yield their full potential of reserves. A rough figure given is that we may have around 40 years left of conventional oil reserves.

As Bartsch and Muller (2000) state in their recent book *Fossil Fuels in a Changing Climate*, 'It is not that we will not have enough oil to take us to 2020 but that the road is likely to be bumpy and subject to a number of economic and political shocks'.

GAS: reserves of natural gas are abundant and current estimates suggest that stocks could last for 65 years at current rates of consumption. Some countries rely on gas for over half of all the primary energy they use and the biggest increase in demand is for gas-powered electricity stations. Gas is a cleaner fuel for the generation of electricity than coal or oil and results in less CO_2 emissions per unit of delivered energy generated because gas-fired power stations are more efficient.

Two interesting characteristics of gas are that:

1 it is difficult to move over long distances without leakage and
2 most of it is located in countries where demand for it is lower.
   For instance, in Europe there are around 3.2 trillion (3.2×10^{12}) cubic metres of proven reserves of natural gas and the Europeans are consuming around 0.38 trillion cubic metres per year, which gives us at this rate just under 10 years of gas left in Europe. However, more reserves may be found. In the USA the situation is more difficult with around 3.2 trillion cubic metres proven reserves left and 0.686 trillion tonnes being consumed a year. At this rate the USA has around 5 years of reserves of their own natural gas left. However, such countries are very aware of the limitations of their own reserves and import large quantities of cheap gas now, with a view to conserving their own stocks for the future. For example if the USA imports three-quarters of the gas they use every year at current rates their own stocks could last for 20 years.

Fortunately there are abundant reserves in other areas of the world of which 77 per cent are in the Middle East (39 per cent) and North Africa (38 per cent). It is estimated that globally there are reserves that will support demand for gas for the next 60 years at least. However, as local reserves of gas are depleted and countries have to buy more and more of their stocks from the global market they will have to pay the global market price. The rate of uptake of cleaner gas technologies, used to reduce CO_2 emissions, for instance, from power stations, will be influenced by the cost of gas, which will increasingly be dictated by the highest bidders. Prices will eventually rise significantly in countries where the fuel is now very cheap, such as the USA, but obviously will be less affected in countries such as Denmark where fuel prices have been kept high and energy efficiency is widely practised. The USA now consumes around 27 per cent of the world's gas (with 4 per cent of the world population) and is responsible for about 23 per cent per year of global gas production.

COAL: the main problem with coal is that it is a dirty fuel and contributes 38 per cent of CO_2 emissions from commercial fuels and is also a major source of sulphur dioxide and nitrous oxides emissions, as well as particulates and other emissions. Coal currently provides only 26 per cent of the world's primary energy consumption, very much less than in 1950 when this figure was 59 per cent. There are abundant reserves of coal in the ground estimated to be capable of lasting over 200 years. Over 50 per cent of the reserves are in the USA, China and Russia. The coal industry does have the additional problems of poor working conditions in some mines and the high costs of transport for the fuel. In France it is expected that all mines will be closed by 2005.

The costs of producing coal vary significantly. Internationally traded coal ranges in delivered price to the European Union (EU) of between US$30 and US$55 per tonne, which in terms of fuel oil is roughly equivalent to US$45–75 per tonne. This compares with the average spot price of fuel oil delivered to northwest Europe in 1997 of US$90–95 per tonne and between US$65 and US$70 per tonne in the first half of 1998. This indicates that coal is very competitively priced against oil but it does have a high environmental impact compared with fuel oil (medium impact) and gas turbines and natural gas combined-cycle power plants (low impact), which will limit its wider use globally in the future for environmental reasons.

The oil crisis of the 1970s resulted in the rise of the solar house movement: homes built to use clean renewable energy from the sun. One such house can be seen in the case study in Tokyo. Such houses used passive solar and solar hot water systems with rock bed and ground storage systems to store heat between the seasons, and provided the foundations on which were developed the blueprints for the ecohouses of the twenty-first century.

In the 1980s came the next big shock – climate change. It was then that the rates of depletion in the ozone layer and the increase in greenhouse gases and global warming became apparent. The predictions made by the Intergovernmental Panel on Climate Change in 1990 have been borne out by the steadily increasing global temperatures over the 1990s, the hottest decade on record.

Just as people dismiss the fossil fuel depletion claims by saying that 'they were wrong in the 1970s about oil, you see we have not run out yet', so climate change predictions are simplistically rebuffed with phrases such as 'the climate of the world has always changed'. It is obvious from Figure 2 that this is indeed correct, but what is deeply worrying is the revealed rate and scale of change that is now happening.

The main greenhouse gas is CO_2 and the main source of CO_2 (ca. 50 per cent of all man-made emissions) is buildings. If we continue to produce greenhouse gases at current rates of increase in a 'business-as-usual fashion', predictions by the UK Meteorological Office indicate impacts will be substantial and by 2080 will include:

- a rise in global average temperatures of 3°C over the 1961–1990 average by 2080;
- substantial dieback of tropical forests and grasslands with resulting loss of CO_2 sink;

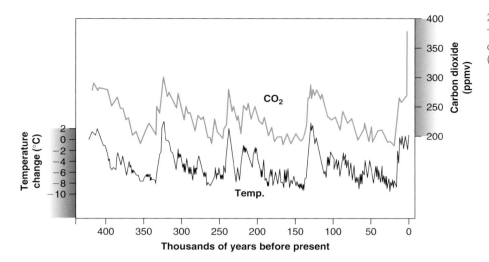

2.
The correlation between historic carbon emissions and global temperature (Woods Hole Institute).

- substantial overall decreases in rainfall amounts in Australia, India, southern Africa and most of South America, Europe and the Middle East. Increases will be seen in North America, Asia (particularly central Asia) and central eastern Africa;
- an increase in cereal yields at high and mid-latitudes such as North America, China, Argentina and much of Europe. At the same time cereal yields in Africa, the Middle East and particularly India will decrease, leading to increases in the risk of famine in some regions;
- sea levels will be about 40 cm higher than present with an estimated increase in the annual number of people flooded from approximately 13 million today to 94 million in 2080. Of this increase 60 per cent will be in southern Asia, from Pakistan through India, Sri Lanka, Bangladesh and Burma and 20 per cent in Southeast Asia from Thailand, Vietnam, Indonesia and the Philippines. Under all scenarios sea level rises will affect coastal wetlands, low-lying islands and coastal lowlands;
- health impacts will be widespread and diverse. By the 2080s an estimated 290 million more people will be at risk from malaria, with the greatest risk in China and central Asia. Fewer people will die in winter in temperate cities and more will die in summer from heat-related problems (www.met.office.gov.uk/sec5/CR_div/CoP5/obs_pred_clim_change.html). Skin cancer rates will soar. In Queensland, where UV-B radiation is the highest, it is predicted that three out of every four people will get skin cancer. In America, in 1935 the chances of getting skin cancer were 1 in 1500, in 2000 the chances are 1 in 75 (www.geocities.com/Rainforest/Vines/4030/impacts.html).

There are so many related impacts of greenhouse gas emissions that we only touch on them here. Yet we see them illustrated daily in newspaper articles on the extinction of species, the increase in number and intensity of floods and cyclones, water shortages and the starvation that results from droughts. What is certain is that we must act now to reduce CO_2 emissions globally and that one of the most effective sectors from which to achieve rapid reductions in emissions is buildings. Houses consume around half of all the energy used in buildings.

A recent Report by the Commission on Environmental Pollution in the UK states that if we are to begin to attempt to stabilise climate change we will have to introduce cuts in all CO_2 emissions of around 60 per cent. This means using 60 per cent less energy to run the home (http://www.rcep.org.uk/). This is actually not too difficult, as demonstrated in many ecohouses. For instance, the Oxford Ecohouse emits around 140 kg CO_2 per year while other, similar sized, houses in Oxford will produce around 6 500 kg CO_2 per year. This is because the Oxford Ecohouse is run largely using renewable solar energy. This demonstrates how important solar technologies are for the 'Low Carbon Lifestyle'.

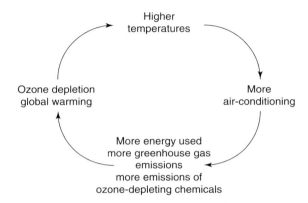

But what is the typical architectural response to the challenge of global warming? It is not to make the building do more of the work in providing better shelter against climate change, nor to use solar technologies, but to install air-conditioning, which is a key element in the vicious circle that is creating global warming.

Air-conditioning systems represent the greatest source of climate change gases of any single technology. In the USA, which has only 4 per cent of the world's population and yet produces around 25 per cent of the global CO_2 annually, over 40 per cent of electricity generated is used in air-conditioning systems. Energy efficiency is absolutely not an issue, in general, with the US architectural profession. Indeed, climate change is not an issue in the majority of architectural offices around the world who have systematically, over the last 30 years, shut the indoor climate off from the outdoor climate, so requiring air-conditioning to make the building habitable. Air-conditioning engineers have traditionally made their profits by putting as much plant as possible into a building. It is not uncommon for heating and ventilating engineers to insist on having fixed windows throughout a building, not least because the calculations for system performance are too difficult if an open-window scenario is adopted. So, many buildings have to be air-conditioned all year round while perhaps for only one, two or three months is the external climate uncomfortably hot or cold. In addition, many 'fashionable' architect-designed buildings contain excessive glass, overheat, create extreme indoor discomfort and can only be saved from becoming hellish environments by huge amounts of air-conditioning plant. When sensible engineers suggest that perhaps the building would be better without, for instance, the glass roof, architects have been heard to retort that engineers cannot understand great design ideas and they should do what they are paid to do and not express opinions about the building's aesthetics.

The world needs a new profession of ecotects, or archi-neers or engi-tects, who can design passive buildings that use minimal energy and that what energy they do use comes from renewable sources if possible. It is the only way forward.

The scenario for future global energy consumption developed in the early 1990s by the Shell oil company demonstrates this well. Figure 3 shows how the demand for energy continues to grow exponentially while conventional fuel sources such as oil and gas begin to show significant reductions in output. The gap is filled by renewable energies such as wind and photovoltaic (PV, solar electric) energy. It was on the strength of such predictions that Shell and BP have invested huge amounts of money in the development of PV production and distribution companies.

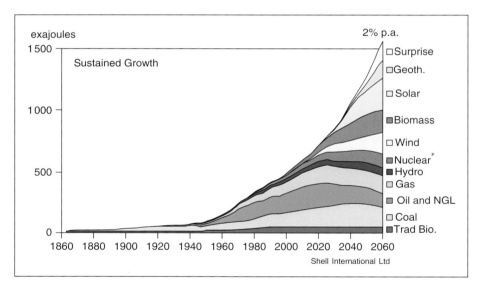

3.
A Shell prediction graph developed in the early 1990s on a 'sustained growth' scenario. It shows the gradual drop-off in fossil fuel supply, the increasing demand for energy and the growth of the renewable energy sector (Shell, UK Ltd, with thanks to Roger Booth).

By the decisions we make on the drawing boards in our comfortable offices the global environment is changed. The world is warming and the ozone layer thinning. Some time in the not too distant future building designers will be made to take into account their own global environmental responsibilities. This will be done through building regulations, fuel price increases and carbon taxes. The sooner we start to change architecture, from an appearance-driven process to a performance-driven art, the better prepared we will be to lay the building foundations of the post-fossil fuel age. The best place to start learning is with an ecohouse.

We have tried to bring together 'How to' information on key issues not well covered in other books. This includes developing technologies, thermal mass, ventilation, cold bridging, materials issues, passive solar design, photovoltaics, cyclone design and grey water systems. The book is not a comprehensive guide to all aspects of low-energy or ecological building. Many subjects have been very well covered in other books; for example, passive solar design (Mazria, 1979; Yannas, 1994), low-energy house design in the UK (Vale and Vale, 2000), materials (Borer and Harris, 1998; Berge, 2000) and timber-frame houses (Pitts, 1989, 2000; Talbott, 1993). We also think that house buyers can choose many elements for their house pragmatically, with a little help from their local building supplies store. For instance, what is the best glass for their windows, based on what is locally available, compared performance data and what they can afford.

We do incorporate the wisdom learnt from ecohouses around the world in the case studies. These are not ordinary houses. The majority are built by architects for themselves and often by themselves, not for clients. They express, in their varied forms, the local climates, resources, culture and the tastes of their designers, as well as the design ethos of the times in which they were built.

The temptation to 'innovate' can often lead us unwittingly into problems, but from them we learn. For example, the early solar houses often overheated because, in the rush to utilise free, clean solar energy, the dangers of the sun were underestimated. The best modern buildings do have excellent solar control and yet it is astounding to see how many still employ glass roofs and walls that not only can cause severe discomfort to people inside but also can result in huge bills for compensatory cooling systems. Some people never seem to learn. Clients should avoid such designers.

Today photovoltaics are already cost-effective in virtually all countries for off-grid systems. In far-sighted countries, such as Japan and Germany, there are already over 10 000 installed domestic PV systems in use. In Britain (where £900 000 000 was spent on the Millennium dome at Greenwich) there are about ten installed grid-connected PV systems on houses. To adapt an old Yorkshire expression, some people are 'all front parlour and no Sunday lunch' when it comes to sustainability and sensibly investing in the future for our children.

It is incredible to note that in many parts of the world including Britain, the challenges of trying to reduce the catastrophic impacts of buildings on the environment are still left to individuals. The challenges ahead seem so enormous that it is difficult to see what we, as individuals, can do. But it was Confucius who said that if each person solved the small problems over which they have control then the larger problems would disappear.

Why are such important issues as the impacts of climate change and fossil fuel depletion ignored by politicians when our species is so obviously at an ecological watershed? We are only one species on the planet, yet we are multiplying exponentially; every day we destroy other species and their ecological niches and, in many parts of the world, we are even destroying our own peoples and their habitats. This was historically demonstrated on Easter Island where the population destroyed all the trees on the island and had to flee to survive, or die. This is happening around us today. Will it be obvious to us that we are the cause, when the first of the Small Islands disappear altogether when sea level rises? Will we register that fact?

Species can adopt symbiotic, parasitic or predatory lifestyles, and they can also literally commit community suicide. There is potentially much to be learnt about how we can develop through the study of ecology, by comparing our behaviour with that of other species on the planet.

ECOLOGY is defined as the study of the interactions of organisms and their physical and biological environment. Organisms have the ability to control the movement of energy and material between their internal and external environments. They adapt in order to use the water, energy, heat, light and resources available in different environments and climates to sustain life in the multiplicity of ecosystems on the planet.

Competition between species is a driving force that can lead to evolutionary divergence between species, to elimination of species and also, more positively, to a co-evolution and the development of mutually supportive relationships. Evolution requires adaptation, not only to adjust to the changing circumstances of climate and environment, but also to changing populations and resources.

The theory of evolutionary ecology begins with Charles Darwin in the late nineteenth century. He regarded the environment as the key agent of 'selective mortality' without mentioning the relationship of birth rate to the survival of species. In 1930 Ronald Fisher's classic book *The Genetical Theory of Natural Selection*, dealt with the importance of population growth rates but this subject was largely marginalised until 1966 when the theory of the 'life histories' of populations became popular. This theory states that adaptation is largely the making of compromises in the allocation of time and energy to competing demands. It introduced the idea that very different 'life history' adaptations are favoured under conditions of high and low population densities in relation to the carrying capacity of the environment. At high densities, selection favours adaptations that enable populations to survive and reproduce with few resources and hence demands 'efficiency' in the way resources are used. At low densities, adaptations promoting rapid population increases are favoured, regardless of efficiency. Natural selection adjusts the amount of time and resources expended not only in accordance with changes in the environment but also with the life history of a population.

So how would this affect us? In times of ecological threat animal species respond in a variety of ways, from becoming spiteful to being altruistic. Ecologists would perhaps expect selfish behaviour to prevail to the exclusion of altruism because it is the selfish behaviours that increase the reproductive success of the dominant species or individual.

Growth, however, is a survival strategy for species with a life history at a low-density phase. At high densities, populations must employ strategies of efficiency to survive. Human beings are unique in the history of the world because of the sheer scale of the impacts we have had on the global environment and in particular on the Earth's atmosphere, and our ability to comprehend, and alter, them.

If we are to survive the challenges ahead of us in the twenty-first century, with some semblance of normality retained, we will have to effect fairly radical changes in what we, as individuals, expect from the infrastructures of our own ecological niches, our houses and settlements, and society. To do this we will have to behave fairly altruistically, not only towards our own families, friends and neighbours but also to the larger family of our fellow human beings. Altruism is not unknown when bonds of loyalty are stretched to encompass larger and larger groups. Humans seldom question that, in times of war, they are asked to die for their country. This they do ultimately to protect their families, through whom their genes are perpetuated.

When faced with the twenty-first century challenges it is the global nature of human being's environmental impacts that make it imperative to see our kin as all the people of the world. If not, few of us will survive. There are no safe islands in the twenty-first century. Europe knows that if the countries of northern Africa suffer from repeated severe droughts it is to Europe that the ravaged populations of these regions will flee. The same is true of America, Mexico and Latin America. The history of humans is one of diasporas, the dispersions of peoples. If there are more people and fewer resources, such movements will surely affect each of our everyday lives?

Buildings are only part of our habitat. Buildings are intimately linked to the local, regional and global environments that are all part of our 'Ecological Niche'. It is the responsibility of our generation to begin to adapt our buildings to ensure that we can stabilise climate change, that we can live without fossil fuels and that we do not unsustainably pollute the environment. Only by so doing can we ensure the survival of our own habitats.

This cannot be so difficult because people survived on the planet for millennia without the miracle fuels of oil and gas. Traditional buildings have much to teach us about how to design regionally appropriate structures.

We can change fast enough. We can mix the wisdom of the master builders, new knowledge, materials and renewable technologies to create ecobuildings, the New Vernacular, to minimise the environmental impacts of buildings. We can now measure those impacts with the new methodologies for counting the environmental costs of buildings. We do need a new type of designer, part architect, part engineer, and to get rid of heating and cooling machines where possible or power them with renewable energy. What you will read in the first section of the book shows that all of this is possible and, in the second section, that it is already being done in many of the case study ecohouses from around the world.

Sue Roaf
August 2000

1 THE FORM OF THE HOUSE: THE BUILDING AS AN ANALOGY

Twentieth-century architecture was influenced by a single analogy coined by the great French architect, Le Corbusier. He proposed that 'the building is a machine for living in'. This is very far from the truth. The mistake, at its heart, is that a machine is an inanimate object that can be turned on and off and operates only at the whim of its controller. A building is very different because, although it is true that it can be controlled by its occupants, the driving force that acts upon the building to create comfort and shelter is the climate and its weather, neither of which can be controlled, predicted or turned on and off.

Machines are fixed, static objects, amenable to scientific assessment. Buildings are part of a complex interaction between people, the buildings themselves, the climate and the environment. The view that buildings are fixed also fits well with certain types of scientific analysis, of daylight factors, energy flows, U-values, mechanical ventilation and so on. But this mechanistic view finds the more dynamic parts of the system (temperature, natural ventilation, passive cooling and all the multitude of human interactions) very difficult to model and, therefore, to understand. In houses it is often these 'difficult' parts of the system that change a house into a home, and the building into a delight.

Considerations of daylight, energy, thermal insulation and the use of machinery, of course, cannot be avoided – but because we can calculate them does not mean that they are our only concern. Figure 1.1 demonstrates, for instance, that buildings have their own thermal life beyond what we can see. If we could see heat, as the thermal imagining camera does, we would probably treat a building very differently. We would know exactly where we need to put a bit more insulation or place a sun shade, which sun shade to use or which corner of the room is cold and needs a little attention.

We have to design for the invisible as well as the visible and so how is this to be done? Buildings have been traditionally designed using accepted premises (propositions that are adopted after reasoning) as well as, of course, on premises (the building and adjuncts set forth at the beginning of a building deed). Three principles on which all building should be based are:

1 design for a climate
2 design for the physical and social environment
3 design for time, be it day or night, a season or the lifetime of a building and design a building that will adapt over time.

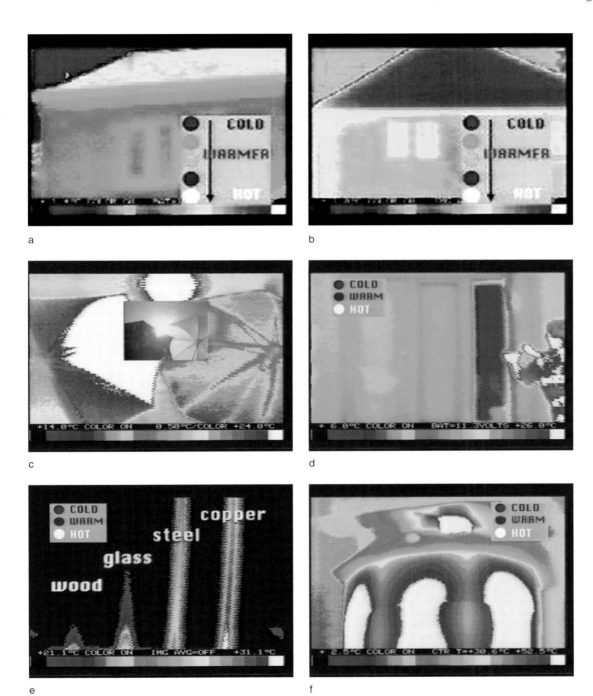

1.1.

Thermographic images: a, The Oxford Ecohouse, built in 1994, on an Autumn morning; b, the house next door built in the 1950s; c, a black umbrella (left) and a white umbrella (right) showing that the black material absorbs radiation and gets hot while the white umbrella reflects the sun from its surface and remains cooler; d, a person opening a window from the inside in the Oxford Ecohouse; e, rods of copper, steel, glass and wood demonstrating that heat is conducted more efficiently in some materials than others; f, the Kacheloven in the Oxford Ecohouse showing the hot ducts in the high mass stove and the hot metal flue passing into the concrete floor above and heating it locally. These images are reproduced with thanks to Glasshead Films Ltd who took the films for Channel 4, and George Jenkinson and Andy Hudson of Oxford Brookes University for their digital re-mastering and transmission of the images (Glasshead Films Ltd).

Humans have been building on these premises for millennia and have evolved house types around the world that are well suited to particular climates, environments and societies. This was done by learning from experience, and with the benefit of repetitive tools and processes that help designers and builders through the complex range of tasks necessary to actually put a building together.

One tool of the imagination that is often used when starting a design is the analogy. An analogy is used where two forms may not look alike but they function in the same way, just as Le Corbusier described a building as a 'machine for living in'. This book starts by considering building form, on which the most powerful influence in design should be the climate. In this chapter, analogies are used to demonstrate how different forms can relate to some of the many different climatic functions of a building. The analogies themselves may seem a little simplistic but you will find that they change the way you look at buildings. To further illustrate the relationship between buildings and climate, a number of examples of vernacular buildings are included.

Finally, at the end of the chapter, a method for evaluating the climatic requirements of a building form in a particular climate is outlined with the Nicol graph. This simply shows what the mean climate of a site is, what the comfort requirements of local people will be and gives an indication of how much heating and cooling will be needed to achieve those comfort conditions in that climate.

THE THIRD SKIN

Buildings are our third skin. To survive we need shelter from the elements using three skins. The first is provided by our own skin, the second by a layer of clothes and the third is the building. In some climates it is only with all three skins that we can provide sufficient shelter to survive, in others the first skin is enough. The more extreme the climate, the more we have to rely on the building to protect us from the elements. Just as we take off and put on clothes as the weather and the climate changes so we can shed skins.

THE HEAT EXCHANGER

The greater the volume of the building the more surface area it has to lose, or gain, heat from. Figure 1.3 shows that different plan forms can have more or less wall area for the same plan area. The surface area:volume ratio is very important in conserving heat transfer into and out of a building. To conserve heat or cold the building must be designed with a compact form to reduce the efficiency of the building as a heat exchanger.

A good example of how not to lose heat because of the shape of a building is given by the ice-house (Figure 1.4). In many countries of the world, before refrigerators were invented, people used to store ice that had been harvested in winter from lakes and ponds in ice-houses. When the hot summer months came it was taken out and used to cool food, drinks and rooms. The only way that ice could be kept so long was to ensure that it had a minimum surface area:volume ratio to lose heat from. Ice-houses were designed so that as the

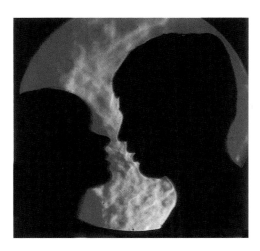

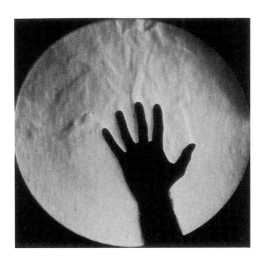

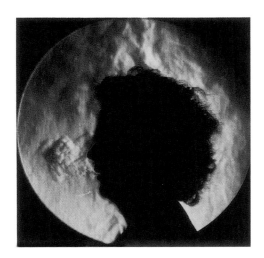

1.2.
People typically generate heat, between 70 and 120 watts each according to how much work they are doing. Figure 1.1. shows the radiant surface temperatures of a person opening a window. This figure shows a thermal image of heat plumes around people, as the heat from our skin warms the air around us it rises, driven by the buoyancy of hot air (Clark and Edholme, 1985).

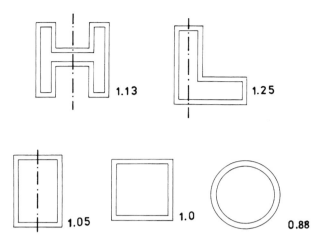

1.13 **1.25**

1.05 **1.0** **0.88**

1.3.
Building can have very different perimeter:area ratios depending on their plan form (Krishan, 1995).

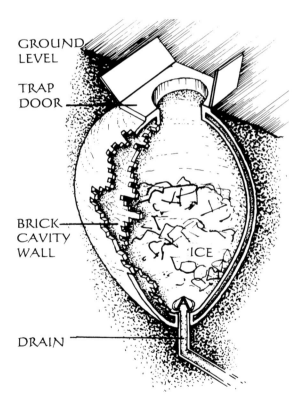

GROUND LEVEL

TRAP DOOR

BRICK CAVITY WALL

ICE

DRAIN

1.4.
The ice-house at Hooke, Chailey, Sussex. Drawn after a 1776 diagram by William Broderick Thomas. This may be the first illustrated cavity brick wall in Britain and here the cavity was used to keep the groundwater away from the ice, rather than for its insulating properties (Beamon and Roaf, 1990).

ice slipped lower down it would retain its ball-like shape. Some ice-houses could store ice for two years without it melting (Beamon and Roaf, 1990).

In warm or hot countries the building must become a good heat dissipater. Just as people who are hot sprawl out to lose heat, so buildings sprawl in warm and hot climates. In many hot climates buildings have a high surface area:volume ratio but the walls facing the sun are protected from direct radiation by verandas, balconies or wide eaves. The shallower floor plan of heat-dissipating buildings also promotes easy cross-ventilation of rooms for cooling, which in compact plan forms is more difficult. House forms in such climates are either long and thin or have a courtyard, or light well, in the centre of the house, to maximise the building's wall area. The relationship between ventilation and cooling is dealt with in Chapter 5.

Do not confuse a hot climate, with mean maximum temperatures below 38°C, with a very hot climate, which is even hotter. In the hottest cities of Saudi Arabia, Iraq, India and Yemen, for instance, houses are very tall with up to seven or eight storeys, each providing another layer of protection against the sun. The courtyards in the very hottest areas are replaced with light wells that allow for cross-ventilation and light penetration but are more shaded against the sun overhead. The outer walls of such buildings are often shaded with shutters, verandas, balconies and mushrabiyah, or ventilated timber cantilevered windows. In such climates rooms can become vertical or horizontal buffers, as can shade elements that keep the sun off mass walls that would transport the heat inwards by conduction. Figure 1.5 shows how a large house, a Havelli, is coupled in the upper floors to the air temperature while in the basement room it is coupled thermally to the more stable ground temperatures.

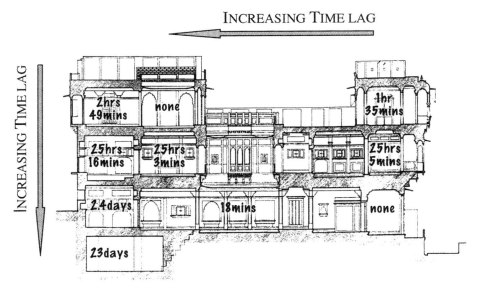

INCREASING TIME LAG

INCREASING TIME LAG

2hrs 49mins — none — 1hr 35mins

2.5hrs 16mins — 2.5hrs 3mins — 2.5hrs 5mins

2.4days — 18mins — none

23days

1.5.
Time lags between indoor and outdoor temperatures in a Havelli in Jaisalmer, India (Matthews, 2000). (South is to the right of this section).

THE TEA COSY

Well-insulated structures are like tea cosies. How quickly the tea cools will depend on how big the pot is, how thick the tea cosy is and how cold the air is outside it. The effectiveness of the insulated envelope depends on a number of variables, not least the area of the envelope in relation to the heating requirements of the occupants in it and the available internal heat sources.

For example, take the tent dwellers of the Mongolian steppes of Siberia to the deserts of Saudi Arabia. The Turkoman yurt (Figure 1.6) is a tent built on a framework of bent wood, with a felt cloth tent, in which ten or more people

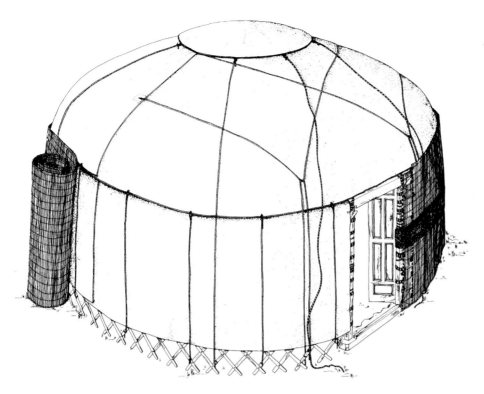

1.6.
A yurt of the Turkoman tribe of Iran
(Andrews, 1997, drawn by Susan Parker).

can live through the freezing winter months. Heavy clothes are worn, even indoors, and a single central brazier provides heat. The yurt is an airtight structure into which there is very little infiltration of cold air from the driving wind. The area of the whole floor is only in the region of 15–20 m² so the body heat of the people in the tent makes up a significant amount of the heat they need to warm the family.

You would probably not survive a severe Mongolian winter in a 300 m² gher with one small brazier fire and ten people. Insulated envelope buildings need constant heating, from a conventional heat source, such as a fire, or from other internal gains such as machines and body heat. The yurt works well because its occupants go to bed very early to conserve heat and light, and sleep at night under thick quilts, often with more than one to a bed, saving considerably on heating. Considerations of the thermal performance of building envelopes are covered in Chapter 2.

THE GREENHOUSE

Imagine living in a greenhouse. There are no climates in which it would be comfortable. Glass lets in light and, with it, heat. Incoming solar radiation heats us to help keep our internal body temperature at 37°C. It can also overheat us. Once solar radiation has passed through glass it hits a surface in the building and is reflected or re-radiated at a changed wavelength that can no longer pass, in the same way, back out through the glass, so causing the inside of the greenhouse to heat up.

This is exactly what is happening with the world's atmosphere. The short-wave radiation can pass through the clear atmosphere relatively unimpeded. But the long-wave terrestrial radiation emitted by the warm surface of the Earth is partially absorbed by a number of the trace gases in the cooler atmosphere above. Since, on average, the outgoing long-wave radiation balances the incoming solar radiation, both the atmosphere and the surface will be warmer than they would be without greenhouse gases.

Once inside the atmosphere or the greenhouse, it is difficult for the radiation to pass back out, and this is why it is fairly pointless to use internal blinds because, although they shade people from direct sunlight, the heat cannot escape from the space. External shading would prevent this problem. Conversely, greenhouses become very cold at night, because they lose heat from the building surface by radiation and eventually become almost as cold as the outside temperature. It would take a fairly brave person to actually try to live in a 'transparent' greenhouse, or suggest to someone else that they should!

Greenhouses are direct solar gain buildings. The ways in which the sun can be captured and used in such buildings is covered in Chapter 7.

THE SWALLOW

Just as swallows move south in winter, so many nomadic families around the world pack up their homes and move towards the sun in autumn and away from it in summer. An excellent example of an adaptable building form is the nomadic tent. Not only are they physically moved from the warmer, lower winter quarters up to cooler, higher pastures in the summer, but the actual form of the tent changes over the year (Figure 1.7). In winter the tent is closed right down to keep out the wind and rain but, as spring turns to summer, its cloth opens up, like wings, to form little more than a sun shade for the people inside. By making the envelope of the tent so adaptable, the range of climates in which its occupants can be comfortable are considerably extended and tents of various shapes and materials are occupied from the Arctic Circle to the Sahara.

THE IGLOO

An important feature of building design in cold climates is the use of stratification of room air. Hot air rises while cold air sinks. This is taken advantage of in igloos, which provide shelter in perhaps the most extreme climates on Earth. The occupants of igloos live on a high shelf, to take advantage of the warmest air in the space, while the cold air sinks down and is contained in the lower entrance area of the building (Figure 1.8).

THE BUILDING AS A BUCKET

Conversely, in hot climates tall rooms mean that the heat and the hot ceiling are far away from the room's occupants. High-level windows can allow the heat to escape from the top of the rooms, thus stimulating airflow even on

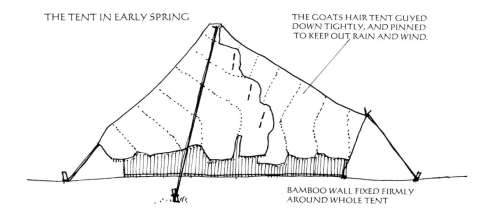

THE TENT IN EARLY SPRING

THE GOATS HAIR TENT GUYED DOWN TIGHTLY, AND PINNED TO KEEP OUT RAIN AND WIND.

BAMBOO WALL FIXED FIRMLY AROUND WHOLE TENT

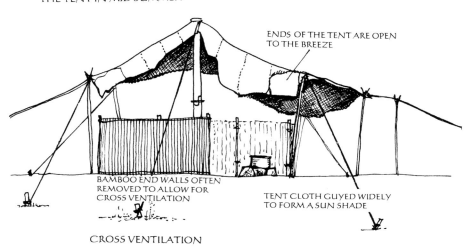

THE TENT IN MID SUMMER

ENDS OF THE TENT ARE OPEN TO THE BREEZE

BAMBOO END WALLS OFTEN REMOVED TO ALLOW FOR CROSS VENTILATION

TENT CLOTH GUYED WIDELY TO FORM A SUN SHADE

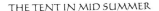

CROSS VENTILATION

1.7.

The changing forms of the black tents of the Luri tribes of Iran over the year. Upper figure: the goatskin tent cloth is guyed and pegged down to keep out the wind and driving rain. Lower figure: as spring progresses the tent cloth is raised to let in the warm breezes and in mid-summer the tent cloth becomes a sun shade (Roaf, 1979).

the stillest days that is driven by the stack effect alone. The stack effect is powered by the buoyancy of air, which depends on the pressure difference between cool and warm air (see Chapter 5). This effect has been compared to water flowing upside down. If the building is a bucket with holes in, filled with water, the water will drain out of the holes at the base. As with heat in a building: the greater the temperature difference, the greater the buoyancy effect; the more water the greater the pressure.

The property of warm air, which can be thought of, almost, as upside-down water flowing around a building, can be used to thermally landscape the ceilings of rooms. Hot air can be channelled around ceilings, in 'banks' or walls, to form rivers or lakes of heat that can move between areas or rooms within a building. This is well illustrated in Figure 1.9.

A BRICK IN A STORAGE RADIATOR

In very cold climates the rooms of buildings, just like people, huddle together to keep warm, often around a central 'hot core', a heat source such as a fire place. Figure 1.10 shows a classic hot-core building from Latvia where an extended

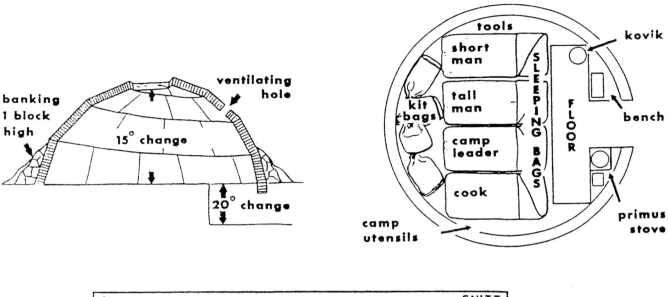

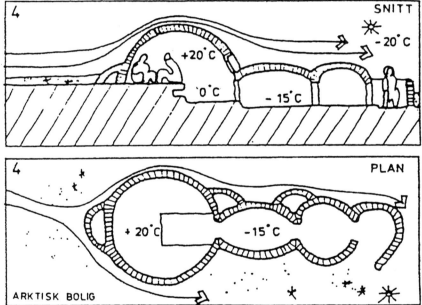

1.8.
Section through an igloo showing the thermal stratification above the raised platform
on which people live (Cook, 1994).

warm wall into the communal room is always a favourite place to sit in winter.
The principle is similar to that of a brick in a storage radiator. The heat comes
from perhaps a fire or the sun, and is absorbed in the thermal mass of the
building, as it is in a radiator brick. Then, gradually, that heat is emitted back into
the room over time. If a material is highly conductive, such as the copper or
steel shown in Figure 1.1, it will not store the heat. If the Kacheloven was made
of steel or iron it would cool down rapidly when the fire had gone out, unlike
the high-density concrete stove that actually stores the heat and will stay warm
for up to 14 hours after the fire has gone out.

1.9.
This Kacheloven is the high mass wood-burning stove at the Oxford Ecohouse. Above it is a cloth skirt, 60 cm deep, which has been attached to form walls for the hot air that rises above the stove. This air is channelled in these walls to the ceiling of the room next door where it warms the concrete floor above. This warm floor then acts as a warm radiator, heating the rooms above and below. Equally, the heat could then be channelled to an outside wall and would flow out of the building through windows above the hem of the skirt. (Nat Rea).

The performance of the thermal mass in a building is dependent on many different factors, including the 'thermal capacity' of the material, location in relation to the other building elements and related ventilation strategies, issues dealt with in later chapters of the book.

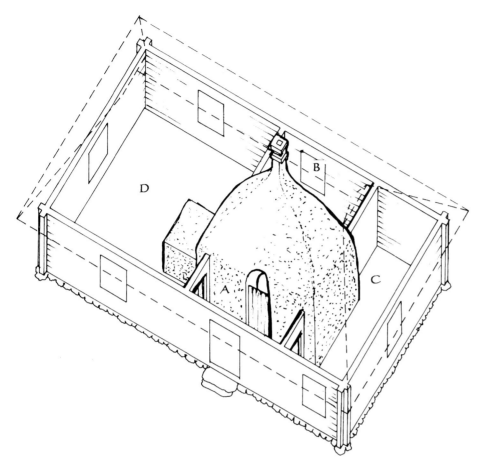

THE BUILDING AS A ROMAN BATH HOUSE

In Roman bath houses the floors were warmed by an under-floor heating system called a hypocaust. A fire would be lit under the great basins used to heat the water for the hot baths and the excess heat from the fire would be ducted under solid floors to heat the bath house itself. So, in such systems, there is a heat source, thermal mass to store the heat in and regulate its dissipation into a space, and a system of heat distribution. This idea uses a convective heat transfer medium, air or water, to a radiator that is part of the building. It can be a horizontal hypocaust under a floor or a vertical hypocaust such as a warm wall, column or Kacheloven.

Even in simple village houses there are some very sophisticated design systems that make our modern Western houses look very ordinary. One of these interesting house forms is found on the isolated island of Ullungdo, in Korea (Figure 1.11). It has a double outer-wall construction with the removable outer buffer zone wall, the 'u-de-gi' (a thatched wall), added to provide protection against the driving winds of the island. The two central winter rooms are made of logs and clay with high thermal performance and good humidity control. The thick thatched roof provides protection against the winter snow and summer

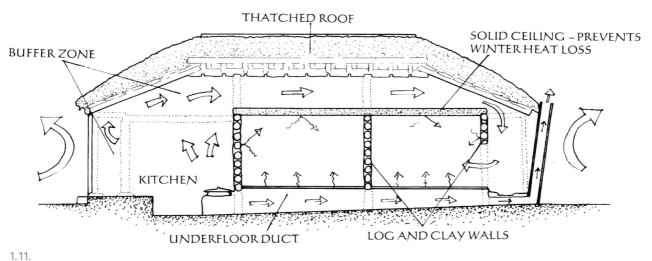

1.11.
Tu-mak-gyp house on the remote Korean island of Ullungdo with a horizontal hypocaust under the floor of the central room.

OPTIMISING THE USE OF WARMTH AND COOLTH

1.12.

Sketch section of the Kacheloven illustrated in Figure 1.1.f that acts like a vertical hypocaust. The oven not only heats the surfaces it can 'see' radiantly but the hot air rising convectively around it collects under the ceiling, so heating the concrete floor above. A 'skirt' dropped from the ceiling 'dams' the heat causing it to move away from the fire on the undammed side. The flue passes up through the concrete wall above and heats the adjacent sections of the wall by conduction.

sun. The really clever trick is the kitchen flue, which is funnelled under the winter living room to optimise the value of the scarce fuel resources to the inhabitants by being used both for the cooking and the heating. While the mean external temperature measured was 1.2°C, the mean temperature in the

Chukdam buffer space was 1.1°C and in the internal room it was a comfortable 15.6°C, with a mean relative humidity (RH) of 44.9 per cent against the external RH of 71.2 per cent. The average floor-surface temperature was 22°C. This demonstrates the excellent ability of the earth walls to control the RH in a space, in a 'breathing wall' (Lee et al., 1994).

THE BUILDING AS A PERISCOPE

Buildings can be periscopes, trained to catch the light, a view, the wind or the sun. If you design them for any of these functions they must face in the correct direction. One of the pioneers of passive building design said that there are three important factors for passive buildings: 1. orientation, 2. orientation and 3. orientation (Docherty and Szokolay, 1999, p. 39).

1.13.
Professor Georg Reinberg's solar development in Sagedergasse, Vienna, making imaginative use of the building form to optimise the solar potential of the site (Reinberg, 1996).

Outside the tropics the best orientation for solar gain, for light and heat, is towards the equator. In the tropics it is best to hide from the sun under a large hat or a roof. If a building faces 15° to the east or west of the solar orientation it will make very little difference to the amount of energy that can be garnered from the sun. Simply by facing the living rooms of a house towards the sun it is possible to save up to 30 per cent on the annual heating bills of a typical house in a temperate climate. Passive solar design is dealt with in Chapter 7 and is often described in terms of ideal sites. Even in the most difficult sites, with careful thought and sometimes inspired design, as we see in Figure 1.13, it is possible to capture the light and heat of the sun. Even if the site has a difficult orientation it is possible to catch the sun with the use of periscopes projecting from the building in the form of upper-floor clerestory windows, bay and dormer windows and roof lights.

The most difficult orientation is west, because the low western sun coincides with the hottest time of day (mid-afternoon), making overheating of west-facing spaces a probability in summer, except in the high latitudes. A western orientation should be avoided if possible, particularly with sun spaces, because of their potential for overheating. Care should be taken to think about what each room in a house will be used for and what type of light and heat it will require from the sun. For instance, it would be best to give a breakfast room access to eastern, morning, sun. Perhaps proper dining rooms may be good rooms for evening sun. A little well-designed light will give more pleasure to the building users than too much.

A TREE IN THE BREEZE

How lovely, on a warm day to sit beneath a shady tree, in a gentle breeze. A building can be like a tree. When the temperature of the air is close enough to local comfort temperatures then, simply by opening up the walls of a building, its occupants can be adequately warmed or cooled in a cross-draught. This is well demonstrated in the Queensland case study where, in the tropical climate, set within the rustling eucalyptus trees, being indoors is as comfortable on a hot day as sitting under a tree in the breeze. In some climates the breeze may be comfortable day and night. In most climates the air temperatures at night are too low for comfort. Many people around the world sleep out at night, in the garden, on the roof or in open-sided buildings or tents, in sight of the stars.

A COOL-CORE BUILDING

Just as the ice-houses used to store cold from the winter months for use in the 'salad' days of summer, the thermal mass of a building can be used to store the cool of the night winds to lower internal temperatures during the day. This is well demonstrated in Jimmy Lim's case study where he has built a modern version of a traditional Malaysian house, with its verandas and balconies around the high-mass core of a pre-existing building. The thermal mass of the inner walls is completely shaded all year and cooled by the air movement over them at night (Figure 1.14). This is a good example of a cool-core

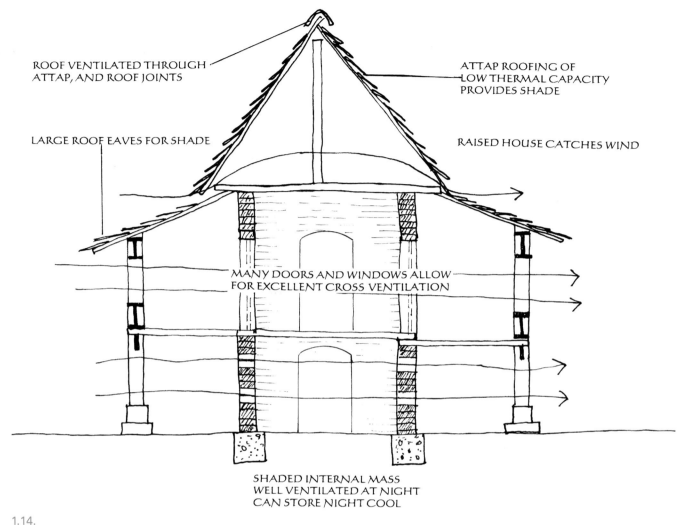

ROOF VENTILATED THROUGH ATTAP, AND ROOF JOINTS

ATTAP ROOFING OF LOW THERMAL CAPACITY PROVIDES SHADE

LARGE ROOF EAVES FOR SHADE

RAISED HOUSE CATCHES WIND

MANY DOORS AND WINDOWS ALLOW FOR EXCELLENT CROSS VENTILATION

SHADED INTERNAL MASS WELL VENTILATED AT NIGHT CAN STORE NIGHT COOL

1.14.
The introduction of a cool core of well-ventilated, shaded, masonry into a traditional Malay house would have advantages in keeping people in the centre of the house cooler on the hottest days.

building. It is simple and works well and, in fact, could be compared to the old colonial bungalows with their surrounding verandas.

AN AIR LOCK IN A SPACE SHIP TO KEEP THE COLD OUT

In temperate or cold regions all outer doors should have a buffer space, or air lock. This acts in five ways:

1 to keep the wind away from the door and the biting draughts out of the house
2 to modify the air temperature, rather as in an air lock, where the air in the buffer space is usually somewhere half way between inside and outside temperature. This is excellent air to use to ventilate the house inside in winter as it is not freezing. Small, openable, windows should be built between

the buffer porch or sunspace and the house to provide natural pre-heat ventilation

3 as a place to leave wet clothes outside the house so removing moisture from inside

4 as a security and privacy feature so people can be heard or seen before they enter the house

5 to protect the floor construction around the inside of the main house door from becoming too cold. In houses without buffer spaces, every time the door opens and cold air comes into the house, heat is drawn out of the floor and walls next to the door. The floor is often constructed with a slab of concrete, making the floor area around the door much cooler than it would be if the door had a porch (Thomas and Rees, 1999).

A HOBBIT HOLE

Some years ago, Michael Humphreys wrote an amazing article that asked us to try and understand what makes a Hobbit's life so comfortable (Humphreys, 1995). He concluded that Hobbits live a very comfortable life for a number of reasons:

- they choose carefully exactly what type of climate and landscape they want to live in
- they choose a sheltered site away from strong winds
- they have a special Hobbit hole design that withstands extreme climates by being largely underground
- they have a simple heating system that they know how to use and to collect wood for
- they have enough opening windows to keep them cool and fresh at any time of the year
- they wear suitable clothes for different times of year
- they change their lifestyles at different times of year to enhance the time in which they feel not only comfortable but also thermally delightful, by being outside more in summer and inside by the fire in winter.

In order to understand how to design a new house for a Hobbit you would have to take all these factors into account from the start, so writing a good brief is an important first start.

THE COST OF 'FORM' IN SITE PLANNING

An interesting case study of a new ecohousing development in Hungary demonstrates that there are very real financial advantages of adopting solar strategies in housing layout. The developers, Aldino Ltd of Budapest, bought a 64-ha site at Veresegyhaz some 30 minutes from the centre of Budapest, in April 1993. The land had few trees and sloped gently to the south. The first design (Figure 1.15A) using conventional housing layouts planned for a maximum density of 380 houses on 100 m^2 plots, but was found to be of too high density and not suitable, both for social reasons and for the unfavourable economic returns offered by the development. The second plan for 330 houses was developed along similar lines but the cost of the infrastructure and

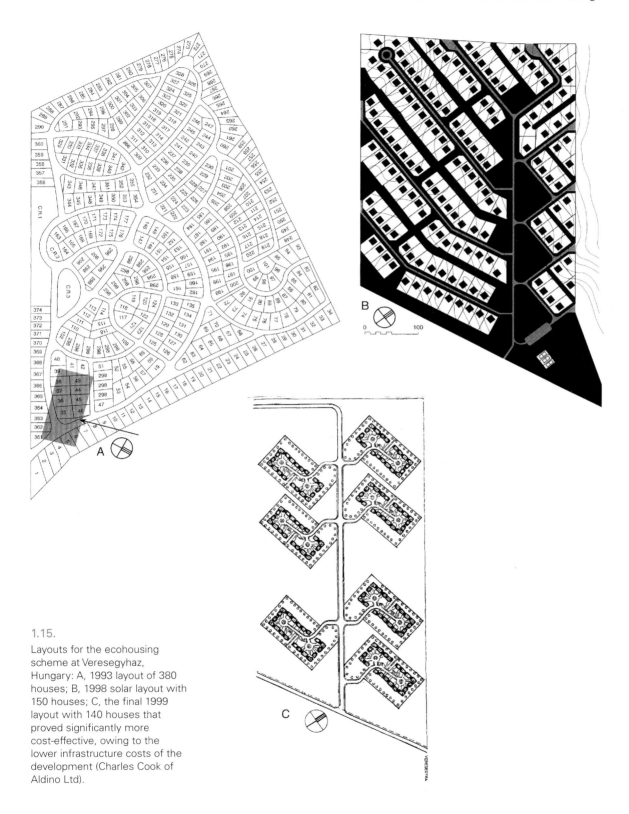

1.15.

Layouts for the ecohousing scheme at Veresegyhaz, Hungary: A, 1993 layout of 380 houses; B, 1998 solar layout with 150 houses; C, the final 1999 layout with 140 houses that proved significantly more cost-effective, owing to the lower infrastructure costs of the development (Charles Cook of Aldino Ltd).

services, which had to be brought from the nearby village half a kilometre away, was found to be double the price of the land acquisition, and therefore that plan was also not feasible.

Some three years later it was decided to re-evaluate the development potential of the site and a third scheme for 300 houses was developed for middle/up-market houses, again with a conventional layout. Again it proved uneconomic using conventional planning. At that time the chief developer, Charles Cook, visited the Oxford Ecohouse and became convinced that a healthy, environmentally friendly development would be a real benefit to the site and region. It would be an important demonstration of what can be achieved for the improved environmental performance of the houses, the quality of life of the householders and the development of solar technologies in Hungary.

It was necessary to create a new site layout that reduced the road area and service lines, provided a green ambience, a secure environment and oriented the houses to the south. After many attempts at site planning he devised a layout of cul-de-sacs of groups of 20 houses that could provide all of the requirements of the brief and a good social atmosphere for the area. The cul-de-sac layouts are served by a single main road that has speed restraining features, so lowering local noise and risks for pedestrians. In so doing, the cost of roads, pavements and lighting has been substantially reduced, as has the cost of the drainage infrastructure beneath the site. As a result of this experience he is convinced that developers should look very seriously at re-evaluating how they develop because, by putting new ingredients into the planning equation, such as solar access, security, the quality of the environment and social ambience he has not only come up with a far more pleasant solution for the people who will live in the houses but has also increased profits. The local council is delighted by the new 'green' agenda and has been very supportive of the project. Surprisingly the council have identified a key benefit of this scheme as being that better housing such as this will put less pressure on their local hospitals' beds, because many local hospital admissions are of people whose health has suffered from poor housing. So everyone benefits, including the environment, particularly when such a development is serviced by good public transport connections to the city.

CHOOSING WHICH FORM TO USE IN A DESIGN

Along with clothing, and later fire, buildings are the primary technology that has allowed man, originally an African animal, to successfully spread throughout the world. One function of the building is to create a 'liveable' climate indoors even when the outdoor climate is hostile. If the building fails then discomfort or even disaster can follow. In the UK some 40 000, mainly old, people die in winter from avoidable cold-related illnesses (many countries with colder climates do not experience this problem). These deaths and the increased cost to the health service of increased disease[1] are the result of

---

[1]Rudge, J. and Gilchrist, R. (2006). Measuring the health impact of temperatures in buildings. *NCEUB Conference 'Comfort and Energy Use in Buildings – Getting It Right'*, Windsor. www.nceub.org.uk

Solar Potential, Poundbury Phase I

Maximum Solar Potential: 95 properties (42%)

Optimum Solar Potential: 92 properties (41%)

Minimum Solar Potential: 37 properties (17%)

1.16.

Plan of Poundbury, Phase I, development in West Dorset. A modern traditional settlement showing that to design settlements for optimal solar gain you do not have to face them rigidly south. Maximum solar gain describes homes within 15 degrees east or west of south and optimal is 30 degrees either east or west of south. On any of these homes solar systems would work well in the UK (Rajat Gupta).

inadequate buildings. In the European heatwave of 2003, 15 000 people died of heat in France alone – 35 per cent of them at home.

So your ecohouse design needs to be not just comfortable to live in but it has to remain habitable and safe despite the worst predictions for climate change. The future of the people who live in the house may depend on whether it stays cool in the summer and warm in the winter and to what extent it can do so without 'outside help' in the form of energy from the gas main or the electricity grid. The cost of energy is not the only problem; as fossil fuels deplete we are facing the problem of the reliability of the energy source. A building that uses a minimum of energy, and preferably generates its own energy, will serve its occupants well in the future.

The first step when approaching your new design should always be to try and understand the overall climate of the site and how much protection the house will need to provide against it. A simple way of doing this is to use a Nicol graph. First of all a graph is drawn with 10°C intervals on the x axis and the 12 months of the year on the y axis. Then the mean maximum (red curve) and mean minimum outdoor temperatures (blue) for each month are plotted showing a double curve for the year with the mean outdoor temperature shown in pink. The green curve is the temperature at which the average person will be comfortable in most buildings (without heating or cooling) at that outdoor temperature. The 'comfort temperature' (T_c) is calculated using the equation derived by Michael Humphreys:

$T_c = 0.534 \, (T_{mean}) + 11.9$
T_c is Comfort Temperature
Where $T_{mean} = (T_{max} + T_{min}) / 2)$
T_{mean} is monthly mean indoor temperature
T_{max} is monthly mean daily outdoor maximum temperature, and
T_{min} is monthly mean daily outdoor minimum temperature.
T_{min} and T_{max} are usually available from Meteorological Office data.

This equation[2], strictly speaking, applies to summer conditions in free-running buildings (not air-conditioned ones) but it gives a general idea of the comfort conditions required by people who have adapted to the local climate.

People can adapt to the most remarkable range of temperatures. One person can be very happy sitting in a pleasant breeze in the warm sunshine and then go inside and feel deliciously cool indoors at 7°C cooler climate.

The T_c line does not represent a single temperature but a running mean of the sort of temperatures that an indigenous person would feel comfortable in. In summer they show that people in Scotland would be happy at 18°C while in Malaysia, Japan, Indonesia and the Caribbean the T_c is around 27°C.

What the Nicol graph (Figure 1.17) can be used for is to give a rough idea of the amount of heating and cooling (if any) the building will require in each month. In a good passive, high-mass building the indoor air will tend to revert to a temperature half way between the mean outdoor and mean indoor

[2]More detailed information on the Nicol graph is given on page 324.

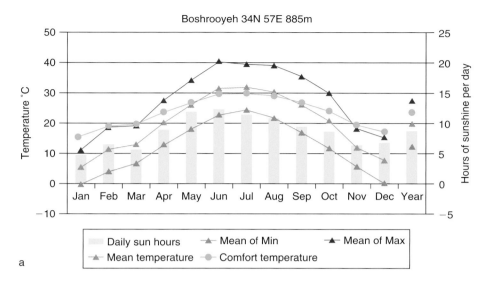

Boshrooyeh 34N 57E 885m

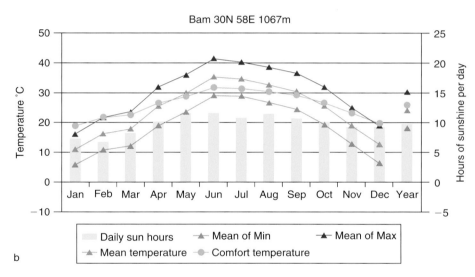

Bam 30N 58E 1067m

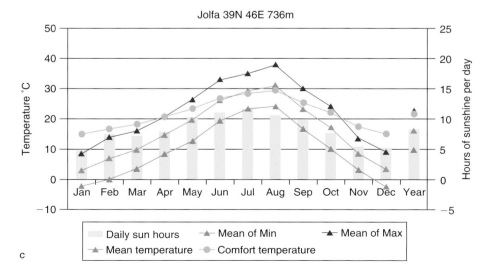

Jolfa 39N 46E 736m

1.17.

Nicol graphs for six different cities in Iran, with their latitude, longitude and altitude showing how very different the climates in one country can be (Fergus Nicol).

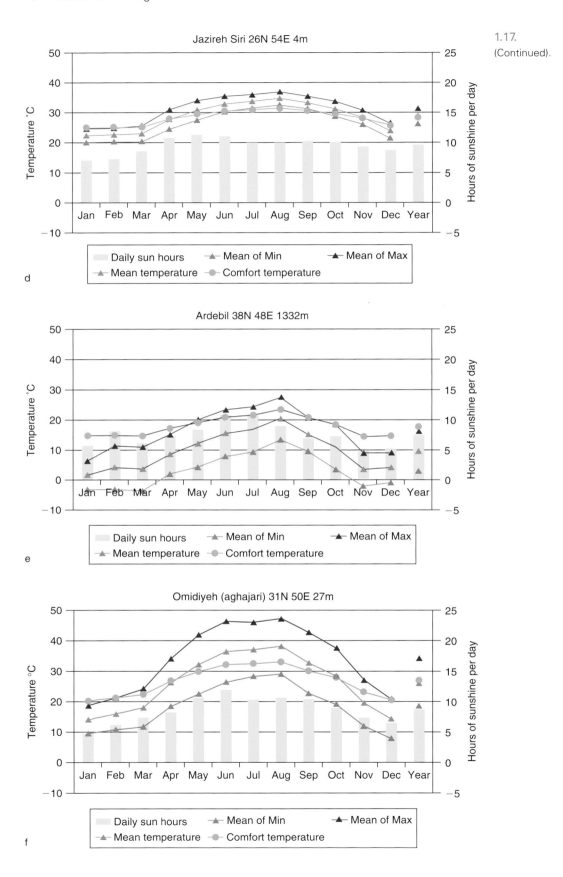

1.17.
(Continued).

temperatures. So a line can be drawn half way between the two to indicate the free-running indoor air temperature. If this is below the T_c, then the building will need heating up to make the occupants warm. If the indoor air temperature line is above the T_c then the building will need to be cooled to make the occupants comfortable.

Figure 1.17 illustrates how much variation can occur in a single country (Iran in this case) with changes in the latitude, the altitude and the proximity to the sea. The graphs include a bar chart showing the number of hours of sunshine available, to give an idea of the possibilities for solar heating (and the problems for cooling in the summer).

If a large amount of heat is required it can be partly supplied by passive systems, such as the rock store in the Bariloche house (see page 396). If a great deal of cooling is required it may be possible to gain it through ventilation, by simply opening a wall of a house, as in the Yarrawonga house in Queensland (see page 377). Convective cooling is effective up to average skin temperature (around 32–34°C) and even above that temperature range it will help with evaporative cooling of the skin. A fan can provide cooling equivalent to a 2–4° drop in temperature in hot conditions with relatively little energy.

Thus, with a simple graph we can tell how much we want to welcome in the external climate at different times of the year, or how much we want to keep it out. The graph also gives a very rough idea of how much extra energy will have to be found in the form of supplementary heating or cooling systems to reach the T_c. This is an effective way of looking at the passive potential of a building in a particular climate and using this knowledge to pick an appropriate building form to optimise this passive potential.

When reviewing the case study buildings in the second section of the book it is worth noting that in no climate shown is the difference between the mean maximum and mean minimum outdoor temperature less than 6°C. This means that a well-designed passive building should be able to give up to 3°C free cooling by using ventilation at the coolest time of day, or heating even in a hot humid climate, as shown for Malaysia or Indonesia. 3°C could well be the difference between discomfort and delight.

Having decided how much shelter from the climate a building has to provide, and roughly what form would be best suited to the task, it is then time to start thinking about what materials you would like to use to build it and how to construct the building. These subjects are covered in Chapters 2 and 3.

2 THE ENVIRONMENTAL IMPACT OF BUILDING MATERIALS

Since the publication of the first edition of *Ecohouse* many of the concepts relating to environmental impact have become more widely known and the availability of commercial environmental impact assessment services has increased. Despite this increase in the availability of information, many architects and designers still have to rely on common sense and deal with constrains of budget and location when specifying materials. This chapter aims to introduce basic concepts and ideas that will help designers develop strategies for specifying materials which minimize negative environmental impact. A reading list at the end of the chapter lists more detailed sources of information about the environmental impact of building materials.

Building materials require processing before they are incorporated into a building; this inevitably requires the use of energy and results in waste generation. The choice of materials therefore affects the environmental impact of a building. The processing may be minimal, as in the case of a traditional cottage constructed from materials found locally, or it may be extensive, as in the case of prefabricated construction.

Even basic materials have an environmental impact. It is estimated, for example, that the production of cement accounts for 5 per cent of global human-made CO_2 emissions, about half of which arise from chemical reactions in the cement-making process and half from the energy consumed in producing cement (Kruse, 2004).

We can calculate the overall environmental impact of a house if we know the impacts that result from its day-to-day use and the manufacture and delivery of its construction materials and components. We can, with this information, see how the choice of materials affects its impact on the environment.

It will become clear that calculations to determine the exact impact of each and every dwelling are, at present, not feasible. This chapter will therefore refer to a very detailed study of the Oxford Ecohouse, which took account of the impact of materials selection. It will also refer to other research in this field and will aim to draw some practical conclusions of use to the prospective house designer, builder or renovator.

MEASURING THE ENVIRONMENTAL IMPACT OF BUILDING MATERIALS

When choosing materials several factors have to be considered, and it is unlikely that absolute rules can be given for all situations. The first question is how environmental impact should be assessed. A material's inherent qualities and the way materials are incorporated into a design (and culture or lifestyle) all determine environmental impact.

2.1.
Living space within a yacht. How much space does one require? The quantity of materials used will have a direct effect on the environmental impact of a dwelling.

Factors determined by a material's qualities are, for example:

- energy required to produce the material
- CO_2 emissions resulting from the material's manufacture
- impact on the local environment resulting from the extraction of the material (e.g. quarry pit, wood taken from a forest, oil spills from an oil well, etc.)
- toxicity of the material
- transportation of the material during its manufacture and delivery to site
- degree of pollution resulting from the material at the end of its useful life.

Factors affected by material choice and design decisions include:

- location and detailing of an architectural element
- maintenance required and the materials necessary for that maintenance
- contribution that the material makes to reducing the building's environmental impact (e.g. insulation)
- flexibility of a design to accommodate changing uses over time
- lifetime of the material and its potential for reuse if the building is demolished.

The following headings for comparing the environmental impact of materials, used in the *Green Building Handbook* (Woolley et al., 1997), provide a good checklist.

- Environmental impact owing to production:
  - energy use
  - resource depletion
  - global warming
  - acid rain
  - toxins.
- Environmental impact owing to use:
  - potential for reuse/recycling and disposal
  - health hazard.

Perhaps the single most important measure of an object's environmental impact is provided by the concept of 'embodied energy'. 'Embodied energy' describes the amount of energy used to produce an object. We can refer to the embodied energy of a brick, a window or of an entire house. The following sections discuss embodied energy and embodied emissions in some detail. As figures for the embodied energy of materials are not yet widely available, it is hoped that understanding the factors affecting it will help the reader to 'ask the right questions' when considering material selection.

Embodied energy is an important measure because the use of non-renewable energy sources is the principal reason for environmental degradation. Degradation is caused in two main ways: 1) resulting from atmospheric emissions, principally CO_2, contributing to global warming; 2) resulting from the effects other emissions have on the atmosphere, such as acid rain.

The concept of 'embodied omissions' is similar to that of 'embodied energy' and refers to the emissions associated with the production of an object, for example the electricity used to produce a window will result in CO_2 emissions associated with that window. In addition, the production of materials, particularly those requiring chemical treatment, can result in the emission of toxins. If accurate embodied-emissions figures are to be calculated, the types of fuels used in any manufacturing process must be known, as each fuel gives a different mix of emissions.

Several different methods exist for calculating embodied energy, and this results in a range of figures published for similar materials. Published data should be treated with some caution, unless it is clearly stated how the figures have been calculated.

CALCULATING EMBODIED ENERGY

The following section will help one research the embodied energy of a particular material or to make some educated guesses.

How has the energy been measured?

When reading figures for the embodied energy of a material or house type, the first question to ask is how has the energy been measured? Energy is measured as either delivered or primary energy. Delivered energy refers to the actual quantity of energy delivered for use to a particular site or building, for example the amount of electricity used and recorded on a bill. Primary energy refers to the amount of energy used to produce a quantity of delivered energy. For example, to create electricity, gas will have been burnt to drive the turbines in a power station. The generators will not be 100 per cent efficient, so the energy content of the gas burnt is greater than the energy content of the electricity generated. Also, the electricity has to be transported from the power station to the consumer, a process that is not 100 per cent efficient. All of these inefficiencies mean that for every one unit of electricity delivered to a consumer, a larger amount of primary energy will have been consumed in its creation.

In the UK, the ratio between primary and delivered energy is greatest for electricity.

It is still the case that embodied energy figures are often quoted without stating if they have been calculated using primary or delivered energy. Where there is uncertainty over the embodied energy figures quoted, it is better to compare materials using embodied emissions figures, as these should take into account the amount of primary fuels used to produce a given quantity of primary energy. In the UK during 2003 electricity supplied from the grid resulted in 0.43 kg CO_2/kWhr being delivered, whereas mains gas resulted in less than half that amount being delivered, i.e. 0.191 kg CO_2/kWhr (Batey and Pout, 2005).

What has been considered when calculating embodied energy?

Once one is clear about the energy measurement, it is important to know where the boundary has been drawn in calculating the energy inputs. For example, consider the embodied energy of a steel-framed window. If the energy inputs are calculated only for the energy used in the factory that assembled the window, figures will differ from calculations that include also

the energy used in the steel works to make the steel or the energy used in the mine to gather the iron ore.

In order to calculate accurately the embodied energy of a material, all stages at which energy is used should be accounted for. An accurate figure will be derived if we consider the energy used for extraction of raw materials, transportation to processing plants, energy used in factories, transportation to site and energy used on site to install the product.

RECYCLING AND EMBODIED ENERGY

For a low-energy house, is it best to construct a new dwelling or refurbish an existing one?

Refurbishment is a means of recycling buildings. Opinion differs as to the benefits of refurbishing buildings (Carbon Vision Building Partnership, 2006); essentially the issue resolves around how well an existing building's energy performance can be improved. If the choice is between demolition followed by new build, or a straight refurbishment, then the energy efficiency in day-to-day energy use will determine which option has the lowest environmental impact. A new building will probably have a lower environmental impact over its lifespan if it requires significantly less running energy for day-to-day use.

Recycling (or refurbishment) is an issue that needs careful thought in relation to environmental impact. It only makes environmental sense to recycle if it can be done easily; that is, without requiring the input of a lot of energy, if the building can be thermally upgraded to a significant extent and if such recycling is not repeated too frequently. As will be seen later, walls and floors (heavy elements) will probably account for the greatest amount of embodied energy; if these can be kept continually insulated at a high level, then refurbishment will be a good option.

As an example, we consider a typical situation found in a nineteenth-century house. Often, internal walls will be constructed using lime plaster on wooden laths fixed to vertical timber posts. After 100 years or so, the lime plaster can begin to separate from the laths, which typically occurs locally. The best solution would be to remove all of the loose plaster. However, once a loose piece is removed, it is difficult both to prevent a larger area coming away and to replace it with new lime-based plaster. Typically, this will be expensive, and it maybe difficult to find a knowledgeable contractor. If you ask a general building contractor they will probably propose to remove all the plaster and replace it with plasterboard (which requires a relatively large amount of energy to manufacture). But if you speak to a plasterer, they will often recommend leaving the original lime plaster in place and reinforcing it with a scrim (fine mesh) and a thin coat of plaster over that. The last option will have the minimum environmental impact, because so little new material is used, even though it uses a modern plaster that will require more energy to produce per unit volume than a replacement lime plaster.

PROCESSING AND EMBODIED ENERGY

The greater the number of processes a material or set of components have to go through, the higher will be their embodied energy and the number of associated waste products. Materials such as metal require very large energy inputs for their production, but so will equipment that requires complex manufacturing, for example a modern gas boiler.

Within reason, one should aim to choose materials and components that are as close to their natural state as possible. So, a high-performance window with a softwood frame will be preferable to the same window with an aluminium frame. Or, as another example, organic paints or those that are water based,

2.3.
External table, Le Corbusier's mother's house at Vevey, Switzerland. An object with minimal use of materials, external spaces allow dwellings to expand seasonally and visually.

particularly if using natural pigments, or waxes are preferable finishes to highly manufactured synthetic paints.

TRANSPORTATION AND EMBODIED ENERGY

Transportation can be a significant factor affecting embodied energy. The further a material has to travel, the greater the energy that is used in its transport. The weight of a material will also affect the energy needed to move it. Some natural products may have travelled great distances, for example polished granite from overseas quarries, the finishing of which may even take place in a second country before delivery to the final point of sale. This kind of information is not always freely available, but asking suppliers about transportation can help you to make decisions while also alerting suppliers to a concern in the market place.

In some situations transportation will have to be weighed against durability. In the UK, you can now purchase natural slate from quarries in Spain. This slate is much cheaper than English or Welsh slate and, though not as durable, the Spanish slate is apparently more durable than artificial slate. On grounds of durability, an imported natural material may be preferable to a local artificial one.

TIME AND EMBODIED ENERGY

Studies conducted in Southern Australia suggest that the day-to-day energy used to run a typical (i.e. non-low energy) residential building, over a 50-year lifespan, is equal to approximately four times the embodied energy of its structure (Pullen, 2000).

This kind of direct comparison between energy in use and embodied energy is not very useful, unless we know how long the dwelling is expected to last. It will always be the case that as energy-in-use requirements reduce, the longer it will take for energy in use to equal the embodied energy of the structure.

2.4.

Recycled buildings, mixed-use housing, Ilot 13, Quartier des Grottes, Geneva, Switzerland. If existing buildings can be reused and upgraded in an energy-efficient manner, they will have a smaller environmental impact owing to a lower material use compared with new buildings. Architects: P. Bonhote, O. Calame and I. Vuarambon.

When considering the embodied energy of a building, we need to take account of the building's expected lifespan, the maintenance requirements of the various building elements and the building's state at the end of its life.

This cradle-to-grave approach is called life cycle analysis. It is used as a way of assessing the total impact of any building and shows the importance of the building's lifespan. The longer a house can last, the lower the impact of the energy and pollution resulting from the manufacture of its materials will be. A simple way to think about this is to consider the initial embodied energy of an entire building and divide this figure over its lifetime, making an allowance for maintenance.

The International Standards Organisation includes a methodology for undertaking life cycle analysis within the ISO 14000 standard. This standard relates to environmental policy within organisations and is not specifically related to buildings, although the methodology is applicable to them.

The following documents within ISO 14000 relate specifically to life cycle assessment:

ISO 14040 Goal and scope (1997)
ISO 14041 Life Cycle Inventory Analysis (1998)
ISO 14042 Life Cycle Impact Assessment (2000)
ISO 14043 Life Cycle Interpretation (2000)

This standard does not provide actual embodied energy figures that can be used in a life cycle analysis – these remain difficult to obtain.

EMBODIED ENERGY AND THE MATERIALS USED IN HOUSES

Generally, if an up-to-date database has been assembled, it will be used commercially. The Building Research Establishment (BRE) has developed a methodology for the environmental profiling of construction materials, components and buildings (Howard et al., 1991; Anderson and Edwards, 2000). This methodology has been used to develop a relative environmental performance rating system using a simple grading – A, B, C – for over 250 building materials and components. The rating system refers to a range of environmental impacts including climate change, toxicity, fossil fuel depletion, levels of emissions and pollutants, mineral and water exaction.

Information on environmental profiles is available in the *Green Guide to Specification* (Anderson and Shiers, 2002) and is used in the BRE's environmental impact estimation tool, ENVEST2, which allows designers to consider the life cycle environmental impact of building materials at the building inception stage.

Due to the specialist knowledge required, and the need to constantly update any embodied energy database, it is normal for specialist consultants to undertake life cycle analysis studies. Architects working on modest projects are likely to rely on general guides such as those listed at the end of this chapter. The website 'EcoSite – Worldwide resource for life cycle analysis' (http:// www.ecosite.co.uk) publishes the list of embodied energy figures, credited to the BRE, shown in Table 2.1.

Table 2.1. Embodied energy of building materials. Range of published figures

Material	Density	Low value		High value	
	$(kg\,m^{-3})$	$GJ\,tonne^{-1}$	$GJ\,m^{-3}$	$GJ\,tonne^{-1}$	$GJ\,m^{-3}$
Natural aggregates	1500	0.030	0.05	0.12	0.93
Cement	1500	4.3	6.5	7.8	11.7
Bricks	~1700	1.0	1.7	9.4	16.0
Timber (prepared softwood)	~500	0.52	0.26	7.1	3.6
Glass	2600	13.0	34.0	31.0	81.0
Steel (steel sections)	7800	24.0	190.0	59.0	460.0
Plaster	~1200	1.1	1.3	6.7	8.0

GJ = giga joule, a unit of energy, 1 GJ = 278 kWh.
Source: Building Research Establishment, 1994.

Table 2.1 illustrates the range of published figures, but it does not state if the figures are for primary or delivered energy. However, previous research (West et al., 1994) has indicated that, for most building types, the following materials will contribute significantly to the embodied energy of a building:

- steel
- concrete
- timber
- bricks
- cement
- aggregates
- glass
- plaster.

These materials account for a large proportion of the volume or mass of most buildings, and the designer can significantly affect a building's embodied energy by paying close attention to their specification. Selecting materials from local sources will reduce their embodied energy and emissions because of reduced transport. The range of values for timber shown in Table 2.1 provides an indication of the impact of transport, amongst other factors.

In a typical house with walls built from brick and concrete blocks and with timber floors, these three materials could account for about 50 per cent of the dwelling's embodied energy, with brick and concrete accounting for about 30 per cent of the total. Sheet materials, for example plasterboards or lining boards to timber-framed walls, can also have a significant impact.

THE EMBODIED ENERGY OF DIFFERENT BUILDING MATERIALS

At present, the few published figures available for embodied energy usually refer to incividual materials, e.g. brick, concrete, timber or glass. These figures are useful for making strategic decisions regarding a house, i.e. should it be built using a timber frame or concrete blocks, but they are less useful when trying to decide if a particular energy-saving feature should be used, for example mechanical ventilation with heat recovery. This is where life cycle analysis becomes important.

As embodied energy is usually quoted per unit weight or per unit volume of a material, one needs to know the weight or volume of the particular material actually used in a building. Certain materials, such as plastics or metals, have very high embodied energies per unit weight but, if used in small quantities, may have an overall benefit by, for example, providing an elegant joint between materials or by increasing the distance a material, such as timber, can span or by increasing the lifetime of an element.

2.5.

Equipment used on a building site for pumping 'Warmcell' insulation, made from recycled newspapers, into a wall. At almost every stage in the production and construction process, energy is used. The sum of the energy from each stage, including the energy used for transport, is called the product's embodied energy.

Plastics, timber and metals are materials about which there is much debate over their environmental impact. There is no consensus as to the advisability of the use of plastics or synthetic materials but, in our view, they are best avoided.

Plastics

The embodied energy of plastics is extremely high. They are, on the other hand, waste products from the production of petroleum. So, it can be argued that by using plastics we reduce the accumulation of waste material. But it can also be said that the use of plastics helps to support the very industry that is responsible for a large amount of CO_2 emissions and for over half of all toxic emissions to the environment. After their production, plastics tend to release gases into the atmosphere. These are referred to as volatile organic compounds (VOCs), which can be harmful if breathed in any quantity. They are found in synthetic compounds in carpets and modern paints, especially oil-based paints such as those with an eggshell finish. The effect of VOCs is usually greatest soon after installation.

One plastic generally thought best to avoid is polyvinyl chloride (PVC). It is particularly difficult to dispose of in an ecologically safe manner but it can be recycled and, in its recycled form, is beginning to appear on the market, generally for low-grade products.

Metals

Metals are another group of materials with a high embodied energy for which the manufacturing process results in local environmental degradation from waste products. Owing to the high price of metals, most waste metal is recycled, although this process is not without its own detrimental environmental cost; the smelting process requires large energy inputs and generates highly toxic dioxin emissions because of the chlorine found in most metals. Until such time when the large-scale use of renewable energies makes their production more environmentally friendly, it is best to minimise the use of metals in construction. Metals should only be used in small quantities or for particular purposes, e.g. for the jointing and fixing of materials.

Stainless steel and aluminium are both very likely to be recycled, but have very high environmental impacts as a result of their initial manufacture. Their extensive use in buildings cannot be considered ecological.

Lead, because of its toxic nature and associated pollution resulting from the manufacturing process, is best avoided. Currently, it is mainly used for roof flashings, where it forms a long-lasting waterproofing element between walls and roof coverings or at junctions between roof coverings. Water collected off roofs with lead flashings is best not used for watering edible fruits or vegetables as these may absorb lead as they grow. Lead may prove a hazard when renovating older properties as paint older than 35 years may contain the metal which was used as a drying agent. Care must be taken to avoid inhaling dust or fumes. It is therefore not a good idea to burn off old lead paint.

Timber

Timber is a material that is generally considered to have excellent environmental credentials. As a renewable resource, its main attributes are that it reduces the amount of CO_2 in the atmosphere until it decays or is burnt, and it is easily worked. There are, however, possible disadvantages associated with timber, the principal one resulting from imported timber. This may have been transported over long distances, for example from Canada to the UK. Another potential problem has to do with the way the timber is grown and if trees are replanted when mature ones are cut. Most commercial softwood comes from forests that will be replanted, however these commercial softwood forests are often planted with very few species of trees and provide little potential for bio-diversity. In the case of imported non-European hardwoods, there is a high probability that these come from tropical rainforests and will not be replaced. The Forestry Stewardship Council, based in the UK, does run a scheme for certifying that timber comes from sustainable forests. Currently, only a small percentage of wood commercially available is certified as sustainable and, practically, this can be difficult to obtain. Anyone contemplating the construction of a new building using timber would be well advised to research the availability of locally grown timber. There are local forests with associated sawmills that can supply good quality home-grown timber suitable for load-bearing construction, such as Douglas Fir, Sweet Chestnut and Oak.

If it is necessary to use imported timber in the UK, then one should aim to use wood imported from Scandinavia, as it will have been transported a relatively short distance. Scandinavian forests are generally considered to be sustainable, but not bio-diverse.

Timber, a note of caution

Timber is a good choice as a sustainable material but, if it is used externally, it must be detailed in such a way as to prevent rot. Currently, most timber suppliers will automatically treat external timber to prevent rot but these treatments are highly toxic and should be avoided in ecological buildings.

2.6.
Recycling a building. Upgrading a typical Victorian terrace house in London. An external wall has been lined with a timber framework, which will hold 150 mm of insulation to achieve 'super insulation' standards. This insulation is cut back where the wall abuts an adjacent heated space, creating a niche. Window frames will be reused but glazed with energy-efficient argon-filled double glazing. Timber details and the ceiling are painted, but plaster is left bare. To justify the reuse of buildings on environmental grounds will, in most cases, require that their energy efficiency is significantly improved. Architects: K. Bohn and A. Viljoen.

Therefore, some untreated species of timber, particularly much low-grade imported softwood, is not suitable for external use. If one can source durable timber, it may be used untreated externally by detailing it correctly. This generally means making sure that, if the timber does get wet, water will rapidly drain away and the timber is well ventilated. One should check the durability of any external timber before purchasing it. Oak and Larch, for example, are durable external timbers, whereas much softwood imported into the UK is not and, if used externally, will not have a long life.

As a general rule for materials, choose local materials that have had the minimum processing. But do check that they will be durable and fit for the purpose intended!

See the recommended reading list at the end of this chapter for publications that provide more detailed information about material selection.

DETAILED STUDIES OF TWO HOUSES IN THE UK

A comparative study between embodied energy and energy in use is a complex task, requiring accurate embodied energy figures and detailed information regarding the construction of the building and its predicted energy requirements. It is not something that every house builder would wish to undertake.

2.7.
Green roof from 1924, Le Corbusier's mother's house at Vevey, Switzerland. A building element can have several environmental functions, for example insulating a roof, increasing bio-diversity, extending nature into a building and giving visual pleasure: 'In spring the young grass sprouts up with its wild flowers; in summer it is high and luxuriant. The roof garden lives independently, tended by the sun, the rain, the winds and the birds which bring the seeds' (Le Corbusier, 1924).

However, detailed study has been undertaken by one of the authors (Viljoen, 1997) of Dr Roaf's Oxford Ecohouse and a similar low-energy house in Suffolk, designed by the architect Roy Grimwade. Conclusions drawn from the study can be applied generally to housing in the UK and further afield. Figures for the primary embodied energy and associated emissions of construction materials were supplied by Nigel Howard, one of the leading authorities on embodied energy in the UK.

The purpose of the study was to assess the relative importance of embodied energy compared with the energy used by a dwelling on a day-to-day basis. Studies were made using several variations of the Roaf and Grimwade houses. The design of each building was altered from being a low-energy house to one that met the requirements of the current building regulations. Then, in a series of steps, each design was made progressively more energy efficient. In the final case, each house was designed as a 'zero-energy house': a house receiving over a year all of its energy requirements for space heating, hot water, cooking and appliances from on-site renewable energy sources. The embodied energy of all materials and components, including solar hot water and photo-voltaic systems, were taken account of in a life cycle analysis calculation.

As a zero-energy house will have more materials and technical equipment built into it, the intention of the study was to find out if this extra equipment

2.8.
Active solar roof from 2000, Centre for Alternative Technology, Wales. Photovoltaic panels used as a roofing material, generating electricity from the sun for use within the building. Systems like this significantly reduce the environmental impact of buildings. Energy used in manufacture is offset by the energy generated while in use.

and its associated embodied energy and emissions resulted in a house with a lower total environmental impact over its lifetime than one that used some non-renewable energy sources. Comparisons between different options were made on the basis of the life cycle analysis, which predicted yearly energy and CO_2 emissions per square metre of floor area for each house, resulting from embodied and in-use energy requirements.

RESULTS FROM THE LIFE CYCLE ANALYSIS

Reducing energy-in-use requirements

The results from this study showed very clearly that zero-energy houses had the lowest environmental impact. The first priority of any design should be to reduce energy-in-use requirements as far as possible using energy conservation techniques and then use active and passive solar systems to supply energy needs. The impact of materials is generally of secondary importance.

Building for a long life

Apart from the embodied energy of individual materials, the study showed how important a building's life expectancy is. The longer the low-energy dwelling can last, the lower the environmental impact of the materials that have gone into its construction.

Choosing materials for walls and floors

Both the Roaf and the Grimwade houses were built to low-energy standards and were similar in form. The one major difference between them lies in the materials used for construction. The Roaf house uses traditional building materials, e.g. concrete blocks and brick with precast concrete floors. The Grimwade house was designed to be built with rammed earth walls, using locally grown timber for a structural frame and wooden floors to the first floor. Also, its section minimises the height of walls and thus the quantity of material required to construct them.

The study showed that, using a life cycle analysis including embodied energy and emissions, one could expect a house built from rammed earth and local timber to have a lifetime energy impact in the order of 20 per cent lower than a house built using medium-density concrete blocks. CO_2 reductions are much greater, at about 50 per cent; see the section below on thermal mass.

While it is almost certainly the case that timber-framed buildings, built using a local source of timber, will have a lower embodied energy than similar houses built using bricks and concrete, this comparison does not take account of the thermal benefits that may arise from using high-mass materials.

Choosing thermal mass

Bricks, concrete and rammed earth have high thermal capacities, which means they can absorb heat over time and release it relatively slowly as the surroundings cool down. The theoretical benefit of high thermal mass is often exaggerated but, for a building continuously occupied, thermal mass can be of some benefit if positioned so as to absorb direct sunlight.

The most environmentally sensitive material for thermal mass is rammed earth. If this is not feasible, concrete blocks will most likely be used. Concrete

2.9.
Wooden cladding and colonnade at mixed-use housing, Ilot 13, Quartier des Grottes, Geneva, Switzerland. Timber, from local sustainable forests, has a low environmental impact. Care should be taken when detailing it to ensure it will not rot. Here, a roof overhang provides protection from rain. The raised timber walkway in the foreground has gaps between the planks to ensure good drainage and ventilation. Architects: P. Bonhote, O. Calame and I. Vuarambon.

blocks are available in a range of densities from low-density insulating blocks (0.6 tons m^{-3}), to medium-density (1.1 tons m^{-3}) and high-density blocks (2.2 tons m^{-3}). The embodied energy and CO_2 of concrete blocks varies considerably and unexpectedly with their density. Owing to the manufacturing process and the materials used, high-density blocks have the lowest and

2.10.
Internal view of a bookshop under construction, Centre for Alternative Technology, Wales. Materials with a high thermal capacity, capable of absorbing and storing heat, are placed below south-facing windows. During the heating season they help to store heat, reducing the need for space heating. In summer, they help tc prevent overheating during the day by absorbing excessive solar gain. The embodied energy of this building is extremely low. The timber comes from local forests, thus minimising the embodied energy resulting from transport. Internal walls (here with sunlight on one of them) are constructed using rammed earth and act, with their high thermal mass, as heat stores. Architect: Pat Borer.

medium-density blocks the highest embodied energy and CO_2 emissions by weight and volume.

The life cycle analysis study showed that a low-energy rammed-earth house would result in CO_2 emissions on the order of $10.3\,\mathrm{kg\,m}^{-2}\,\mathrm{year}^{-1}$, compared with $12.9\,\mathrm{kg\,m}^{-2}\,\mathrm{year}^{-1}$ for a building using dense blocks (2.2 tonnes m^{-3}) or $20.9\,\mathrm{kg\,m}^{-2}\,\mathrm{year}^{-1}$ for a house using medium-density blocks (1.1 tonnes m^{-3}). Compared with using rammed earth, and depending upon the type of block chosen, the CO_2 impact of a concrete house can change by between 25 per cent and 100 per cent!

An interesting strategy for housing is to use a mixture of high thermal mass and lightweight timber-framed construction. Normally, high-mass walls are constructed internally and are surrounded with well-insulated timber-framed external walls. There is a clear analogy with a person wrapped up in a warm coat.

Generally, a well-insulated high-mass house is less likely to overheat in summer than a low-mass one. In lightweight timber dwellings, care is required to prevent summer-time overheating, usually by means of solar shading and ventilation.

Integrating photovoltaic and solar hot water systems

Photovoltaic and solar hot water systems significantly reduce a building's overall environmental impact. The life cycle analysis study showed that a photovoltaic system reduced the total embodied and in-use energy impact of the Roaf house by about 40 per cent and the CO_2 emissions by about 35 per cent.

Integrating whole-house mechanical ventilation with heat recovery

Based on the Roaf and Grimwade house life cycle analysis studies, mechanical ventilation with heat recovery for the whole house makes sense, resulting in energy and CO_2 reductions in the order of 10 per cent. However, recent studies of low-energy houses by the International Energy Agency (Hestnes et al., 1997) have noted that the electricity used by fans in mechanical ventilation systems can be significant. If larger amounts of electricity are used, the energy advantages of a mechanical ventilation system with heat recovery will be less than suggested above, and perhaps these systems have an overall negative impact. Within the UK, the jury remains out on this point. Notwithstanding energy and CO_2 considerations, there is a question regarding the internal air quality delivered by such systems. Whole-house mechanical systems require horizontal pipe runs connecting inlet and outlet points that are generally not cleaned and can, over time, build up deposits of dirt and dust, which may lead to poor air quality.

Comparison with current Building Regulations

The total embodied and in-use energy impact of the Roaf house, as built, is about half that of the equivalent house built to current Building Regulations. CO_2 emissions are reduced by about 60 per cent.

Where to find building materials with a low environmental impact?

Germany appears to manufacture the greatest range of ecological building materials. As the market expands, variety and availability increase. Currently, in the UK the quantity of ecological building materials available is increasing, but many are imported. Although import adds to the material's embodied energy, it seems a good idea to use these products as, apart from their envir-onmental benefits, using them will demonstrate that a market exists. This should stimulate local manufacture, which in the long term would result in significant environmental benefit.

Solar hot water and photovoltaic systems are available in most countries; both systems can significantly reduce the environmental impact of a dwelling.

2.11.
Small theatre building built of straw, Centre for Alternative Technology, Wales. A timber frame supports the roof. External walls are constructed using straw bales, which provide high levels of insulation. A render protects the straw bales from moisture. This is a building with low thermal mass; it will cool down and warm up quickly. For a building used intermittently this can be a good strategy but care needs to be taken to prevent summertime overheating, by providing effective ventilation and shading. Architect: Pat Borer.

The cost of photovoltaics remains relatively high, but is dropping all the time. Solar hot water systems are considerably cheaper and, given their environmental benefits, should if possible be used.

Other building materials with a low environmental impact, which are generally available in the UK, include paints and stains (water based), plasters (clay based), thermal insulation (using recycled paper, flax, wool or cork), local sustainable timber (often available if researched), earth wall construction (local soil types need to be tested to see if suitable) and straw bale construction (if space permits and finishes are acceptable, it can be quite rough).

Materials that will save energy (mainly double or triple glazing with low emissivity coatings or insulation) almost always make sense. Low-impact window frames with different glazing types are relatively easy to obtain in the UK.

Windows should be considered in relation to daylight and thermal insulation. A poorly daylit room will require the use of electric lighting with its associated negative environmental impact. One should also remember that double or triple glazing will reduce the amount of light passing through a window as each pane of glass will absorb some of it. Nineteenth-century houses give a good idea of window sizes required for adequate day lighting. Insulation materials with low environmental impact, as well as skilled contractors, are beginning to appear on the British market.

Within the UK, as a rule of thumb, 150 mm of insulation in walls, 250 mm in roofs and, say, 100 mm expanded polystyrene under a concrete ground floor are considered to result in a 'super-insulated' house (Olivier, 1992).

These amounts of insulation equate broadly to the Association of Environment Conscious Building (AECB) Silver Standard Energy Performance Standards for Building (see: www.aecb.net). The AECB estimate that the Silver Standard, applied to an 80 m^2 semi-detached dwelling in the UK, would result in 23 kg/m^2 yr CO_2 emissions, compared to 57 kg/m^2 yr for the same dwelling built to 2006 Building Regulations, or 73 kg/m^2 yr for one meeting the UK average for dwellings.

Synthetic insulations should be avoided, unless waterproof qualities are necessary (see recommended reading list for further reading).

Ventilation and insulation must be considered together. There is no point in heavily insulating a dwelling if it is not also airtight. Too much background ventilation results in great heat loss in the winter, too little leads to a risk of condensation and stale air or, at worse, excess CO_2. Adequate background ventilation, usually through 'trickle ventilators' built into window frames, is essential for health and condensation avoidance in most houses. Trickle ventilators for all types of window frames are easily available in the UK, as well as more complex whole-house natural ventilation systems.

CONCLUSION

As a first priority, a design should aim for a dwelling that uses the minimum amount of energy to run. This can be supported by, for example, applying conservation techniques and passive solar design principles. Where possible, the use of solar hot water and photovoltaic systems is highly advisable to generate on-site energy (wind or water power may be appropriate in some situations).

Once the design strategy is clear, local building materials and those requiring the minimum processing should be selected in preference to highly processed materials and those from further afield. (You can learn more about such materials in Chapter 14.) Non-toxic products should replace chemically treated materials and those containing toxins. The durability of materials is also very significant as it will affect the lifespan of a building and, the longer a low-energy house lasts, the less relative impact its materials will have. Ideally, all building materials should be easily recyclable. Finally, the potential for flexible occupancy will help to extend the useful lifetime of a building.

2.12.
A chair at the Tipu Sultan's Summer Palace in Bangalore, India. Avoiding artificial finishes in interiors is a good strategy for reducing environmental impact. Modern synthetic paints and carpets generally have high embodied energies and are often environmentally unfriendly. Their frequent replacement also contributes to the negative environmental impact of finishes and fittings.

ACKNOWLEDGEMENT

Embodied energy and embodied emissions figures used to perform the life cycle analysis calculations for the Roaf and Grimwade houses were supplied by Nigel Howard.

RECOMMENDED READING LIST

Anderson, J. and Shiers, D. E. (2002) *Green Guide to Specification.* Blackwell Publishing, ISBN 0632059613.

Anink, D., Boonstra, C. and Mak, J. (1996). *Handbook of Sustainable Building: An Environmental Preference Method for Selection of Materials for*

Use in Construction and Refurbishment. James and James, London, ISBN 1-873936-38-9.

Asko, S. (2002). *Integrated Life Cycle Design of Structures.* Spon Press (UK), ISBN 0415252350.

Association of Environment Conscious Building (2000). *The Real Green Building Book 2000, Yearbook of the Association for Environment Conscious Building.* AECB, Nant-y-Garreg, Saron, Llandysul, Carmarthenshire, SA44 5EJ (http://www.aecb.net).

Berge, B. (2001). The Ecology of Building Materials Architectural Press, ISBN 0750654503.

Borer, P. and Harris, C. (1998). *The Whole House Book, Ecological Building Design and Materials.* The Centre for Alternative Technology, Machynlleth, ISBN 1 898049 21 1.

Snell, C. and Callahan, T. (2006). *Building Green.* Lame Books, ISBN 1579905323.

Talbott, J. (1993). *Simply Build Green, A Technical Guide to the Ecological Houses at the Findhorn Foundation.* The Findhorn Press, Findhorn, ISBN 1 899171 90 8.

Woolley, T., Kimmins, S., Harrison, P. and Harrison, R. (1997). *The Green Building Handbook.* E & FN Spon, London, ISBN 0 419 22690 7.

Woolley, T. and Kimmins, S. (2001). *Green Building Handbook, Volume 2.* Spon Press (UK), ISBN 0419253807.

http://alcor.concordia.ca/~ raojw/crd/concept/concept000324.html (accessed August 2006). Embodied energy links provided by the Conceptual Reference Database for *Building Envelope Research.*

http://www.brighton.ac.uk/environment/research/sustainability/CSBE/index.htm (accessed August 2006). Low-energy construction and design reports provided by the Centre for Sustainability of the Built Environment.

3 PUSHING THE BUILDING ENVELOPE

In this chapter we give some detailed information on the thermal performance of specific elements of the construction of a house. These include the insulation, cold bridging in windows and walls, infiltration, and other aspects of window design. This material, very detailed in places, is an important part in the jigsaw puzzle of low-energy house design.

INSULATION

The colder the climate, the more insulation iCommunitys needed. The Inuit people of the Arctic get most of their insulation from the skin and fur clothes they wear that can keep them warm even when living in houses made of ice.

In a similar climate, in the Antarctic, a Mantainer (container for people) was designed for Robert Swan's expedition to the South Pole. The design brief was for a facility that had minimum environmental impacts and used, where possible, local resources including ambient energy. The vapour barrier envelope of the unit includes enough insulation to keep people warm in the severely cold Antarctic climate (Figure 3.1). In this case the external vapour barrier was rigid and formed from a polyamide honeycomb panel (thickness ranging from 6–12 mm). In modules where weight is less critical, honeycomb and panel skins are of cellulose fibre. The panel supports 150 mm thick external wool insulation contained by a fine mesh net. The use of compressible insulation lends itself to more efficient transport when the module is 'packed down'. Greater thickness of insulation must be considered in conjunction with air change requirements and latent heat losses. In wet climates certain inorganic insulation can also be contained by netting and in some circumstances the cage is of copper mesh which contributes to the formation of a Faraday cage, as a protection against lightning strike! Organic insulation, such as leaves, straw, shredded paper, etc., requires an impermeable external skin. The Antarctic Mantainer unit assisted in maintaining an internal minimum temperature of 5°C by storing water, from melted ice, below the habitation level. In similar units, such as those used to assist farming in the Swiss Alps (Figure 3.2), their success depends on choosing exactly the right insulation, that is light and highly efficient. In the alpine pod, heat gained from daytime solar radiation is

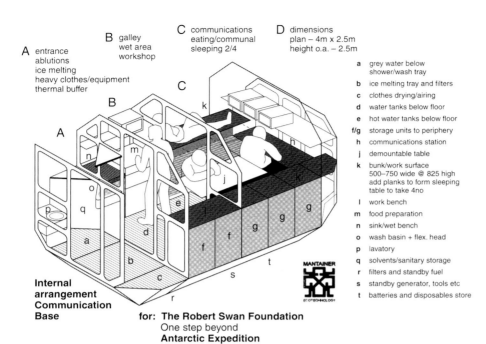

A entrance
ablutions
ice melting
heavy clothes/equipment
thermal buffer

B galley
wet area
workshop

C communications
eating/communal
sleeping 2/4

D dimensions
plan – 4m x 2.5m
height o.a. – 2.5m

a   grey water below
    shower/wash tray
b   ice melting tray and filters
c   clothes drying/airing
d   water tanks below floor
e   hot water tanks below floor
f/g storage units to periphery
h   communications station
j   demountable table
k   bunk/work surface
    500–750 wide @ 825 high
    add planks to form sleeping
    table to take 4no
l   work bench
m   food preparation
n   sink/wet bench
o   wash basin + flex. head
p   lavatory
q   solvents/sanitary storage
r   filters and standby fuel
s   standby generator, tools etc
t   batteries and disposables store

MANTAINER
ECOTECHNOLOGY

**Internal
arrangement
Communication
Base**

for: The Robert Swan Foundation
One step beyond
Antarctic Expedition

3.1.
The Mantainer pod designed for Robert Swan's Antarctic Expedition. The pod uses photovoltaics to generate electricity and a gas microwave cooker. A multifuel cooker is included where waste can be burnt. Water comes from snow melt. The WC is composting, and those wastes not compostible or combustible are removed at the end of the habitation (Ian Guilani, Mantainer, Ecotechnology, Henley, UK. Email: ecotech@mantainer.co.uk).

controlled by a combination of thermal insulation and reflecting panels combined with air vents.

The specification of insulation in our own homes may be quite different. The trick with insulation is to choose the right insulation for the climate and the available local energy sources. The Mantainer unit designed for the Antarctic employed five, 100 W, wind generators to provide electrical power for ice melting, microwave heating of food and radio communications. Although during the duration of the expedition daylight was present for twenty-four hours a day, the use of solar electric systems was precluded, due to a low solar projectory, through 360°. Where location and resources permit, as in the Alpine example, heating can be provided by a 'multi' fuel stove, utilising local carbon or incinerating 'waste'. Human effluent is, wherever possible, treated by composting, where temperatures and time-scale allow. So with the right building envelope and a little human ingenuity, people can live almost anywhere using minimal fossil fuels!

But there, is a wide range of insulation products on the market at a wide range of prices (Table 3.1). How does one choose the right type for the job? The properties of each different insulation product should be evaluated and, if necessary, checked with the manufacturer. A clear specification for what job the insulation has to do in a building should be drawn up. Does the insulation have to be waterproof? Is it best to use a reflective board, a high-mass wall or a bulky insulation product? How much room in the construction is available for it? How toxic is the product and does it matter? Is it to be put on the exposed side of a house where there is driving rain or on the sheltered solar elevation? How fire resistant does it have to be? For instance, if the insulation is to be used internally in a room, then a fire-resistant type is essential; this subject is covered under the section on 'Fire' in Chapter 6. Where the insulation is in well-sealed cavity walls this may not be such an issue.

3.2.
A Mantainer pod placed by helicopter in the Swiss Alps for all-season use (Ian Guilani, Mantainer, Ecotechnology, Henley, UK. Email: ecotech@mantainer.co.uk).

Table 3.1. Some properties of insulation materials

Type of insulation	Thermal performance	Moisture resistance	Mechanical performance	Chemical properties
Expanded Polystyrene Insulation	0.033 W/mK	Not considered a vapour barrier. Low water vapour transmission, no capillary action, and high resistance to moisture absorption.	10% compression strength of 110 to 150 kPa.	Resistant to diluted acids and alkalis. Not resistant to organic solvents. Can chemically interact with polymeric single ply membranes such as PVC.
Rock Mineral Wool	0.034–0.036 W/mK	Does not absorb moisture. At 95% RH, hygroscopic water content is only 0.02% by volume, 2% by weight. No capillary action.	10% compression strength of 120 to 180 kPa.	May need isolating board under asphalt.
Cellular Glass	0.042 W/mK	0.2% by volume. No capillary action.	10% compression strength of 230 to 500 kPa. Average compressive strength is 600 kPa (87 psi).	Pure glass without binders or fillers. Totally inorganic, impervious to common acids except hydrofluoric acid. May release hydrogen sulphide and CO in a fire.
Cellulose	0.033 W/mK	Not given (presumed low moisture resistance).	Not given (presumed poor mechanical strength).	Treated with inorganic salts for fire protection.
Flax Isovlas	50 mm: 0.035 W/mK	Absorbs 12% moisture – not prone to mould.	Natural flax fibres held together with natural binders.	No chemical or fibre irritants.
Microporous Silica	0.020 W/mK	Moisture content of 1–3% by weight.	Tensile strength is low. 5% compression can be fully recovered.	Leachable chloride content is low, less than 50 ppm. Leachable silicate content is high, greater than 1500 ppm.
Sheep's Wool	0.037 W/mK	40% water absorption (by dry weight) at 100% RH.	Not given (presumed poor mechanical strength).	Not mentioned.
Flexible Melamine Foam	0.035 W/mK	Undergoes significant dimensional changes with increased moisture content due to its open cell structure.	'Foam does not have a particularly high strength'.	Resists hydrolysis, alcohols, hydrocarbons, most organic solvents, and dilute acids and bases.
Cork	0.037 W/mk	Water repellent with zero capillarity. Relatively high rate of vapour transmission.	Compressive strength up to 20 kN/m^2 without deformation. Bending strength 140 kN/m^2.	Unaffected by water, alkalis, and organic solvents.
Isonat Hemp and recycled Cotton fibre batts	0.039 W/mK	Average 10% increase with relative humidity 50–85%. Can absorb and release without decay.	Poor.	Non toxic.
Recycled Fabric	R-value/inch: 2.8–5.5	Water absorbent.	Poor.	Non toxic.

Type of insulation	Fire behaviour	Toxicity	Embodied energy	CFC emissions	Effects of age
Expanded Polystyrene Insulation	Melts and shrinks away from small heat source. Ignites with severe flames and heavy smoke when exposed to a large heat source.	Thermal decomposition products are no more toxic than those of wood.	120 GJ/t.	Does not use CFCs, HCFCs or CO_2.	None reported. See Chapter 4.
Rock Mineral Wool	Non-combustible to 2000°C. Practical limit is 1000°C due to the additives.	None.	25 GJ/t.	Does not use CFCs or HCFCs.	None (batt) Settling (loose fill).
Cellular Glass	Non-combustible.	None.	27 GJ/t.	Does not use CFCs or HCFCs.	See Chapter 4.
Cellulose	Withstands direct heat from a blowlamp.	None, fully biodegradable.	0.63–1.25 GJ/t.	Does not use CFCs, HCFCs, or VOCs.	None reported.
Flax Isovlas	Euroclass C. Treated with natural based fire retardant – chars.	None.	1.6 MJ/kg.	None.	Durable.
Microporous Silica	Non-combustible with zero flame spread.	Safe to handle. Avoid breathing dust from cutting or machining.	Not given.	Not mentioned.	None.
Sheep's Wool	Ignition point 560°C. Fire resistance B2.	None, fully biodegradable.	30 kWh/m³ energy consumption in manufacture.	None reported.	Will degrade if left exposed to sunlight or water for extended periods.
Flexible Melamine Foam	Can withstand up to 150°C with no reduction in performance. Rated as Class 1.	Non-carcinogenic.	Not given.	CFC-free.	See Chapter 4.
Cork	No cyanides, chlorides or other toxic gases are produced. Rated as Class 1.	None mentioned.	Can be harvested every 9–12 years during the tree's 160–200 years productive lifetime.	None reported.	None reported.
Isonat Hemp and recycled Cotton fibre batts	Treated with boron salts. Euroclass E rating. Complies with Building. Regulations.	None.	Not given.	None.	Prolonged exposure to moisture causes decay.
Metisse recycled fabric	Treated with natural fire retardant.	None.	Not given.	None.	Durable.

(Continued)

Table 3.1. (Continued)

Type of Insulation	New Buildings	Existing Buildings	Prices	Lifetime	Recycling
Expanded Polystyrene Insulation	On or below sub-floor slab, between timber floor joists. Partial or full fill wallboards. Flat or pitched roofs.	Granular and bead forms of EPS can be injected into existing cavity.	Range £2.50–£6.50/m² Board 50 mm £2.50 100 mm £5.00 Cavity Fill 65 mm £3.50 (including labour).	None given.	Easily melted and reformed. Low bulk density precludes long distance transport.
Rock Mineral Wool	Roof or ceiling, walls, floor or foundation.		£3.50–£6.20 m².	60+ years.	Recycling programmes in place in the UK.
Cellular Glass	Roof or ceiling, walls, floor or foundation.		'Expensive'.	None given.	Reclaimable on demolition.
Cellulose	Roof or ceiling, walls, floor or foundation.		£8.00 m².	None given.	100% recycled and recyclable.
Flax Isovlas	Wall, floor and ceiling.	Wall floor ceiling.	50 mm £4.29 m² 100 mm £7.54 m².	Long.	Can be recycled.
Microporous Silica	Mostly industrial applications.		None given.	None given.	Not mentioned.
Sheep's Wool	Roof or ceiling, walls, or floor.		50 mm £4.76 m² 100 mm £9.50 m²	None given.	Can be fully recycled.
Flexible Melamine Foam	HVAC pipes, ducts, plant. Plant rooms, offices and conference suites, theatres, cinema auditoria, and recording studios.		50 mm £30.00 m².	None given.	Cannot be melted and reused.
Cork	Single layer system or as part of a composite board.		None given.	None given.	Not mentioned.
Isonat Hemp and recycled Cotton fibre batts	External walls in timber and steel frame buildings and internal applications, walls, floors, lofts, roofs.		50 mm £4.16 m² 100 mm £8.30 m².	None given.	Yes.
Metisse recycled fabric	Walls, roof spaces and encased, suspended floors		50 mm £5.53 m² 100 mm £7.43 m².	None given.	Is made of recycled fabric.

The usual basic rules for materials choice should apply: use materials that are as natural as possible and as local as possible. However, in some cases, such as in Mantainer modules, the choice of materials, essentially made on the basis of minimal impact on the environment, will attempt the balance between the use of local and imported, and possibly high technology, alternatives. It might be possible to justify the transport energy costs of moving insulation long distances because of the cost of the energy it will save when used on location. The capital cost of the Mantainer unit for Antarctica is less than the cost of supplying fuel for a similar period to a conventional tented encampment.

The most often asked envelope question is how much insulation to put into the roof, walls and floors of a building? This decision should be made early on in the design as it determines how thick the house envelope will be and, in turn, what is the most suitable construction detailing for the house. This choice is often made on the basis of cost.

In 1997, Peter Warm explained calculations to evaluate the optimal thickness of insulation. He based the first equation on a semi-detached house, in the UK, with space heating, over a 60-year lifetime with fuel costing £0.164 kWh^{-1} (Warm, 1997). Normal mineral wool batts at current costs, the cheapest insulation available in the UK at present, and the results showed that the most economical thickness is at around 200 mm but in terms of the energy balance of what is produced and what is saved he recommends 500 mm+!

However, these calculations are based on present fuel prices and insulation costs. We also know that over the next 20 years the price of energy must go up, though by how much is not known. What happens to the cost of insulation materials if the cost of oil and gas doubles or triples over the next 20 years? Warm also redid the calculations independently of prices. He looked at how much energy it takes to manufacture the insulation in comparison with how much energy the insulation saves over a 60-year lifespan. It does suppose that the fuel types are equivalent, but it gives a rough tool for answering the question. This changes the picture completely and the most economical thickness of insulation becomes around 650 mm! So the limitations on how much insulation we put in our homes are possibly the practical details of the mounting and fixing systems we use, rather than economic ones.

Already we have introduced a number of variables into the process of choosing the right insulation for a job, including type, fire resistance, time, local material availability, cost, and micro-location, i.e. is it an exposed or sheltered wall. Each of these factors will vary around the world because the amount of insulation required to ameliorate the climate inside a building depends also on the climate of the location (for instance, maritime or continental), latitude and also altitude.

In his Doctoral study on energy-saving guidelines in South Africa, Piani (1998) calculated the amount of heating energy needed by each person to keep warm in the different geographical regions of South Africa (Figure 3.3). He recommended that wherever the heating demand was 2.20 kWh m^{-2} or less, insulation in the roof for winter heating was not required, but in those areas where more heating was needed roof insulation would be necessary as standard. This, however, does not cover the need for insulation in the roof to keep the heat out in summer. Many readers will have suffered from the 'hot top floor' problem caused by thin uninsulated roofs that act as heat collectors during the day. Occupants have to wait until late at night for the upstairs bedrooms to be cool enough to get to sleep in. This is true in countries such as India and Pakistan, where the high costs of electricity mean that only the rich can afford AC, making many houses uncomfortable in summer.

Insulation is put around buildings to keep the heat in. Heat is a form of energy that is measured in the same units as any other type of energy, i.e. in Joules. Heat always flows from a hotter to a colder state, and it cannot be destroyed. In our homes we merely change the state of the energy, or degrade it, when we burn wood or heat a kettle.

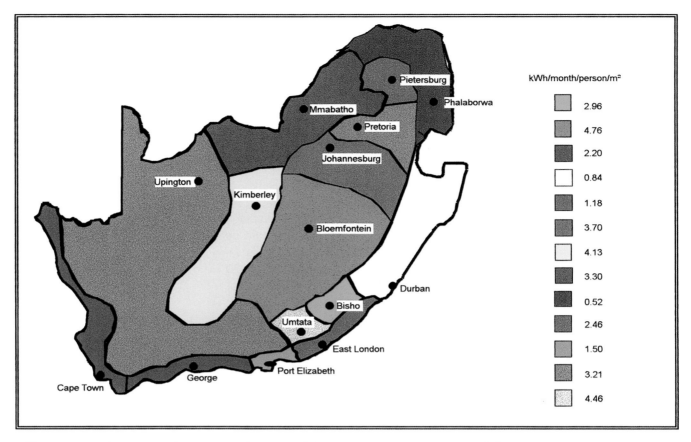

kWh/month/person/m²

	2.96
	4.76
	2.20
	0.84
	1.18
	3.70
	4.13
	3.30
	0.52
	2.46
	1.50
	3.21
	4.46

3.3.

Proposed maximum required heating energy for different South African climatic regions in kWh m⁻² per person (Piani, 1998, p. 123).

Temperature is commonly measured on the Celsius or centigrade scale, graduated into degrees Celsius (°C), with 0°C being the freezing point of water. However, the Kelvin scale is widely used in scientific measurement, for which the freezing point of water is taken to be 273.15 Kelvins (K). Because the interval of one Kelvin is the same as that of one degree Celsius, temperature in Kelvins is thus equal to temperature in degrees Celsius plus 273.15.

The specific heat capacity of a substance is a measure of how much energy it can store. For different materials, it can be described as how much heat energy is required to raise the temperature of a kilogram of the material by one Kelvin. Materials can store very different amounts of heat, have very different densities and be better or worse conductors of heat (Table 3.2).

There are three different ways in which a wall can be insulated:

- **Resistive insulation.** This is what most of us think of as insulation. These are the 'bulk' insulation products which include mineral wools, strawboard, wood–wool slabs, glass fibre products, kapok, wool, and cellulose fibre. They also include expanded and extruded polystyrene, polyurethane, urea-formaldehyde, vermiculite and perlite. This type of insulation is based on preventing convection, which in turn depends on the conductivity and viscosity of the liquid or gas in the gap or contained in the material, the temperature difference, and to some extent the thickness of the gap, these are all factors that are taken into account in the design of new high performance windows (Figure 3.4).

Table 3.2. The relative density, conductivity and thermal capacity of a range of materials. Note the excellent thermal capacity of water. This makes it an excellent storage medium for heat

Type of material	Thermal capacity $(J\,Kg^{-1}\,K^{-1})$	Density $(kg\,m^{-3})$	Conductivity $(W\,m^{-1}\,K^{-1})$
Lead	126	11 300	37
Expanded polystyrene slab	340	25	0.035
Polyurethane	450	24	0.016
Steel	480	7800	47
Mineral fibre batts	920	35–150	0.35–0.044
Brick	800	1700	620–840
Glass	840	2500	1.100
Plasterboard	840	950	0.16
Marble stone	900	2500	2.0
Adobe	1000	2050	1.250
Concrete	840–1000	600–2300	0.190–1.630
Wood wool slab	1000	500	0.100
Dry air	1005		
Strawboard	1050	250	0.037
Timber hardwood	1200	660	0.120
Chipboard	1300	660	0.120
Timber softwood	1420	610	0.130
Urea formaldehyde foam	1450	10	0.040
Phenolic foam	1400	30	0.040
Cork	1800	144	0.038
Water	4176	1000	

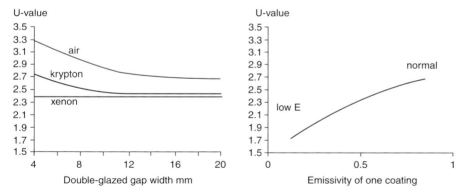

3.4.

Insulation issues affecting the design of high performance windows. (a) Convection dependent on the gap and the gas; (b) radiation dependent on the surface emissivity of the glass (Peter Warm).

- **Reflective insulation.** This requires a highly reflective material, such as aluminum foil, to face into a cavity. Foil has an extremely low emissivity (about one-thirtieth that of common building materials) and thus radiant heat transfer between the walls of the cavity is much reduced. Performance is compromised if the face of the foil is touching the opposite wall as conduction of heat is then allowed. The amount of heat a material can radiate depends on its surface emissivity, i.e. how easily it allows heat to move through its surface, and the temperature difference between its surface and that which it is radiating to. Its thickness is irrelevant. So a 'low E' window will radiate far less heat than a normal one so helping to conserve energy in the home.

- **Capacitive insulation.** This is often described as 'thermal mass' and is found in buildings as heavy walls. Heat is conducted through the solid material of the wall and the rate of the heat flow depends on the conductivity of the material the wall is made of, its thickness and the difference in temperature between the air on the two different sides of the wall. Load-bearing insulation materials are important when designing to avoid cold bridging.

While resistive and reflective insulation work instantaneously, using a high capacity insulation affects the timing of the heat flows. The difference is best illustrated by the comparison of:

1. 10 mm polystyrene slab ($U = 2.17\,\mathrm{W\,m^2K}$)
2. 400 mm of dense concrete slab (also $U = 2.17\,\mathrm{W\,m^2K}$).

Under steady state conditions there will be no difference in heat flow through the two slabs (Zold and Szokolay, 1997). A significant difference will, however, occur if these slabs are exposed to a periodically changing set of conditions. Figure 3.5 shows the variation of the heat flow rate over 24 hours at the inside face of the two slabs, exposed to the same external temperature variation whilst the indoor is kept constant. The daily mean heat flow is the same but the two sinusoidal curves differ in two ways:

1. The heavy slab's heat flow is delayed: the term *time lag* is defined as the difference (in hours or days) between the peaks of the two curves.
2. The amplitude (mean to peak) of the heavy slab's curve is reduced well below that of the lightweight material. The ratio of the two amplitudes is called the decrement factor.

A simple rule of thumb to use when sizing mass in a very passive building, designed to minimise heating and cooling loads, is that the optimal depth of

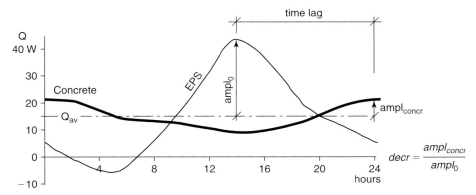

3.5.
The periodic heat flow through a light and heavy wall of the same U-value (Steve Szokolay).

mass for diurnal use is 100 mm for each exposed surface (Figure 3.6). So if there are rooms backing onto each other the walls should be 150–200 mm thick. In more extreme climates just increase the time lag, or decrease the decrement factor, by increasing the width of the mass wall further.

In a colder climate, for instance in Glasgow, the heavyweight building ensures more even and comfortable conditions than the lightweight building and uses slightly less energy to do so if the heating and occupation are regular on a daily basis. If a heavyweight house is left unoccupied and then has to be reheated, the lightweight version uses less energy. During the heating OFF

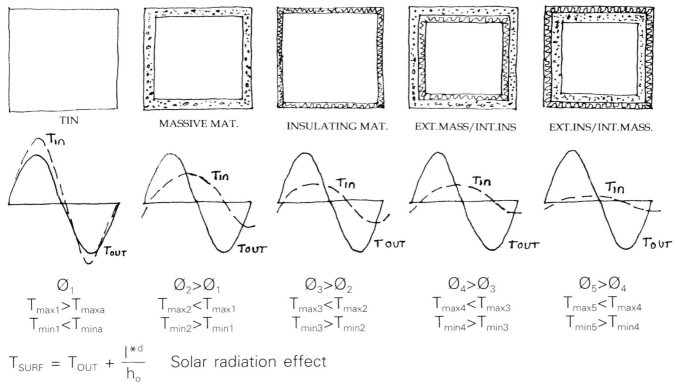

3.6.

The location of the insulation in relation to the cold mass of a building is extremely important (Isaac Meir).

period the house will cool down considerably. However, with intermittent heating (e.g. night shut-down) but continuous occupancy, as in most residential buildings, the heavyweight version would maintain acceptable conditions during the OFF period (Szokolay, 1997). This is why so many of the older houses in Britain, and many other countries, had such thick walls: to keep the warmth in during winter when they were continuously occupied, and the heat out in summer. This does not work when they are used as weekend cottages.

A more flippant rule of thumb for the optimal thickness of insulation could be 'Think of a number and double it'. Insulation will pay dividends for years to come when the price of heating energy rises and the price of insulation materials with it. It is not uncommon in some countries such as Switzerland to use up to 500 mm of bulk insulation in the roof and 300 mm in walls. For these thicknesses, traditional rafters are difficult to detail and new materials such as pre-formed masonite beams that can be specified to such depths are often used (Vale and Vale, 1999). Nylon wall ties up to 300 mm wide are available for cavity walls from K. G. Kristiansen of Denmark.

It is very important to get the construction details correct, and to build right on site. Very close site supervision is needed to ensure that the insulated cavities are not filled with dabs of mortar from the walls that will form cold bridges across the cavity. When sprayed insulation is used great care must be taken that corners are properly filled. Wall batts must be fixed so they do not sag in cavities or in the roof space and insulation properly cut to fit snugly against surfaces. In cold climates the water tanks must be included within the insulation envelope to prevent them freezing.

Corners are particularly difficult to get right and their filling should be supervised to ensure that the most vulnerable elements in the building are not

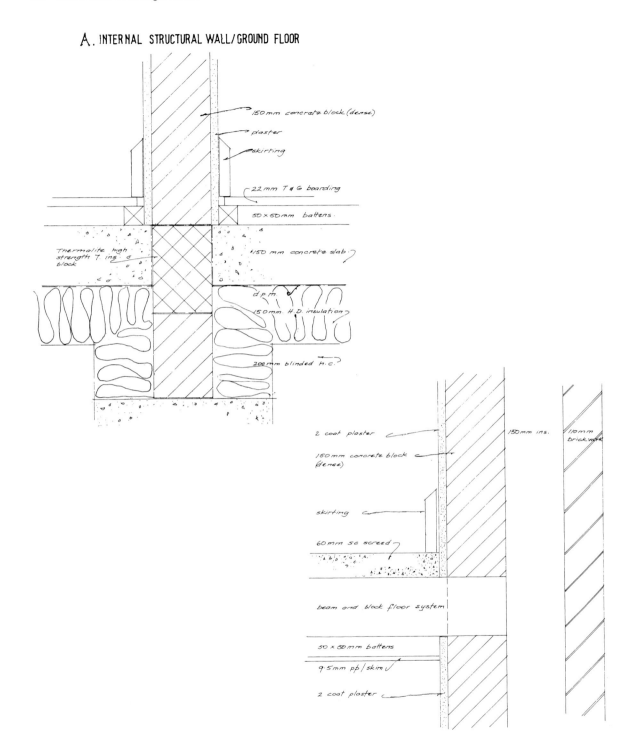

A. INTERNAL STRUCTURAL WALL/GROUND FLOOR

150mm concrete block (dense)

plaster

skirting

22mm T & G boarding

50 x 50mm battens.

Thermalite high strength T. ins. block

150mm concrete slab

d p m.

150mm. H.D. insulation

200mm blinded h.c.

2 coat plaster

150mm concrete block (dense)

skirting

60mm sc screed

beam and block floor system

50 x 50mm battens

9.5mm pb/skim

2 coat plaster

150mm ins.

110mm brickwork

B. FIRST FLOOR/EXTERNAL WALL

3.7.
Constructional section through the ground floor wall of the Oxford Ecohouse demonstrating how to eliminate cold bridging (David Woods).

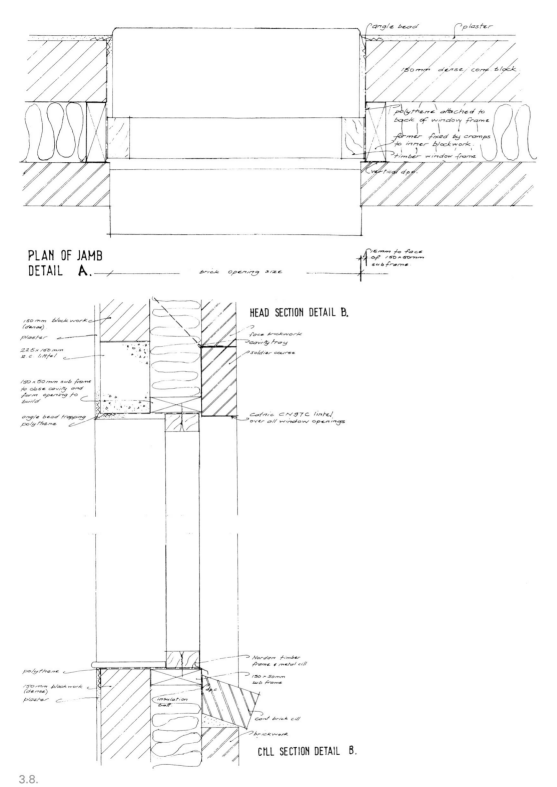

PLAN OF JAMB DETAIL A.

brick opening size

angle bead · plaster

150mm dense conc block

polythene attached to back of window frame

former fixed by cramps to inner blockwork

timber window frame

vertical dpc

16mm to face of 150 × 50mm subframe

HEAD SECTION DETAIL B.

150mm blockwork (dense)

plaster

225 × 160mm R.C. lintel

150 × 50mm sub frame to close cavity and form opening to build

angle bead trapping polythene

face brickwork

cavity tray

soldier course

Catnic CN97C lintel over all window openings

Nordan timber frame & metal cill

150 × 50mm sub frame

polythene

150mm blockwork (dense)

plaster

insulation batt

cont brick cill

brickwork

CILL SECTION DETAIL B.

3.8.
Plan through the window of the Oxford Ecohouse demonstrating how to eliminate cold bridging with timber sub-frames around the window (David Woods).

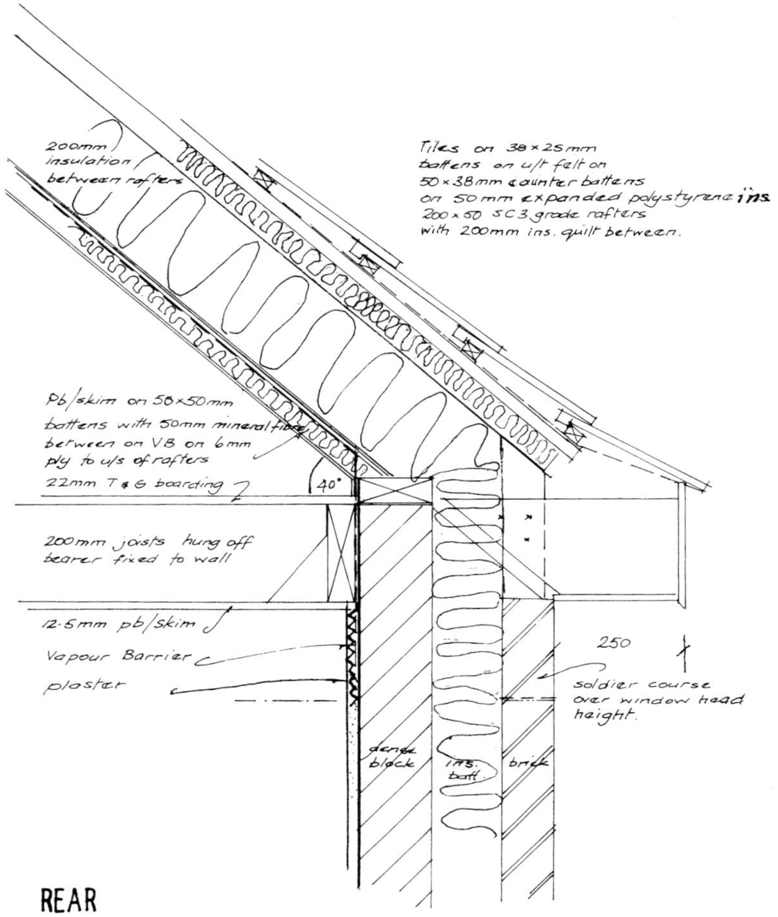

200mm insulation between rafters
Tiles on 38 × 25mm battens on u/f felt on 50 × 38mm counter battens on 50mm expanded polystyrene ins. 200 × 50 SC3 grade rafters with 200mm ins. quilt between.
Pb/skim on 50×50mm battens with 50mm mineral fibre between on VB on 6mm ply to u/s of rafters
22mm T & G boarding
40°
200mm joists hung off bearer fixed to wall
12·5mm pb/skim
Vapour Barrier
plaster
250
soldier course over window head height.
dense block
ins. batt
brick
REAR

3.9.
Constructional section through the roof/wall junction of the Oxford Ecohouse (David Woods).

exposed with poorly fitting insulation (Figures 3.7–3.9). In areas with driving rain care should be taken to place a cavity between the insulation and the outer skin of the buildings down which water can run without soaking the insulation. If one side of a cavity only has insulation then proper wall ties must be used and installed to hold the insulation in place to maintain the cavity in its right location in the wall.

It is no use putting in very high levels of insulation when the windows have a much lower thermal performance so very good walls should have very good windows. Check with locally operating window manufacturers about the performance data for available ranges of windows and choose the best windows you can afford because these will pay dividends over the years.

The key ecological issues related to the choice and design of insulation relate to:

- ozone depletion
- sustainability of the sources – is it naturally produced/can it be recycled?
- the embodied energy of the material, how much energy has been used in its manufacture and transport? (Table 3.3).

Table 3.3. The ZODP, the Zero Ozone Depletion, Insolence listings with prices from 2000

Insulation samples	k-value	cost £ m² @100 mmk = 0.04 W mK	Gas	Comments
Air-based all ZODP				
Loft quilt – mineral fibre	0.037	2	air	
Cellulose fibre	0.036	3	air	
Loose fill cavity fill	0.039	6	air	Estimate includes installation
Cellulose batt viscose	0.034	10	air	
Partial cavity batt – mineral fibre	0.033	10	air	
Wool	0.038	11	air	
Flax	0.037	12	air	
Sarking batt – mineral fibre	0.036	15	air	
Woodfibre board	0.050	21	air	Load bearing for semi-floating floors
Cork	0.042	21	air	Radiant barrier, air gap and non-dusty
Expanded clay	0.015	33	air	critical variables
Multi-radiant	n/a	n/a	air	
Foamed ZODP				
Expanded polystyrene white, 'beadboard'	0.037	5	pentane	
Expanded polystyrene white, high density	0.033	10	pentane	
Foamed urethane	0.025	15	propane	Plus radiant barrier, big discounts for bulk
Extruded polystyrene	0.034	16	CO_2	
Foamed glass	0.040	30	CO_2	Load bearing
Foamed non-ODP				
Foamed urethane	0.019	5	HCFC	Plus radiant
Foamed urethane	0.019	5	HCFC	
Extruded polystyrene	0.028	12	HCFC	
Specials				
Aircrete blockwork	0.110	19		Load bearing
Transparent insulation	n/a	n/a		
Double-glazed insulated spacer	n/a	n/a		
Plastic wall ties	0.300	n/a		
Stainless steel	17.000	n/a		
Breather membranes	n/a	2		

Peterwarm@aecb.net, July, 2000.

COLD BRIDGES

Cold bridges are the most invidious of all problems that are designed into a building. They are invisible, and yet can cause enormous damage to the building and the health of people in it. Cold bridges have been, along with too much glazing, the thermal nemese of 'modern architecture'. A cold bridge is a pathway between the outside cold surface of a building and the internal warm air of the room. A cold bridge, most usually made of metal or solid masonry, conducts the heat out through the wall so cooling the internal wall surface of the building. But even timber forms an effective cold bridge if not dealt with by careful detailing (Figure 3.10).

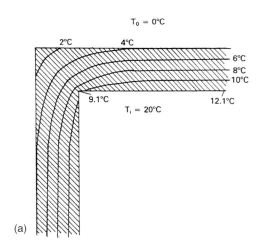

Between Joists
U = 0.2

Over joists
U = 0.17

3.10.
Timber forms a cold bridging element in the roof and requires careful detailing. (Peter Warm, Boxhedge Horsley, Stroud, Gloucs, GL6 0PP, UK; tel +44 (1453) 834060; fax +44 (1453) 834065.)

A wall can be a cold bridge if it is built of solid masonry. Studies have shown that in, say, a 100 mm solid brick wall the internal surface temperature can be very similar to the external temperature. Walls are particularly vulnerable to cold bridging on corners, where they have more than one surface exposed to the elements, as shown in Figure 3.11. Cavity insulation can significantly improve the thermal performance of a wall. The most common cold bridges in buildings are metal lintels, wall ties, window frames and concrete and metal columns and beams that link the internal and external leaves of walls.

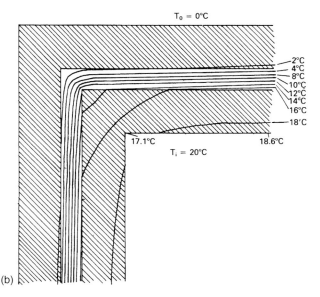

3.11.
Corners of walls lose heat very rapidly as they are exposed on two sides. This figure shows isotherms and Temperature Difference Ratios (TDR) at the corner of an insulated and uninsulated wall showing the impact of good insulation on wall temperature. A, 100 mm brick, $U = 3.3\,\mathrm{W\,m^{-2}\,K}$, TDR – 0.54. B, 100 mm brick/50 mm insulation/100 mm brick, $U = 0.6\,\mathrm{W\,m^{-2}\,K}$, TDR – 0.14 (Oreszczyn, 1992).

The effectiveness of a cold bridge is dependent both upon its geometry and the conductivity of the material of which it is made. Figure 1.1 (page 25) shows that while copper and steel are very good conductors of heat, timber and glass less so. To show how much difference in the conductivity of materials there is, aluminium conducts heat 4× better than steel, 170× better than glass, 1200× better than timber and PVC, and 8000× better than air.

There are a number of reasons why cold bridges should be avoided:

- They cost the building owner money because they are an effective path for heat out of the building or, in hot countries, heat into the building, so requiring more money to be spent on the heating or cooling of buildings.
- They can cause serious discomfort in buildings by creating cold (or hot) walls, windows or areas in a room.
- They cause condensation. Because, when the outdoor air temperature is lower than the indoors, the cold bridges are colder than the internal surrounding wall and room air. So, they cause the adjacent wall and air to cool rapidly. As cooler air can hold less moisture than warm air, so moisture condenses out on the surface of the cooler wall. This moisture can damage the structure of a building and provide a substrate for the growth of mould. This is why mould is typically found on the edges of metal window frames, or wall corners, and in patches on the wall in front of a cold bridge. Mould is very bad for health, as described in Chapter 6.

In order to prevent cold bridging in new buildings care should be taken to ensure there are no metal or concrete elements that span from the inside to the outside leaves of walls:

- Replace metal wall ties with nylon ones.
- Do not return the brick work around doors and windows but use a timber sub-frame detail as shown in Figure 3.12 (see also Vale and Vale, 2000, pp. 162–166).
- Eliminate the need for through-wall metal ducts by sensible design of opening windows and vents, and the use of passive stack ventilation systems.
- Split lintels so there is an external lintel for the outer leaf of a wall, a timber sub-frame for the insulation and a separate internal lintel for the inner leaf of a wall. Single metal lintels across the wall should be avoided.
- Choose the windows carefully to have a *U* (or *R*) value in keeping with that of the walls. If there is a single glazed window in a very well-insulated wall it will attract condensation owing to its internal surface temperature being much lower than that of the wall. Try to avoid all metal window frames.

Numerical modelling of building details can be used to assess the severity of cold bridging for a particular configuration. For instance, Part L of the UK Building Regulations (Conservation of Fuel and Power) requires that, unless details conform to an approved set of robust standard details, numerical modelling must be used to determine linear thermal transmittance (additional heat flow due to the cold bridge) and surface temperature factor. Temperature factor f_{Rsi} is calculated as:

$$f_{Rsi} = \frac{\text{Minimum internal surface temperature} - \text{external temperature}}{\text{Internal temperature} - \text{external temperature}}$$

3.12.

A window is often the largest cold bridge in a wall. The top row are aluminium frames. Second row left is simple timber. The next three are timber/aluminium combinations. Centre in the third row down is all PVCu and the last 4 frames are PVCu/aluminium combinations. Thermally broken spacers (with 4 internal lines) improve performance. (Richard Harris, 1995 and the Centre for Window and Cladding Technology, Bath).

The lower the temperature factor, the higher the risk of condensation and possible mould growth (if the surface is absorbent). Guidelines relating to minimum values of temperature factor to avoid surface condensation and mould growth in different types of building are given in Table 3.4 (BRE Information Paper 17/01):

Table 3.4. Guidelines for minimum temperature values for avoiding surface condensation and mould growth in different types of buildings

Building type	Minimum f_{Rsi}
Storage buildings	0.30
Offices, retail premises	0.50
Residential buildings, schools	0.75
Sports halls, kitchens, canteens, buildings with un-flued gas heaters	0.80
Buildings with high humidity, such as swimming pools, laundries, breweries	0.90

CONDENSATION

Interstitial condensation is caused when water vapour produced in the building escapes through the external wall and as the vapour cools on its way out it condenses thereby forming water, often in the building cavity. One way of removing this moisture is to ventilate the cavity on the inside of the outer wall so that the moisture will run down the inner face of the external wall, and not touch the insulation on the outer face of the inner leaf. Another way of dealing with condensation is to place an effective moisture barrier on the inner surface of the inner leaf of the wall, thus preventing the moisture penetrating into the wall.

However, it is very dangerous to have the internal and the external surface of a wall both completely watertight, because if the water does then get into the wall it cannot get out again – causing mould growth and unhealthy conditions to arise. This problem can be seen in the majority of American timber stud homes, where the inner walls were sprayed with waterproof paint and the outer surface with waterproof render so ensuring that when the water does penetrate into the cavity, usually through service pipe or nail holes, a common source of interstitial condensation arises from the movement of moist air through the construction via such cracks. This dampness allows certain toxic varieties of mould to grow in buildings. Combined with modern building materials and construction methods, this mould can lead to serious respiratory problems and, according to one claim, even deafness. A number of buildings in the USA where the mould was out of control have had to be demolished altogether, often as a result of interstitial condensation and resulting mould growth.

Building renovation projects, such as old brick barn or warehouse conversions are particularly susceptible, because they are old buildings which have never before been heated. Once installed with central heating and partitions put in, ideal breeding conditions for interstitial condensation and mould are created. The sudden heating draws moisture out of the building's structure

Description	f_{Rsi}
Uninsulated solid wall	0.765
25 mm drylined solid wall	0.675
Solid wall plus 187 cm floor and ceiling drylining	0.855
Solid wall only ceiling and wall drylined	0.685
Solid wall external insulation	0.885
Solid wall partial external insulation	0.825
Uninsulated cavity wall	0.760
Insulated cavity wall	0.790
Insulated cavity wall with floor and ceiling insulated	0.750

3.13.
The TDR for various insulated and uninsulated constructions consisting of a brick wall penetrated by a concrete floor slab. The cavity wall is built of 105 mm brick/50 mm cavity/105 mm brick. The solid wall is 260 mm brick, the floor is 150 mm dense cast concrete and the insulation is 25 mm drylining or external (Oreszczyn, 1992).

and these older buildings, which have been converted and unevenly insulated, have a problem with condensation. Dealing with interstitial condensation can be a very expensive exercise.

In a vapour-balanced construction the inner source of the wall or roof will have a vapour check, while the external surface will have a breather membrane that allows moisture trapped in the construction to escape to the outside air.

Description	f_{Rsi} No fin	f_{Rsi} Plus fin
Uninsulated cavity wall	0.760	0.765
Insulated cavity wall	0.790	0.795
Solid wall	0.735	0.740
Drylined solid wall	0.675	0.680
External cladding solid wall	0.825	0.830
(insulation over edge of floor)	0.885	

3.14.
The TDR for a concrete floor slab both with and without fins or balconies. The cavity wall is 105 mm brick/50 mm cavity/105 mm brick, the solid wall is 260 mm brick, the floor is 150 mm dense cast concrete and the insulation is 25 mm drylining or external.

Of course, if the site is very exposed, you may need to design against the driving rain. The amount, speed and direction of the rain hitting your walls will be affected by the location of the site, its roughness, topography, obstructions around it and the actual design and construction of the wall. In extreme locations the height of the wall, the width of cavities and the surface finishes and quality of the pointing will be important in keeping out the driving rain. These issues are included in the British Standard BS8104 which explains how best to design for extremely wet and windy sites.

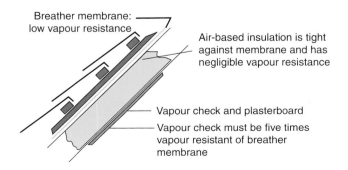

Breather membrane: low vapour resistance

Air-based insulation is tight against membrane and has negligible vapour resistance

Vapour check and plasterboard

Vapour check must be five times vapour resistant of breather membrane

3.15.
Vapour-balanced roof constructions with the 5:1 rule of thumb. (Peter Warm, Boxhedge Horsley, Stroud, Gloucs, GL6 0PP, UK; tel +44 (1453) 834060; fax +44 (1453) 834065.)

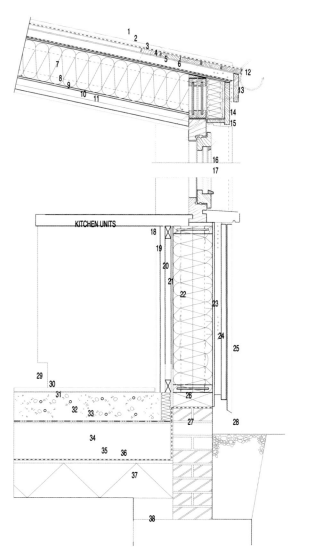

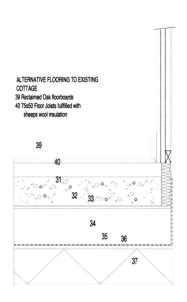

ALTERNATIVE FLOORING TO EXISTING COTTAGE
39 Reclaimed Oak floorboards
40 75x50 Floor Joists fulfilled with sheeps wool insulation

Limecrete floors and foundations used in a small extension to the Croquet Pavillion at Druidstone Hotel, to create an Eco Cottage in a clifftop setting on the Pembrokeshire coast.

JULIAN BISHOP - R.I.B.A.   ARCHITECT
Dan-y-Garn, Mountain West, NEWPORT, Pembrokeshire SA42 OQX
Tel and Fax: 01239 821 150
Client: Jane Bell, Druidstone Hotel, Broad Haven,
                                          Pembrokeshire
Job: Eco Cottage, Druidstone Hotel
Drawing: Typical Construction Details   Scale: 1:10   Date: Nov '01

3.16.

A good building section is designed to take into account all the important small issues from wind-proofing to insulation, damp paths, cold bridges, and the embodied energy and health implications of materials in addition to the shape or location of the wall, floor or roof itself. This is demonstrated by this section of a new house wall by Julian Bishop on an exposed cliff in Wales.

Key – ROOF: 1, Titanium Zinc Sheet Roofing with stand seams; 2, Separation quilt; 3, 100 × 20 Penny Gap D.F. boarding; 4, 50 × 50 Douglas Fir Battens; 5, Breathing sarking felt; 6, 9 mm Panel Vent Sheathing; 7, 200 mm Welsh unprocessed sheeps wool insulation; 8, 9 mm Oriented strand board; 9, 25 × 50 Douglas Fir battens/Service Zone; 10, 25 mm Heraklith, wood wool magnesite bound slabs; 11, 20 mm two coat Lime/Sand render & Natural paint finish; 12, Half round Zinc guttering; 13, Oak Fascias Ex. 150 × 25; 14, 20 mm Ventilation gap; 15, Oak Soffit & Lower Fascia. **WINDOW:** 16, 4-18-4 Double Glazed Sealed Argon filled Super Low 'E' unit; 17, Oak Cill with min. 38 mm overhang. **WALL:** 18, 20 mm Lime/Sand render; 19, 25 mm Heraklith; 20, 38 × 50 Douglas Fir battens/Service Zone; 21, 9 mm Oriented strand board; 22, 200 mm Masonite, timber I beam studs at 600 c/c fully filled with Welsh sheeps wool quilt; 23, 38 × 50 diagonal Douglas Fir battens at 400 c/c and Ventilation Zone; 24, 100 × 25 sawn Oak boarding; 25, 50 × 25 sawn Oak coverboards; 26, 200 × 75 Sole Plate bolted down through DPC and DPM; 27, Class B Engineering brickwork; 28, Ground Level. **FLOOR:** 29, Quarry tiles; 30, Lime mortar bed; 31, 150 mm Limecrete floorslab; 32, Light Metal mesh grid to stabilise LECA; 33, Geotextile; 34, 200 mm LECA (Lightweight Expanded Clay Aggregate) Insulation; 35, Dampproof membrane; 36, 25 mm Sand blinding; 37, 150 mm Hardcore (reused excavated Rab); 38, Limecrete Footings

THE LEAKY ENVELOPE

It is apparently normal for up to 50 per cent of the heat loss from new buildings in the UK to come from uncontrolled air leakage (Olivier, 2000). Moreover, the effectiveness of porous insulation materials (e.g. Warmcel, mineral and glass fibre) rely to a great extent upon trapped air. The impact of substantial air leakage can be to reduce to half or less the resistance to heat loss provided by such layers.

Preventing air leakage requires both good design and good workmanship. There are common risk factors which can be addressed at the design stage, but poor workmanship can rapidly compromise the envelope of a building. To achieve an airtight building, better site supervision and more management input is inevitably required.

Three of the major risk factors for air leakage are:

1   Building upper floor joists into a masonry inner leaf
2   The use of plasterboard drylining over unsealed masonry
3   Opting for a cold roof construction, where insulation lays flat across the upper ceiling of the dwelling and the loft space is unheated.

Figure 3.19 shows how gaps around floor joists can allow air leakage paths to connect into the centre of a house. Some builders have addressed this issue by moving to joist hangers, whilst more recently we have seen the development of 'joist boots' – plastic end caps which seal around the end of a joist, thereby ensuring that it does not breach the air barrier provided by a masonry inner leaf.

Figure 3.19 also illustrates how voids behind drylining can permit air to move around inside the walls of a dwelling, eventually finding a connecting leakage path. This is an inevitable weakness of drylining and can only be reliably prevented by using a 'scratch coat' to seal the inside face of blockwork inner leafs before drylining is applied. Many low-energy builders consequently opt to use wet plaster finishes, making airtightness much easier to achieve.

Cold roof construction, where the air barrier is usually formed by the plasterboard upper ceiling, has numerous factors associated with it that make delivering an airtight envelope harder. There are likely to be spotlights fitted in the ceiling, and also a loft hatch, where there can be a 1–40 ratio between the leakage associated with good and bad products and installations – some obviously being very leaky. Opting for a prefabricated loft hatch does not eliminate this risk – on occasion these have been found to be worse than a timber site-built hatch! If there are water tanks in the loft, there are likely to be gaps around the pipework through the ceiling, and electrical cabling will often have leakage associated with it – including connections to solar panels (thermal and/or PV). Another common problem is the large hole around the soil vent pipe rising up from the bathroom and connecting with the cold loft space.

Having minimised the risk of leakage through good design, great care must then be taken to ensure a satisfactory level of workmanship. Great care should be taken that every time a hole is put through the structure the remaining air gaps are sealed up, using robust materials. Watch out for gaps that form beside timber beams as drying out occurs, and also around pipe inlets and outlets through walls.

At the same time care must be taken to ensure that the vapour and wind barriers around the house are kept intact throughout the building process to ensure that walls, and poorly built masonry or timber joints, do not leak (Mould, 1992). Beware, in particular, of the poor bricklayer who does not fill

3.17.
Leakage around and through spotlights mounted in an upstairs ceiling.

the mortar joints properly but uses dabs of mortar that will allow air leakage into the cavity.

Where ventilation is needed, a range of different sized vents, and windows with suitable handles, latches and locks that permit varying, opening sizes, can be included to enable residents to control the amount of air movement in a range of different ways. This is much more thermally efficient than having the heat pour out of the house like water from a leaky bucket through holes in the envelopes and via metal ventilation ducts that act as very effective cold bridges across the external wall. Air leakage from buildings is even more of a problem in areas where there is driving wind and rain and special care should be taken in these areas to seal up the building tightly, and use buffer spaces such as porches and sunspaces for the external doors of the house. Chapter 5 outlines how moisture problems can be avoided by proper ventilation, house form and the use of correct materials in the house.

AIR LEAKAGE

Mainstream UK construction has become much more aware of airtightness over the past five years, and the latest revision to the Building Regulations (England & Wales), which came into force in April 2006, will accelerate this trend. Scottish requirements have also been tightened in May 2007.

Nevertheless, dwellings and other buildings waste vast amounts of energy through the uncontrolled escape of warmed air to the atmosphere. Uncontrolled air leakage, known as infiltration, is wasteful and is also damaging to our dwellings and other buildings. As levels of insulation have risen over recent decades, escaping hot air has come to dominate the energy lost from new dwellings. If you attempt to be more sustainable and adopt more stringent insulation standards, and yet fail to address infiltration, the amount wasted will be substantially higher.

Moreover, air passing through the external envelope – walls, floor and roof – of a building carries moisture with it. This causes significant damage in buildings, particularly to timber, and can substantially shorten the useful life of a building. Hence a sustainable building *must* be an airtight building – and for breathing wall constructions to work effectively such buildings must also minimise uncontrolled air movement.

Infiltration versus ventilation

Infiltration is the technical term we use for the uncontrolled movement of air through buildings. Infiltration is driven by the wind, or by the buoyancy effect which causes hot air to rise, particularly in multi-storey buildings, known as the stack effect.

Excess air movement through infiltration:

- Makes heating systems inadequate
- Gives rise to cold draughts and discomfort, particularly at ground level
- Increases fuel bills and CO_2 emissions
- Allows potentially damaging moisture to penetrate our building fabric
- Reduces the effectiveness of insulation.

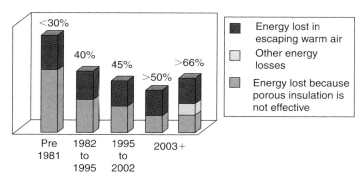

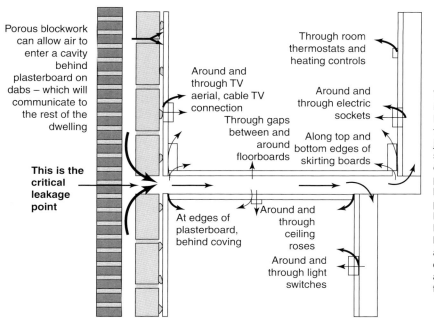

3.18.
Graph showing proportion of energy lost through the escape of hot air (Paul Jennings).

Date building constructed (to England & Wales B regs/common practice)

Porous blockwork can allow air to enter a cavity behind plasterboard on dabs – which will communicate to the rest of the dwelling

This is the critical leakage point

Through room thermostats and heating controls

Around and through TV aerial, cable TV connection

Around and through electric sockets

Through gaps between and around floorboards

Along top and bottom edges of skirting boards

When there is major air leakage into a floor void, every joint, edge, socket, switch or other penetration becomes an air path into the heated volume. Moreover, hollow walls and floors are cooled by the airflow, leading to discomfort.

At edges of plasterboard, behind coving

Around and through ceiling roses

Around and through light switches

Even when the cavity is filled with insulation, air will leak through it – just more slowly. This will also reduce the effectiveness of the insulation – by up to two-thirds.

3.19.
Illustration of some connecting leakage paths into a dwelling (Paul Jennings).

Unfortunately, there are numerous examples of supposedly energy-efficient buildings that require supplementary – and usually expensive – heating because of excessive air leakage.

Ventilation is the controlled removal of pollutant-laden air and its replacement by fresh air. Ventilation can be provided merely by opening windows, or by using more sophisticated passive stack and mechanical ventilation systems, sometimes fitted with heat recovery units. However, MVHR (mechanical ventilation and heat recovery) systems are only sensible in well-sealed dwellings where a large majority of the heated exhaust air passes through the system; in leaky dwellings they are largely a waste of money.

We do need some fresh air in our buildings. We need it to:

- Remove moisture generated by breathing, washing, cooking and drying
- Dilute and remove smoke, cooking fumes, odours and other pollutants

- Provide combustion air to appliances without a direct source of fresh air (although these are increasingly rare)
- Breathe.

The biggest pollutant we have to deal with in our dwellings is moisture – plain old H_2O. Minimising the build-up of moisture helps prevent condensation and mould growth, and discourages dust mites. A relative humidity of between 50 and 65 per cent will provide the most comfortable and healthy living environment. If we have open-flued appliances, such as wood-burning stoves, we need more ventilation for safety, and if people smoke we need lots more ventilation. Nevertheless, in general we need at least 10 times as much fresh air to remove moisture as we do to breathe – hence, except where combustion air is required, it is effectively impossible to get air leakage down to a level which threatens health. Rampant condensation and black mould would set in much sooner! However, particularly when tackling existing buildings, we must always consider fresh air requirements – carbon monoxide from incomplete combustion continues to kill a few unfortunates each year.

AIRTIGHTNESS TESTING

Anyone interested in sustainable construction should appreciate that the targets for airtightness set in the 2006 revisions to the UK Building Regulations are very lax – not at all suitable for low-energy construction. However, the regulations for new buildings – ADL1A for housing, ADL2A for non-domestic buildings – do strengthen the requirements for airtightness testing to be carried out. Figure 3.20 illustrates the principle of airtightness testing.

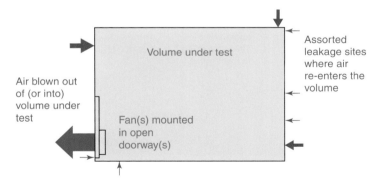

Air blown out of (or into) volume under test

Volume under test

Fan(s) mounted in open doorway(s)

Assorted leakage sites where air re-enters the volume

3.20.
The principle of air airtightness testing.

The key variable in most airtightness testing in the UK and Ireland is the *Air Permeability*, with the Canadian Super-E houses using a different leakage characteristic, the *Air Change Rate*. These are explained in the box below. The 2002 Building Regulations set a maximum air permeability value of 10 for all new building in England and Wales, and this remains in the 2006 Regulations, with a minor exception for very small housing developments.

The key change in the 2006 Regulations is the introduction of the Target Emission Rate (TER) of carbon dioxide as the measure of compliance with Building Regulations. In calculating the TER one must apply an air permeability value – which then must be achieved in practice and proven by an airtightness test carried out by a competent tester. The maximum value of the air permeability assumed in calculating the TER is 10, except for developments of two or fewer houses, when 15 may be assumed and the excess CO_2 compensated for by additional insulation and/or renewable energy sources.

> **Air Permeability** Units: m^3/hr (of airflow) per m^2 (of total surface area) at an imposed pressure differential of 50 Pascals (equivalent to 5 mm of water column, typically a 20 mile-an-hour wind), summarised as $m^3/hr/m^2$ @ 50 Pa. The target AP of 10 equates to an average air velocity through the entire walls, floor and roof of a building of 2.8 mm per second, substantially slower than one can walk – and that is the maximum.
> **Air Change Rate** Units: air changes per hour at an imposed pressure differential of 50 Pascals, summarised as ACH @ 50 Pa. For houses, the air permeability and the air change rate are typically similar, generally within 10 per cent.

However, meeting the AP target of 10 is very much a minimum, particularly for an ecobuilder. After all, all you have to do to meet this Building Regulations target is to build a dwelling where heated air remains inside for 7 minutes in

3.21.
Retrotec twin-fan blower door system maintained in a fire escape doorway whilst testing a low-energy Sports Centre (Paul Jennings).

the hour when a 20 mile-an-hour wind is blowing! This is neither energy-efficient nor sustainable, by a substantial margin. Hence the advanced energy standards set by the Association for Environment Conscious Building, AECB, of an air permeability of 3.0 for their silver standard and 0.75 for their gold standard. The first of these is the lowest air permeability we would recommend for naturally ventilated buildings, whilst the higher gold standard is comparable with the German PassivHaus standard and is more onerous than the Canadian Super-E standard.

Airtightness testing is carried out using portable fan equipment, annually recalibrated and in the UK is undertaken to TS1, Technical Standard 1, developed by ATTMA, the Air Tightness Testing and Measurement Association. The equipment is temporarily located in an opened doorway, and a series of steady state measurements of imposed pressure differential against the airflow required to produce it are taken. These are then entered in a suitable software program to check the data consistency and accuracy and generate the results, normally expressed as the *Air Permeability*.

ACHIEVING AIRTIGHT BUILDINGS

Some builders and designers are ambivalent about sealing up buildings, concerned that indoor air quality will suffer. The key point to understand is that whilst we minimise the uncontrolled air leakage that gives rise to draughts and discomfort, and of course inadequate heating and excess fuel use and CO_2 emissions, we also need to provide effective ventilation.

Build Tight, Ventilate Right is the slogan that has been adopted for many years to encourage us to improve our buildings and reduce our shameful waste of energy as warm air escapes into the atmosphere. So we do our best to prevent draughts by sealing up our buildings (and incidentally thereby making breathing wall constructions work), but also provide controllable ventilation using openable windows, trickle vents, extract fans, etc. Most UK dwellings have too much air leakage (draughts) when the wind blows and not enough ventilation on calm still days. Because we cut down the diluting effect of air movement through our new buildings, we are also wise to cut down the loading of indoor pollutants during construction and fit-out, for example by opting for organic paints and the careful selection of furniture, fixtures and fittings.

COMMON LEAKAGE SITES

Figure 3.22 shows most of the most common leakage sites in housing, although it is likely that many readers could add to the list from their own experience of UK housing.

Key to leakage sites (including additional common ones):

1 Around floor joists and joist hangers;
2 Beneath window cills and around window frames;
3 Through windows and/or hollow window frames;
4 Through and around doors, particularly double doors;

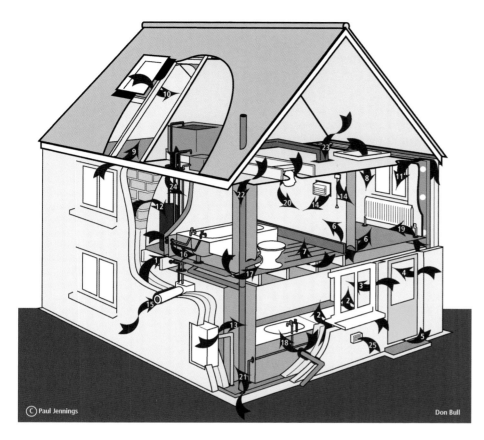

© Paul Jennings

Don Bull

3.22.
Axonometric showing common paths for air infiltration into a house (Source: Paul Jennings).

5 Beneath doors and doorframes;
6 Along the top and bottom edges of skirting boards;
7 Between and around sections of suspended floors;
8 Around loft hatches;
9 Through the eaves;
10 Around rooflights;
11 Through gaps behind plasterboard on dabs or hollow studwork walls;
12 Cracks and holes in a masonry inner leaf;
13 Around supplies from external meter boxes;
14 Around wall-mounted fan or radiant heaters; around and through fused spurs and pull switches;
15 Around boiler flues;

16 Around water and heating pipes that penetrate into hollow floor voids and partition walls;

17 Around waste pipes passing into floor voids or boxed in soil stacks;

18 Around waste pipes passing through walls;

19 Gaps around heating pipes;

20 Around and through recessed spotlights;

21 Around waste pipes, gas and water supplies, and electrical and other cables, all of which may penetrate the lower floor;

22 Hole around the top of a soil stack;

23 Through MVHR or warm air heating systems; around terminals;

24 Gaps around pipes to cold water and/or heating header tanks;

25 Around and through wall-mounted extract vents, cooker hood vents, tumble drier vents.

In order to deliver an airtight building we must:

a design for airtightness

b build for airtightness, and

c test to confirm airtightness.

Designing for airtightness requires an appreciation of where buildings can leak and how the junctions between elements can be made airtight, at a very detailed and basic level. Unfortunately it is still routine to have to remind site managers that mastic does not stick to dust, and that it needs to be tooled into place to achieve robust adhesion and provide an effective seal! The passage of services through the building envelope must also be evaluated. Moreover, buildability and the practicality of constructing the design on site must be considered.

Key principles to remember when attempting to design and deliver an airtight building are:

1 Identify your principal air barriers and make them accessible. Membranes or other elements buried in the middle of a complex wall construction are a hostage to fortune and frequently fail to deliver the planned airtightness. Be aware that taped joints are only robust if trapped beneath a batten or other element;

2 Provide air barrier drawings and clear specifications for the materials forming the air barrier, and how they interface. Check for gaps or voids where the air barrier is non-continuous;

3 Plan your penetrations and group them together where possible. Ensure there is a rigid substrate around penetrations (e.g. a timber pattress) to help effective sealing;

4 Think about what can go wrong ahead of time; adopt robust and checkable solutions rather than normal practice. Beware of on-site variations to services – these will generally give rise to additional leakage;

5 Allow plenty of time for supervision and agree critical 'check' and 'hold' points at which satisfactory inspections are required before further works can proceed. For example, the sealing around a soil vent pipe connecting to a cold roof space should be checked and approved before the pipe is boxed in;

6 Incorporate information on air leakage and airtightness testing into site inductions to ensure the whole workforce is aware – most will co-operate. Over-communicate – never allow a builder to say 'I assumed'. And hold your builder to account – be clear what the airtightness target is and let him know he'll have to achieve it – even if he has to take the roof off to redo the eaves detail!

In short, to achieve the major reduction required in carbon dioxide emissions from our buildings we need to substantially reduce the air leakage from them. Tackling existing buildings is even harder than tackling new-build. So far we have largely made a hash of the new-build sector, where the average house built since 2002 probably fails to meet the maximum air permeability target set then – just 10 – and this is very much more lax than truly sustainable targets such as the AECB Gold standard and the German PassivHaus standard.

GETTING LIGHT INTO THE HOUSE SAFELY

A window is an important element in the building envelope. As with insulation, the greater the difference in temperature between the outside and the inside of a house, the better the windows will have to be. Look carefully to see what are the relative performances of the windows that are used in the different case study buildings around the world. For details of different windows there are a number of excellent sites on the internet listed under 'window performance'. The key things with window design are:

- To ensure they are similar in thermal performance to the adjacent walls so that they do not become too prone to condensation.
- In temperate, or colder climates, the side of the building facing the sun should have more windows, and the polar orientation very few to prevent excessive heat loss from the cold side of the building.
- To design the window for a specific purpose.
- To illuminate the centre of the house as well as its peripheral rooms. This can be done with internal windows, skylights, light tubes through the roof and other clever ideas. One idea that was very popular in the 1930s was to use glass ceilings in the upper floor which took the light from the sunny side of the building to the darker ceilings on the dark side of the house, often above stair wells.
- To not make unshaded windows too large. It is important to prevent overheating in a house. With climate change the sun will get stronger and rooms that are exposed to the direct sun in summer will have a problem. Shade all windows in summer. Only in the colder climates should the sun be allowed to penetrate into the house in summer. It is very important to design for solar control through windows but also in their external surroundings. Take into account highly reflective pavements outside the window that will bounce light back into a room, as will glass walls next to or opposite the window.
- A window can have many layers. A sunspace, with its second layer of glass, will keep the cold away from the internal windows. Light can result in heat and, in very hot climates, dark interiors will keep rooms cooler.

3.23.
Krister Wiberg sitting at his kitchen table in Sweden. Light is a powerful design issue and very important in creating the 'spirit' of a place (Source: Paul Jennings).

Shutters can be used externally to control solar gain in hot climates at different times of the day and year. Shutters can be used internally in cool and temperate climates to keep excessive sunlight out but some warmth in. Shutters can be wind-permeable but still keep the sun out. Once the light has passed through the glass the heat it contains is trapped inside the room and will not escape back out. Heavy curtains can be used to keep light out in summer (but not heat for the same reason) and warmth inside in winter.

- Consider the problem of glare in rooms. In particular, high glare levels will make it difficult to read computer screens and view the TV. Glare is also an indication of very high daylighting levels which may indicate that rooms will also overheat in summer.
- Capture the view. Careful consideration should enable the designer to make maximum advantage of the views on offer from the site. If there are particular features of interest ensure that they are captured in the centre of the window frame rather than the foreground in front of them or the sky above them (Lynes, 1992).
- Make sure that the positions of windows are such that this enables you to arrange the furniture easily – if you have low chests of drawers you want to place against the outer wall, make sure the window sill level is above them.
- If you want to get light deep into a room use high windows.
- Think about the psychological effect of a window or door in a room. What will a window do for the degree of privacy you require? Do you want everyone in the street to be able to see you in a particular room? Will a large patio door type window turn a room into a corridor?
- Think about light as a sculptural medium that changes every daylight hour of the year. You can create dynamic sculptures in shade and light to great effect on floors and forms within the house. Grade light through the house with darker and lighter areas to create visual interest.

All the techniques above provide ways in which we can understand, and design for, the invisible workings of a building. There are, however, also issues which cannot be calculated, that are very important in creating that other invisible factor: the spirit of a place, and these are dealt with, by Christopher Day, in the following chapter.

4 BUILDING-IN SOUL

Building is expensive – though not half, perhaps not one-fifth, so expensive as having something built for you. It also takes a lot of energy. But most importantly, you invest your soul in what you build, which is why self-built homes are so soul-rich to live in.

It is just this – the soul in buildings – that makes all the effort worthwhile, much more than just a cut-price roof. And self-built homes have infinitely more soul-potential than contractor-built houses. If we cannot build a house ourselves, how can we build-in soul through design and, once constructed, how do we introduce 'soul' into the way we live in buildings? But to have a self-built house or to be built-for, does this issue conflict with ecological concerns?

Buildings are substantive – what they are made of is very much part of their character. Wood, earth, brick, concrete, steel, glass or plastic buildings are totally different from each other to see, to live in, to build and in the forms their construction logically and characterfully demands. Their influence on microclimate, air quality, physical health and psychological state is also very different. So, very important in terms of their pollution and environmental costs, are their manufacturing biographies and how they end their life – do they return to nature or become refuse?

Buildings are primarily made of bulk materials. Though some, such as concrete foundations, are invisible, most are in daily view. Secondary materials range from drainage pipes and windows to small bits and pieces such as draught seals, light fittings and so on. While environmental cost is something to consider in every material choice, there is a need to be pragmatic; it is obvious that there is a lot more PVC in floor tiles or wallpaper than in electric cabling so the relative impacts of choosing tiles/wallpaper and the electric cabling will be very different. Fortunately, alternatives to both exist, though they are not always easy to obtain.

A building's furnishings also need serious thought as they are replaced many times in the life of the building. They tend to be newer, and also are often in warm places. So, as well as seeing and touching them, we breathe them: as materials get warmer they tend to give off more of their chemicals.

How do building (and furnishing, maintenance and cleaning) materials affect us, and the wider world? Every material has some environmental cost; some have compensating environmental benefits, as has been shown in Chapter 2.

These can be measured in terms of embodied energy or, more meaningfully, embodied CO_2. This, however, is an imprecise science and values are seldom transferable from country to country. Timber in Britain comes mostly from the pacific side of Canada; in Central Europe from managed forests only a few kilometres away. Whatever its source, and however cruelly the forests are raped, building timber locks up carbon as do other carbon-rich materials such as straw and cellulose fibre, so diminishing the CO_2 emissions from the building.

Contrast this with steel, the cost of which is equivalent to that of 300 times its weight of water and five times its weight of coal – multiplied again by some nine times as much soil excavated as both coal and iron ore. But this is nothing compared with plastic, made at the price of 5000 times its weight in raw materials.

In terms of how we relate to these materials, wood is approachable, easy to work with, absorbs airborne toxins and moderates temperature and humidity. It is sensitive to environment and needs to be maintained and protected from sustained moisture by careful design. Aging adds character. It is easily repairable. It can be recycled or allowed to compost back to earth. Steel is hard, can be worked with hand-scale, semi-industrial tools (such as welding apparatus) and is neutral in health terms. It needs protection from water, but is unaffected by light, insects or aging. It can, with suitable tools, be repaired and recycled. Abandoned, it will rust back into ore – though this does not apply to its (usually toxic) paints and platings. Plastic is generally unappealing to touch and emits toxins. It is unaffected by the environment (except abrasion, UV light and organic solvents) and appears ageless except for scratching, cracking and crazing, which compromise both appearance and performance. It is effectively unrepairable. Little is recycled, some types cannot be, and most types effectively are never broken down – beyond breaking up and slow toxin release.

Not coincidentally, wood is a material from life. Iron is from the earth, but by way of intense heat and heavy industrial rolling. Plastic is from oil and coal deep beneath its surface, after so numerous chemical synthesis operations that it is totally removed from life. These materials connect us to the world from whence they came: living and life-cycle bound by nature, or lifeless, dead industrial processes. Whereas plastic needs industrial equipment suited to mass production to form, wood needs only a pocket knife. It is more appealing, accessible and healthy to work with. Indeed, you can put your heart into what you make out of it.

We use thousands of materials in modern building, but a general rule is that the nearer something is to life, the more compatible it is: the healthier to live with, the more recyclable back to earth, thence living matter again. It also needs more care for longevity – but this care, like the care given to its making, is imprinted into its substance and emanates from it, to nourish those who live next to it. Mass-produced products can never do this; the imprint of care given by an individual maker is, by definition, absent. So the materials of which a building is built, and the extent to which they are imprinted by care and love through hand-work, imprints spirit – or the lack of it – into buildings, even before occupation. This care is something self-builders can easily afford, while those sufficiently well off to get others to build for them rarely can.

4.1.
Light from two directions in every room
(Christopher Day).

One technique I use often is hand-finished rendering. Lime-rich mortar (9:2:1) applied unevenly to walls, preferably with a round-nosed tool so it is a little mounded, but then smoothed by (gloved) hand as soon as it is firm, removing all tool marks and contrived form. This forms a gentle, undulating and sand-textured surface. But more: it has been shaped by the hand. On one hand-plastering course I taught, a massage therapist told me, 'There is no part of the human body that a part of the hand is not shaped to fit'. So this technique imprints our hands into our physical surroundings. And it is impossible to work for long engaging the hands (not just repetitively using them) without the heart becoming involved. Thus, in a hand-plastered room you are surrounded by hand-imprinted heart forces. This works on us in the same way as food prepared with love – as distinct from mass-produced, routinely, institutionally cooked meals.

Another technique I enjoy is repair – inserting a patch of new wood into old. Working with second-hand materials you have to do this quite often. Of course, we use our hands to some extent for everything we make, but the fewer devices between hand and work, the more direct the link between hand and heart.

However, buildings are only part of places. Even 'home' is only part house. It is also entry, gateway and garden – and is enmeshed in street and neighbourhood. Every place has a unique spirit. Part of that spirit comes from how the place is used – the actions, thoughts and values of those who inhabit it. And part comes from how it was formed – the geology, weathering, forces of living nature, the elements and human interaction. Part also comes from how we meet it, the concept of place we then form and how this then influences our thoughts and actions.

How do we meet places? What do they say to us? And how can we transform the negative – all too common in our decrepit cities and their compromised fringes – into the positive, spirit-uplifting?

First impressions tend to influence what we subsequently see, feel and think. The welcome or fortified defensiveness of an entry door colours our expectations – and meaningfully so, for we gain an intuition of the essence of a place. And this impression is repeated every time we re-arrive there. Whether or not we are commencing a new building or altering an old one, there is some kind of place already there. We are converting a place. What is already there limits what we can do, so how can we ensure the first impressions reflect the spirit we wish to establish there?

4.2.
The inside of the sunspace of David's house in Wales (Andrew Yeats).

There is a technique for this that works with the connections with spirit and matter. To overcome the tendency of individuals to be led by their own ideas, it is a listening technique, so it is easier to do this as a group. We identify and work along the arrival route, from the point that you first meet a building. The first walk is for first impressions if you don't know the place, consciousness of the journey as an entity in its own right if you do. We walk in silence, without judgement, meeting at the final destination, say the kitchen, to reconstruct the journey. This we do at the end of each walk. We then repeat this walk, recording only what is physically there – no feelings, judgements, causes or suggestions. Next, we re-walk the route, focusing only on sequential space: how the space and light expands, contracts, breathes and turns, the gestures of forms and flow of our movements. Our next walk focuses on the moods and the feelings they induce along the journey. Now we can ask how the place would describe itself. What is its essential message? As this message, this spirit of place, is central to why we build, how we wish to live in a place and the nourishment we hope it will feed us will colour our individual ideas of what this message should be. With existing buildings, used for new purposes, there can be harsh discrepancy between the spirit that is and what it should be. A school building, for instance, may well speak of controlling little vandals, not loving and inspiring children on their journey to independent adulthood.

But when we know what a place should say, we can re-walk our route asking: what moods would support this? And then, on our next walk: what journey sequences, qualities of flow, would support these moods? And finally, re-walking to ask: what physical changes would support these qualities of flow?

Invariably these changes are small: pruning trees to form an archway, re-aligning an entry path, pivoting past a bush, easing an abrupt corner with furniture or a plant, flowing ceilings into each other, unifying colour and such like. Small, affordable, material changes that have a major impact on what a place says and how it reflects and reinforces the spirit we wish to grow within it.

But what if there is as yet no building? Where should it go? What place should it help make? How can it contribute to, rather than compromise, what is already there?

We use a similar process, starting with silent first impressions and then the physical here and now. But then, instead of looking at time experiences through space (its flow), concentrate on space through time (its biography). How was this place formed in geological process? How was it before the agricultural, then industrial, revolutions, last century, last generation, a decade, a year ago? And continuing into the future, what will it be like next season, year, decade and century? We can thus enter into the flow of time through a place and ask what changes are set in motion when we intervene, postulating various actions and imagining their chain of consequences unfold. We then return to moods and spirit-of-place as before.

We now ask what spirit stands at the heart of what we are about to establish. What activities will this manifest in – and where, in the light of what we know about the place, should these be located? These 'zones of activity' we peg and string on the ground, then record on a site plan. We need now to identify the moods appropriate to each area, and to modify the layout for both this and for appropriate relationships between places, paths, gateways and views. We can next lay paper rectangles representing room areas onto this drawing, confirming its layout more meaningfully. The next step is to replace paper shapes with clay rectanguloid volumes – which rapidly become moulded into more living forms. All this is group work, just one family and myself, or 20 or 30 people. It can be a very strong experience as shared imagination of the future becomes almost substantial amongst the group.

For a single house this is simple (except that small, simple things tend to end up as being the most complicated!) but this process especially suits something larger or a group of buildings. Few larger projects, however, are built all at once. Nor should they be. Disruption to the spirit-of-place is excessive and the greater this is, the more buildings are imposed, not grown. And anyway, cash flow is rarely as predictable as we hope at the outset, so often only half a project gets built. We need to unravel the design to find a sequence so that every phase of building seems perfect – but the next stage makes it even better!

Space need doesn't only grow. In houses, for instance, it also contracts as children grow up and leave home. This doesn't just leave parents with mortgages still to pay, but also with big, lonely empty nests to rattle around in. From working with a Swedish eco-village group, I learnt to design homes that can expand – for instance, into garages, workshops and stores – and contract by division into house and disabled-accessible flat.

Growth is a key to how to blend the new (such as buildings) into the old – be it rural landscape or urban street. Anything that doesn't grow has a different spirit to its surroundings. If they don't talk to each other, can we expect social or ecological harmony, not to mention soul harmony?

With or without human intervention, no place is static. It is changing in response to the living and elemental forces of nature. Socially and economically, it waxes and wanes under these interacting forces; and grows or withers from nodes of growth activity or blight. New buildings feel right in place if they grow in accord with these forces. We can learn from the place study method just described how places want to grow – how they would do so without our intervention. Also what qualities of a place need enhancement and what need balance – so how this growth is asking to be steered.

We also learn about the arrival journey – of central importance to every building, whether home, hospital or work place. 'Home' has an active meaning: 'arriving home' – and a passive one: the state of 'being at home'. Haven and oasis roles. Different parts of the journey: front gate, entry hall, social rooms, bedrooms need different moods, need to meet us with different gestures – which we can gesture with our bodies – and link into different patterns of relationship: front door with street community and socially outward-looking; back garden to neighbour community, yet protectively private and linked into local wildlife habitat.

All these parts of the whole have time- and season-related needs. Bedrooms to wake up in, bathed with optimism for the day ahead. Evening rooms to unwind in. Winter hearth and summer breeze-freshened openness. Sunlight when children return from school or adults from work, not to mention orientations for view, skyscapes, sunsets and qualities of weather.

Rooms within the house range from family to individual realms, each different. Once we start to think of small children's needs as distinct from just practical space planning, new things come up: 'secret' spaces under stairs, in lofts or all the 'lost' spaces architects prefer to hide, with moods of privacy, enchantment, mystery, but also warm security. Then, teenagers need their own 'realms' that they themselves can, to some extent, form. An older person has needs for stability and an anchoring lifespan of memorabilia – along with warmth and sun and the life invigoration of nature's moods, which they can less and less actively partake in. One thing these rooms are not is just rectanguloid volumes – appropriate soul mood is the primary reason they are there.

But no building or garden is just an interior. It links into a wider community, economy and ecology. It links into the infrastructural system of a place. Yet drains and pipes and wires aren't place-related but transporters to and from invisibly distant sources and destinations. Composting, on-site greywater treatment and autonomous energy link us to ecology, water flow patterns and microclimates. As these have aesthetic implications from water gardens to shelter planting and conservatories, they are also soul links to the forces of nature, interactions unique to every place.

Linkage to place also demands meaning in why we live somewhere and what we do. But our lifestyle and activities relate to where we are – unlike picturesquely preserved holiday cottages, appropriate only in visual appearance but otherwise alien, unrelated and dissociated from place-responsibility.

It also requires local materials. At first sight, many materials – such as stone and brick – don't seem sufficiently energy-efficient – but they can be made more so. Almost certainly, however, local traditional materials are durable in local climatic conditions and have a local skill-base familiar with local, climatically appropriate construction detailing.

The more local and unprocessed materials are, the less the transport and manufacturing energy and pollution, the more health-benign, and the better for local employment. Also, the more localised within the community does the money cycle. Local traditional materials also connect us with the cultural continuum of the past and enable us to connect it to a future inspired by different ideals. New technologies and forms can blend harmoniously with the old if given substance in traditional materials and bound by the constructional limitations inherent in them. Giving value to that which has formed the character of a place is also to value its culture, the keystone of community and individual self-esteem. So local materials have energy, minimum pollution, social economic, cultural, self-esteem and spiritual benefits – and shape, of course, the character of a place – its identity.

Materials connect us to a place. Traditionally taken from the ground, its vegetation and even animals, they are raised into human habitation – connecting those who live there with our roots in place. This is still so, even when we use these materials in less traditional forms: straw as building blocks, timber as round poles tensioned into unfamiliar curves, earth as free-formed cob.

However soul warm are vernacular forms, we should not gloss over the restrictive, narrow conventionality that comes with unnaturally prolonged past ways of life. Turning our back on them, however, merely dissociates us from where we have come from and in so doing blinds us to all we can learn and obscures where we are going to.

The traditional way was to raise the physical materials of a place to be a home for the human spirit. Largely unconsciously, totemic and elemental echoes remained in stone, earth, tree, straw and hide. Matter, in vernacular times, could not be divorced from spirit. Nor can it be today – however widespread its apparent negation. In every aspect of buildings, matter and spirit are cyclically linked.

The materials of which a place – land, town, building, room – is made have effects in multiple directions unified, however, by the 'essence' at their heart. They used to, and still can, link us with locality at several levels, giving substance to a spirit-of-place growing out of that locality. We can develop these places in accord with the life-generating energies latent within it, and colour its moods to be appropriate to our soul needs, increasingly individualised and different from a generation ago. We can imprint human energy and care – a gift of spirit – into the material substance of buildings, thus inspiriting matter and building-in soul.

5 VENTILATION

Ventilation is the movement of air within a building and between the building and the outdoors. The control of ventilation is one of the most subtle and yet the most important concerns of the building designer. How to make air move about the building in a way that satisfies, and even delights, the occupant.

There is, of course, a simple solution – to use a fan – but this can be a noisy and expensive business and is not the preferred first option for an ecohouse in which mechanical systems should only be used as a last resort.

So how does air move without a fan? Actually, air moves very easily and always down a pressure gradient. Positive pressure exists on the windward side of a building where the air is pushed with some force against the building. Negative pressure occurs on the leeward side of a building, in the wind shadow, and sucks air from the structure.

The trick is to create that pressure gradient. This can be done in two ways:

1 using pressure differences around the outside of the building caused by wind
2 using pressure differences caused by the pressure variations within the house. Warm air is less dense than cold air, therefore pressure variations that cause warm bodies of air to rise also cause cold bodies of air to fall. This is called the stack effect and can be used to ventilate a space. It can also be in conflict with wind-driven cross-ventilation.

Using wind pressure to ventilate is common, particularly if the house is in a windy part of the world. There are many challenges in designing properly for ventilation including the variability of the wind, its speed and direction, but if carefully handled and understood it can be of real benefit to the indoor climate of a house, for most of the time.

Wind and ventilation are not the same thing. Wind is very variable and can present itself in many different guises.

A wailing rushing sound, which shook the walls as though a giant's hand were on them; then a hoarse roar, as if the sea had risen; then such a whirl and tumult that the air seemed mad; and then with a lengthened howl, the waves of wind wept on. Dickens.

How different was Dickens' description of the wind from that of Longfellow:

The gentle wind, a sweet and passionate wooer, kisses the blushing leaf.

The wind can be an agent of terror or delight, it can soothe or destroy and it is one of the most important of the invisible building blocks of architecture. This chapter begins by considering the wind, and its usability for a building for a particular site and form. The reasons why and how to use air in buildings for maximum effect are then outlined. Finally, a section is included on how to protect a house from strong winds, such as those that result from hurricanes and cyclones. A major impact of global warming over the last decade of the twentieth century has been the increase in wind speeds and damage experienced in many countries of the world (Headley, 2000). We cannot predict how badly climate change will affect any of us, but we have taken this opportunity to include design for extreme wind environments, just in case. This section is complemented by a case study building in cyclone-prone St Maarten in the Caribbean (see page 403).

To ventilate a house well you first have to develop a relationship with wind. To do this you need to understand the regional and local climate of the site, the form and surroundings of the site and building. Key, also, are the building's occupants and their comfort requirements.

STEP 1 – CHOOSE YOUR WIND CAREFULLY – AND NAME IT

Every region or location in the world has its own winds. In the old days, builders knew the name of every wind, its personality and its potential for benefit or harm. In fact, a single wind would probably have two or three names. One name may denote the direction from which the wind comes, the part of the day in which it arrives or the name of the town, region or country from whence it hails. Another may refer to the quality of the wind, such as cold, hot or wet. If it is very important wind regionally, it may have its own grand name like Mistral or Sirocco, words that in many countries conjure images of the unique aeolian character of that particular wind. For instance, in the Naples region of Italy wind names include:

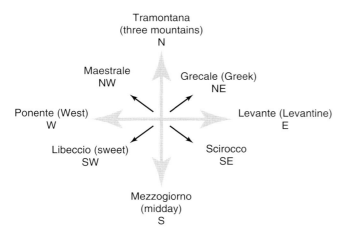

Local geographical conditions will have a large influence on local winds. In Naples the cool Tramontana wind sinks down from the hills to the north and east of the city, flushing the heat out of the long streets running down to the sea. As the land and city warm up on summer afternoons they draw the cool sea breeze up the same streets to replace the warm air in them as it rises.

For every site and area designers should get a clear idea what winds exist, which they would like to use in order to heat or cool their buildings and which they wish to exclude as too hot or cold. This can be done by looking at a wind-rose that shows how much wind comes from different directions every month or year. However, it will not tell you the properties of that wind; this can be worked out by looking at the geography of a region. An easier way is to ask a local builder about the winds around the site.

Traditional settlement patterns can reveal a great deal about the wind. The ways in which buildings are arranged in a settlement will indicate if the wind is welcome inside or not. A staggered arrangement means that buildings are spread out to ensure each house can capture some of the wind, as are the great wind catchers of Yazd in the Central desert of Iran, shown in Figure 5.1. Linear patterns indicate that one building is used to shelter the next from unwelcome winds and will show from which direction the unwanted winds come.

5.1.
Windcatchers on the skyline of Yazd, staggered to catch the prevailing winds (Roaf).

WINDSCAPING BUILDINGS

There are many ways to sculpt a building into the landscape and the wind.

- Nestle the building into the landscape. This simple device of hiding a building behind a feature of the landscape is very effective. However, bear in mind that if the wind is needed to cool the building, siting it behind a spur in the landscape may cut it off from the breezes. In some cases people take bulldozers to the landscape to ensure that the winds from the refreshing directions are channelled around their houses and the hot winds are excluded by features in the landscape.
- Split the winds. A single flagpole 20 m from a building in the direction of a strong prevailing wind can split the wind vertically before it arrives at the building and considerably lessen its impact on the structure. In the St Maarten house an open porch has recently been placed in front of the house with vertical columns supporting it to split the winds before they reach the building. Wind can be split vertically to reduce wind speeds and turbulence on the face of the building; in the wind towers of the Iranian Desert the wind is very neatly sliced horizontally to throw some wind over the top of a tower while forcing some air down the wind catcher shaft. Beneath the vent the wind is again split cleanly to force wind below the shaft down the face of the tower.
- Shape the roof carefully. Figure 5.2 shows how much difference there is between different roof shapes in the negative pressure they generate. It

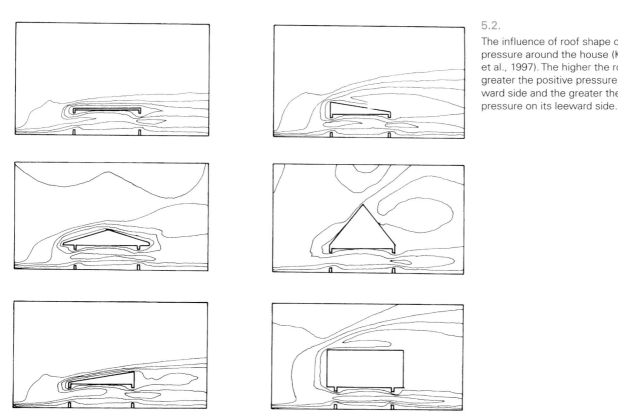

5.2.
The influence of roof shape on the air pressure around the house (Kindangen et al., 1997). The higher the roof the greater the positive pressure on its windward side and the greater the negative pressure on its leeward side.

is this negative pressure that typically rips roofs off buildings (Kindangen et al., 1997).

- Mould the wind impact of wind pressure on façades with features such as balconies. The use of features on building façades will cause an increase or decrease in pressure at different heights on the building façade as shown in Figure 5.3. Note the lack of pressure variation on the leeward side of the building (Chand et al., 1998).
- Use planting as wind breaks.

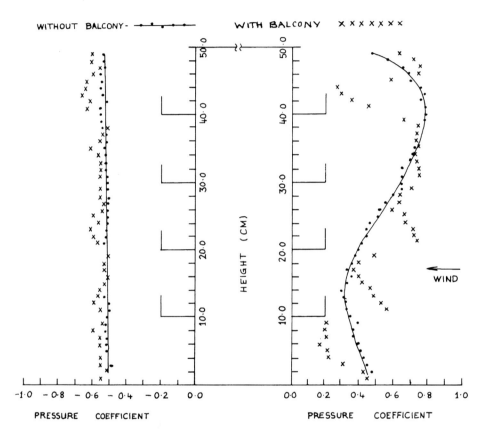

5.3.
Pressure difference on the windward façade of a building with balconies (Chand et al., 1998).

WHY VENTILATE A BUILDING?

For each room of a house you should ask: why is ventilation needed in this space? Three possible reasons are:

- for fresh air supply
- for direct comfort ventilation to cool or heat the occupants of the space by convection
- for indirect comfort ventilation, for heating and cooling the actual structure of a building to indirectly enhance the comfort of the room's occupants and to use 'free energy' more efficiently. In this way, day-time solar warmth can be stored in the structure and used at night, or coolth from night air can be stored to cool the people indoors during the day.

FRESH AIR

The need for fresh air ranges from the nominal amounts needed for breathing (2 litres s^{-1}) to the much higher ventilation rates necessary to control odours (up to 16–32 litre s^{-1} is a commonly quoted figure for fresh air needed to mitigate the effects of smoking smells). In houses, care can be taken to provide zones for smokers where the smell of a cigarette can be dealt with by opening a window. This may be more easily said than done. Studies have shown that homes with smokers use significantly more energy to heat or cool because the windows are continually opened to get rid of the smell. This should be taken into account and the problem designed out by sensible zoning of spaces.

How the room is furnished will affect lingering odours, with smells collecting more easily in the soft fabrics of curtains and carpets. Different activities in the house may be associated with different smell levels, so finishes can be chosen appropriately. The need for fresh air can be influenced very much by the chosen room finishes. It should be noted that building regulations are typically not designed to mitigate against the impact of smells or the transmission of diseases. It is not possible to regulate against air-borne diseases, although many indoor air quality regulations have evolved to deal with condensation risks in buildings that do have indirect health implications.

Fresh air is also needed to prevent the build up of moisture in a room. This is obvious for kitchens, bathrooms and utility rooms but there can be a real build-up of moisture in bedrooms as well. There are six ways to design out moisture as a problem in housing.

1 Provide wet zones in the house outside the main envelope of living rooms. Build a front porch/lobby/air lock in which the temperature of the outside air can be modified to be warmer or cooler before it enters the house. All wet clothing, coats and shoes can be left there, so keeping a great deal of moisture outside the house on wet days.
2 Build an outdoor drying space where clothes and bath towels can be left outside the main body of the house in winter. Wet clothes are a main source of excessive moisture in winter.
3 Build a high-level vent window above the kitchen stove that can be easily opened to immediately remove the hot, wet air generated by cooking. A good, non-cold-bridging window is much better than a mechanical vent above the stove as metal vents across a wall act as one large cold bridge and will cause condensation to collect in the wall at one of the wettest points in the house.
4 Bathrooms should either have a window that can be opened after a bath or shower or a very good passive stack outlet that will carry the moist air out of the room, which may, or may not, have a small fan to assist its draw.
5 Design out cold bridges from the walls of the house.
6 The wall-surface finishes of rooms should be chosen to be capable of absorbing some moisture. Where possible use an organic water-based paint on walls. These can range from the traditional white-washed walls and natural wood products to the use of modern, sophisticated, water-based paint products. The room finishes can play a significant part in controlling moisture build-up in the room as well as smell.

A common-sense approach is needed to estimate the best ventilation strategy for a particular building. For example, a high-volume low-occupancy house with all the above features and wet-plastered high-mass walls or exposed timber walls with a natural finish could, on some days, get all the fresh air necessary from people intermittently opening doors.

However, a low-mass, small-volume, high-occupancy room with hard finishes may need significantly more. For a well-designed house, even with low mass, hard finishes and normal occupancy but where the moisture problem has been removed from the interior of the house to a wet zone, most problems of air quality will disappear when the air change (ac) rate is 0.2 ac h^{-1}. That means that one-fifth of the air of a room is changed every hour. Humidity control can be achieved with a rate of 0.3 ac h^{-1} or more (Marshall and Argue, 1981). Actually, this level of air change can be achieved almost with door-opening air intake only. In many houses the air leakage rate through the structure will be of this order. Robert and Brenda Vale recommend an air change rate of around 0.45 ac h^{-1} as acceptable but, again, there is little reason not to design to the lower levels (Vale and Vale, 2000). Attention should be paid to houses where radon or carbon monoxide problems from open fires may exist, see Chapter 6.

DIRECT COMFORT VENTILATION

The comfort and thermal delight of the occupant is what makes a great house (Herschong, 1979). Issues of comfort should certainly dictate how to ventilate a building. If you think about times when you have been blissfully comfortable in a house, the feeling is probably either associated in winter with being near a warm radiant heat source, perhaps a fire, or in summer being in a cooling breeze. Sue Roaf remembers a summer's evening in Baghdad, coming out onto the freshly watered veranda at around 7 p.m. with an iced drink, wearing a cool cotton dress, sitting chatting in the early evening breeze and thinking that 'this is bliss'. Only on looking at the thermometer was it seen to be 42°C! It had been almost 50°C all that day.

People acclimatise to ambient temperatures. How warm or cold they feel depends on what the temperature has been over the last three or four days. It can take two to three weeks to adapt to a whole new climate.

If it is too hot or cold people do something about it. They may put on or take off clothes, they may change places within a room or move from one room to another. They may open a window, close a door or take a cold or hot drink. In extremes they may change buildings or even move to a different region with a more pleasing climate. They adapt their circumstances. It is only at the very extremes that people die of heat or cold. One of the key strategies they adopt in adapting the building to improve the indoor climate is to open a window to let in warm or cool air, another is to go to sleep.

Passive building design is driven by the relationship between the outside and the inside air temperatures. Michael Humphreys demonstrated this over 20 years ago with his classic diagram (Figure 5.6) showing that people who

5.4.
The cool, shaded, naturally ventilated living room of Jimmy Lim's house in Malaysia, giving thermal delight (Jimmy Lim).

live in hotter climates are comfortable at higher temperatures. In this book we adopt his simple, but effective, equation to show, very roughly, at what temperatures locally adapted people are comfortable:

$$T_c = 0.534 \, (T_{mean}) + 11.9$$

Where $T_{mean} = (T_{max} + T_{min})/2$ and is monthly mean outdoor temperature; T_c is comfort temperature; T_{max} is monthly mean daily outdoor maximum temperature; and T_{min} is monthly mean daily outdoor minimum temperature. T_{min} and T_{max} are usually available from Meteorological Office data.

This equation, strictly speaking, applies to summer conditions in free-running buildings (not air-conditioned ones) but gives a general idea of the comfort conditions required indoors by locally adapted populations.

Where the comfort temperature lies somewhere between T_{max} and T_{min} in a well-designed passive building with good levels of thermal mass and no excessive solar gain it should be possible to open windows for comfort cooling where T_{max} is 35°C or below. Comfort warming from the window breeze should be achievable in a good passive building when T_{max} is over 22°C and T_{min} is over 15°C.

5.5.
Environment and attitude of a person on a hot day (Sab Ventris).

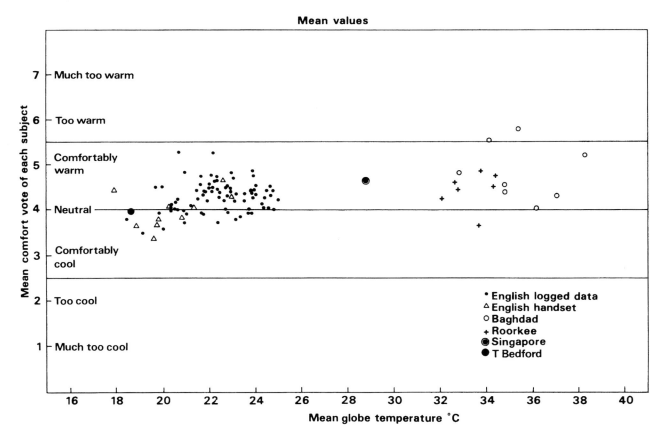

Mean values

5.6.
People who live in hotter climates are comfortable at higher temperatures (Michael Humphreys).

In temperate or hotter regions, a well-designed passive building should keep out direct solar gain (or too much indirect gain re-reflected from pavements and adjacent buildings) in summer. If it is necessary to reduce summer peak temperatures, or shift them to later in the day, then more thermal mass is necessary.

As the air temperature increases more air movement is necessary, as can be seen from Figure 5.7. This shows the effect of air movement on the probability of being comfortable. With air movement almost 100 per cent of people will be comfortable at 30°C and around 80 per cent at 35°C (this is only true for people who have adapted to the local climate. You could not really take Inuits to the Sahara and expect them to be happy at such high temperatures).

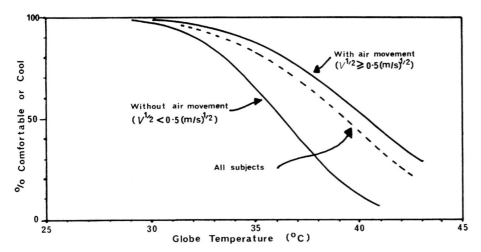

5.7.
The probability of being comfortable with and without air movement at higher temperatures (Fergus Nicol).

Convective cooling only works when the air temperature is below skin temperature and an average mean maximum skin temperature is around 35°C. In fact, at temperatures above 32°C the body begins to lose more heat by evaporative cooling, where the moisture on the skin is removed by the air passing over it. As this moisture evaporates off, it cools the skin because the process of turning the moisture into a gas requires heat and draws it from the surrounding air and skin. This is why the most difficult climates to be cool in are very hot humid ones where there is already so much moisture in the air that the only way to remove more from the skin is to pass ever more air over it. More air and higher air speeds are necessary for comfort in hot humid climates, as can be seen in Figure 5.8.

Inhabitants of the Florida Keys who insist on living in naturally ventilated houses find it difficult to understand the fuss, made by their air-conditioning-accustomed friends when they come to dinner, over how hot it is. It is simply that both groups have acclimatised to different temperatures. If the air-conditioning-accustomed group wanted to wean themselves off the 70°F all-night habit they would have to slowly raise the temperatures until the indoor and outdoor air temperatures were the same. In so doing, for much of

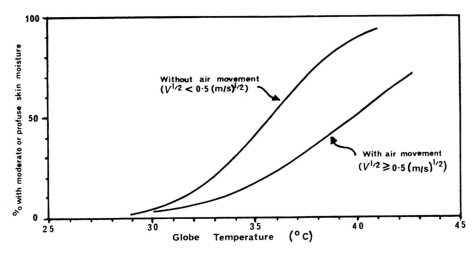

5.8.
The probability of moderate or profuse skin moisture with increasing temperature (Fergus Nicol).

the year they could kick an expensive habit. In extreme spells of heat, of course, the air-conditioners could go back on but, because the inhabitants had adapted to the ambient outdoor temperatures, the units could be run at much higher temperatures and still give comfortable conditions, so saving lots of money.

A study some time ago by Terry Williamson and Sue Coldicutt, at Adelaide University, Department of Architecture, showed that people in Darwin, Australia, often have air-conditioners in their houses for use in the hot humid season. However, the units were, because of the high cost of running them, typically only used when neighbours came to visit as a sign of status.

If the air coming into the house is too warm to use as a convective cooling medium for people inside then one solution may be to passively air-condition the air before it enters the house.

PASSIVE CONDITIONING OF OUTDOOR AIR

1 **Wind breaks.** These can be used not only to lessen the impact of strong hot or cold wind but also, if shrubs and trees are used, the air will pick up moisture from the leaves and so increase its humidity, thus cooling the air.

2 **Dust.** Use air that has passed over natural planted groundcover to reduce dust levels. Ensure that land on the windward side of the site or settlement is planted or maintained so that the earth's crust is not broken because, if it is, this produces erodible dust particles that will be carried on the wind to the house. Avoid exposed land and replant natural vegetation if possible, even on unused plots in the centre of towns. Adopt compact plans for groups of houses in hot dry areas to avoid the formation of dust. In addition, a small plot size will increase the likelihood of more of the site being landscaped, so reducing dust. Compact plans also provide more shade (Erell and Tsoar, 1997).

3 **Natural air-conditioning.** Use air that has travelled over water or vegetation, for coolth. If you are lucky enough to find a site downwind of a body of clean water this will cool it evaporatively and provide little resistance to the wind, so ensuring that the house gets a breeze that cannot be eliminated by other buildings. Do not forget that leisure water users can be noisy. Also, because the surface of water is flat, wind speeds can be very high over water because of the lack of surface resistance. Make sure the wind coming in over the water is not uncomfortable because of its high speeds. Trees around a house can lower the air temperature by several degrees.

4 **Sound barriers.** If the site is noisy build a substantial garden wall to keep the noise out. Sound is very persistent and will slip through any holes in a barrier so make sure the barrier is continuous.

5 **Coolth ponds.** Sunken gardens are a classic example of a coolth pond into which the cooler air descends. Garden walls can act as pond walls. Cool, moist, well-shaded gardens within such walls around a house (not too large that the intrusive wind above will stir up the cool air) can lower the air temperatures by 2–5°C in hot dry climates.

6 **Sun traps.** If higher air temperatures inside the house are required, expose the ground surface in a sheltered sun spot facing towards the south or west, and shelter from the incident wind. The actual ground temperature can be significantly increased by doing so and will warm the air

5.9.

Cross-section through a windcatcher showing the temperatures of the external air, the ground floor living room (the Talar) and the basement air. Air forced down the tower and pushed through the basement cools and humidifies before flowing out into the courtyard, which it cools. In turn, when that courtyard air is drawn back across the ground floor living room it cools its occupants.

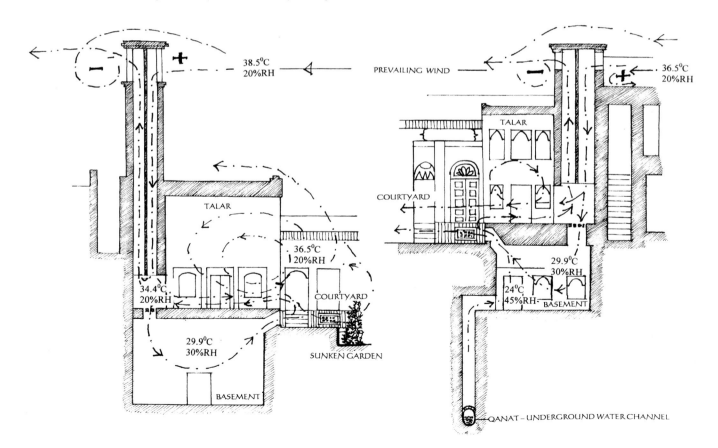

above it. Using deciduous planting over such a space means that in winter one could have a sun trap and in summer a coolth trap in the same space.

7 **Basement coolers.** Use the prevailing wind and the coolness of a basement to lower the temperature of the air around the house before it is taken in to ventilate the building. This is shown in Figure 5.9.

8 **Windcatchers.** Windcatchers or ducts through which air travels before reaching the house can reduce or increase the temperature of the air entering the building, as air issuing from ducts in the wall can be cooler or warmer than the incoming air.

9 **Pavements.** Use pavements around the house to condition the air. Hard, light surfaces with a high reflectivity directly adjacent to the building will not only reflect light indoors but will also heat the air directly above this hot pavement convectively before it moves into the house. If the object is to reduce the temperature then ensure that the ground surfaces adjacent to the house are shaded and absorptive, or planted. Shading, such as awnings, verandas or deciduous planting, around the building can be designed to allow sunshine in, in winter and to keep it out in summer.

10 **Breeze walls.** Use 'breeze walls' around the garden of the building or on roof parapets. Well-placed holes can be placed in the walls to allow the pleasant wind in, while obstructing the view. Walls facing unpleasant winds have no holes through them.

11 **Heat-scape.** Heat-scape the external envelope of the building (Figure 5.10). People often think that heat only travels into the building via the windows but it can also enter the building through the walls by conduction through the wall. Shade walls to keep them cool in summer if necessary. A wall in the sun will, in still conditions, heat the air adjacent to it, which then rises and can be caught and funnelled into the window above the hot wall. If there is a sun shade above the window, this will trap the rising warmer air in which the pressure will build and so force it in through the window. Vent solar shades to remove this heat if it is unwanted. This may be an excellent thing in winter where the heat will add to the internal comfort of the occupants. Windows can be designed to take advantage of this winter heat if required. A good way of keeping walls cooler is to place planting against the wall that will dissipate the heat before it reaches the wall. If deciduous species are used then the wall can be warming in winter and cooling in summer (Sandifer, 2000).

12 **Location, location, location.** Choose your location in the street carefully: are you on the sunny side or the shaded side? Are there trees in the street? What alignment is the street in relation to the sun and the prevailing winds? How wide is the street? And so on. All these factors will influence the temperature of air coming in to the house from the street. Extensive work has been done by Isaac Meir and the team at the Institute of Desert Architecture Unit at Sede Boker in the Negev, who are worth contacting for advice on town planning in hot dry climates.

Design strategies for using the breeze also to fit with the lifestyle of the house occupants. For instance, in Naples there is a traditional window shutter for the full-height French windows that commonly open onto the balconies overlooking

5.10.
Heat-scaping the outside of a building. The wall temperature of a building will be significantly altered by the use of plants to shade walls, as at the Oxford Ecohouse. The deciduous Wisteria cools and humidifies the air passing into the high-level vent, slightly open in the sun space. Note the washing drying in the sunspace (Susan Roaf).

the street. These full-height shutters often open in two halves, top and bottom. There are a number of possible functions of the combination of wind access and solar gain that can come into play over the year but one delightful function is as follows. On hot summer afternoons the top pair of external shutters are closed during siesta time, so allowing the sun to fall only on a small patch of the floor adjacent to the balcony, not deeper inside as it would do if the top shutter was open. The afternoon breeze flows in through the open door and open lower shutter, over the people sleeping on the bed, and out through the door opposite. If the top shutter was open the air flow across the room would be above the prone people. This illustrates the need to design for a particular lifestyle to create thermal delight. In many countries where people do not take siestas this particular design strategy would be of no consequence. In many tropical areas of the world windows are louvred and different sections of them can be open to optimise the air flow over a person seated in a particular position in a room (Figure 5.11).

5.11.
One section of a glass louvred window open to direct air over a seated person in Chetumal, Mexico (Sue Roaf).

How far into a room the breeze will reach depends on whether there are openings on one or more sides of the room. The most effective systems is one where there is a good direct cross-current of air across the room, so preventing the breeze from dissipating. In hot climates single-sided ventilation is not sufficient and more can be effected either by windows in opposite or adjacent walls, by a roof window or skylight, which may also act as a wind-catcher (Figure 5.12). In the lower latitudes, such a roof window should be roofed as in a dormer. This would work in the same way as a windcatcher by letting in the air but keeping out the hot sun from the rooms below.

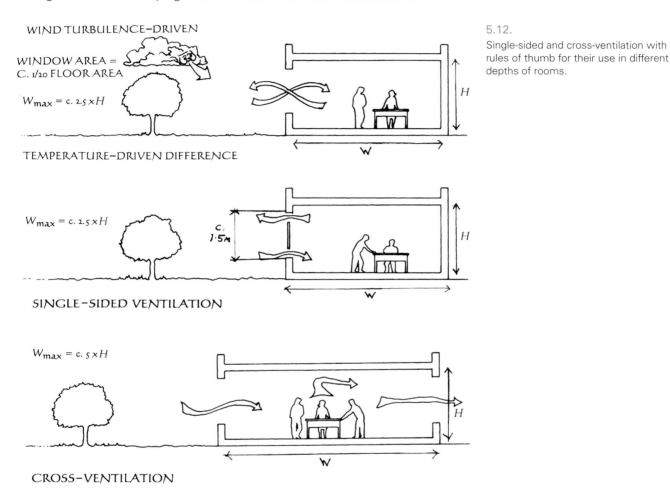

WIND TURBULENCE–DRIVEN

WINDOW AREA = C. 1/20 FLOOR AREA

$W_{max} = c.\ 2.5 \times H$

TEMPERATURE–DRIVEN DIFFERENCE

$W_{max} = c.\ 2.5 \times H$

c. 1.5M

SINGLE–SIDED VENTILATION

$W_{max} = c.\ 5 \times H$

CROSS–VENTILATION

5.12.
Single-sided and cross-ventilation with rules of thumb for their use in different depths of rooms.

CEILING FANS

In hot areas the ceiling fan is commonly used. A ceiling fan simply moves the air in a room around, so increasing the wind speed over the skin and increasing heat loss from the skin either by convection or conduction. If the walls of the room have some thermal mass and can store heat, then the fan may move the warmer air from the middle of the room and mix it with night-time-cooled air from near the walls. This causes the daytime air temperature to drop by a degree or two. The ceiling fan may also increase the rate of air movement across a room and draw in air from a cooler source so lowering the air temperature a little. It is important in rooms with ceiling fans to avoid creating a pool of hot air directly beneath the ceiling that is then blown down by the fan to heat the room's occupants. Vents near the ceiling would remove this hot air.

PASSIVE CONDITIONING OF INDOOR AIR

Every building has a structural temperature, just as human beings have a body temperature. In the core of the human body the temperature typically stays around 37°C, give or take a degree. At skin level it is a very different picture with very large variations caused by a myriad of reasons (sex, weight, health, exercise, clothing location and so on). Armpits are very warm and hands and feet coldest because they are further from the heat pump of the body, the heart.

Buildings are similar. The core of the building will typically have temperatures that fluctuate less than those in the spaces around the edges that are more exposed to the diurnal and seasonal variations in climate. Every room within a building will have its own metabolism, or internal structural temperature, with daily and seasonal rhythms. Ventilation in houses can be used at different times of the day and year to modify the core temperatures of a building to enhance the comfort of its occupants. The main ways in which this is done is by warming the building through passive solar heating (see Chapter 7) and cooling it using night-time ventilation.

NIGHT-TIME COOLING OF BUILDINGS

This is the process by which heat is removed from the structure of a building by passing cooler night air over the surfaces of the building, thus lowering the temperatures of the walls, floors and ceilings of rooms. For a successful night-time ventilation system it is important that the air inlets and outlets can be left securely open at night.

A good rule of thumb is that for sufficient thermal storage to be built into a house, the walls of each room should be at least 100 mm thick (that is 150–200 mm if rooms are back to back) and made of a high-density building material. Night-time cooling of internal mass is useful where the mean value of the diurnal external temperature range of a building in summer is above the comfort temperature (see Nicol graph in case studies).

Compartmentalisation of a building impedes the free flow of air around it and therefore decouples the building from the outside climate. This is true of buildings with banks of rooms with single-sided ventilation only. Windows in one wall do not evenly distribute heat through the building. In banks of rooms that are not connected, heat builds up unevenly in the room facing the sun and is excluded from the room facing away from the sun. Alternatively, if the rooms are joined, for instance by a door, then the heat can be distributed more evenly across the building, meaning that the sun-facing room may not overheat while the cold room may avoid the need for heating. However, one common problem does still exist and this is the heat pond that builds up beneath the ceilings of both rooms. The air becomes buoyant as it heats and rises, collecting under the ceiling as a heat pond. This is often not removed by cross-ventilation as the pressure that keeps it aloft is greater than the pressure of the wind-driven ventilation. The problem is that as the air beneath the ceiling gathers heat during the day it also heats the ceiling above that then becomes warm and begins to radiantly heat the people in the room below. Cool night air flowing along the floor of this space may not affect the hot pool of air on the ceiling. Do note that, in this situation, adding insulation to the ceiling would only exacerbate the problem here (Figure 5.13 and 5.14).

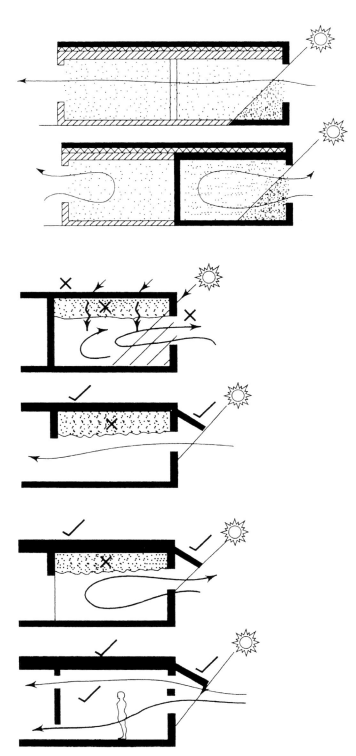

5.13.
Diagram showing the potential difference in performance of a single-sided and cross-ventilated space in distributing solar heat build-up through the building.

5.14.
Ceiling heat pond problem.

This case demonstrates the need to look at the thermal design of a building and its ventilation holistically. To solve this problem single-sided ventilation can be replaced with cross-ventilation by making a door between the two rooms. To remove the hot pool beneath the ceiling, either the door should nearly reach to the ceiling or there should be a higher-level window out of which this heat can flow during the day. In so doing it draws the air from the night-cooled floor up over the room occupants, so increasing their comfort. An alternative, not so good, solution is to use angled louvres on the windows that will direct the wind up to the ceiling so disturbing and dissipating the heat pond beneath it. However, the night cooling will not work if the window is improperly shaded and during the day the floor is continually heated, forming a radiant and convective heat source that will make the room occupants even more uncomfortable.

DESIGN OF WINDOW OPENINGS FOR VENTILATION

There are many considerations for the uses of windows for ventilation. Think carefully about the way a window opens in relation to the ventilation needs of the room behind it, its occupants and the small and large wind-flow patterns around the building. Would the room best be served by a sash, side or centre hung, sliding or hopper window? Avoid conflict with opening regimes and furniture, curtains and blinds. Do not forget that one of the most important considerations is the performance of the window over time. The longer it can be kept

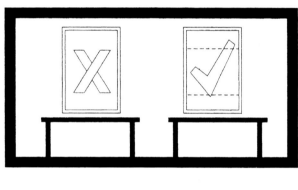

5.15.
Window types.

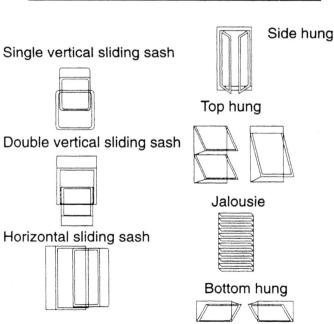

in good repair the better the life time value of the window will have been. Make sure the window can be cleaned and maintained easily and can be secured. It should be easily accessible and openable by the room occupants and be sized intelligently for the function for which it was designed. There is no use opening a patio door for a little ventilation. The disastrous shift to having huge windows has made buildings much less people friendly over the last 30 years. Do not design large windows when small ones will do. In many countries, for ventilation requirements in different seasons, large windows are not necessary. In other climates entire walls are not necessary at certain times of year.

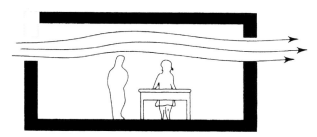

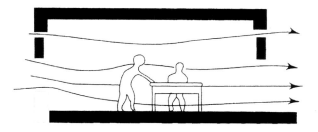

5.16.
Always consider the occupant of the room. Do you just want to remove excess heat from the room, or do you want to pass air over the seated or standing body?

There are many lessons to be learnt from the case studies at the end of this book that show how amazingly rich is the design vocabulary for windows in buildings and how important they are to the metabolism of the home. Do not forget that ventilation in the home should be, above all, about creating delight (Figure 5.17).

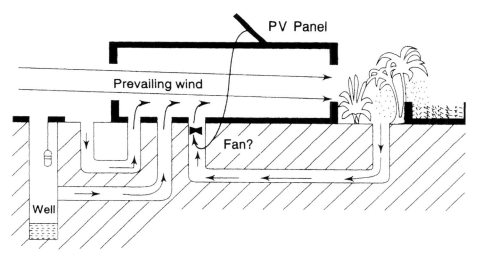

5.17.
PV panels can be used to run simple ceiling fans at 70–100 watts or even complex passive cooling systems in hot weather.

BUILDING HOMES IN CYCLONE AREAS

Stephanie Thomas

If you live in a cyclone belt, ventilation occasionally is less about delight and more about survival. Winds, as they get stronger, begin to do damage to buildings. By the time that wind speeds reach 65 m.p.h. they can become really dangerous. Winds of this speed in a 'closed circulation', meaning they go around in a complete circle, are classified as hurricanes or typhoons. The terms *hurricane* and *typhoon* and regionally specific names for a strong *tropical cyclone*: they are called typhoons to the west of the International Date Line and hurricanes to the east of it (Dommin, 1999).

In the Tropics the cyclone season occurs officially between 1 June and 30 November, yet most hurricanes occur in August, September and October (Galambos, 1990) once the land and water have warmed up over the summer. The hurricanes that originate in the Atlantic basin originate in the area around the Cape Verde Islands and head west towards the Caribbean islands. Their frequency ranges from none up to around five per year, with an average of two. In the last decade the number and intensity of cyclones has increased significantly and in 1999 in the Caribbean there were 12 named tropical cyclones (Headley, 2000), over twice the annual average for the preceding decades.

Hurricanes are classified according to sustained wind speeds, and the Saffir–Simpson scale explains the categories of hurricanes in accordance with their wind speeds (Table 5.1).

Most people who live in hurricane-prone areas can remember at least one major hurricane in their lifetime. When a hurricanes hits land, it can leave a trail of devastation, of fallen power lines and trees, strewn debris, damaged structures and human and animal casualties. For example, in Florida last century, Hurricane Andrew, a Category 4 Cape Verde classified hurricane, is used

Table 5.1. Saffir–Simpson Scale for Hurricane Classification

Tropical cyclone classification

Tropical depression	20–34 knots (kts)				
Tropical storm	35–64 kts				
Hurricane	65+ kts or 74+ m.p.h.				

Strength	Pressure (inches Hg)	Wind speed (kts)	Storm surge (ft)	Wind speed (m.p.h.)	Pressure (millibars)
Category 1	28.94	65–82	<5	74–95	>980
Category 2	28.50–28.91	83–95	6–8	96–110	965–979
Category 3	27.91–28.47	96–113	9–12	111–130	945–964
Category 4	27.17–27.88	114–135	13–18	131–155	920–944
Category 5	27.16	>135	>19	>155	919

as the benchmark for comparing hurricanes. On 24 August 1992, southern Florida was directly in the path of Hurricane Andrew, which came ashore with sustained winds of 145 m.p.h. and gusts of up to 175 m.p.h. By the time and storm moved on into the Gulf of Mexico, 41 people had been killed and hundreds of thousands were homeless. The winds and the 12 foot storm surge caused approximately US$25 billion of damage in Florida alone, and US$26 billion in total, making this storm the most expensive natural disaster in US history until Hurricane Katrina in 2005 broke all records at a predicted $200 billion (Rappaport, 1993).

Another noteworthy storm is Hurricane Luis (August 1995). This storm left behind a pathway of destruction on the island of St Maarten (an island of 37 square miles located about 300 miles southeast of Miami). Luis was a Category 4 Cape Verde hurricane that wreaked harm and havoc on the north-easternmost edge of the Leeward Islands, with an estimated 16 dead and causing US$2.5 billion dollars in damage, US$1.8 billion dollars on St Maarten alone.

Whether you live amongst a population of 14 million (1998 Census for Florida population) or 100 000 (Census from St Maarten Tourist Bureau) hurricanes can devastate both developed and underdeveloped countries in the same proportions. For Caribbean islands such as St Maarten, hurricane-resistant buildings are mandatory because any damage to the island can result in a significant impact on the tourist industry of that island. Hundreds of thousands of tourists visit islands in the Caribbean such as St Maarten every year. But when homes, hotels and restaurants are damaged, the economy can often suffer beyond repair. In Case Study 16 David Morrison describes how he tries to upgrade the defences of his own home against hurricane damage annually.

Following hurricane disasters such as Andrew and Luis, the governments, insurance industries and the public have demanded a review of what could be done to minimise the destruction and suffering caused by hurricanes. This has led to a realisation that building codes, enforcement and products are seriously in need of improvements. Key elements to hurricane-resistant design are: compliance to the latest code requirements (if applicable); protection of building envelope; and the use of approved missile impact and cyclic windload-tested materials.

The degree of damage to a building will depend on the strength of the hurricane (Table 5.2).

When clients rely on architects to design their dream homes in areas of potential hurricane activity, far too often too much money is spent on how the building looks and not enough on protecting it against the threat of hurricanes. To make a house design able to sustain winds of 100 m.p.h. may cost 10–15 per cent extra. To make it safe in winds of 150 m.p.h. will cost another 10–15 per cent on top. It is a false economy in a hurricane zone to think that you may be able to escape the wind. Many people rely on insurance policies to cover the costs of rebuilding, but insurance cannot bring back peoples' lives.

With winds around the globe getting stronger, many house designers would be well advised to take note of the following light-hearted advice

Table 5.2. Hurricane Damage According to Category

Category 1	Wind damage to unanchored mobile homes and foliage; some coastal flooding.
Category 2	Wind damage to some roofing, doors and windows; significant damage to mobile homes; small craft could break moorings.
Category 3	Extensive hurricane. Structural damage to homes; mobile homes destroyed; flooding at elevations lower than 5 ft above sea level (asl).
Category 4	Extreme hurricane. Major structural damage; extensive beach erosion with flooding at elevations lower than 10 ft asl.
Category 5	Catastrophic hurricane. Massive structural damage; some complete building failures; flowing at elevations lower than 15 ft asl; evacuation necessary.

for minimising wind damage on buildings taken from *Design for Tropical Cyclones* (Macks, 1978):

• Avoid roof overhangs	Lose your shade
• Avoid flat roofs	Pitch all roofs 30°
• Avoid large windows	Buy paintings to look at
• Don't use aluminium, asbestos cement and galvanised iron	Build everything in concrete
• Don't use nails or glue	Bolt everything to the floor (which is concrete)
• Avoid wave surges	Build in the hills
• Avoid exposed sites	Don't build in the hills
• Don't build near the sea	Enjoy the desert view
• Don't build near trees	Cut all the trees down
• Don't have roof penetrations	Use invisible vent pipes
• Don't have fancy roof shapes	Live in a box
• Avoid cyclones/hurricanes	Live in Adelaide.

A task list that may help if you are thinking of building a house in a hurricane area is given below. The list has been compiled from personal experience and a variety of sources that include building code offices, *Design for Tropical Cyclones* (Macks, 1978) and *Tropenbau, Building in the Tropics* (Lippsmeier, 1980).

Site selection
• Identify site, and proximity to the sea.
• Establish flood heights and possible surge levels.
• Is site in a flood plain?
• Is evacuation possible immediately prior to a hurricane arriving (landfall)?
• Is the site in a heavily populated area and susceptible to future growth that may hinder evacuation?

- Check possible effects of damage by debris of both trees and neighbouring properties.
- Where a site is near rivers and open spaces, establish what are the local turbulence effects of wind patterns.
- Study the history of hurricane activity over past 100 years.
- Study the prevailing wind patterns of site.

Landscaping

- Study the topography of the immediate area.
- Can advantage be taken of mounds, etc., to give protection or reduction in wind loads?
- Can trees be planted that are more resistant to fracture and collapse?
- Can tree foliage be easily pruned to reduce wind effects?
- Note any screen walls that can break up wind patterns and act as debris barriers.

Floor levels

- Study the topography and drainage in storm rains to determine flood-free floor levels.
- Evaluate the implications of the number of floor levels needed; one, two or split level (also note local building codes; some regulations may have a first-floor habitable minimum height and a total height maximum).
- Remember that rises in roof heights increase wind loads.
- Ground-level floors can introduce flooding.

Windows and doors

- Check their size and the loads they are to carry.
- Design frames to connect to walls to which wind loads can be transferred.
- Consider the implications of windows breaking in high winds.
- Consider impact-resistant windows.
- Are openings on opposite walls able to funnel the wind through the building without affecting other areas?
- Design shutter fasteners to be part of structural drawings (do not install them after construction is complete).
- Louver blades leak under pressure and may reduce wind loads.
- Resolve the eternal conflict of wider windows for view and smaller windows for safety.
- Consider balconies and porches for protection – to split the winds.

Structure

- Design for structural integrity.
- Consider a structural grid system of posts and beams to provide stiffness.
- Keep structural systems simple.
- Have generously dimensioned foundations, widening at the base so that the ground pressure can absorb a portion of the forces that arise.
- Extra strong joints between foundations and walls by means of steel reinforcement, bolts, etc.
- Examine large spans and cantilevers.

Shape

- Consider shapes to be adopted and optimise them for wind protection while reducing 'alcoves' in which pressure can build up.
- Can roof profiles be designed to transfer wind loads more evenly over whole roof?
- Design carefully areas where roof projections and shapes cause local turbulence – e.g. chimneys, vent pipes, sharp direction changes, outriggings, roof-mounted solar water heaters, etc.

General planning

- Consider using posted verandas to catch or deflect debris.
- Division of the plan into many smaller rooms increases structural stability.
- Check interior half-height walls and their stiffness.
- Good interior cross-ventilation can be an advantage.
- Stiffen and reinforce the structure around most secure rooms.
- Disposition and planning of internal spaces should fit into a firm structural system or vice versa.

Costs and estimates

- Evaluate costs of alternative solutions (including sustainability and embodied energy).
- Are bolts cheaper than metal fasteners (in areas of high corrosion, evaluate galvanised and stainless steel products for long life performance and lower maintenance)?
- If a post and beam structure is used, size members for optimal safety as well as cost.
- Are grilles on windows cheaper than shutters and do they give adequate protection?
- If impact-resistant windows are chosen, is it cost-effective to include shutters as well?

Selection of finishes

- Are wall and ceiling linings suspect when wet and, if they lose stiffness, can remaining structures maintain stiffness?
- Is it wise to place carpets throughout and up to windows where water damage can ruin carpets?
- Are external walls debris-resistant and to what degree of impact?
- Is there adequate bracing in wall planes, ceiling and roof planes, and in internal partitions for lateral stability?
- Select type of wall cladding appropriate for climate.
- Check higher-pressure areas at walls and roofs near corners and profile changes.
- Check spans and warranty of roof cladding with manufacturers.
- Check type of sheeting, thickness and fixing.
- Are secret fixings to roof sheetings adequate or are screw fixings needed in addition?
- Check that manufacturer's instructions match terrain category of site and verify warranties.
- Check windows selected, and glass size, for the correct thickness to match the pressure to be resisted.

Details
- Check door and window frames, stops, catches and their fixings into walls.
- Check weak joints such as half-height walls with windows above, where joint of vertical cantilevered wall and window needs stiffness to resist breaking or overturning.
- Check flashings to roofs and ensure adequate fixings are provided as loss or damage to flashing often leads to degradation of adjacent material.
- Parapets should be reinforced.
- Tying down of roof members should extend down into foundations in a single element or at least in a straight line.
- There are technical solutions available to fix windows into frames but the actual fixings are seldom made correctly.

Claddings
- When selecting claddings for walls and roofs examine thickness of material for the proposed use.
- Examine manufacturer's instructions and verify that the claddings are suitable for the job.
- Check method of fixing and type and number of fixings used: nails, screws, glue.
- Is the material impact-resistant and to what degree of impact?
- What happens to the material when it breaks? (Does it still have strength?)
- Does the material add stiffness to the frame?

Codes
- Designers should use the most up-to-date local design codes available.
- If government does not require code compliance, or code is not sufficient, work to the codes of another country where good codes do exist.
- Do not expect builders and tradesmen to build to a list of codes specified if the specifier does not have the code, has not read it and does not fully understand it.

A building in hurricane storm area must be able to withstand extreme winds that blow from every direction during a single storm. Good design and workmanship are essential. Rapid and extreme changes in air pressure can be a further cause of damage. For example, if a well-sealed air-conditioned building is hit too quickly by the extremely low-pressure centre of a storm the building can explode (Lippsmeier, 1980). In the Porpoise Point Ecohouse (Case Study 20), steps have been taken to ensure that this airtight building can release such pressures by cracking the window but leaving the perforated storm shutters in a locked and closed position. The perforations allow the internal building pressure to equalise.

According to some people in the hurricane regions of the world the most effective line of defence against the winds is to leave a message to the hurricane, often painted on the plywood boards used to protect windows. There are a number of more permanent hurricane shutter types used other than these boards, including the most popular aluminium accordion types, Bahamian wooden shutters and metal rolling doors. The important factor to remember about hurricane shutters is that they are only as good as their installation, and they must be well secured to the wall or they become missiles themselves.

After a hurricane has made landfall, it usually decreases in strength. Although it may seem safe once the hurricane has been downgraded to a thunderstorm, tornadoes often develop and are the most damaging weather patterns to deal with. It is almost impossible to economically build for the shear force of a tornado's direct hit. Sometimes the wind speeds reach 300 m.p.h. During a major tornado hit, wind pressure loads can build up to over 0.5 ton m^{-2} (P > 100 p.s.f.). Only reinforced concrete structures are able to withstand these pressure levels. When high-density mobile home areas are subject to a tornado the most inherent danger to people and property is flying debris carried in high winds. In 250 m.p.h. winds, a 2 ft × 4 ft timber can cut right through a building.

As wind speeds increase with climate change, standards for design for the wind will have to improve in many areas. While no building is completely free from hazards, these can be minimised by proper design, good construction, careful selection of materials and homeowner awareness. There are many good books and websites available to learn more about this subject, of which one of the best is the book on *Design for Tropical Cyclones*, by the Department of Civil and Systems Engineering at James Cook University, Queensland Australia (1978). Also try the website http://www. aoml.noaa.gov.

However, we cannot absolutely predict the climate, which no doubt has plenty of surprises in store for us in the twenty-first century.

6 HEALTH AND HAPPINESS IN THE HOME

There are many different health risks in the home. They range from earthquakes and house fires to methane poisoning from a poorly vented gas stove. Many of them can be quite simply designed out, once they have been recognised as a problem.

Think carefully about how to design, not only for the more obvious aspects of health but also for peace of mind, restfulness and delight in your buildings. The mind and body are closely linked; a person at ease, comfortable and peaceful in a house, is likely to be healthier for it. For instance, in Ecolonia at Apeldoorn in the Netherlands, groups of houses in the 1980s and 1990s were constructed, each with a range of different eco features. The most popular of them all proved to be, surprisingly, the quiet house. This suggests that designing noise out of a building should be near the top of the list of priorities and yet it is a seldom-mentioned item on housing specifications for green buildings.

There can be a global dimension to the impacts of health issues, as well as being about the safety, health and happiness of the people who live in the house. Because the subject is so large we have simply listed alphabetically a number of the most important issues that may concern householders. Some of the issues are touched on in other chapters. Once homeowners are aware that there may be problems in one particular area of their house design, many different local and national organisations can be contacted for more information on each area. Local government offices and building research establishments are often good places to start. Many issues will be covered by the local building regulations and can be discussed with the relevant authorities. The internet is also a great place to search for detailed information on individual hazards and issues. All information from the Web should be thought through to ensure it is backed up by the common-sense intuitions of designers and that it is not simply pushing a certain line of thought in order to sell a particular product.

It is advisable to read through this chapter before starting to design the house as it may significantly affect how you go about the design. In design, as in so many other parts of life, the best decisions are made on the basis of the most information. If you are employing someone else to design your house make sure they can justify, to your satisfaction, the health implications of their design.

6.1.
Low-allergen design requires careful thought. Floors are best without carpets, walls of water-based paints and soft furnishings should be made of natural materials that can be easily washed. This view of the balcony at the Oxford Ecohouse shows the French door and vent windows that provide a variety of different ventilation opportunities into the buffer zone of the sunspace, these make dust-collecting ducts unnecessary in this house (Nat Rea).

ALLERGENS

An allergen is a substance that causes a reaction by the body's immune system against an otherwise harmless foreign protein. People are allergic to many different proteins, from milk to wheat. For allergens that affect breathing the immune reaction occurs when the allergen has been inhaled. Initially the body becomes 'sensitised' against a particular allergen causing the body to generate antibodies against the inhaled protein. These antibodies are Immunoglobulin E (IgE). Certain families are genetically prone to generate more IgE than others and have a tendency to develop more asthma, hay fever or eczema than other groups. The common allergens in houses relate to dust mites and domestic pets.

ASBESTOS

Avoid this material completely. Do not use it in new build and when having it removed employ a registered expert. Asbestos causes lung cancer and mesothelioma (rare tumours) of the lungs, chest and abdomen. Asbestos comes in three forms:

1 **White.** In board or sheeting products, surface treatments or as thermal and acoustic insulation.
2 **Brown.** In laminated boards and pipe lagging.
3 **Blue.** In fire insulation on steel frames or thermal insulation to heating systems. Also mixed with other forms of asbestos in boards or in asbestos cement mixes.

ASTHMA

An increasing number of people around the world are suffering from asthma, a condition with symptoms of chest tightening, coughing, difficulty breathing and wheezing. Symptoms will vary from day to day and place to place. When it is poorly controlled people often wake at night, breathless and distressed. Many different things can cause a narrowing of the airways and asthma, including exercise, cold air, exhaust fumes, cigarette smoke, aerosol sprays, chemicals and strong smells. It is important that sufferers identify what makes their asthma worse so they can deal with its causes. In the home dust mites, organic solvent vapours, wood preservatives, formaldehyde and even certain garden plants are key triggers.

Choose plants for the garden that are pollinated by insects and exclude those pollinated by the wind, such as ash, birch, hazel and oak trees. Some insect-pollinated plants can cause problems because of their scent, such as geraniums, or because they produce large quantities of pollen, such as the daisy family, or for both reasons, such as Buddleias and honeysuckle. Other plants to watch are those that cause skin allergies; some people find that by gardening in gloves they can avoid the problem. Large areas of grass may cause problems and avoid mulches that may harbour mould spores.

CANCER OF THE SKIN

Ozone depletion has already resulted in an enormous increase in the incidence of skin cancer in the Southern Hemisphere. In Queensland, Australia, where

Step by step guide to asthma avoidance in the home

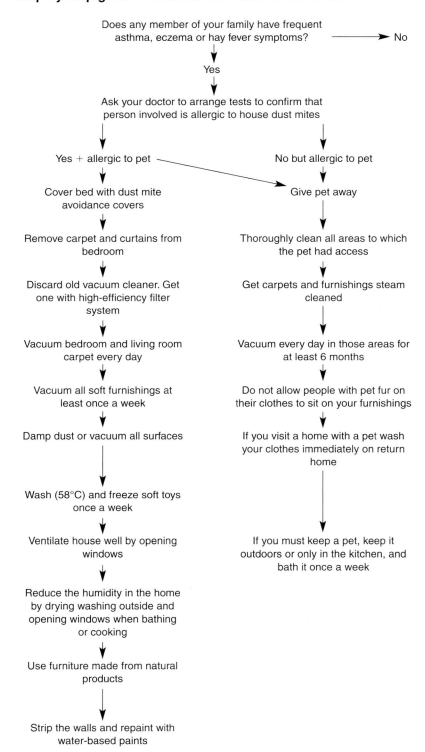

the most damaging UV-B radiation is highest, three out of every four people can expect to get some form of skin cancer during their lives. With the rapidly thinning ozone layer over the Northern Hemisphere, ozone depletion is expected to account for a 10–20 per cent increase in skin cancer in the Pacific Northwest in the next few decades. In the USA in 1935 the chances of developing the most serious form of skin cancer (malignant melanoma) was 1 in 1500. In 2000 it was 1 in 75 (http://www.geocities.com/RainForest/Vines/4030/impacts.html).

So do people sitting beside large areas of glass or even under glass roofs in buildings have an increased risk of developing skin cancer? The situation here is as follows. There are two different types of wavelength that have been identified as causal in the development of skin cancer. These are UV-A and UV-B. UV-B is ten times stronger than UV-A as a cancer trigger. UV-B is almost totally eliminated by most glass currently on the market. UV-A does penetrate glass but one would need to sit next to large areas of glass for considerable periods to be exposed to significant amounts of UV-A. Because UV-A has around one-tenth the effect of UV-B, sitting near a large glass window could be considered equivalent to being outside all the time with a Sun Protection Factor 10 sunscreen on. In other words, the effects would gradually build up but would probably not be noticeable during the lifetime of the person exposed, particularly in higher latitudes. It is possible that UV-A has special effects that have not yet been investigated. While UV-A has not been identified as a potential carcinogen it is responsible for the ageing of the skin. UV-A would largely enter the building from the exposed, visible, blue sky, so if a person is seated away from a window and receives only reflected light then there is no possible problem. The basic research into this issue has not yet been done but it is not perceived to be a problem by the medical profession (personal correspondence with Professor J.L. Hawk at the Department of Photobiology, Guy's, King's and St. Thomas' School of Medicine, London and Dr James Slusser, Research Scientist Director, UVB Monitoring Network, Natural Resource Ecology Laboratory, Colorado State University, USA).

CARBON DIOXIDE – INDOORS IN HOUSES

In breathing we expire carbon dioxide (CO_2). This can build up in the air of a room. In the home, in rooms where there are several people and consequently very high levels of CO_2, simply opening a window or door is the most effective way of purging the room of CO_2 in a short time, no more than 15 minutes or so.

CARBON MONOXIDE

Carbon monoxide (CO) is a colourless, odourless, deadly gas. When CO is present it rapidly accumulates in the blood displacing the oxygen needed for the cells to function. Inhaled in sufficiently large quantities its effects are rather like suffocation. CO is a common by-product of appliances run on flammable fuels such as gas, oil, wood and coal. CO poisoning often results from blocked chimneys or flues, or improper venting of rooms. Symptoms of CO poisoning include headaches, giddiness, drowsiness and nausea. If these symptoms are experienced a doctor should be asked to carry out a carboxyhaemoglobin test.

To ensure that CO poisoning does not occur in your home:

* have all stoves, fires and appliances that burn fuel such as gas, coal, wood, etc., properly and regularly maintained
* avoid using flueless gas or paraffin heaters.

CHLOROFLUOROCARBONS (CFCs)

CFCs are a group of man-made gases that are largely responsible for destroying the ozone layer above the Earth that shields the planet from incoming radiation. CFCs are used in buildings in insulants, aerosols, refrigerants and fire extinguishers. The main CFCs are CFC11 and CFC12. In addition to their role in the destruction of the ozone layer they are 17 500 and 20 000 times, respectively, more potent as 'greenhouse' gases than CO_2. Because they are in a stable form they will take many decades to break down and so the impacts of CFC pollution today will only be felt later on in this century. This is what makes them so dangerous. In 1987 the world's prime consumers and manufacturers of CFCs signed the Montreal Protocol written to reduce and phase out emissions of CFCs into the atmosphere. CFC production had ostensibly stopped by 2000 but the black market in CFCs is still buoyant, largely because of the huge cost of replacing them in refrigeration systems. Their main uses in buildings were in roof and wall insulations, dry linings and pipe sections and, above all, in air-conditioning and refrigeration systems. Do not use any building materials or systems that are made with CFCs, HCFCs, R11, R12 and, if possible, use only R22 products as this is considered a less hazardous material. In temperate and cold climates air-conditioning should not be used and if specifying a cooling system for a warm or hot climate insist on minimal ozone impacts for the system you choose.

The seriousness of the ozone problem cannot be over-emphasised. Not only are the potential health hazards enormous but the occurrence of the ozone holes over the Arctic and the Antarctic – where the freezing atmospheric air is necessary for the breakdown of CFCs into chlorine which destroys the ozone layer – means that below the holes radiation levels are higher, thus escalating the rate at which the ice caps are melting.

CONTAMINATED LAND

With increasing pressure on building land many new housing developments are sited on contaminated land. The first task is to find out how the land was contaminated and with what. Local government offices should have records of the history of sites and, if necessary, hire a specialist consultant to determine the hazards posed by the land. The land may then be treated in situ with neutralising chemicals, removed altogether and replaced with clean top soil, or by sealing the base of sites with horizontal and vertical barriers to prevent the movement of contaminated groundwater into the adjacent land. Seek specialist advice and see Roaf et al., 2004.

DISABLED ACCESS

All houses should be capable of easy access by wheelchair users and ground-floor toilets should be provided. A good way of approaching this particular design challenge is to imagine oneself becoming unexpectedly disabled and still wanting to live in the house. Also, you may still want to live in the house at the age of 95! If it is a proper ecohouse you will not want to leave it before then because its annual energy bills will be so low. The price of conventional fossil fuels and insulation materials may be so high you will not be able to afford the bills in a non-ecohouse alternative anyway.

DUST MITES

Dust mites contain a leading allergen that causes and worsens asthma. Many studies around the world have been done on how to reduce dust mite populations because of the high increase in the incidence of asthma worldwide. Dust mites are found particularly in bedding, furniture and at the base of carpets where the humidity is higher and the temperature more stable. They are very small and up to 2 million of them can live in one mattress.

The best conditions for mite growth are temperatures of around 25°C with 80 per cent humidity. How to avoid them:

1 move to high alpine pastures as they cannot survive in the cold, dry air up there
2 lower the humidity in a room until it becomes too dry for the dust mites to survive. This can be done by removing wet objects such as washing, raincoats and wet towels from the house; and putting a good ventilation window above and/or beside the cooker
3 the first line of attack should be to remove their habitat, so out go the wall to wall carpets and curtains, and special asthma covers can be bought for bedding. Barrier covers can be placed beneath the sheets and inside pillow covers. Modern covers are made of materials that are permeable to water but impermeable to dust mites
4 beat rugs thoroughly.

EARTHQUAKES

The basic rectangular, single-storey, wood-frame house is one of the safest structures in an earthquake. The amount of damage incurred should be minimal if the house is properly engineered and built. The key to a well-designed building is the ability of the structure to withstand an earthquake as a single unit.

Houses built on steep hillsides, or with split-levels, second storeys over garages, or pole foundation systems, cripple walls higher than 1 m; too many windows or irregular features can represent even greater risks. In such situations, a structural engineer should be consulted. Avoid sites with high groundwater tables and/or Lacustrine clay soils that tend to turn liquid during earthquakes. Get advice on the geology of your site before purchase.

The shaking and lateral forces of an earthquake will separate building components at their weakest points. Therefore, all structural elements must be securely tied together:

- the structure must be tied to the foundation with anchor bolts to keep it from sliding
- the wall studs must be sheathed (tied) with plywood or some other material to reduce deflection and provide strength
- the floors and roof must be fastened securely to the walls to tie the structure together.

Almost all existing structures can be strengthened to be more earthquake-resistant (but not earthquake-proof). Masonry chimneys should be reinforced with steel and tied to the roof and upper-floor framing with steel straps. Un-reinforced masonry chimneys should either be removed and replaced with a properly braced metal flue and enclosure system (e.g. a wood-frame), or measures should be taken to mitigate the effects of potential damage.

Clay and concrete tile roofs can weigh five to ten times as much as lighter roof systems, such as composition shingles. The increased weight results in significantly larger earthquake loads for the roof and walls. Heavy new roofing should not be added to existing structures without consulting a structural engineer.

Boilers should be strapped to walls. Tall furniture should be fixed to walls with L-shaped brackets. Keep heavy objects on lower shelves. Install shelf guards to hold objects on shelves. Install strong latches to all doors and windows. Ensure that all gas pipelines in the home are flexible. Have very clearly located meter points for turning off gas, water and electricity into the property. Have a clear point in the house for the storage of a medical kit. Have well-serviced fire extinguishers in the home. Have a post-earthquake plan ready for all members of the family. If you live in an earthquake area contact local authorities for advice on making your own house safe in earthquakes. They will have lots of experience.

EARTH SHELTERING

In earth-sheltered structures all or part of the building is sunk into the ground. They are typically built to keep buildings warm or cool, with their internal temperatures modified by the surrounding ground temperature, and to minimise the impact of a building on the landscape. In addition they provide excellent fireproof qualities in high fire-risk areas. Because of their low energy demands for heating and cooling they are buildings that very much promote the health of the global atmosphere by their very low emissions of greenhouse gases. An excellent introduction to the principles of earth sheltering is *Sod It*, by Peter Carpenter (1992).

EPOXY RESINS AND GLUES

These can lead to various forms of dermatitis. A no-touch policy should be employed when using them.

FIRE

This is one of the worst health risks that any house should be designed against. With global warming the risk of houses being engulfed by external fires is increasing year by year. Around the world there have been unprecedented numbers of major bush and forest fires in recent years. If you are in a high-risk area for such fires great care will have to be taken to protect the house as best you can. In some areas it has been shown that judicious placing of earth banks around houses can cause fires to jump buildings. If the site is in a really high-risk area, where annually fires lick up the sides of hills, then an extreme measure would be to earth-shelter the house and sink it completely or partially below ground.

In terms of the envelope of the building there will be very different fire implications if one is building in masonry or timber, and the various pros and cons of each material type will have to be weighed by designers. The roof is often the first element of the house to ignite. Contact local authorities for advice on fireproofing houses.

Care should be taken to consider the fire risks of any design. All local regulations for fire compartments and escapes in buildings should be noted before the design begins. It is difficult to overemphasise the need to design out fire risks from buildings. A major source of fire risk in buildings is insulation materials; the following advice can be offered on the fire implications of different types.

In cavity walls airflow is often limited or prevented by cavity barriers, so lowering the risk of spread of flame in the cavity. This may cause fire to then burst out and ignite adjacent rooms. Please note that this is another good reason to make sure that cracks and holes between the cavity and the room are well sealed. Where the cavity is not capped, air can enter the combustion zone and it has been found that the performance of different materials here depends more on their form, i.e. board, granules or infill, than their basic composition. It is advisable to cap all cavities filled with bead or granular materials but it is essential to do so where a board insulant is fixed into the cavity adjacent to a continuous air gap, as fire can spread quickly up such voids. The use of in-situ foamed materials, particularly thermosetting plastics such as polyurethane and urea formaldehyde, reduces the risk of airflow and keeps smoke or flame spread to a minimum. The flow of bead or granular materials into the fire area, following the breaching of a masonry wall, will increase the heat potential of the fire and the release of smoke and toxins into the room. However, the risk arising from infill materials in cavities is unlikely to occur until the fire has reached major proportions.

Some foamed plastic insulants, once ignited, will burn with considerably greater intensity than cellulose products and will require a thicker protective cover between the insulant and the room that restricts the flow of air to the product or prevents rapid emission of flammable volatiles (e.g. volatile organic carbons, VOCs). Even composite products should be investigated; recent tests in the UK have shown that composite sandwich panels with a polyurethane core can burn very rapidly and cause flashover, achieving very high temperatures.

Materials made of loose fibre granules can be either used as poured or blown insulation in cavities, as a blown foam, or as boards or rigid sheets. The combustible types are often not difficult to ignite and can cause fires when ignited even by a cigarette. Organic materials often produce toxic combustion products, frequently accompanied by thick smoke. Particular care is needed where insulating materials are used as room finishes. Such finishes can create ideal conditions for the spread of surface fire, irrespective of whether the insulating low-density substrate is combustible or not. Plastic materials will usually ignite or decompose when subjected to heat or fire and, as a result, produce heat, smoke and combustion gases. Thermoplastic materials will soften and flow on heating, often before ignition takes place. This can then collapse and ignite. Examples are polystyrene, polypropylene, PVC and acrylics. Thermo-setting materials do not soften but undergo localised charring, possibly flaming with combustion. Examples are urea formaldehyde, polyurethane and polyisocyanurate.

With few exceptions no insulation material should be left exposed directly in the habitable areas of a building. It should be protected at all times from sources of heat that could be likely to cause ignition. Many foamed plastics, for instance, can be separated from the room by a layer of plasterboard. Any protection over insulating materials that soften at low temperatures should be independently fixed (e.g. nailing and battening) so that softening of the insulation does not result in premature collapse of the protective material (BRE Digest 233).

Before wet-pumped insulations are added to cavities the house electrics should be checked as faults in the system could cause major fire risks. PVC and electric cables are also best left apart. Electric wiring should be kept above the level of loft insulation to reduce the risk of overheating. Painting the surface of an insulating material such as polystyrene can increase its fire risk and gloss-painted ceiling tiles should be removed; matt-finish flame-retardant paints or water-based emulsion paints should be used.

Mineral wool and glass fibre materials with a low resin binder content can be rated as non-combustible. However, products such as canvas are combustible and, although the addition of a fire-retardant may improve its performance, it may still be a hazard. The same is true of a finishing film of PVC or polythene or any thin film supported on an insulating substrate. If plastic-finished wallpapers are used ask about their fire ratings. Also, take care where combustible materials, for instance around ducts, penetrate into room spaces as they could carry fire with them.

Before choosing any material think carefully about its behaviour in fire. If you do not have information on how it performs, ask for it or look it up on the internet. Non-combustible materials are safer. Be careful of electric wiring, equipment, candles and blowtorches and, if in doubt, ask the local building inspector for advice. Do not underestimate the health risks of fire (BRE Digest 233).

FLOORS

One of the three largest surfaces in the home is its floors. The choice of flooring material is very important. There are many ways of judging which is the best choice for the environment but really the main question is which is best for your house. If there is an asthmatic in the house avoid wall-to-wall carpets. If you do want a wall-to-wall floor covering follow the two main rules for choosing materials:

1 choose the most natural material possible
2 choose the most local material possible.

These could be pure wool carpets or rugs, or sisal or hemp matting. If you want a heat-absorbing passive solar floor choose ceramic tiles or natural stone floors. If you want to use a renewable material choose cork or reused timber or solid timber from a local sustainable source, with an oil-based finish. If you need a durable flooring choose Linoleum, made from renewable raw materials such as wood and cork powder and linseed; its degradability is also good. Vinyl flooring is less good as it contains harmful substances, asbestos and mercury that are released during its manufacture and chlorine that involves risks of accidents in transport. Vinyl flooring is a petroleum-based product and, as such, is using a finite and scarce resource (Jonsson, 2000). Choices are difficult but think the alternatives through carefully.

FORMALDEHYDE

Many wood-based panel products, such as chipboard, are made with glues that give off formaldehyde, especially when new. In addition, urea-formaldehyde foam (UFF) insulation in the wall cavities may be a source of formaldehyde vapour. This is a colourless gas with a pungent odour. Low concentrations of the gas may irritate eyes, nose and throat, possibly causing running eyes, sneezing and coughing. These products are widely used in the home for flooring, shelving and kit furniture. Some types of foam-backed carpets may also release formaldehyde. The amount of this gas released from these products will decrease over time.

Ways of avoiding this substance include:

1 use blown mineral fibres or expanded polystyrene beads for cavity-fill insulation rather than UFF
2 if you are exposing UFF in building works plan to expose it for a short time only and cover it up again promptly
3 make sure there is no possible air leakage through cracks or holes into the house from cavities filled with UFF
4 repair any damp patches in walls adjacent to UFF-filled cavity or materials.

LEAD

Lead is a poison. Avoid it. Remove all lead pipes from the home. Most house paints and primers dating from before World War I are likely to contain lead. Lead paint is most dangerous when it is broken and flaking. Either paint over it with modern non-lead-based paint to seal it or strip it completely. Do not dry sand it as inhaled dust can be poisonous. Do not burn strip it as this releases fumes. Hot air tools that soften the paint so it can be scraped off may be used but avoid overheating the paint as it will then give off fumes. Wet sanding is the least dangerous but the slowest and messiest method to strip it. Chemical strippers are costly, give off hazardous fumes and are caustic to the skin.

Always use lead-free solder. Older putty contains lead so be careful when removing it. Avoid dry sanding of old lead putty. Avoid lead flashings if the rainwater is collected for drinking purposes.

LEGIONELLA

Legionella pneumophila is a bacterium found in all natural fresh water where it poses little threat to health. In buildings' water systems it grows into high concentrations and can be dangerous when inhaled in droplets of water from sprays, as found in showers, hot and cold taps and ventilation and air-conditioning systems. When inhaled it gives rise to Legionnaires' Disease, which is a type of pneumonia that typically causes death in one in ten of those who contract it. Legionella grows best in stagnant water at temperatures between 20 and 50°C with an optimum of 30–40°C. Organic material in the system also enhances growth rates. Thermostats in water tanks should be set to 55°C or be regularly flushed with water above this temperature. The bacterium will not grow significantly at temperatures below 20°C. Lipped, fitted lids should be placed securely over water tanks. Domestic systems are less of a problem as they have a regular turnover of water. Spa baths and jacuzzis should be drained and cleaned daily, with the strainer removed and cleaned at the same time.

MINERAL WOOL

A wide range of man-made mineral fibres is now used in the construction industry for insulation and reinforcement. These typically look like glassy fibres and are made from molten blast-furnace slag, rock or glass by a combination of blowing and spinning processes to turn the melts into fibres. The normal diameter of mineral wool fibres being manufactured today is around $6\,\mu m$. The main health effects of working with this material are skin and eye irritation; protective goggles can be used if irritation persists. A high degree of exposure to mineral wool can lead to irritation of the upper respiratory tract but this is not considered to be a long-term health risk, although many countries have legislation that specifies maximum permitted exposure levels. There is ongoing research to establish if there is a link with cancer from these fibres. If there is, it has not been proved to be a strong one.

In the home, rock and glass wools are used for insulating loft and wall cavities. Mineral fibres are also compressed into bats or boards, pipe insulation and roof tiles. The main thing to avoid is the inhalation of the mineral wool fibres and this can be achieved with a little common sense, not allowing cracks in the construction where the fibres can infiltrate a room, such as through down-lighters or around pipes. Care should be taken not to disturb the fibres during maintenance. Also, ensure that any water tank exposed to possible pollution by fibres has a firm lid. Simple protective measures, such as the use of suitable clothing, gloves, glasses or disposable respirators, can be used while working with mineral wool if skin, eye or respiratory tract irritations occur.

MOULDS

Is mould the new asbestos? This question was posed by the *Independent*, a UK newspaper, on 16 August 2002. A leading insurance broker had warned that toxic mould has led to a growing number of claims in the United States and the problem is beginning to become apparent in the UK. In the US, a 'toxic mould syndrome' case led to a court award of $32 m (£15.5 m) to a Texas resident, Melinda Ballard, after her insurer failed to recognise the problem or acknowledge that its policy covered such issues. The insurance industry in the US is braced for billions of dollars of similar claims against builders. Mould feeds on the organic materials of a building, such as carpets, wood and wallpaper and eats into wallboard and brickwork. In many areas of the world the problem will have been exacerbated by recent flooding which soaks the fabric of the building, leaving in its wake the ideal damp conditions necessary for mould growth. Mould can be very toxic indeed, leading to allergies; sick building syndrome and even death, can result from exposure to high concentrations of some moulds that grow on wet building materials. They can also shorten the life considerably of many products in the home.

So serious is this growing problem that we asked for some advice from Dr Dave Anderson (drdave@envirostress.com), Ph.D., who is a Toxicologist, and known as the famous Washington 'Mould Detective'. Here are tips for all house-holders to look for:

> *'Beware! The first sign of mould is not what you see. It's a change in how you feel. Sick building syndrome really is a building related illness. No one complains about air in the building unless the air actually bothers them. Once the air starts to bother you, you already have symptoms that are most likely the result of the combined effects of all of the chemicals in the air. The air you breathe can make you feel sick and tired. One of the most common complaints in buildings with poor Indoor Air Quality (IAQ) is fatigue and lethargy.*

What is mould?

From a human perspective, there are two kinds of mould:

* pathogenic moulds that infect you like bacteria, and
* those that don't infect you.

Unlike bacteria or viruses, moulds can affect how you feel even if they are not pathogenic. Even if you are exposed to moulds only for a short time they can have an effect on you. Ask anyone who has a mould allergy. Just walking into a mouldy room can make them sneeze. To an allergist the definition of allergy is based on beta-glucan. Beta-glucan is part of the make-up of the outside wall of mould spores or mould branches (hyphae). To test if you have allergies, a physician sprays some Beta-glucan into your nose and if you react you have an allergy by definition. The way in which non-pathogenic moulds affect people varies. Mould spores are between 0.1 and 10 microns or about 1/40 diameter of a human air. Not all moulds are bad for you; for instance, antibiotics are often based on mould, and Penicillin itself is a mould.

Our perception of odour changes with age. Our sense of smell is very good as a child, but after reaching 30 years it starts to diminish. The rate it decreases is not the same for everyone. Men's sense of smell continues to diminish with age but women's stays relatively constant. Participants of 'Odour Panels' are selected based on the ability to smell some standard chemicals at low concentrations. There are very few older men that can pass the screening tests.

The difference in the ability to detect odours at low concentrations is often the cause of disputes about poor IAQ. While women can smell faint odours men are convinced there is no odour because they are unable to detect any. Nasal fatigue often occurs after a few minutes – it's as though the odour has disappeared but is actually still there. Leaving the room for 5 minutes then re-entering will check for nasal fatigue. The odour will seem stronger than before.

Mould grows on some building materials quickly, while other materials are naturally resistant to mould growth. Composite materials that are used today have adhesives which can often be digested by fungi. Mould also digests starches and sugars in wood fibre if the cell walls are fractured. Part of the process of making paper from wood pulp is to mechanically break up the structure of the wood and to reform it into sheets with adhesives. In solid pieces of wood, the protective oils and whole cell walls combine to resist mould growth. It is difficult for mould to penetrate the surface of solid wood although it finds it easy to digest the adhesives in particle board and chipboard, which are made up of lots of particles of sawdust or chips of wood – mould grows on surfaces, and the sawdust or wood chips have thousands of times more surface area than a solid board.

There are thousands of mould species. Some that are causing real problems in buildings in the US at the moment are *Stachybotrys chartarum* and toxin-producing species of Aspergillus such as *Aspergillus versicolor* and *Aspergillus niger*. Moulds have evolved as specialists in digestive enzyme production although each species requires specific conditions in order to grow: the type of substrate and the amount of available moisture are the key factors in determining where each kind of mould grows. Mould and bacteria can grow on virtually anything when there is enough water, which often leads to intense competition between mould species and bacteria on the substrate surfaces. Mould competes by using chemical warfare techniques. It produces chemicals or mycotoxins to target other moulds or bacteria and prevent them from growing. Alexander Fleming was the first to discover the bactericidal effects of *Penicillium*. It is these mycotoxins that so often have negative side effects on people's health.

So for anyone who is not feeling well in a building, the cure may depend on finding and removing outcrops of mould, but where do you look for *hidden* mould? The answer is simple: where the water is! This can be done by using Dr Dave's 'Hidden Mould' mapping technique. Here is how you do it:

1 **Sketch out the map.** Create a building history of past water leaks and mark the location and date on a drawing of the floor plan (map). Roof leaks, flooding, broken pipes, washer overflows, leaking plumbing under sinks, and leaky valves or seals. Did you know that the wax ring seal at the base of a toilet is only designed to last for a few years? The best ones are only warranted for 10 years. Leaks in the seal only occur when the toilet is flushed so they are much harder to see than a leak in a pressurised pipe. But a periodic supply of water over weeks or months creates perfect conditions for mould growth. Seals should be changed before they leak. The cost of a seal is much less than replacing the floor around the toilet!

2 **Collect clues.** What parts of the house do you feel uncomfortable in? Is there a room where it is uncomfortable to take a deep breath, or you take a nap and wake up as tired as when you went to sleep? Pay attention! Even if you cannot smell mould it affects other senses.

3 **Investigation and observation.** Water flows downhill then spreads out on horizontal surfaces. If the leak is from above the wall, the area next to the ceiling will be soft or wet as will be the wall near the floor. The mid-wall does not usually show an effect unless there is a lot of water. Evidence of water damage in ceilings is detected by unevenness where the nailboard is nailed. The wallboard swells when wet, then shrinks somewhat when it is dry. The hydraulics of the swelling are strong enough to slightly dislodge the nails from the wood. When the ceiling shrinks and dries the nail is left protruding. If the hydraulics are not great enough to pull the nail out of the wood, or if screws were used, then there will be an indentation in the surface of the swollen wallboard.

4 **Measure moisture.** If you don't have a moisture meter to detect the relative saturation of the floor or walls then test for softness. Water damage to wallboards will leave them soft even after it has dried out. To check for this, first find a portion that you know is undamaged, to determine how soft the normal wall board in your house is. Firmly pressing your thumbnail in soft wallboard will leave a mark.

5 **Dig for results.** Don't cut holes in the wallboard unless you are prepared with plastic and tape to seal the hole immediately. Aluminium foil works best but plastic looks better. Hidden mould contained inside the wall may be released into the room. The spores are small and easily disturbed by the mechanical action of cutting the wallboard. This is when the most serious mistakes are made, so plan ahead to contain the spores and to avoid exposing yourself to the mould.

6 **Repair, revise and reconstruct.** Stop the water leak. Fix the plumbing, roof, window, foundation, etc. Take precautions to maintain good air quality. Remove the mould. If it is mouldy cut it out and throw it out! Reconstruct with materials that don't contain fractured cellulose (paper).

The ACGIH has written a book, *Bioaerosols: Assessment and Control* (Macher, 1999), which is an excellent reference on what precautions should be taken during the investigation to avoid unnecessary exposure. It also deals with testing strategies, interpretation of test results, and remediation protocols.

Testing

Only test when the test results will answer any question that you don't already know the answer to.

One good question would be: has the mould gone? It is an important question to answer after you have removed mouldy materials and before you start reconstruction. There may be *hidden* moulds. Another good question would be: is the mould the reason why a person feels ill? This can be tested by using the 'Symptom Survey Screening' method (however, chemical or analytical methods

6.2.
Dr Dave inspects an outbreak of mould in his own home!

are insufficient to define the quality of indoor air in relation to people's breathing problems if they are in the same room all the time, for weeks on end). Each time you breathe you are measuring, or 'assaying', the quality of the air by the symptoms you have. Exposure over long periods is known as a chronic bioassay or long-term bioassay. The results are often difficult to interpret because they have been exposed to varying qualities of air: at school or work, in cities, in cars, or underground transit, so the real problem of mould exposure may arise anywhere. But using this 'Symptom Survey' technique you may help identify the source of the problem. If you think you may have a mould problem, see Dr Dave's 'Detailed Symptom Survey' on his website www.envirostress.com. The results can help your own doctor evaluate your symptoms or diagnose fungal syndrome.

Thank you Dr Dave. Design advice we can add includes:

- Eliminate cold bridges in the external and internal walls so that there are no patches of cold wall on which moisture will condense and mould develop (Chapter 2).
- Remove moisture in the home (Chapter 5) with good zoning of wet activities and a range of good opening windows and vents, and repair any cracks in the structure.
- Have moisture-absorbing walls such as a plaster finish with a water-based eco-paint finish which can cope with a little internal room air moisture without causing moisture to collect.
- And don't forget Dr Dave's advice – if you have the symptoms your building probably already has the problem!

NOISE

Sound is generated by creating a disturbance of the air, which sets up a series of pressure waves fluctuating above and below the air's normal atmospheric pressure, much as a stone that falls in water generates expanding ripples on the surface. Unlike the water waves, however, these pressure waves propagate in all directions from the source of the sound. Our ears sense these pressure fluctuations, convert them to electrical impulses and send them to our brain, where they are interpreted as sound.

There are many sources of sound in buildings: voices, human activities, external noises such as traffic, entertainment devices and machinery. They all generate small rapid variations in pressure about the static atmospheric pressure; these propagate through the air as sound waves. Sound is usually measured in decibels (dB).

Decibels are related to the response of the human ear, which responds logarithmically to sound. For example, a 10 dB increase in sound pressure level would be perceived as a doubling of the loudness. In practical situations, level changes of about 3 dB are just noticeable. It is very important to remember that decibels and similar acoustical quantities have properties different from more conventional units. Sound pressure levels, for example, cannot be added together as can kilograms. The combination of two noises with average levels of 60 dB does not give a sound pressure level of 120 dB, but 63 dB.

Table 6.1.

Typical sound levels	dB
Jet takeoff, artillery fire, riveting	120 or more
Rock band or very loud orchestra	100–120
Unmuffled truck, police whistle	80–100
Average radio or TV	70–90
Human voice at 1 m	55–60
Background in private office	35–40
Quiet home	25–35
Threshold of hearing	20

In building acoustics, it is important to know the frequencies that make up a sound because different frequencies behave differently.

For most noise control work in buildings, the two most important acoustical properties of the materials and systems used are sound absorption and sound transmission loss.

Noise from footsteps and other impacts is a common source of annoyance in buildings. Sound carries easily through the structural components of a building. If noise is a problem in the design then some quiet spaces can be zoned into the house by isolating them from areas of most activity, which may be the stairs or front hall.

One method for controlling the sound level within a room is through dissipation of the sound energy in absorptive materials. Sound is absorbed when a portion of the sound energy striking a surface is not reflected, but passes into the material and is converted into heat energy. Generally, higher frequencies are more easily absorbed than low frequencies. Materials that are good absorbers permit sound to pass through them relatively easily; this is why sound absorbers are generally not good sound barriers. They reduce the level of noise inside an enclosure. However, it requires large thicknesses or many passes for the sound energy to be significantly reduced. It is important to understand the difference between sound absorption and sound transmission loss. Materials that prevent the passage of sound are usually solid, fairly heavy and non-porous. A good sound absorber is 15 mm of glass fibre; a good sound barrier is 150 mm of poured concrete. Sound barrier materials are used to reduce the level of steady sound in a room, from a machine for example, and to reduce the reverberance. A solid concrete wall would be used to keep traffic noise out of a room. Solid masonry construction is quieter than timber frame. Make sure that having a quiet peaceful home is high on your wish list at the briefing stage and if you have further questions seek expert advice on sound-proofing your home.

PAINTS

Paints affect health in two main ways: they can be toxic and they can exacerbate humidity problems in a room. A good paint breathes and allows the wall to breathe. It is permeable to air and moisture movement and it allows moisture in the wall, plaster, render and/or joints behind it to evaporate out. The great advantage of a breathing paint is that it reduces the build-up of moisture in a room that can be a major source of health problems. Many modern acrylic paints trap moisture in the walls and also impede the movement of heat between the room air and the wall. Traditional paints with a lime base allow the wall to breathe. Be careful when applying lime washes because lime is a caustic substance.

Some of the new water-based eco-paints also perform very well. They are made from substances such as resins, water, pigments, opacifiers, waxes and water. They should not contain solvents, white spirits, turpentine, VOCs, heavy metals such as lead, cadmium or mercury, or formaldehyde. Check the contents of the paints you are offered and if they contain such substances think again. Avoid all paints with any chromium in them, as it can cause dermatitis, ulceration and cancer. One of the most polluting products in paints is titanium dioxide, excavated largely in Australia and processed often in China. Its production processes use chlorine and sulphuric acids, which produce greenhouse and ozone-depleting emissions. However, it is the most common of all paint colourings and it is very difficult to find a paint without it.

Also be aware of the fire risk of different paint types. Gloss paints, for instance, can perform badly in fires, exacerbating the ignition times of various products, while water-based paints present less fire risk. If in doubt make enquiries from manufacturers on the ignition times for different paints.

PETS

Around 40 per cent of children with asthma are sensitised to cat allergens. Only 1–15 per cent are sensitised to dog allergens. No pets should be acquired if children in the home have either asthma, eczema or hay fever. If a much-loved pet predates the child's arrival some doctors recommend that the pet be kept out of the bedroom or the house. Pets should be washed regularly, as should the house, to remove their allergens. Do not resort to strong drugs to make life with the pet tolerable. Find your pet a new, loving home and allow occasional visits.

PLANTS IN BUILDINGS

Plants modify the environment in buildings by three processes:

1 **photosynthesis**, during which a green plant converts CO_2 and water to sugars and oxygen for growth
2 **respiration**, the reverse process to photosynthesis. This releases CO_2 back into the atmosphere and in so doing makes energy available for cell metabolism
3 **transpiration**, which is the evaporative loss of water from a plant, a process that turns large amounts of energy into latent heat, so producing a net cooling effect from the plant.

Studies have found that plants can indeed not only reduce the CO_2 and the relative humidity of a room but also they can lower the temperature of the room. However, different plants perform very differently and their ability to modify the environment in a room will be affected by the amounts of solar radiation being intercepted by the plant. These properties of plants have already been tested in office environments where, particularly in air-conditioned offices, people often suffer from symptoms of sick building syndrome, such as headaches, dry throats and eyes, lethargy, skin irritation and respiratory problems (thanks to Gaynor Coltman for much of this information). Pearson et al. (1994) conducted a range of studies of the impacts of plants in non-domestic buildings and found that there was a great difference in the impacts of different plants. For instance, Yucca plants and, best of all, Ficus Benjamina produced significant drops in CO_2 levels in the offices. Hibiscus and Cordyline plants reduced the internal temperature of the space by several degrees centigrade and also increased the relative humidities in the spaces by 5–10 per cent during the middle of the working day. These effects were most significant when the plants were placed on the windowsills, so ensuring that the plants could take advantage of the most sunshine during the day. It is rather nice to think of putting a living machine in the form of plants into buildings to clean up the internal air quality. Any good horticulturalist should be able to help choose the best plants for a particular indoor air-quality problem.

PLASTER

Gypsum plaster applied wet or dry has excellent absorption and diffusion properties for heat and moisture. It must be natural gypsum, not phosphogypsum, which is radioactive. When using plasterboard check that it does not contain adverse chemicals. Sand and lime plaster may also be used, possibly with a final coat of gypsum. Do not use cheaper cement-based plaster if possible as it is a poor insulator and is less permeable to heat and moisture. Mud plaster is also excellent and can be made more waterproof by mixing well-fired wood ash into the wet mix before kneading. It should be left for soaking and kneading for several days. Over all plasters an eco-paint should be used.

POLYURETHANE RESIN AND FOAM

When this is applied in situ high-efficiency personal respiratory protection is required – not just simple muslin pads. The problems of this material are for the construction worker and casual DIY person rather than the householder.

POLYVINYL CHLORIDE (PVC)

This polymer is widely used in construction and is known to be a carcinogen for animals and humans. In its early use, high levels of monomers were measured when the material was stored but more recent development of the technology has reduced their emissions substantially. The main concern is for the householder exposed to high levels of newly installed PVC in an airtight home for a long period of time. A number of fairly toxic substances are also combined with the PVC in the manufacture stage. Use timber windows if possible rather than PVC ones and avoid PVC furniture.

RADON

In 1985 an engineer at a Pennsylvania nuclear power plant underwent a routine radiation check at the plant entrance and set off the radiation alarm. The remarkable thing was that he did so upon entering the plant, not leaving it. After an investigation the Environmental Protection Agency recorded very high levels of the radioactive gas called Radon in the air in his home.

Radon is a naturally occurring radioactive gas that is tasteless, colourless and odourless. After its discovery in 1900 by the German chemist Ernest Dorn it became a popular health fad and was marketed in products such as chocolate, bread and toothpaste as a really healthy substance. As late as 1953 it was used in contraceptive jellies, blasting away at all those sperm in the cervix! Today its cell-killing properties are used in cancer treatment. Unfortunately it is also linked to many deaths from lung cancer, myeloid leukaemia, melanoma and DNA breakdown.

The amount of radon emitted into a home depends on the rocks on which the home is built and how much soil or other material covers the radon-emitting rocks. Sedimentary rocks, except for black shales and phosphate-rich rocks, are generally low in the uranium that emits the radon, and metamorphic rocks such as gneiss and schist are richer in uranium than marble, slate or quartz.

Radon has three main routes into the house:

1 groundwater pumped into wells
2 construction materials such as blocks that emit radon
3 gas that emanates up from the soil and rocks into basements and lower floors of houses.

Radon levels vary also with altitude (increasing radon with increasing altitude, owing to the thinner atmosphere and higher radiation levels) and with the time of year, readings usually being lower in summer when house windows are open.

In risk areas (check with your local council) radon concentrations can be reduced by placing an unperforated, impermeable membrane between the concrete lower floor slab and the ground, or a well-ventilated crawl space beneath the floor. Sealing all cracks and openings into the basement will prevent the entry of radon into the house and the use of exhaust ventilation can remove any that does. The warm air in a house will tend to draw radon into the home and care should be taken to avoid a build-up of the gas in the house.

Radon is measured in grays or sieverts (Sv) and impacts on human health at the following levels:

- 5000 mSv – lethal to all exposed
- 1000 mSv – vomiting, fatigue, induced abortions, sterility
- 500 mSv – physiological damage
- 5 mSv – US maximum permissible annual dose. Natural background radiation averages around 1.0–2.5 mSv per year. See U.S. Protection Agency, *A Citizen's Guide to Radon* and BRE (1999).

RUBBER

Historically, natural rubber has been used extensively in roofing sheeting, flooring materials and underlays. While in position they pose no threat to occupants. During fires their fumes are very toxic in confined spaces. The use of latex-based adhesives does require considerable care, the solvents in them may cause skin irritation and are dangerous; they should not be used in unventilated spaces and may cause serious health problems. Synthetic rubbers contain more carcinogens and their fumes are lethal in fires.

SECURITY AND PRIVACY

A sense of peace in a home is very important to the quality of life of the people who live there. It is awful to live in a house where you lie awake at night listening for the sound of the door or window being forced or of intruders in the house. A very important part of feeling peaceful is to feel secure at home. As with many aspects of design it may simply require a little thought at the design stage and the house, or housing estate, can be made much more secure through good design and perhaps a little extra investment. A number of websites deal with such issues, including http://www.securedbydesign.com.

Most robberies involve a rear-door entry and escapes are made easier when houses have pathways that are not overlooked. A first step is to design the whole housing development so that everyone in it feels a sense of ownership and responsibility for every part of the development. Clear and direct routes through an area are desirable but should not undermine the defensible space of neighbourhoods. Underused and lonely routes should be avoided. Crime is always easier to commit where offenders cannot be recognised so properties are usually entered from a door that is not overlooked. Communal areas should be designed to allow natural supervision. A sense of defensible space around a house is effective using real or symbolic barriers, i.e. change of road surface texture or colour, to encourage a feeling of territoriality among the residents. Houses can be sited in small clusters or interacting with each other. The front boundaries of properties should be well defined as private property. Strong, lockable gates should be included on the front build-line of a house in the worst areas. Avoid design features that allow climbing and access points. Utility meter cupboards should be located externally, as close as possible to the front building line and should be overlooked. Car parking should be located within view of residents and road users.

For front doors glazed panels, which should be laminated glass, will enable residents to see who is at the door and entries with two doors give added protection. Good locks should be specified on outer doors with entry by key only. Doors should have three hinges and, if the occupants still feel vulnerable, a chain latch device can be installed. Special care should be taken to protect French doors with adequate security devices and do not forget to put a good lock on the door between a house and garage too.

The position of ground floor windows and those easily accessible above ground floor level should be carefully thought out to get a balance between

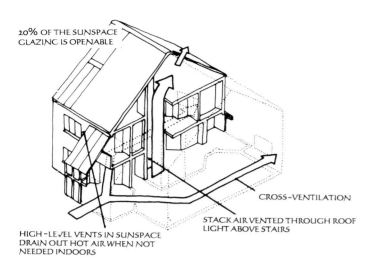

20% OF THE SUNSPACE GLAZING IS OPENABLE

CROSS-VENTILATION

STACK AIR VENTED THROUGH ROOF LIGHT ABOVE STAIRS

HIGH-LEVEL VENTS IN SUNSPACE DRAIN OUT HOT AIR WHEN NOT NEEDED INDOORS

6.3.
A, ventilation.

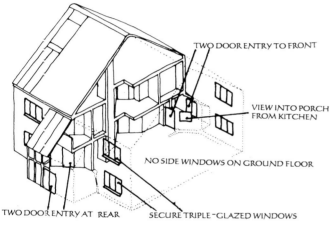

TWO DOOR ENTRY TO FRONT

VIEW INTO PORCH FROM KITCHEN

NO SIDE WINDOWS ON GROUND FLOOR

TWO DOOR ENTRY AT REAR

SECURE TRIPLE-GLAZED WINDOWS

6.3.
B, security.

Add to this the challenge of choosing safe, healthy and environmentally benign materials, and one begins to see what an amazing job the ordinary practising architect undertakes every day, without even having a brick laid on site.

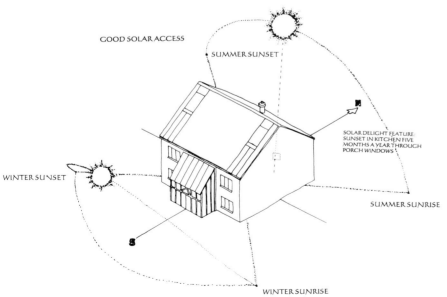

GOOD SOLAR ACCESS

SUMMER SUNSET

WINTER SUNSET

SOLAR DELIGHT FEATURE: SUNSET IN KITCHEN FIVE MONTHS A YEAR THROUGH PORCH WINDOWS

SUMMER SUNRISE

WINTER SUNRISE

6.3.
C, solar gain.

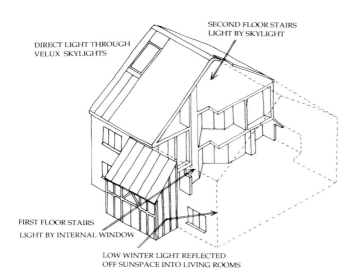

SECOND FLOOR STAIRS
LIGHT BY SKYLIGHT

DIRECT LIGHT THROUGH
VELUX SKYLIGHTS

FIRST FLOOR STAIRS
LIGHT BY INTERNAL WINDOW

LOW WINTER LIGHT REFLECTED
OFF SUNSPACE INTO LIVING ROOMS

6.3.

D, natural light.

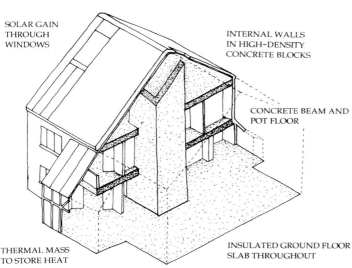

SOLAR GAIN
THROUGH
WINDOWS

INTERNAL WALLS
IN HIGH-DENSITY
CONCRETE BLOCKS

CONCRETE BEAM AND
POT FLOOR

THERMAL MASS
TO STORE HEAT

INSULATED GROUND FLOOR
SLAB THROUGHOUT

6.3.

E, sketch axonometrics of the Oxford Ecohouse showing the wide variety of considerations that have to be taken into account at the outset of a building design, including considerations of energy storage from passive solar gain.

security and privacy. Opaque glass can be used to prevent view into some windows that are overlooked. Frames should be securely fixed into the wall. Double- and triple-glazed windows provide a much greater deterrent to intruders than single-glazed ones.

Security alarm systems come in two forms; they can either be tripped by motion in the house or be designed to go off when the perimeter of the house is broken into, with movement sensors by doors and windows. The problem with internal motion-sensor systems is that they only trigger once someone is already in the house, so perimeter systems are safer. It is better to consider security issues right at the outset of the design because the design of the building form can have a significant impact on how safe you feel in the house once it is built.

TIMBER

There are a number of fairly failsafe ways to make sure you are specifying sustainable timber for your home:

- Do not use endangered species. A list of these can be found on: http://www.wood-worker.com/properties.htm#sectA
- Give preference to timber products that carry the Forest Stewardship Council's trademark or equivalent and for this see: http://www.fscoax.org/
- Where this is unavailable, timber is to be specified from a sustainable source with documentation from the suppliers and the contractor giving evidence of the fact.
- Where specifying hardwoods, preference should be given to certified hardwoods and you must make your own mind up if you want to use any certified tropical hardwoods yourself, but they should only be used as a second resort in any case.

However, not everybody can actually get FSC trademarked, for a variety of reasons, so again we advise the common-sense approach. You can seek out what local sources of timber are in your region, if there are sources of recycled timber, or local timber processing yards. A few enquiries will lead you to where the timber you want is actually grown. I was lucky enough at the Oxford Ecohouse to be recommended by Jewsons in Norwich to one of the most sustainable timber merchants in the Midlands, Jeffrey Walker & Co. Ltd of Harworth, Doncaster. Walkers is an old family business who felled the trees for my house from sustainably managed stands in Sherwood Forest, and then dried them in new high-efficiency kilns, and delivered them the few tens of miles to my house, so I know where it came from – and that's rather nice. Other timber in the house, used for the stair and balcony railings, was purchased from Richard Burbidge Ltd in Oswestry and again they knew where all their timber came from, how it was processed, and treated. Many businesses are really keen to promote responsible environmental practices and can prove it. These are the types of suppliers and contractors that really make a difference in that you can be sure of their products.

Timber specification practices are becoming a litmus paper test of environmental credentials for many businesses, and clients are becoming passionate about having green buildings. Even local authorities are going green, and leading these is the Lambeth Council in London who have recently won an award for their sustainable timber policies. The secret, they believe, is to actually tie down the specification procedures for ensuring that the wood that arrives on site is sustainable. They have a lot of sensible advice on the subject of sustainable design issues on their website, which is www.lambeth.gov.uk, and in Table 6.2.

VOLATILE ORGANIC COMPOUNDS (VOCs) AND ORGANIC SOLVENTS

VOCs are found in many everyday materials in the home, including carpets, underlays, adhesives, caulks, sealants, thermal insulation materials, paints,

Table 6.2. DRAFT Lambeth Council – Guidance on actions and specifications to meet the sustainable timber policy

Action/specification	Does action meet policy requirements	Evidence required
Both contractor and component manufacturer with Forest Stewardship Council (FSC) Chain of Custody (CoC) certification or equivalent, and sustainable timber used.	Fully meets policy requirements.	Copy of CoC certification.
Timber from a component manufacturer with FSC CoC certification or equivalent.	Partly meets policy if the contractor can demonstrate that the components from the manufacturer were delivered to and used on site.	CoC information from manufacturer. Description of how materials are used on site and paper work, e.g. delivery note.
Timber specified by component manufacturer from a timber mill with FSC or Pan European Forestry Certification (PEFC) chain of custody.	Partly meets policy if the contractor can demonstrate that specified timber was used by the manufacturer for the components delivered to and used on site. PEFC.	As above, with additional paper work to demonstrate that the component manufacturer purchased and used CoC timber.
Timber from suppliers/manufacturers who are signatories of Forest Forever or similar scheme.	Partly meets policy if contractor can demonstrate that their suppliers had checked that the environmental policies of their timber mills were being implemented. Also if the contractor had sought FSC or equivalent certified timber.	Copies of all environmental policies in the chain and information on checks carried out. Delivery note from supplier. Inquiry letters and responses to suppliers.
Timber – from UK or Scandinavian forest.	Does not automatically meet policy as higher levels of sustainability are now commonly available unless other evidence can be provided.	Documentation that timber is from a local source which is well managed, e.g., coppiced chestnut from Kent. Inquiry letters and responses to suppliers showing that certified timber was sought.
Timber – soft wood specified.	Does not meet policy as timber could be from old growth forest or harvested in an unsustainable manner.	
No action.	Does not meet policy.	

FSC, Forest Stewardship Council; PEFC, Pan European Forestry Certification; CoC, Chain of Custody (independently).
Note: for tropical hardwoods, the requirement for certification is the only practicable assurance of sustainability because of the extent of timber smuggling in many areas and the high risks to rainforests.

coatings, varnishes, vinyl flooring, plywood, wallpaper, bituminous emulsions and waterproof membranes.

A wide range of VOCs can be emitted, including solvents or plasticisers used in the manufacture of building products. As the weather gets hotter so the rates of emission of VOCs increase. They can cause discomfort because of their smell and, worse, provide health hazards in the home and initiate symptoms of sick building syndrome.

Organic solvents include white spirit, which is found in many household products such as cleaning fluids, varnishes, glues and paints. Dry cleaned clothes also contain very high levels of solvent residue, so air them outside if possible before wearing and keep them in a nylon cover bag in the wardrobe. In large quantities organic solvents can cause dizziness and in smaller quantities they can exacerbate asthma problems. Avoid them by:

- using water-based eco-paints and varnishes that do not contain ammonia (see the section Paints (page 156))
- if you are using glue, paint strippers or varnishes, open the windows wide and ventilate the rooms really well
- keeping only small quantities of them in the house
- if you have bedding dry cleaned, air it thoroughly before using.

WALLPAPERS

If you must use them, choose wallpaper that is made of paper and not a synthetic material such as vinyl. If you paint over it make sure you choose an eco-paint that does not contain solvents, vinyls or fungicides.

WOOD PRESERVATIVES

Many different chemicals are used to protect wood from insect or fungal decay and many are potentially very harmful. They should be handled with care and contact with skin should be avoided. Any product for protecting buildings from woodworm should be applied only by an expert. Avoid their use in enclosed spaces and do not use rooms where a smell of the chemical product lingers. Avoid storing these chemicals in rooms in the house.

WOOD PELLET HEATING SYSTEMS

Ian Bacon of TV Energy

Wood is broadly a *carbon neutral* because, as trees grow, they remove CO_2 from the air; and so by burning wood, we are only putting back the carbon that has been taken out. One environmentally benign way of delivering heat into an ecohouse is by using a wood pellet boiler feeding into a 'wet'-based radiator, or under floor heating system. Wood pellets are made as a by-product of the traditional timber industry so one is also heating a house on waste!

Pellet boilers are generally free-standing and flued to the outside. They come in a range of sizes from the domestic to the industrial in scale. The pellets are stored in a hopper and fed automatically into the grate of the boiler. The hopper size will dictate the frequency required for refilling but, in the winter, a domestic system may need topping up every two to three days. Ash constitutes less than 1 per cent of installed mass and can be disposed of on the garden or with the household waste.

The boilers operate in the same way as a conventional fossil fuel boiler and can be turned on and off in the same manner. They also require an annual maintenance check.

Pellet supply is a reasonably new market in the UK, but several British companies now offer a supply. At the beginning of 2006, one of these companies was selling pellets at £1.95 + 5 per cent VAT for a 10 kg bag, with 100 bags fitting on a pallet and constituting a tonne. Delivery was an additional £45 + 17.5 per cent VAT. When viewing the cost comparison in Table 6.3, it is clear that wood pellets are a cheaper option than electric, oil or LPG-based heating.

Table 6.3. Cost of delivered energy as at November 2005

Electricity	3.9 to 7.6 p/kWh (1)
Heating oil (in condensing boiler)	4.2 p/kWh (2)
LPG (in condensing boiler)	4.7 p/kWh (3)
Coal (anthracite grains)	3 p/kWh (4)
Natural gas	2.8 p/kWh (5)
Logs in stove	0 to 5.1 p/kWh (6)
Woodchip	1 to 2 p/kWh (7)
Pellet	3.0 p/kWh to 3.5 p/kWh (8)

Pellets should preferably be stored inside a dry building, but a pallet could be stored outside with a tarpaulin secured over it.

The issue for this heating solution is upfront costs, with a domestic wood pellet boiler likely to cost in the region of £8 000 installed, although a grant of £1 500 can be accessed towards this expenditure from the government's Low Carbon Buildings Programme (LCBP) – see: http://www.est.org.uk/housingbuildings/funding/lowcarbonbuildings/.

There needs to be enough space on the site to both install the boiler and for a storage hopper of reasonable size – a minimum area of around 1.5 m by 1.5 m may be sufficient. This can be either in the location of an existing boiler, with the hopper outside, to the rear of the property, or in an adjoining building.

If you are seriously thinking of installing a pellet burner, and many people in rural locations who find their heating oil bills are soaring are, then it is worth getting an understanding of the full costs and ongoing maintenance and fuel requirements of a conventional oil-based boiler and comparing these over the lifetime for a wood pellet alternative. This will require detailed quotes for both options and for either you, or a local energy consultant, to put together the cost–benefit analysis on both options, not forgetting to look at the choices with a doubling and tripling of oil prices, which may well happen before the new boiler needs replacing.

ECOKITCHEN DESIGN

After a decade in residence at the Oxford Ecohouse the time had come to replace the £250-worth of budget units I first installed. They had rotted in places with the moisture round the sink, broken, peeled and were about to join the millions of tonnes of other discarded kitchen units in the landfill of England (see: http://www.wrap.org.uk/). When I first built my house I put what money I had into the solar energy systems and kitchen white goods that have helped me save enough money to be able to invest in building a real ecokitchen. So I had to think hard about what I really wanted:

- easy to work in
- easy to clean
- easy to access pots, crockery and food
- has enough storage
- easy to recycle in
- easy to get access for repairs
- low-impact materials
- low waste in construction
- low-energy appliances
- cosy but well lit
- fresh air

with materials that are:

- recycled
- low embodied
- local
- from sustainable sources
- low-toxicity materials and finishes
- low-energy appliances.

Let me explain how I achieved all these things starting from the bottom up! The floor was originally cork and that has been warm and wonderful but I decided to cover the existing floor with a medium coloured, moderately priced lino that was not too expensive, not so light that it shows all the dirt and not so dark that you can't see it at all! By laying this over the cork I get a warm, wipe clean, finish and rather than ending it at the front of the kitchen unit, I have extended it right up to the wall beneath the worktop.

All the original units have been sent to landfill (never again) and Nigel Aust, the carpenter who built much of the ecohouse in the first place, constructed a timber frame of second-hand and new timber, with shelves under the new worktops high enough off the floor that the floor can be easily cleaned when necessary. There are a couple of drawers for the cutlery but all the other utensils, crockery and pans now either go directly on or under these shelves, or are stored on them in baskets and wooden trays that can be easily removed for cleaning.

The worktops are all of sustainably-sourced beechwood and have to be well oiled with Danish or Norwegian oil, a job to be repeated once a year to keep them in good condition. There are many different low-impact surfaces you could be using but it is only important for you to know exactly why you have chosen that particular surface over others on offer – in ecokitchens there are no 'right' answers. In ecokitchens it is just as in all other eco-design – the best choice usually 'all depends' on the circumstances.

In the kitchen I have a shelf above the worktop, on which I can put those things one uses every day like tea and coffee, sugar and salt. The shelf provides easy access to these everyday items and helps keep the work surface below clean and tidy. Beneath the work surface I have returned to the old fashioned method of a curtain strung between the supporting uprights, just beneath the worktop, that can be easily pulled back or up for access to the shelves behind and which can be taken off for regular washing or replacement. I have also lined the shelves to protect their surfaces.

I have reused the original Belfast sink with two waste bins beneath the sink for general waste and compost, in a bucket that gets emptied when full on the compost heap in the garden. The recycled waste goes in the porch and the general waste bin from beneath the sink is emptied into the big green wheelie bin outside that the council empties once every two weeks. Plastics, tins and cardboard go in the blue bin in the porch and good paper is stored in the green bin, with each of these being collected once every alternate week with the wheelie bins.

The large cold north-facing porch is also used as a cold larder for vegetables and bulky items that one wants to keep cool; people seldom realise that it was only in the 1960s that councils began to create a space in council house kitchens to put a fridge in. Before then cold larders were used instead. The porch also houses bicycles, wet coats, shoes and buggy storage, as well as acting as a draft lobby to keep cold air out of the house in winter.

I am lucky to have a good dry pantry off the kitchen where a new shelf adds to the space available for food storage and this time I have decided to keep a clearer distinction between food storage – pantry, porch and fridge – and the crockery, cutlery, pots and pans beneath the worktops. Let's see if this works!

As one moves up, one of the most important things in a kitchen are its windows. Some of you will notice that I have moved the cooking hob from the blank east wall to the north worktop beneath the 'tilt and turn' windows. If you are very lucky you will have windows above your hob that will enable the steam to travel directly out of the window; a small opening window light or a tilt and turn window is ideal What you don't want is a huge window that you have to open such a large bit of that it puts you off opening it.

We need a revolution to put an end to the patio door mentality that designs opening windows that are so big that no one uses them. Long live the opening top hung vent window (and I don't mean trickle!). I also think that if you have a good window above the cooker you don't want a huge hole in your kitchen wall lined with an extract duct and fan that is simply a huge heat drain from a building. You open the window when you need to. The Building Regulations people argue that with a fan it works whether you remember to use it or not. Not if it is turned off it doesn't. The same applies to a window and the more that fans are relied on the worse the windows in our buildings have become. My advice in ecohomes is get rid of the fans and open the well-designed windows.

Looking further up the walls the paint is, as always, water-based to help the walls to 'breathe' so that even quite large amounts of moisture in the room air can be absorbed by the plastered walls.

Lighting is key for kitchens and it is important to have good lighting levels where one is doing things like cutting with sharp knives and trying to identify good products, either before or after cooking, by sight. Key tasks that have to be well lit include the storage, preparation, cooking and eating of food and the cleaning of the kitchen to maintain high levels of hygiene in it. I chose to use a range of flexible spotlights so I can adapt the lighting levels according to what I am working on. Just be careful to ensure that you think carefully about what you need to light in your space and how you do that.

Just as I chose to make the body of the kitchen very utilitarian in my original kitchen, the same is true for this refurbishment, with robust resilient fitting and, as before, first rate 'white goods'. In Europe, electricity used for appliances, largely in kitchens, accounts for more than 4 per cent of total CO_2 emissions. This includes the emissions produced as a result of making the products as well as running them but it is a huge amount nonetheless. Around 80 per cent of the environmental impact of white goods used in the kitchen occurs during use, and around 20 per cent is accounted for by the embodied energy of the products. The pressure is now on for white goods manufacturers and companies to respond to such pressure by setting ambitious targets for improving the energy and water efficiency of their products.

I have taken an amazing step forward by choosing this time to cook with an 'induction hob' (see: http://en.wikipedia.org/wiki/Induction_cooker). Before talking to a friend, Susan Dean, I knew nothing about them, but it turns out that they are really quite amazing and because I am generating away with my solar PV electric roof I can actually do quite a bit of my day-time cooking free! Now that I like.

An induction hob automatically senses how large each pot is and only uses the actual amount of energy required to cook that much food. Magic! A magnetic field heats the pot only and not the hob itself. The pot heats the food by conduction and very little heat is transferred back to the hob. The system is so efficient that the manufacturers claim that the induction hob will save over 50 per cent of energy used to cook compared with gas.

I still have my dishwasher and I have always thought that this was a really efficient way to do lots of dishes. I wait until the dishwasher is full then run it during sunlight hours. I was interested to find out that an independent study by the University of Bonn showed that in tests that involved washing the same

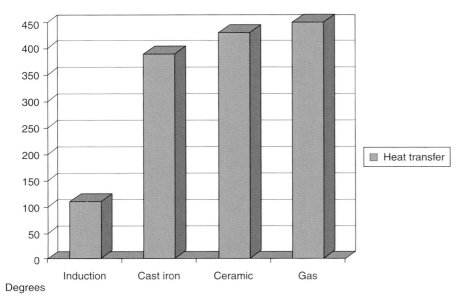

Degrees

6.4.
This graph show the outer temperature of a pan on an indication hob compared with those on a cast iron, a ceramic and a gas hob showing how minimal the heat transfer from the food to the pan is in an induction system. Based on a pan contents of 1 litre of water at 100°C (Source: Electrolux).

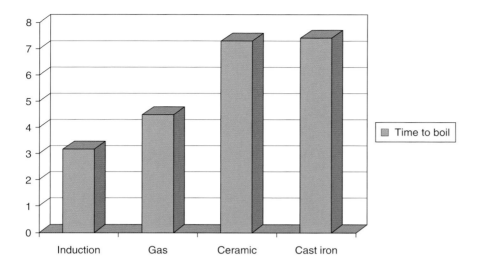

6.5.
The time taken to heat food in an induction hob is a fraction of that for other hobs (Source: Electrolux).

sized loads, the dishes that were hand washed used 2 kWh of energy (hot water), whilst using an efficient dishwasher uses as little as 1.05 kWh; so one could save over 209 kWh per annum using a dishwasher based on around 220 wash cycles. This does not of course take into account the embodied energy of the machine. These benefits do not include the water efficiency you get from both the dishwasher and the washing machine, which are so water-efficient they use up to ten times less water than some other side-loaders but hundreds of gallons less than the amazingly inefficient top-loaded machines.

This time around I have added a few more things to my white goods wish list and one of them is to have a very quiet spin cycle as we spend a lot of time in the kitchen when the washing is on. In addition I have chosen delay start features so that I can load my machine before I leave the house and set it to start when the sun is strongest so I use as much of my own energy as possible. Every little helps in a world of rapidly rising energy prices. The desire to get my energy bills to an absolute minimum has really coloured my choice of kitchen appliances because this is where most of the energy is used in the house. I began to notice for instance that there can be a huge difference in performance between even different 'A' rated machines. When you next go shopping for a new washing machine actually take the time to look at the exact footprint rating for each machine – you could save a huge amount on your household energy bills by doing so!

The combination of efficient kitchen appliances in conjunction with solar hot water systems and a PV roof really makes a radical reduction in the energy running costs of the house and the CO_2 emissions from it. Look at the very different performance of the following houses and ask yourself about the wisdom of investing now to future-proof yourself against the problems of rising energy prices and helping the planet at the same time.

House no.

1 3 bedroom, 160 m^2 semi-detached house built to 1995 Building Regulations standards.

Table 6.4. Amounts of CO_2 that can be saved by buying efficient white goods and running them on a solar roof (Source: Sue Roaf)

House no.:	1 3 bed 160 m² Typical	2 3 bed 160 m² Zero CO₂	3 3 bed 160 m² Zero E	4 6 bed 232 m² Oxford	5 Oxford Ecohouse Ox + D plus PV	6 Ox + A no PV	7 Ox + D no PV	8 Ox + A plus PV
Space heating	7926	3172	240	3000	3000	3000	3000	3000
Hot water	4548	2319	1660	1500	1500	1500	1500	1500
Pumps and fans	175		200					
Cooking	656	330	330	1000	1000	1000	1000	1000
kWh total gas imported	13305	5821	2430	5500	5500	5500	5500	4700
CO₂ gas total gas (× 0.19)	2528	1105	462	1045	1045	1045	1045	893
Lights/appliances total	3000	2700	2100	3500	4816	3500	4816	2600 [5]
Elec imported @ Oxford [4]				2500	3816	3500	4816	1600
CO₂ total elec imp × 0.43	1290	1161	903	1075	1641	1505	2071	688
PV elec made @ Oxford [6]				3000	3000			3000
PV elec made + used @ Ox				1000	1000			1000
Ox. PV elec exported [2] minus CO₂ for expt.				2000	2000			2000
PV	1290	1161	903	−860	−860			−860 [3]
Total electricity CO₂ (×0.43)	1290	1161	903	215	781	1505	2071	−172
Energy total kWh	16305	8521	4530	9000	10316	9000	10316	7300
CO₂ total kgCO₂	3818	2266	1365	1260	1826	2550	3116	721
Total energy used per m² p.a.	102	53	28	39	45	39	45	31
kgm CO₂ per m² p.a.	24	14	9	5	8	11	13	3
Cost of gas per annum	532	233	97	220	220	220	220	188
Cost of electricity imported	360	324	252	300	418	420	578	192
minus 4 p for exported 2000				80	80			80
Total electricity cost	360	324	252	220	338	420	578	112
Total energy bills p.a. in £	892	557	349	480	558	640	798	300

(Continued)

Table 6.4. (Continued)

House no.:	1 3 bed 160 m² Typical	2 3 bed 160 m² Zero CO₂	3 3 bed 160 m² Zero E	4 6 bed 232 m² Oxford	5 Oxford Ecohouse Ox + D plus PV	6 Ox + A no PV	7 Ox + D no PV	8 Ox + A plus PV
Energy bills × 2	1784	1114	698	960	1116	1280	1596	600
Energy bills × 3	2676	1671	1047	1440	1674	1920	2394	900
Energy bills × 4	3568	2228	1396	1920	2232	2560	3192	1200
CO₂ saved in 20 yrs	76 tons [1]	45 tons	27 tons	25 tons	37 tons	45 tons	62 tons	14 tons

[1] 76 tons is nearly 5 times more CO_2 than the 14 tons of the PV Oxford ecohouse with ecokitchen that is an 80% reduction on emissions – but without the eco-appliance that is only a 60% reduction so the ecokitchen makes a 20% difference in emissions of CO_2 from the house!

[2] Exported PV electricity is used in adjacent buildings replacing imported energy from the grid so CO_2 for this displaced electricity is deducted from the house total CO_2.

[3] It is the solar-generated electricity that makes the greatest contribution to reducing emissions from the Oxford Ecohouse along with the efficiency improvements made in white goods for the ecokitchen.

[4] If all the appliances are D rated (not A rated) this adds a further 1316 kWh/a. This means $1316 \times 0.4 = 526$ kgms CO_2 difference.

[5] In the ecokitchen we change the gas cooking for a more efficient gas oven and an electric induction stove. The efficient gas oven goes down to 200 kWh/a from 300 kWh/a. The electric hob adds 200 kWh/a to the electric total and takes 700 kWh/a off the gas total. 200 kWh extra is taken off for increased efficiency the electricity load for the more efficient white goods.

[6] For electricity bills of the PV house you calculate the cost of the imported electricity at 12 kWh/a and then subtract the cost of price paid for the exported electricity (4 kWh/a in 2007 – this doubles with the doubling of the price of energy etc. – it also gives a good idea of the advantages of reverse metering).

2 3 bedroom, 160 m^2 semi-detached house built to Zero CO$_2$ Standards (UK Government definition of a zero carbon home is one with 'zero net emissions of carbon dioxide from all energy use in the home'). The definition encompasses all energy use in the home (including energy for cooking, TVs, computers and other appliances) rather than just those energy uses that are currently part of building regulations (space heating, hot water, ventilation and some lighting). It means that over a year there are no net carbon emissions resulting from the operation of the dwelling. This could be achieved either through steps taken at the individual dwelling level or through site-wide strategies. So it will not be necessary for each dwelling to have its own micro-generation capacity where development level solutions would be more appropriate. In fact few houses can be zero CO$_2$ but the column shows the figures given for this standard.

3 3 bedroom, 160 m^2 semi-detached house built to zero-energy standards (even better than No. 2 above).

4 6 bedroom, 232 m^2 Oxford Ecohouse, with D rated kitchen appliances and a 4 kWp PV roof.

5 6 bedroom, 232 m^2 Oxford Ecohouse, with A rated kitchen appliances and no PV roof.

6 6 bedroom, 232 m^2 Oxford Ecohouse, with D rated kitchen appliances and no PV roof.

7 6 bedroom, 232 m^2 Oxford Ecohouse, with A rated kitchen appliances and no PV roof.

8 6 bedroom, 232 m^2 Oxford Ecohouse, with A rated kitchen appliances and a 4 kWp PV roof.

So the bottom line is that not only can you build a beautiful ecokitchen, with the only construction waste being woodwork shavings you burn on the fire, but the investment in buying or reusing low-energy appliances, used in conjunction with renewable energy, can help you future-proof yourself against the inevitable rise in energy prices that will happen because of the Peak Oil issue. If energy prices go up four times you save a stunning £2368 a year in home running costs while losing nothing in quality of life. I knew it made sense to use renewables when I built this house – not only is this table proof but the scary thing is that in January 1996 I generated only 2 kWh of PV electricity because it was a dense cloudy month and over the January/early February 2007 month I have generated over 140 kWh, more than I need to keep the whole house going. Is this a trend to sunnier winters? If so, the sooner you get your solar ecokitchen the better! I heard a well-known green architect recently describe solar panels on a building as 'eco-bling'.

'Hullo – is there intelligent life out there…?'

Solar panels and ecokitchens, and the way we eat and the way we live our lives, are all important parts of a larger strategy to reduce our impact on this planet before we destroy it completely. This book, however ordinary the issues and ideas in it are, isn't about bling – it's about survival.

6.6.
The Oxford Ecokitchen has done away with all the prefabricated units that end up so quickly in landfill. The simple design by Sue Roaf and Oliver Bridge and built by Nigel Aust uses a softwood frame in-filled by tongue and groove walls with plywood shelves. The solid timberwork surface is finished with eight coats of oil and a simple shelf behind the sink carries everyday items in use. By eliminating the vertical dividers of the units the shelf space is increased and dry food is stored in the larder (Photograph by Chris Honeywell). See also Oliver Heath's website on Eco-Kitchen design: http://www.blustinheathdesign.com

6.7.
The white goods in the kitchen can use up to a third of all domestic energy. By using the new high-efficiency electric induction hob during the day when the PV roof is generating, it is possible to do 'carbon free cooking'. This is a way to optimise the value of the renewables in the house by perfectly matching the loads to the energy generated. We are all waiting now for the fridge that uses thermal mass to store enough coolth to keep food cold overnight but only draws electricity during the day! (Photograph by Chris Honeywell).

7 PASSIVE SOLAR DESIGN

DESIGNING WITH THE SUN

The first step in creating comfort and thermal delight in buildings is to understand the relationship between the climate and our need for shelter. There is an enormous variation in climates that buildings experience. These can be at the scale of global climates, from the Arctic to the Sahara. They can be regional climates in the centre of a continent or on the seashore. They can be local climates on the sunny or the shady side of a hill or street. All will influence the way in which a building should be designed in relation to the sun.

The sun can be a friend or an enemy in buildings. Poor climatic design of buildings, all too often seen in 'modern' architecture, causes many buildings to overheat, even in temperate or cold climates where such problems traditionally never existed. The power of the sun should be understood and respected by good designers of well-designed, passive solar buildings in which the free energy of the sun is used to power the building but not allowed to interfere with the comfort and economy of the building's occupants.

The five things a designer needs to know for a good passive solar design are:

1 how strong the sun at the site is at different times of the year
2 where the sun will be at different times of the year in relation to the site
3 how much of the sun's heat a building will need, or not need, at different times of the year to enable the building occupants to be comfortable
4 how much storage capacity the building should have in relation to the available solar gain at the site to meet those needs
5 what the additional requirements are for controlling the heat gain from direct solar radiation, convection or conduction in a design and how they can be met by envelope performance, building form and ventilation.

There are a number of factors that influence the incidence, or strength, of solar radiation at the site including:

- the latitude of the site
- the altitude and azimuth of the site
- how much shade will be given by any obstacles that exist between the building and the site
- the weather above the site.

AZIMUTH AND ALTITUDE OF THE SUN AT A SITE

The angle with which the sun strikes at a location is represented by the terms *altitude* and *azimuth*. Altitude is the vertical angle in the sky (sometimes referred to as height); azimuth is the horizontal direction from which it comes (also referred to as bearing). Altitude angles range from 0° (horizontal) to 90° (vertical: directly overhead). Azimuth is generally measured clockwise from north so that due east is 90°, south 180° and west 270° (or −90°).

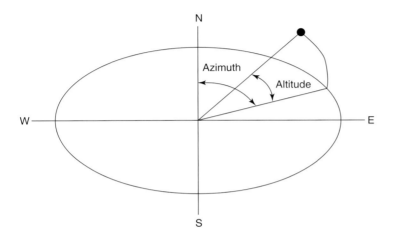

7.1.
The altitude and azimuth of the sun at a site (Andrew Bairstow).

Because the Earth revolves around the sun once a year, we have four seasons. The Earth's axis remains in a constant alignment in its rotation so twice a year the incoming solar radiation is perpendicular to the latitude of the equator and only once a year is it perpendicular to the tropics of Cancer and Capricorn, as shown in Figure 7.2.

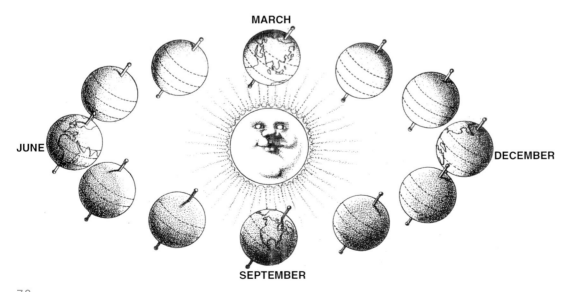

7.2.
The Earth revolves around the sun once a year, as well as around its own axis once a day (Mazria, 1979).

The changing values of azimuth and altitude angles are predominantly a reflection of the changes in the relative positions of Earth and sun. These are governed by:

- the rotation of the Earth around the sun
- the rotation of the Earth about its axis.

One of the simplest tools we can use for the derivation of altitude and azimuth angles is a graph using Cartesian coordinates (Figure 7.3). Figure 7.3 incorporates two types of line. Firstly, those representing the variation in altitude and azimuth over the period of a day (given for the 21st or 22nd day of each month). Secondly, those joining the points on the altitude–azimuth lines for a specific hour. Thus the solar angles for 11 a.m. on 21 March may be read off on the horizontal and vertical axes where these two lines meet (altitude 36°, azimuth 19°). Values for other days may be read by interpolating between these lines.

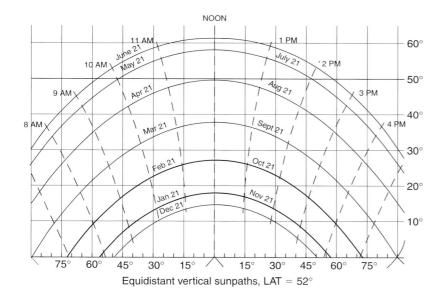

Equidistant vertical sunpaths, LAT = 52°

7.3.
Sunpath diagram for 52°N on cartesian axes (Andrew Bairstow).

It may appear that these are the only determinants of angular position, however we are actually concerned with the direction of the sun's radiation rather than the Earth–sun position. Also, radiation does not travel in an entirely straight line but is bent slightly by the Earth's atmosphere.

The distance between the Earth and the sun is approximately 150 million km, varying slightly through the year with the variation of the azimuth and altitude angles with time.

All passive solar features involve the transmission of solar radiation through a protective glazing layer(s) on the sun side of a building, into a building space where it is absorbed and stored by thermal mass (for example thick masonry walls and floors or water-filled containers). The typical processes involved are:

- **collection** – to collect solar energy, double-glazed windows are used on the south-facing side of the house

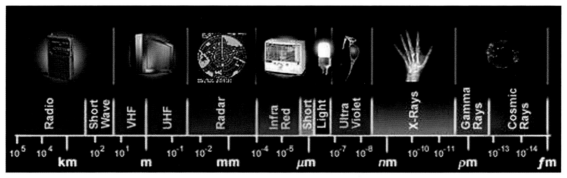

7.4.

The sun emits solar radiation that arrives at the Earth in the form of a number of different wavelengths ranging from infrared, the hot end, through the visible light spectrum to ultraviolet light (http://www.fridge.arch.uwa.edu.au/).

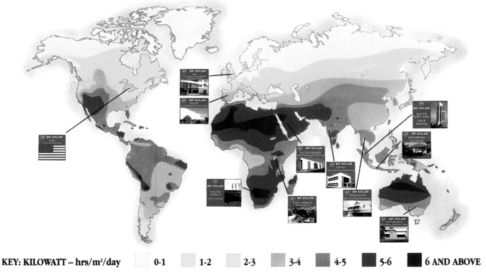

KEY: KILOWATT – hrs/m²/day   0-1   1-2   2-3   3-4   4-5   5-6   6 AND ABOVE

7.5.

Solar incidence at different latitudes. Closer to the equator, where the sun is more directly overhead, the sun is 'hotter' because the energy density is determined by the angle of incidence (Mazria, 1979).

- **storage** – after the sun's energy has been collected, some heat is immediately used in the living spaces and some is stored for later use. The storage, called thermal mass, is usually built into the floors and/or interior walls. Mass is characterised by its ability to absorb heat, store it and release it slowly as the temperature inside the house falls. Concrete, stone, brick and water can be used as mass
- **distribution** – heat stored in floors and walls is slowly released by radiation, convection and conduction. In a hybrid system, fans, vents and blowers may be used to distribute the heat.

There are several types of passive solar system that can be used in homes. The most common are direct gain, indirect gain and isolated gain.

SYSTEM COMPONENTS

There are three key components to all passive solar systems for heating:

- collector
- mass
- heated space.

DIRECT GAIN SYSTEMS

Direct gain systems are most commonly used in passive solar architecture. The roof, walls and floor are insulated to a high level. Solar radiation enters through the windows and is absorbed by the heavy material of the building. The whole building structure gradually collects and stores solar energy during the day. Heavy building materials provide thermal storage. The collected solar energy is gradually released at night when there is no solar gain.

Direct gain systems commonly utilise windows or skylights to allow solar radiation to directly enter zones to be heated. If the building is constructed of lightweight materials, mass may need to be added to the building interior to increase its heat storage capacity. The proportion of a building's heating needs that can be met by solar energy increases as the area of sun-facing glazing increases. Additional mass must therefore be used to reduce interior temperature swings and delay the release of solar energy into occupied spaces. While the mass that is directly illuminated by the incident energy, sunshine, is the most effective for energy storage, long-wave radiation exchanges and convective air currents in the solar heated rooms allow non-illuminated mass to also provide effective energy storage.

THERMAL MASS

Thermal storage mass plays a vital role in the effective performance of direct gain buildings. Thermal mass is needed to store the solar energy for subsequent release into the interior space as heat. It is necessary because the sun's energy is not always emitted in phase with heating requirements. This is why the heat gained must be stored for future use, rather as a brick in a night storage radiator is heated at night using cheap energy and re-radiated as heat out into the space during the day. In passive solar systems the cheap energy comes from the sun.

Thermal mass in a building does two things, it reduces the peaks of the temperature swings (decrement factor) and shifts them to a later time than the air temperature peaks (time lag). The more mass there is, the lower and later the indoor air temperature peaks (see Figure 3.5).

As a general rule, buildings that contain very little thermal mass are unable to store heat for night-time use; thus, only the day-time portion of the heat load can be met by solar gains, and overheating can be a serious problem if the solar gains are excessive. Furthermore, heat losses through an aperture whose effectiveness is impaired by insufficient thermal mass can exceed the useful solar gain. Lightly constructed stud-wall buildings with no floor slab (or a carpeted floor slab) are the worst offenders in this category.

The effectiveness of thermal storage mass in direct gain buildings depends on its thickness, surface area and thermal properties (volumetric heat capacity and

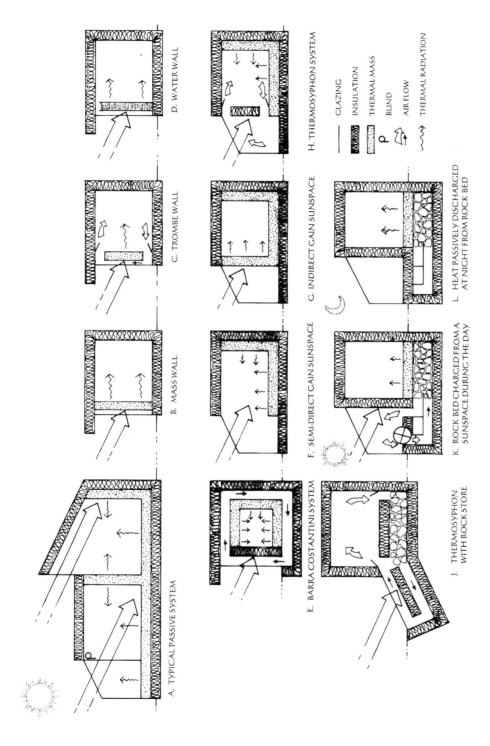

7.6.

Passive solar systems: A, a typical passive solar system; B, mass wall system; C, Trombe wall system; D, water wall system; E, Barra Constantini system; F, semi-direct gain sunspace; G, indirect gain sunspace; H, thermosyphon system; J, thermosyphon system with rock bed; K, underfloor rock bed actively charged from a sunspace during the day; L, underfloor rock bed passively discharged by radiation and convection at night.

Legend:
- GLAZING
- INSULATION
- THERMAL MASS
- BLIND
- AIR FLOW
- THERMAL RADIATION

A. TYPICAL PASSIVE SYSTEM
B. MASS WALL
C. TROMBE WALL
D. WATER WALL
E. BARRA COSTANTINI SYSTEM
F. SEMI-DIRECT GAIN SUNSPACE
G. INDIRECT GAIN SUNSPACE
H. THERMOSYPHON SYSTEM
J. THERMOSYPHON WITH ROCK STORE
K. ROCK BED CHARGED FROM A SUNSPACE DURING THE DAY
L. HEAT PASSIVELY DISCHARGED AT NIGHT FROM ROCK BED

thermal conductivity). The best materials are those that are capable of storing large quantities of heat (high volumetric heat capacity) and that can readily transport heat from the mass surface to the mass interior for storage and back again to the surface to meet the building's heat load (high thermal conductivity). As a general rule, mass surfaces should be relatively dark in colour compared with non-massive surfaces in order to promote preferential absorption of solar radiation by the thermal storage medium and, for optimal effectiveness, should be located in building zones that experience direct solar gains. Mass located in zones not directly illuminated by solar radiation entering through south-facing windows will be ineffective unless care is taken to ensure adequate free convective exchanges with directly heated zones or unless a forced-air distribution system is employed. In either case, remote thermal storage mass will be less effective than that located in direct gain zones.

Some rules that apply to high-density masonry (roughly 2000–2500 kg m^{-3}:

- Performance variations for mass thickness between 10 and 20 cm are small. The thickness may be reduced to 10 cm without incurring significant performance penalties. This generalisation is independent of location, configuration and mass surface area.
- The range of mass thickness between 5 and 10 cm can be considered a transition region. In this region, performance penalties for reduced thickness are becoming significant but, in some cases, may be considered acceptable as design cost trade-offs.
- For mass thickness below 5 cm, performance falls off much more rapidly than in the transition region. Under most conditions it is not advisable to employ mass thickness of less than 5 cm for passive solar building assemblages.
- Lower-density masonry has a lower thermal conductivity and, therefore, has a smaller effective thickness for diurnal heat storage. The same heat storage capacity must, therefore, be achieved with material spread over a larger area.

INDIRECT GAIN SYSTEMS

These are passive thermal systems that collect and store the sun's energy. The storage is directly linked to the comfort of the interior space. In winter, energy is collected and stored to be released later in the day. This allows better control of indoor temperatures and heat distribution. In summer, the systems reverse their operation preventing overheating.

A building component can be heated by absorbing heat radiated from warmer components (walls, floors) or by convection from the surrounding air. The storage is influenced by the component temperature difference, location and emissivity. Indirect gain systems may be characterised by the placing of a sheet of glass in front of, and quite close to, a solid masonry wall or other building element that has a high thermal storage capacity. These systems are designed to capture and store a large fraction of the indirect radiation for subsequent release into the adjoining occupied space. When a wall is used for thermal energy storage in an indirect gain system it is called a solar wall or a mass wall.

A mass wall relies on conduction to transfer heat. For better thermal efficiency mass storage elements are located within a building, taking up some space that could be used for other things. Commonly a large wall is constructed on the sun-orientated face of the building. The sun warms up the mass of the wall during the day. After sunset, the stored heat is emitted for a period of time that depends on the thickness of the wall and its thermal characteristics. The glazing on the external face reduces heat loss to the outside. After sunset, the stored heat is emitted for a period of time that depends on the thickness of the wall and its thermal characteristics. The glazing on the external face reduces heat loss to the outside. There are several variations of the mass wall principle, as follows.

The Trombe-Michel wall

The Trombe-Michel wall (also known simply as the Trombe wall) is a variation of the mass wall principle. Here the mass wall has controllable vents at high and low levels to allow convective heat transfer. Solar radiation heats the wall. The inclusion of vent holes through the heated wall permits some convection to take place, as a means of circulating heat to the building during the day.

The water wall

The water wall is a variation of the mass wall where water replaces the solid wall. This is attractive in situations where a low-mass wall is required. Water-filled containers take the place of a masonry wall. Tall fibreglass tubes are often used. Water has a greater unit heat capacity than brick or cement so, for a given volume, a water wall works more efficiently than a solid wall.

The Barra-Constantini wall

The Barra-Constantini system uses lightweight glazed collectors mounted on a wall. The glazed wall panel acts as a heat collector. Ducts in the building circulate the warm air by natural convection. The heated air warms heavyweight ceilings, walls and floor.

> **ROOF STORAGE SYSTEMS**
> Roof storage systems are a variation of the storage wall principle for indirect heat gain. Movable insulating decks can be situated over the roof (storage medium). These are used to cover the roof during winter nights and summer days.

SUNSPACES, SOLAR GREENHOUSES, CONSERVATORIES

One of the most attractive passive solar features is the use of an attached sunspace (also known as solar greenhouse or conservatory) to gather energy and pre-warm ventilation air for the parent house. An attached sunspace is a solar collector that is also a useful space capable of serving other building functions. Occupants not only have the benefit of lower energy bills but also it can be a most comfortable area of the house on sunny winter days. In winter they make an excellent place to store fire wood or, more importantly, to hang clothes to dry, saving on the need to have an electric clothes dryer. This also removes unhealthy moisture from the house during winter. They also provide a more secure double-door rear-entry to the house.

The sunspace performs its passive solar heating function by transmitting solar radiation through its glazing and absorbing it on its interior surfaces. The solar radiation is converted to heat upon absorption. Some of the heat is rapidly transferred by natural convection to the sunspace air and some of it flows into massive elements in the sunspace (floor, walls and water containers) to be returned later. The sunspace is, thus, a direct gain space in which heat is used directly to maintain a temperature suitable for its intended secondary function, such as occasional living space. But the primary purpose of the sunspace as a solar heating system is to deliver heat to the adjacent building spaces. This may be by conduction through a masonry common wall, by natural convection through openings (doors, windows or special vents) in the common wall. The sunspace system then resembles an indirect gain, thermal storage wall. The common wall may also be insulated so that heat transfer occurs only by natural convection through openings. Then the sunspace system is in the isolated gain category.

Some sunspaces are operated as hybrid systems in which a fan is used to transfer heated air from the sunspace to other building spaces or to storage. Sunspaces have become very popular building features, both for the attractive space they provide and for their ability to deliver solar heat to adjacent spaces. The solar heating performance can indeed be very effective, often exceeding the performance of any other passive solar system occupying the same area of south-facing wall. The sunspace designed in the Bariloche solar house (see page 396) is a typical case of hybrid sunspace.

The sunspace works in many different ways. On sunny days it collects solar energy that can be transferred into the house. At night and during cold days it acts as a buffer, reducing heat loss. If the sunspace itself is heated or cooled by other means to normal comfort levels with auxiliary energy, the buffering characteristic of this isolated-gain passive solar system is lost. In this case, the benefits of solar heating are lost, and the total energy consumption of such a sunspace may be almost as much as that of the house itself. Sunspaces are popular because of their spatial and architectural qualities.

Semi-direct gain sunspace

This system incorporates a double-glazing system where the sun's rays absorbed by the internal surfaces of the sunspace and living areas are transferred into heat, with a marginal contribution of convective and storage effects.

Adjustment may be critical. Automatic control of openings and screens is expensive and not always reliable. Solar radiation can easily overheat the sunspace and the interiors. This can occur during sunny days of intermediate seasons (spring and autumn). Overheating must be reduced by ventilating the sunspace and, if necessary, part roofing the space.

Indirect-gain sunspaces

In this energy storage system a massive wall is placed between the sunspace and the building interior. The wall absorbs solar radiation and converts it into heat, gradually transferring the heat by conduction into the building mass and the interior spaces of the house. This sunspace configuration works well in winter. It can be difficult in summer when radiation levels are high and the collecting surfaces are not sufficiently shaded. Movable shading devices on the wall's external surface can avoid overheating. Such shading devices can find use throughout the year.

Storage walls have a high thermal capacity and a low conductivity rate. A means of controlling the high winter heat losses of the system, particularly during the night, is by using insulating shading devices on the external surface of the wall. Double glazing further reduces heat losses from the sunspace.

Thermosyphon sunspaces

Thermosyphon sunspaces absorb solar radiation, heat the sunspace air and increase the internal temperature of the sunspace. The sunspace air is transferred to the building interior using automatic shutters or valves at the top of the background wall. Valves at the bottom of the wall recover the cooler interior air. A convective effect is produced, exploiting the thermal stratification in the sunspace and optimising the heat gain in the house. A regulation system simultaneously controls the sunspace and interior room temperature levels, and allows air to flow from the sunspace to the interior rooms at appropriate temperatures. The main problem with any automatic system is that it presumes that there is one comfort temperature whereas, in reality over the year, people find very different temperatures comfortable. With a manual system that relies on opening top and bottom windows the house occupants can decide for themselves if the sunspace air is sufficiently warm to be used in the house.

Hybrid systems

The term *hybrid systems* is used to describe ideas and techniques that are not easily described by 'active' or 'passive' systems. Hybrid systems usually contain some active and some passive system characteristics. An example is the thermosyphon system. These passive solar convection systems use the buoyancy effects of heated fluids to transfer solar heat into building spaces or storage by convection. When they use mechanical assistance (pumps, ventilators), they are called hybrid systems. Air or water is the most common heat transfer medium of passive and active solar energy.

One type of hybrid convection system is the thermosyphon air panel. It uses flat-plate collectors mounted on the outside of an exterior sun-facing wall to heat air. Automatic vents located at the top and bottom of the panel allow hot air to flow directly into the space to be heated. The hot vented air is replaced at the bottom of the panel by cooler interior air.

ROCK BEDS

An effective and favourite hybrid application is the use of a rock bed in conjunction with a passive solar building. In many applications the rock bed is located beneath the source of hot air and thus natural convection cannot be used to transfer the heat. In this case a fan is normally employed, resulting in that part of the system technically being an active element. Rock beds can be used effectively in situations where there is an excess of energy in the form of air that is heated above the comfort level. It is desirable to remove this overheated air for three reasons:

1 to reduce the air temperature in the space and improve thermal comfort
2 to store the heat thus removed for later retrieval, and
3 to redistribute heat from the upper south part of the building where hot air tends to accumulate into the lower north part of the building that normally tends to run colder.

Imbalances in temperature in the building, which might be created by the passive elements operating alone, can be corrected.

It requires very careful design to remove heat from the rock bed in the form of warm air. This air is then blown into the space to be heated. The air temperatures that can be achieved are low, and the flow rates that would be required are therefore high. The effect of a high air-velocity at low temperatures may be cold and unpleasant. A much preferred approach is to remove the heat from the rock beds by means of radiation and convection from the rock bed container surface. In this case the rock bed is thermally coupled to the space that is to be heated, rather than being thermally isolated from it. A convenient approach that is often used is to place the rock bed underneath the floor of the building, although it would also be possible to place it behind one of the walls. Distribution of heat from the rock bed to the space is entirely passive. The floor temperature or wall surface temperature will only be a few degrees above the room temperature. If the installation is properly designed the net result will be a very comfortable situation, heating the house slowly from a large radiant panel.

Experience with under floor rock beds has been very favourable. Comfort is greatly improved by keeping the floor temperatures 3–6°C above what they normally would be. By increasing surface temperatures and thus increasing the mean radiant temperature within the space, the air temperatures can be reduced and energy savings that are even greater than the actual amount of heat released from the rock bed can be realised.

A technique that is suitable for residential applications is to divide the building into two thermal zones and accept fairly large temperature swings in one zone in order to stabilise temperatures in the other. In Zone 1, which is a direct-gain space, large temperature swings can be expected because there is a large excess of heat. Heat storage is in the mass separating the zones and in the floor of Zone 1. Depending on the size of Zone 1, its enclosing mass surface area and the glazing area, temperature swings of 12°C to 17°C can be anticipated. However, such swings can be completely acceptable (and perhaps even advantageous). Uses of such a space could be as a greenhouse, sun room, atrium, conservatory, transit area, vestibule or as an airlock entry. A principal advantage of this approach is the reduced temperature swings in Zone 2. This is a buffered space protected from the extremes of Zone 1 by the time delay and heat capacity effects of the mass wall. With a little care in the design, one can phase the time of heat arrival into Zone 2 so as to maintain an almost constant temperature. An example of the effective use of the two-zone approach is the house in Bariloche.

7.7.
The newly installed rock bed at Fuentes House in Bariloche, showing the concrete walls of the bed and the heat supply and extract ducts (Manuel Fuentes).

TIPS: ROCK BED SIZING

1a The rock bed volume should be $0.6\,m^3\,m^{-2}$ of sun-orientated glazing.
1b The airflow rate through the rock bed should be $0.03\,m^3\,s^{-1}$ for each m^2 of sun-orientated glazing.
2a More than one-third of the net heat should not be transferred out of the space to the bed rock.
2b The working bed temperature drop should be one-half of the working air drop.
3   The air velocity should not exceed $3.5\,m\,s^{-1}$ and $10\,ac\,h^{-1}$.
4a The pressure drop across the rock bed should be in the region 40–75 Pa.
4b The pressure drop across the ductwork should be less than one-fifth of the rock bed pressure drop.

THE IMPORTANCE OF THE ORIENTATION

A major part of the Oxford Ecohouse (see page 330) project involved the house's thermal performance, the simulation of its fabric, form and materials, and the subsequent iteration of the simulation to interrogate and understand the success of the thermal and energetic aspects of the house design. We were extremely fortunate to have been able to carry out the project in conjunction with one of the most experienced modellers of passive solar buildings, Dr Chiheb Bouden of the Tunisian Solar Energy Institute who developed the model and ran the simulations. With computer modelling of this sophistication, much of the success of the project depended not only on the model, but the skill with which it was developed and operated.

One of the aspects studied was the importance of the orientation in the thermal performance of the house. To this end, a simulation program called

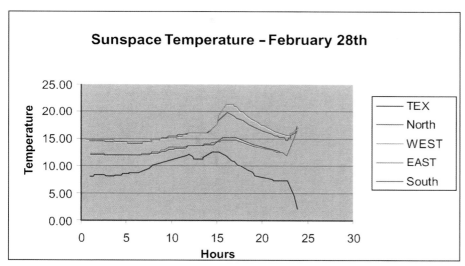

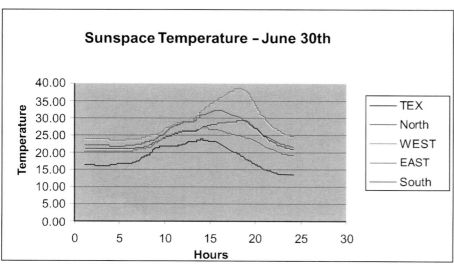

7.8.
Graphs showing the internal temperatures in sunspaces orientated to the cardinal points for the months of February and June.

TRNSYS was used. This program is widely used for modelling passive solar systems. TRNSYS is a very versatile tool because it can allow you to simulate a wide range of different systems. This makes the tool very powerful, in particular, for parametric simulations. TRNSYS is used by the majority of solar laboratories around the world and has been extensively validated for solar uses.

For studying and simulating the effect of the orientation, the existing south-facing orientation of the sunspace and house have been rotated, and simulated when the sunspace is facing west, then north, then east, requiring the rotation of the whole building to be simulated when facing, respectively, 90, 180 and 270 degrees.

Figures 7.8 and 7.9 show sunspace temperatures for the four orientations to the cardinal points and clearly demonstrate the advantages of the southerly aspect over most of the year. The north-facing sunspace is the coolest – closely

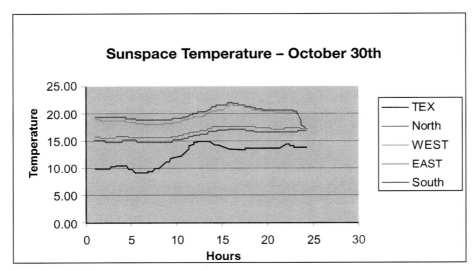

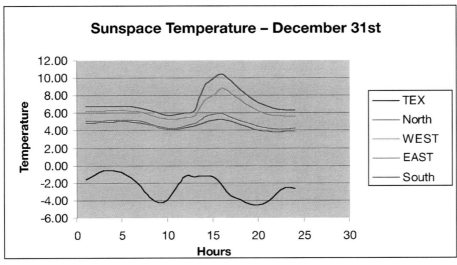

7.9.
Graphs showing the internal temperatures in sunspaces orientated to the cardinal points for the months of October and December.

followed by the east-facing sunspace – except for mid-summer when the sun sets in the north-west, and after 3 p.m. when heat from the sunspace air is above that of the east-facing sunspace, although still no better in performance than the south-facing sunspace. The east-facing sunspace is slightly warmer in summer when the solar gain coincides with the hottest time of day. Therefore, for summer performance of the house the east-facing sunspace is best although it has a poor winter performance.

In spring and autumn, the south- and the west-facing sunspaces are very similar in temperature, although in spring, the west-facing sunspace gets warmer than the south-facing sunspace after 3 p.m. It is in winter and summer that the advantages of the south-facing sunspace become apparent. In mid-summer afternoons the west-facing sunspace can get up to 8°C warmer – at nearly 38°C in late afternoon and early evening – than the south-facing sunspace which generally peaks at 32°C and falls off in temperature steadily after around 3 p.m. In winter, when the heat is most needed, the south-facing sunspace is warmer in mid-afternoon by around 2°C and is steadily

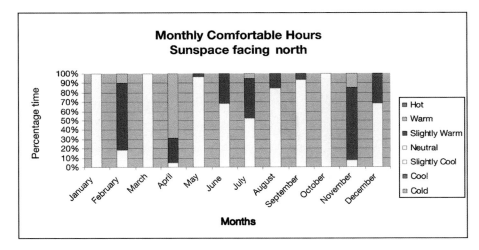

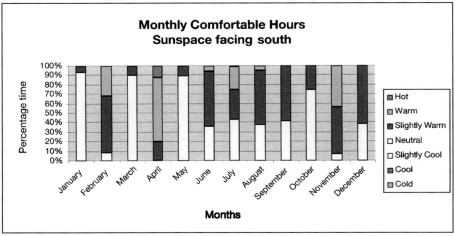

7.10.
Graphs showing the MCH for the sunspace facing north and south.

warmer than the west-facing sunspace over 24 hours. Thus, correct orientation can significantly alter the usefulness of the sunspace as a comfortable living area and as an effective buffer against the external climate when it is too hot or too cold.

Figures 7.10 and 7.11 demonstrate what difference the performance of the sunspace in the south (actual), north and west orientations make to the internal comfort of the house. The north orientation results in the lowest temperatures inside the house being achieved all year round. The orientation to west creates more warm and hot hours in summer, with some overheating beginning in the month of April, resulting in lower thermal comfort indoors. The east orientation gives cooler temperatures than the south orientation which is characterised by a lower number of 'slightly warm', 'warm' and 'hot' hours. Surprisingly, the hottest months indoors are April and November, due largely to the comparatively warm sun and the intermediate sun angle that still penetrates into the heart of the house.

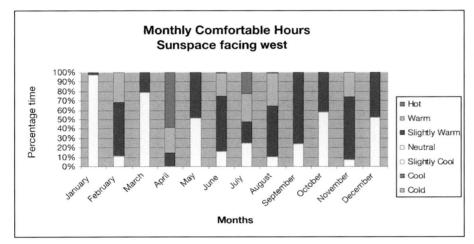

7.11.
Graphs showing the MCH for the sunspace facing west and east.

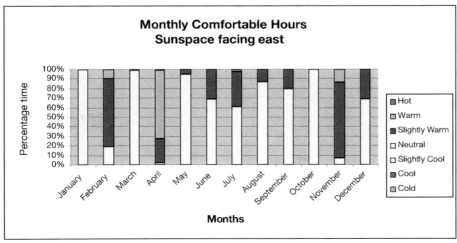

HOW MUCH DOES IT COST TO USE PASSIVE SOLAR SYSTEMS?

Today's passive solar heating systems can typically provide 30–70 per cent of residential heating requirements, depending upon the size of the passive solar system, the level of energy conservation being employed in the building envelope and the local climate. At the upper end of this range the use of specialised components is often required. These performance results are typical for single-family residential buildings, and small commercial and institutional buildings.

The economics of some passive solar techniques are difficult to determine because many features are part of the fabric of the house itself. Take the sunspace for example. The building owner may want to build a sunspace into the house. The capital cost for energy savings would then be zero. Where economic analysis is performed including capital costs, passive solar techniques often offer a good payback.

Passive solar systems have demonstrated their competitiveness with conventional fuels by saving 30 per cent and more of a building's space heating requirements in some climates, though their effectiveness varies from site to site.

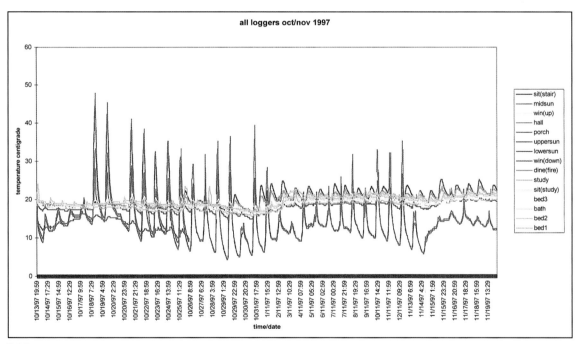

7.12.

Graph showing the temperatures in different spaces of the Oxford Ecohouse. These show that the temperatures in the sunspace can fluctuate considerably while the internal rooms maintain a much more steady temperature because of good design and high levels of thermal mass.

GOOD PUBLICATIONS ON PASSIVE SOLAR DESIGN

Balcomb, J. D. (1979). 'Designing fan forced rock beds'. *Solar Age*, November, p. 44.

Balcomb, J. D. (1980). *Passive Solar Design Handbook. Volume I*. National Technical Information Service, 5285 Port Royal Road, Springfield, VA 22161, USA.

Balcomb, J. D. (1982). *Passive Solar Design Handbook. Volume II*. National Technical Information Service, 5285 Port Royal Road, Springfield, VA 22161, USA.

Balcomb, J. D. (1983). Conservation and Passive Solar Guidelines for New Mexico. Los Alamos National Laboratory, Report No. LA-UR-83-1452, USA.

Balcomb, J. D. (1983). Heat Storage and Distribution Inside Passive Solar Buildings. Los Alamos National Laboratory, Report No. LA-9684-MS, USA.

Building Research Station Digest 41 (1970). HMSO, London.

Curtis, E. J. W. (1974). 'Solar energy applications in architecture'. *Low Temperature Solar Collection of Solar Energy in the UK*. UK Branch of the International Solar Energy Society, London.

Duffie, J. A. and Beckman, W. A. (1977). *Solar Engineering of Thermal Processes*. Wiley Interscience, New York and London.

Hastings, S. R. (ed.) (1995). *Solar Low Energy Houses*. International Energy Agency Task 13. James & James (Science Publishers) Ltd, London.

Hestens, A. G., Hastings, S. R. and Saxhof, B. (eds) (1997). *Solar Energy Houses,* Strategies, Technologies and Examples. IEA, James & James (Science Publishers) Ltd, London.

Kreith, F. and Kreider, J. F. (1975). *Solar Heating and Cooling*. McGraw-Hill, Washington, DC.

Lebens, R. (1980). *Passive Solar Heating Design*. Applied Science Publishers.

Lebens, R. (1983). 'Documents of Second European Passive Solar Competition, 1982'. In *Passive Solar Architecture in Europe 2*. The Architectural Press, London.

Littler, J. G. F. and Thomas, R. B. (1984). *Design with Energy, The Conservation and Use of Energy in Buildings*. Cambridge Urban and Architectural Studies, Cambridge University Press, UK.

Mazria, E. (1979). *The Passive Solar Energy Book*. Rodale Press, Emmaus.

McFarland, R. D. and Stromberg, P. (1980). *Passive Solar Design Handbook*. Editors Balcomb, J. D. and Anderson, B., Department of Energy, Washington, DC.

Olgyay, V. (1963). *Design with Climate*. Princeton University Press, Princeton, NJ.

Page, J. K. (1976). *Solar Energy – a UK Assessment*. UK-ISES (International Solar Energy Society).

Wright, D. (1978). *Natural Solar Architecture*. van Nostrand Reinhold.

8 PHOTOVOLTAICS

WHAT ARE PHOTOVOLTAICS?

Photovoltaic cells convert sunlight directly into electrical energy. The electricity they produce is DC (direct current) and can either be:

- used directly as DC power
- converted to AC (alternating current) power, or
- stored for later use.

The basic element of a photovoltaic system is the solar cell that is made of a semiconductor material, typically silicon. There are no moving parts in a solar cell, its operation is environmentally benign and, if the device is correctly encapsulated against the environment, there is nothing that will wear out.

Because sunlight is universally available, photovoltaic devices can provide electricity wherever it is needed. Since the power source will last for hundreds of thousands of years, and it is very hard to interfere with its delivery, photovoltaic (PV) is widely expected to become a major source of power worldwide in the long term.

Photovoltaic systems are modular and so their electrical power output can be engineered for virtually any application, from low-powered wristwatches, calculators, remote telecommunications systems and small battery-chargers to huge centralised power stations generating energy only from the sun. PV systems can be incrementally built up with successive additions of panels easily accommodated, unlike more conventional approaches to generating energy such as fossil or nuclear fuel stations, which must be multimegawatt plants to be economically feasible.

> **HOW PV CELLS WORK**
> Although PV cells come in a variety of forms, the most common structure is a sandwich of semiconductor materials into which a large-area diode, or p-n junction, has been formed. In the presence of light an electric charge is generated across the junction between the two materials to create a charge similar to that between an anode and a cathode. The fabrication processes for making the cells tend to be traditional semiconductor processes, the same as those used to make microchips,

by 'doping' the silicon with different elements using diffusion and ion implantation of the elements into the silicon. The electrical current is transferred from the cell through a grid of metal contacts on the front of the cell that does not impede the sunlight from entering the silicon of the cell. A contact on the back of the cell completes the circuit and an anti-reflection coating minimises the amount of sunlight reflected back out from the silicon, so maximising the light used to generate electricity, as shown in Figure 8.1. See 21ADPV for a more detailed account of how a cell works.

Photovoltaic panels have been commercially available since the mid-1970s and were initially used to power some early demonstration buildings, such as those that are still working at the Centre for Alternative Technology in Wales. However, it was the 1990s that saw the first great boom in PV buildings around the world. Germany and Japan lead the way with Japan installing 110 MWp in 2001, Germany installing 77 MWp and USA installing 18 MWp. These three programmes accounted for over half the world PV production in 2001. The Netherlands and Spain came next in the table of installations. Some countries are way behind in the solar race. Britain installed around 300 KWp in 2001.

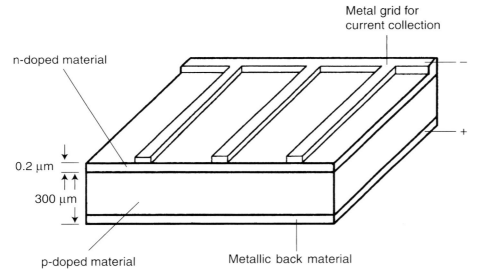

8.1.
Cross-section of a solar cell.

WHAT IS A PV SYSTEM?

PV cells are typically grouped together in a module for ease of use. A PV system consists of one or more PV modules, which convert sunlight directly into electricity, and a range of other system components that may include an AC/DC inverter, back-up source of energy, battery to store the electricity until it is needed, battery charger, control centre, mounting structures and miscellaneous wires and fuses.

> **WARNING**
> Direct current (DC) electricity is much more dangerous to handle than alternating current (AC) electricity, which is typically used for all household appliances. This is because there is no break in the flow of a DC current and, if you grab hold of an exposed DC wire, the muscles contract and it is very difficult to let the wire go again. Great care should always be taken when dealing with DC electricity.

WHY PV IN BUILDINGS?

Even in cloudy, northern latitudes, PV panels can generate sufficient power to meet all, or part of, the electricity demand of a building. The Oxford Ecohouse (see page 330), for example, incorporates 48 PV panels on the roof that generate enough energy to lower the household electricity bills by 70 per cent.

The flexibility of PV enables its use in many building products, such as solar roof tiles, curtain walls and decorative screens, which can directly replace conventional materials in the building fabric. These products serve the same structural and weather protection purposes as their traditional alternatives but offer the additional benefit of generating the power to run the house.

WHAT'S GREEN ABOUT PV?

The electricity produced by every square metre of PV can effectively displace emissions of more than two tonnes of CO_2 to the atmosphere over its

8.2.
The photovoltaic roof at the Bariloche Ecohouse (Manuel Fuentes) (see page 396).

Table 8.1. Environmental impacts of PV manufacture

Burden	PV (monocrystalline silicon)	UK electricity generation mix
Energy ($kWhth\ kWh^{-1}$)	0.38	0.61
CO_2 ($g\ kWh^{-1}$)	74	672
SO_2 ($g\ kWh^{-1}$)	0.43	4.20
NO_x ($g\ kWh^{-1}$)	0.21	2.10
Particles ($g\ kWh^{-1}$)	0.03	0.32

Table 8.2. Environmental benefits of PV systems

Energy and emissions	PV (monocrystalline silicon)	UK electricity generation mix	Total avoided emissions (in 25 years)
Energy (GWhth)	29	47	18
CO_2 (tonnes)	6	52	46
SO_2 (tonnes)	0.03	0.32	0.29
NO_x (tonnes)	0.02	0.16	0.15
Particles (tonnes)	0.002	0.02	0.02

lifetime. Few now dispute that CO_2 emissions can continue to increase at current rates without dire consequences, such as global warming. Wider use of PV power in buildings can help to reduce such environmental impacts of buildings that are responsible for generating over 50 per cent of all emissions of greenhouse gases globally.

Let us use the Oxford Ecohouse as an example. In order to calculate the environmental impacts of the PV system it is necessary to know the UK energy generation conversion values, the amount of CO_2 released into the atmosphere for every unit of energy delivered to a house. It has been estimated that an average energy conversion efficiency for thermal electricity generation plants in the UK is around 37 per cent. This results from an electricity mix generated from 65 per cent coal, 15 per cent gas, 22 per cent nuclear and 9 per cent oil. For the PV manufacture assumptions see Energy Technology Support Unit (1996).

Based on the monitored data, the PV system produces 3093 kWh per year, that is around 77 000 kWh in its 25-year life cycle.

The Oxford Ecohouse PV system avoids the release of 1.84 tonnes CO_2 per year. These values can be extrapolated to give the avoided emissions in the case of a massive programme of installing PV on residential building. A system one-eighth of the size of the Oxford Ecohouse would avoid 230 kg CO_2 per annum.

WHAT WILL IT COST TO USE PV IN BUILDINGS?

Solar electric PV systems are now an economic and viable technology in many parts of the world. More than that, they are a sensible economic investment for ordinary householders who want to begin to protect themselves from future changes related to energy and the climate. They should begin to consider the following:

- Climate change is driving the move towards carbon taxes that will make energy more expensive.
- Fossil fuel depletion will push up oil and gas prices. We have around 40 years of conventional oil reserves left and around 60 years of gas left. By 2020 oil and gas scarcity will make future energy prices very unpredictable.
- Climate change may well make heating and cooling our houses more expensive in energy terms as the climate gets warmer or colder.
- Security of energy supply. PV systems can provide electricity during conventionally produced electricity blackouts resulting from poor supply conditions or bad weather. There is already a range of uses for which a secure energy supply should be essential; these include, water pumping, electric garage doors and gates, lift safety systems, smoke and fire alarms, emergency lighting and security systems, computer UPS systems and communications systems.

Investment by people now in their high-earning years in energy efficiency and renewable energy will pay dividends in, say, 10 years when they retire and must inevitably face higher energy bills they are less able to afford. Anyone with a £500-a-year electricity bill would be wise to envisage at least a doubling of electricity costs in 10–15 years time. Will your pension cover £1000 a year for one bill?

Costs of installing PV systems today vary significantly according to the technology used and the application and the efficiency of the system. Capital costs of PV panels are broadly similar to prestige cladding materials, ranging from £350 to £750 per m^2 depending on the technology and its detail. Prices are expected to fall significantly over the next decade as demand grows and the PV industry achieves economies of scale in production. In parts of Germany and the USA (Sacramento municipality) the cost of installing one watt of PV power into a home has already fallen to around £2.75 per watt, which is very low compared with current UK estimates of £6 per watt for an installed system. In those countries, the impact of early investment in the technology by national and local government bodies has paid dividends for consumers while people in countries such as the UK have to suffer because of short-sighted investment policies in this, one of the most important technologies of the twenty-first century.

Your own investment decision should also take account of the marginal cost of the PV system (capital cost minus the cost of the alternative material) and power output. PV systems are not difficult to install and, if maintained properly (annual washing), have an expected lifetime of around 25 years.

What is certain is that today PVs should be an essential feature of a real ecohouse, because ecohouses are setting the agenda for building in a changing climate and helping to prepare society for the 'post-fossil fuel age'. PVs have a very important role to play, like solar hot water systems, in the new agenda for buildings; the earliest PV 'pioneers' in the twentieth century often installed PV systems for ecological reasons rather than economic ones. However, in some farsighted cities, such as Aachen in Germany, a green tariff on every electricity bill enabled the local utility company to pay every house-holder with a PV roof DM2 per kW exported. This enables householders to pay back the installation costs in around 10 years for systems that will last for 20 years.

But it is no use placing a PV system on an energy-profligate building and expecting it to solve the problems wrought by the building designer. This is just throwing good money after bad. Forget PV for air-conditioned buildings for the foreseeable future. PVs will work well with low-speed fan-assisted passive cooling systems, such as earth-coupling and the night cooling of buildings (see Chapter 5 on ventilation).

To use PVs properly the building electricity loads should be as low as pos-sible, and only then should the system be designed to meet part or all of those loads to give you a magic building that generates its own energy.

ADVANTAGES OF PHOTOVOLTAICS AS A DOMESTIC SOURCE OF ENERGY

- It is a clean green energy source. It does not produce CO_2, NO_x or SO_2 emissions.
- The silicon PV panels are non-toxic in production.
- The energy payback (the time for the PV to produce as much energy as is required for manufacture) is 2–5 years, while the working life of a PV panel can be well over 20 years.
- Energy is generated on site so there are very few losses in transport, unlike remotely generated supplies relying on long supply lines.
- It is reliable. You just put them on the roof and they work. Panel war-ranties are now typically for 20 years.
- They are silent.
- They are low maintenance. Once installed they will simply require their surfaces to be cleaned, especially in dusty environments.
- They can provide power in locations remote from the grid.
- PVs are a transportable technology and can be moved between buildings.
- They can provide power during blackouts.

THE PROCESS OF DESIGNING A PV SYSTEM

There are many different types of PV systems available with different fea-tures, capabilities and costs. It is important to follow the steps described here to get the PV system that fulfils your own particular needs.

Step 1. Choose your system

What type of system do you require? Do you want batteries? Do you want to power DC or AC equipment? Do you want to grid-connect the system to use the National Grid as a store so you can export the excess during the day when you are out at work and then draw in electricity from the grid when you need it at night? This is called a grid-connected system. Do you want to use PV and wind to cover all your power needs? The different system types are outlined in Figures 8.3 to 8.6 (Source: www.windandsun.co.uk.).

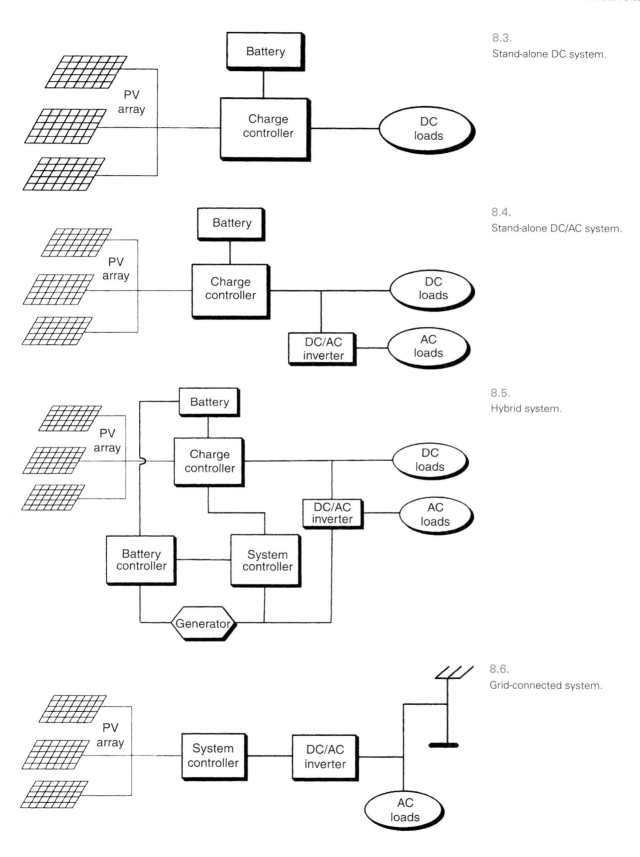

8.3.
Stand-alone DC system.

8.4.
Stand-alone DC/AC system.

8.5.
Hybrid system.

8.6.
Grid-connected system.

Step 2. Determining the average daily sunlight hours at your site

At the meteorological station closest to your site, look up the average sunlight hours for each month of the year at your site location. Determine the Minimum Monthly Sunlight Hours at your location for the months that you expect to be using the PV system.

The Minimum Monthly Sunlight Hours is the number of sunlight hours for the month with the lowest average number of sunshine hours. It is generally best not to consider the winter months among your months of use when determining Minimum Monthly Sunlight Hours, even if you are installing a PV system in a permanent residence, as the number of sunlight hours in these four months tends to be low. Unless a very large system is purchased, some form of back-up power, such as a generator or a grid supply, will be needed for the four winter months. The most frequently used approach is to design a PV system for a full-time residence to operate optimally for the eight months of the year when the sunlight hours are greatest. The month with the lowest number of sunlight hours out of the eight brightest months is selected as the Minimum Monthly Sunlight Hours month.

If you definitely do not wish to have a back-up source of energy, or the number of sunlight hours at your location during the four winter months is high, you can use all 12 months to determine your Minimum Monthly Sunlight Hours.

Divide Minimum Monthly Sunlight Hours by 30 to get the Average Daily Sunlight Hours.

Simple sizing tools are available on the internet, and are continuously being improved and updated. The freeware programs are often quite accurate, enough for a small building calculation, and any good PV supplier should be able to confirm your calculations too.

> **Note:** Keep in mind that the PV array should be located so that it receives the most hours of sunlight. Avoid obstacles, such as trees or buildings, blocking direct sunlight.

Step 3. Determining your total daily energy load

Make an Energy Budget Chart as shown below. Begin in the 'Electrical loads' column by listing all the devices in your home that consume electricity. Make sure to include everything from the hairdryer to power tools.

Energy Budget Chart sample

Electrical loads	Rated watts	Hours/day	Daily watt hours
Colour television	330	3	990
Microwave oven	1000	0.25	250
Vacuum cleaner	800	0.75	600

The rated wattage of each device can be determined either by using the list of power ratings of common tools and appliances given in Table 8.3 to find the typical power consumption values for common appliances, or by looking at the back panel of each device to determine its specific rated wattage. If the rated wattage is not listed on the device, it can be calculated by multiplying the amps (A) of the device by the voltage (Vac for alternating current and Vdc for direct current).

Example: if a blender is 2.45 A and 220 Vac, multiply 2.45 A by 220 Vac to get 540 rated watts.

Table 8.3 does not provide rated wattages for refrigerators or freezers. This is because they cycle on and off automatically thus making it difficult to estimate the hours per day they are operated. Instead, the table provides the typical daily consumption in watt-hours. Alternatively, if your refrigerator or freezer has an EnerGuide label on the front indicating the number of kilowatt hours (kWh) the appliance uses per year, or per month, you can use this to calculate Daily Watt Hours. Divide the kWh value by 365, if it provides the yearly number, or by 30 if it provides the monthly number. Multiply the result by 1000 to determine the Daily Watt Hours of the appliance.

Example: if a refrigerator has an EnerGuide rating of 768 kWh year^{-1}, divide by 365 to get 2.104 kWh day^{-1}. Multiply 2.104 kWh day^{-1} by 1000 to get 2104 Daily Watt Hours.

Add the Daily Watt Hours for all devices to determine Total Daily Watt Hours. Divide the Total Daily Watt Hours by an assumed Inverter Efficiency Factor (see box) of 0.85 to get the Total Daily Load.

> PV cells generate direct current (DC) and the PV system batteries store electricity as DC. Most common appliances, however, require alternating current (AC). As a result, an inverter is needed to convert DC to AC power. Some power will be lost in the conversion, as inverters are on average 75–90 per cent efficient. For the purposes of this calculation, assume that your Inverter Efficiency Factor is 85 per cent.

Total Daily Watt Hours divided by Inverter Efficiency Factor of 0.85 equals Total Daily Load (Watt Hours).

Table 8.3. Typical power ratings (in watts) of common tools and appliances[*]

Blender	700	Lighting (60 watt bulb)	60
Block heater	500	Lighting (fluorescent, 15 cm single ended)	9
Bubble jet computer printer	40	Lighting (fluorescent, 1.2 m double ended)	50
Clock	2	Microwave oven	1000
Coffee maker	900	Radio, solid state	5
Computer/monitor	75	Satellite receiver	25
Deep well pump	1350	Saw, circular	950
Washing machine (automatic)	500	Saw, jig	400
Fan (portable)	115	Vacuum cleaner	800

(Continued)

Table 8.3. (*Continued*)

Stereo	30	Furnace fan motor	350
Television (black and white)	200	Gas clothes dryer	250
Television (colour)	330	Hairdryer	1500
Toaster	1150	Hand drill	300
Iron	1000	VCR	120
Laser printer	700	Dishwasher (excluding hot water)	1300

Typical daily electricity consumption (watt-hours) of refrigerators and freezers (pre-1993 and later)

Freezer (15 cu. ft)	2500	1600
Freezer (15 cu. ft, frost-free)	3600	2500
Refrigerator/freezer (12 cu. ft)	2500	1600
Refrigerator/freezer (12 cu. ft, frost-free)	3100	1700

*Please note these are approximate values only. For exact numbers, consult the appliance, its accompanying instructions or the product supplier.

Table 8.4. Typical Daily Watt Hour consumption at hourly intervals in winter

Load type	Watts	Min/hr	6	7	8	9	10	11	12	13	14	15	16	17	18	19	20	21	22	23	24	1	2	3	4	5
Hoover	500	30						250		(once per week only)																
Bed radio	7	60	7																							
Food mixer	100	10						17																		
Fridge	200	10	33	33	33	33	33	33	33	33	33	33	33	33	33	33	33	33	33	33	33	33	33	33	33	33
Kitchen radio	7	60			7				7					7	7											
Fax	250	4					17					17			17				17							
Game Boy	5	60		5							5															
Stereo	200	0																								
TV	64	60		64								64		64	64	64	64									
Water pump	50	20																								
Fire system	50	60	50	50	50	50	50	50	50	50	50	50	50	50	50	50	50	50	50	50	50	50	50	50	50	50
Boiler	10	60	10	10	10	10	10	10	10	10	10	10	10	10	10	10	10	10	10	10	10	10	10	10	10	10
Dishwash m/c	1200	20								400																
Iron	500	60							500																	
Kettle	0	20			0		0					0		0				0								
Toaster	800	10			133																					
Washing machine	500	20		167																						
1st landing lamp	10	60	10	10	10										10	10	10	10	10	10	10	10	10	10	10	10
Bathroom lamp	10	30		5									5			5										
Main bed lamp	13	60		13											13			13								
Top landing lamp	10	60			10										10	10	10									
WC & wash lamp	10	30			5			5					5			5			5							
Kitchen/diner lamp	13	60		13							13	13	13	13	13	13	13	13	13							
Study lamp	12	60			12	12	12	12	12	12	12	12	12	12	12	12	12	12	12	12						
Totals	4521	924	103	377	270	105	122	360	629	105	505	135	192	130	158	224	202	197	210	128	120	103	103	103	103	103

Step 4. Determining the load profile

Once you have made the calculation for the total load draw up a graph of when those loads will be used. Put hours of the day along the y axis and the loads on the x axis and plot the hours when each piece of equipment will be used and the wattage for that hour. When you have done this, it can be totalled to make a graph of your projected daily electricity use profile. A load profile such as this will have two characteristics that are important when designing your system:

- The typical **peak load** of your house. This is the most electricity you will need at one time.
- The typical **base load** of your house. This is the energy that is needed constantly for items such as your refrigerator and fax machine.

Now you have your first load table sit down and go through it and practice a little of:

- **Load reducing or shaving.** Get rid of all the electric appliances you think you can do without, can replace with lower-energy items or simply have less of them. This may include items such as an extra light in the hall, or four side lamps in the sitting room. Change all the light bulbs to low-energy ones and decide if now is the right time to buy a new low-energy washing machine or fridge. These actions will reduce the total load of the system as well as its peaks and base load.
- **Load shifting.** Where previously you had the washing machine and the iron on at the same time start a new habit of doing only one high-energy chore at a time. You will find that your peaks are often significantly reduced, although the base load and the total load will not change. This is why in Germany it has been found that the people who use their PV electricity in homes best

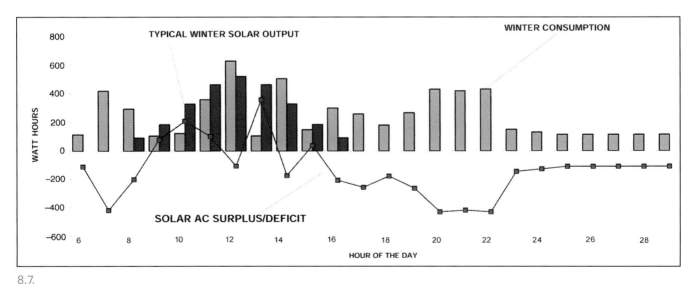

8.7.

Load profile of the Oxford Ecohouse showing the electricity generated in winter.

are retired people who are at home all day and can manage their chores to reduce peak loads.

REDUCING THE LOADS IN YOUR HOME

Reducing loads by low-energy lighting

- Do not over-light the house. Use a careful selection of background lighting, task lighting and feature lighting to make sure that you are not wasting money and energy. Light the floor where you want to walk, not the ceiling, and the desktop where you want to study, not the walls.
- Use lower general lighting levels.
- Avoid dark lampshades that absorb the light.
- Always use energy-saving fluorescent bulbs that cost more to buy but work out cheaper in the long run. Traditional filament bulbs convert around three-quarters of the energy they consume into heat and not light, which may be good in winter but is silly in summer.

Reducing loads by careful selection of equipment

- **Freezers.** Get rid of the second freezer and use a chest freezer if possible, not an upright one from which the cold air tumbles when opened. Look for low-energy-rated freezers, with thick insulation around them and good door seals; these can be checked with a bit of paper at the shop. If the paper slips easily out of the door when it is cold the door is poorly sealed. Damaged door seals should be replaced in older models. Do not site them next to heat sources such as cookers or tumble dryers. Allow air to circulate freely around the heat exchange element so heat does not build up around it.
- **Fridges.** Check very carefully for the energy rating of the fridge and buy the lowest-energy fridge you can afford.
- **Fridges and freezers using CFCs and HCFCs** should be avoided. Look out for hydrocarbon-based models using butane or propane that neither destroy the ozone nor produce greenhouse gases.
- **Disposal of old fridges** and freezers should be arranged through the local council if possible as they may have schemes to prevent the release of dangerous gases into the atmosphere.
- **Washing machines** should use a hot water supply not heat their own water, which uses a lot of electricity. They should also have a half- or low-load setting to save wasting electricity on a small wash. Side-fill machines use 50–70 per cent of the water used by top-fill machines and are lower in their energy consumption as well. Buy a machine with a high spin-speed of, say, 3000 r.p.m. as these take less time to spin clothes than the 1000/1500 r.p.m. machines.
- **Spin dryers,** where adequate, are much more electrically efficient than tumble dryers, which dry the clothes with electrically-generated heat. New EU spin dryers will dry clothes to a 35 per cent moisture content rather than the older models that retained up to 80 per cent moisture content.
- **Tumble dryers.** Gas models dry up to twice as fast as electric models and running costs are around one-third of those for an electric dryer. Good temperature and time controls are essential to prevent overdrying of the clothes. Much better still, build a winter drying space for clothes and save yourself lots of money in the long run.

- **TVs, radios, music players, microwaves, computers.** Check the plated energy rating on the machine before you buy it and choose a low-energy model.
- **Kettles.** Choose gas for your kettle, if possible, because of the lower CO_2 emissions for this fuel, taking into account that the kettle will more often be boiled at night and in winter than in summer so the PV electricity may not be used to heat it.

See: *Save Energy Save Money* booklet (1995) from CAT; *Lower Carbon Futures* (2000) from ECI.

Step 5. Sizing the PV system

The optimum size of a system depends on a number of external factors, such as cost of the system, the available budget, government subsidies, the energy payback policy of the local utility company and the amount of PV energy to be used in the building. Here are some options.

- **A base load array.** This generates over the year typically just above your building base load for, in the UK, around 9 out of the 12 months of the year. A base load system will rarely export anything to the grid and can be designed never to do so. However, the base load of the building can work out to be a substantial proportion of your annual electricity consumption and, in countries such as Britain, the price paid for exported electricity is very low. Generating and using as much of your own electricity as possible is currently the most economic way of using PVs in the UK. A typical nominal size for such system is 500 Wp.
- **A stand-alone system.** For stand-alone systems batteries are used to store the energy from when it is generated until it is needed. The total array output should exceed the domestic loads as calculated previously.
- **Zero-energy house grid-connected supply.** The total annual domestic load should be equal to, or less than, the array output over 12 months.

Step 6. Choosing the modules

There are six important considerations when choosing a panel type:

1 power output required of the panel
2 size of the available roof for panels
3 what colour you wish the roof to be
4 the appearance/texture of the panels
5 what size panels fit into the architectural image of the building
6 the desired durability of the panels.

The required PV array area (A_{PV} in units of m^2) can be calculated from the chosen nominal PV power using the formula

$$A_{PV} = \frac{P_{PV}}{\eta_{PV}}$$

where P_{PV} (KW) is the nominal power of the PV array and η_{PV} (fraction) is the efficiency of the modules.

The amount of electricity to be generated from your roof as a fraction of the domestic load is dealt with above. If you know the peak wattage required then a review of the panel outputs will determine how many of each of the different types you will need to achieve the necessary wattage for the system. If you choose the lower efficiency, and cheaper, amorphous silicon panels then you will need more roof area to support them. If you want to use the more efficient polycrystalline modules then less roof space is required; the most efficient panels, monocrystalline modules, not only require less space to generate the same wattage but are also more durable.

Table 8.5. Choosing the module type

Module type	Appearance	Colour	Efficiencies (%)	Durability (years)
Monocrystalline	Module composed of circular polygonal shapes	Blue black	10–16	25–30
Polycrystalline	Sparkling crystal chaotic surface	Blue black	8–12	20–25
Amorphous	Matt dull surface	Red, green, orange, blue black, yellow	4–8	15–20

When designing the array, do think carefully about the colour of the cover strips that will link each module. Are the cover strips to be the same colour as the modules or form part of the elevational features of the building with contrasting colours? Panel manufacturers may be able to produce special modules for your building cut to specification. Discuss this with manufacturers. In the development of elevations of new solar buildings the rhythms of the solar panels can form a strong design feature. Use the modules to influence the size of other features in the house, such as doors and windows. Line up, both horizontally and vertically, the proportions of the solar features to introduce balance and harmony into the appearance of the house.

Step 7. Choosing the inverter

An inverter is needed in most residential PV systems to convert the DC power from the array to AC power. The inverter size needed will depend on whether:

HOW TO CHOOSE AND SIZE AN INVERTER
The optimum power ratio (inverter/PV module power) for a given inverter depends mainly on how much sunshine hits the array at what times of day. This gives the shape of the irradiance distribution, which is determined by local climate and the slope of the PV generator.

The selection of an inverter for a **grid-connected system** generally only takes into account the relative size of the inverter to the PV array. Since PV generators very rarely deliver their full nominal power, results obtained from the monitoring of the German 1000-roof programme show that inverters can be undersized with respect to the PV generator to reduce cost. Output power rating of the inverter for an optimally orientated PV roof generator should be 80–90 per cent of the generator rating. For vertical facades, even values around 50–60 per cent are sufficient. The websites of the main suppliers (e.g. SMA) have a simple sizing routing which enables selection of the best match of inverter to any make, model or technology type of PV panel.

In **a stand-alone system** the size of the array and the inverter must be matched to the watts required for the largest load that will be operated on the system at one time. To calculate this first determine the device with the largest rated wattage of all of the devices to be operated on the system. This could, for example, be the microwave, which can have a rated wattage of up to 1500 W. If you plan to be very careful about only running one device at a time, then you will need an inverter large enough to handle the largest load. If you think that there is a possibility that you will be running more than one load at a time, then you must have an inverter large enough to handle the largest possible combination of loads.

IMPORTANT ATTRIBUTES OF INVERTERS

- Maximum output
- Rated power factor
- Input/output voltages
- Number of phases
- Frequency: 50 Hz
- Protective apparatus:
  - protection against overvoltage and overcurrent
  - protection against islanding
  - fulfil local utility company's requirement
- Performance aptitudes:
  - high efficiency
  - low harmonic distortion
  - maximum power point capabilities
  - low self-consumption.

1 A stand-alone system or a self-sufficient system is desired
2 Base loads are going to be matched.

For the second option, an inverter which matches the PV and the voltage DC output is needed. It must also conform to the electricity regulation of the country in which it is used. In the UK small domestic systems must meet the G77 regulations, so check with your supplier which models have been approved. In some cases a system with 'AC Modules' may be designed by using the new single-module inverters.

An example of how to size a stand-alone system is as follows: assume a deep well pump (1350 W) and a washing machine (500 W) are operated at the same time, and there is a possibility that other items, such as the stereo (30 W) and a light (60 W) will also be in use. You will need an inverter that can handle 1350 + 500 + 30 + 60 = 1940 W at once. The larger the inverter needed, the more expensive it will be. You might want to try to schedule certain operations so that you do not have too many devices operating at once. This will reduce the largest potential combined wattage that the inverter is required to handle.

Once you have determined your largest combined potential wattage, select an inverter wattage and find a suitably priced corresponding inverter. Be sure to choose an inverter wattage that exceeds your largest potential combined load. Select a price on the basis of the range given.

Step 8. Installing the system

Photovoltaic modules generate the most electricity when they face the sun directly. Integration of PV modules in a building surface may influence the size of the module used, the size of the array, its inclination and its direction.

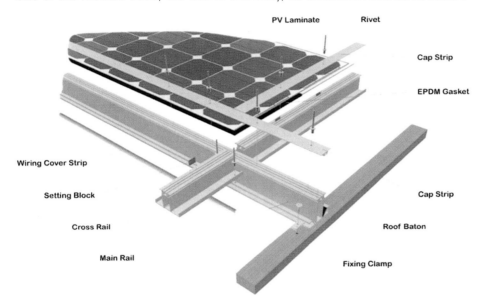

PV Laminate   Rivet

Cap Strip

EPDM Gasket

Wiring Cover Strip

Setting Block

Cross Rail

Main Rail

Cap Strip

Roof Baton

Fixing Clamp

8.8.
A typical mounting system (Bruce Cross).

Several mounting techniques are available with a number of roof structures, styles and designs. Installing the array requires mechanically mounting the modules, attaching the electrical interconnections and checking the performance of the completed array source circuits. All phases of array installation involve working with electrically active components, which can be particularly dangerous with DC supplies. Each option for mounting and wiring an array will present its own special installation requirements.

HOW TO GET THE ANGLE RIGHT FOR YOUR PV ARRAY
This issue depends on the design concept of the particular PV system:

1 If the intention is to maximise the PV output over the year, the PV modules need to be inclined with an angle equal to the site's latitude (from the horizontal).
2 If the intention is to maximise the PV production during winter, the PV modules have to be inclined 10° higher than in case 1 to catch the low winter sun.
3 If the intention is to extend the 'solar' season (where PV production is at its maximum), the PV modules have to be inclined 10° less than in case 1.

8.9.
Details of the mounting system at the Bariloche Ecohouse, as designed by Marshall and Associates (Manuel Fuentes).

Useful design and construction tips for people wanting to install PV

- Make sure everyone is clear who has responsibility for wiring and wire sizing of the:
  - module wires to the string connectors
  - string connectors to the inverter
  - inverter to the domestic loads board
  - electric loads board to the house export and import meters.
- Make sure you comply with the lightning protection requirements of the local utility company. The inverter should always be earthed.
- Ensure that you have a simple way of determining which module on the roof is attached to which wire coming in through the ceiling for later testing in case of module failure.
- Make sure that nowhere in the system does the wiring come into contact with damp or condensation, for instance adjacent to uninsulated cold water pipes.
- Locating the inverter near the DC array minimises power losses.
- The mains supply should always be disconnected before the PV supply before working on the system and vice versa for reconnection.
- Make sure that the mounting frame is weather sealed.

These features, and many others besides, are dealt with in the DTI publication *Photovoltaics in Buildings – Guide to the Installation of PV Systems*, DTI/Pub URN 02/788. This guide also gives drafts of installation certificates, inspection and test procedures, plus guidance for electrical connection application and regulations for the UK.

OTHER WAYS OF USING PHOTOVOLTAICS IN HOUSES

PV shades

Sunshading is an important part of many designs, and the shading member can be utilised as a PV panel since the mounting structure is already provided. Caution must be exercised when calculating the spacings, lest the units shade each other at some times of year.

PV tiles

PV roof tiles have been manufactured in several countries. The advantage of using a traditional roof product is that normal building trade practice can be used, and there is little resistance to the concept from the naturally conservative building trade. However, tiles are small components and a large number is required for an installation – this implies that large numbers of interconnections and a mix of building trades are needed (e.g. electricians must be prepared to work on a roof, or roofers must be able perform an electrical function).

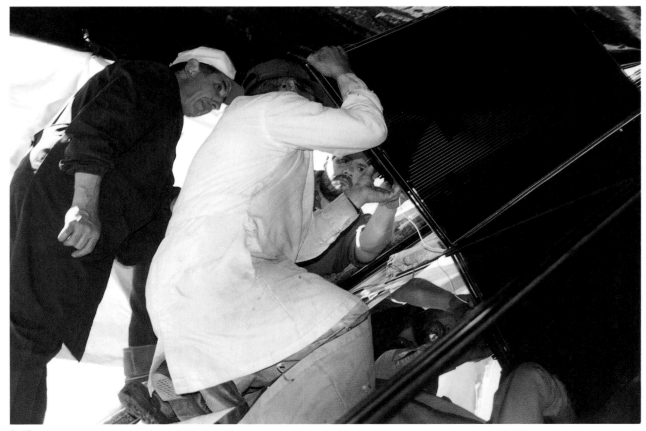

8.10.
Installing the PV system at the Bariloche Ecohouse (Manuel Fuentes).

Translucent PVs, e.g. over sunspaces

These are frequently adaptations of standard face-sealed sloping glazing systems, where the PV may optionally be built into a double-glazed sealed unit. These are particularly suitable to buildings where the PV is visible from the inside, and can provide a varying degree of transparency for internal daylighting needs.

SYSTEM MAINTENANCE AND CHECKS

- Examine the PV array structure for signs of deterioration.
- Check PV modules for cracked cells and glazing.
- Check wiring for rodent damage, indicated by cracking or fraying of wires.
- Check electrical leakage to ground.

CASE STUDY: THE OXFORD ECOHOUSE

In order to take readers through the process of building a PV array on their own house the example of the Oxford Ecohouse will be used to describe from experience what is involved in building a PV array, designed by Energy Equipment Testing Services in Cardiff.

The Oxford Ecohouse is owned and was designed by Sue Roaf and David Woods, with David Olivier, who provided some of the theoretical input into its detailed design.

The design for the PV array on the house was influenced by the following considerations:

- the PV source must be integrated in the house both technically and architecturally
- the PV array should have a peak power output of 4 kW to ensure that the house generated more electricity than it used over the year, based on the results of the load analysis done by Alan Dichler (1994)
- the system should operate in a normal grid-connected mode, with the grid providing back-up power when needed, for instance at night, in winter or in poor weather.

The house is situated in an area that receives approximately 4.0 peak sun hours in summer, but only 0.6 peak sun hours in winter (Dichler, 1994). The variation in output from winter to summer is therefore significant and the array size was specified to achieve a reasonable level of diurnal autonomy for the house for around nine months of the year.

During the summer months, energy surpluses were predicted to be around 12 kWh per day, which is greater than the house energy deficit in winter. The house is therefore expected to have a positive energy balance. It was known by the time of design of the PV system what the footprint of the house was and the slope of the south-facing back roof was designed to be optimal for the generation of electricity from the PV array at 39° from the horizontal. The project was worked up with Rod Scott from BP Solar who helped in choosing the best panels on the market – the robust, monocrystalline, high-efficiency BP Saturn 585 cells.

The 48 modules required a flat roof size of 6.8 m × 5 m and would be arranged in four vertical rows of 12 modules in each row. Thus, with the optimal angle of tilt and these dimensions now available, we could fix the ridge height of the building just above the top PV panel, so deciding the slope of the north-facing roof as the ridge height was fixed.

Description of the system

Electrical power is generated in three strings of BP585 panels. Each string consists of 16 panels, giving nameplate figures as follows:

- open circuit voltage, $V_{oc} = 16 \times 22.03\,V = 353\,V$
- short circuit current, $I_{sc} = 3 \times 5.00\,A = 15.00\,A$
- at maximum power $V = 288\,V$ and $I = 14.16\,A$.

The panels are connected in series in the ducting and each string is then linked to its own 6-A miniature circuit breaker (MCB) connector, two of which are in the ducting in the upper bedroom and the third is situated in the small attic space above the stairwell. The three +ve and three −ve cables then run through the insulated roof space in a conduit and emerge in the small attic room containing the boiler system. The six cables pass through a junction box on the left-hand side of the inverter and then the power flows to a DC power metering box consisting of Hall effect transducers, current shunt and a voltage divider. DC energy is also measured here. From there the DC power flows into the SMA 5 kW inverter and emerges as 240 V AC. It then flows through an AC power metering box where AC current, voltage and energy are measured. It then continues down through the main concrete-block ducting to the house distribution board. A third power metering box, where house power demand, energy and current are monitored, is situated here. This box also contains an MCB for inverter isolation. A simplified block diagram of the PV system is shown in Figure 8.11.

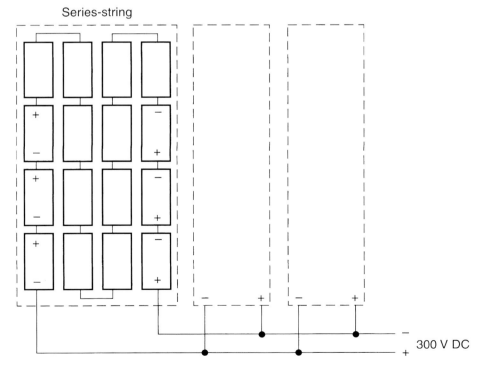

Series-string

8.11.
Single line schematic of the Oxford Ecohouse PV installation.

300 V DC

Because DC electricity is dangerous, the DC wiring has to have a series of control switches and fuses so that each string from the modules can either be cut out or turned off if the system fails on the roof or the inverter side of the system. In addition, the main cable to the domestic load board is fused to ensure that if the system fails on its house or grid side the roof will be isolated immediately. One problem we did suffer was surges in the grid voltage that shut the inverter down temporarily; in countries such as Germany this is not such a problem.

Electricity from the inverter is cabled down to the domestic load board and then either used in the house or exported, via an export meter, to the grid. In Oxford, for each 1 kW of electricity exported the local electricity company pays around £0.02 and, for every 1 kW imported to the house via the standard import meter, 0.6p approximately is paid to the company. This is not the case in many areas where common practices include:

- **Net metering.** A single meter is employed that either runs backwards or forwards and the same price is paid for imported as well as exported electricity. This practice is widely used in the USA and some European countries, such as Germany and Austria among others.
- **Rate-based incentive schemes** where a premium price is paid for exported PV electricity to help the homeowner pay back the cost of the PV installation. These schemes were pioneered in the German city of Aachen where a nominal percentage increase on every electricity bill helped the local utility company pay back around DM2 for every 1 kW exported. On a house such as the Oxford Ecohouse this would produce an income of around £2000 a year, which would pay off the installation of the 4 kWp system at current prices over 10 years. Not bad for a system that could, and may, last for 30 years before it needs replacing.

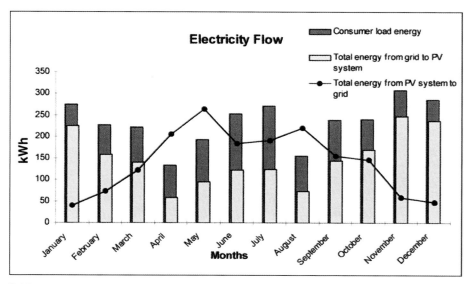

8.12.

Graphs showing PV consumed in the Oxford Ecohouse, exported and imported on different days of each season and the annual inputs and outputs.

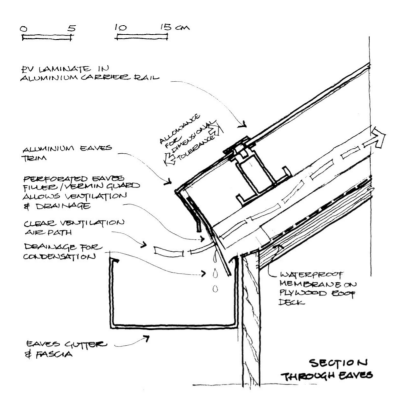

0   5   10   15 CM

PV LAMINATE IN
ALUMINIUM CARRIER RAIL

ALLOWANCE FOR DIMENSIONAL TOLERANCE

ALUMINIUM EAVES
TRIM

PERFORATED EAVES
FILLER / VERMIN GUARD
ALLOWS VENTILATION
& DRAINAGE

CLEAR VENTILATION
AIR PATH

DRAINAGE FOR
CONDENSATION

WATERPROOF
MEMBRANE ON
PLYWOOD ROOF
DECK

EAVES GUTTER
& FASCIA

SECTION
THROUGH EAVES

8.13.
Section through the eaves of the Oxford Ecohouse PV system (Jeremy Dain).

However, in the UK there has been no such support for the PV industry. On the contrary, as you will see below, the solar pioneers have had to work hard to stay in business.

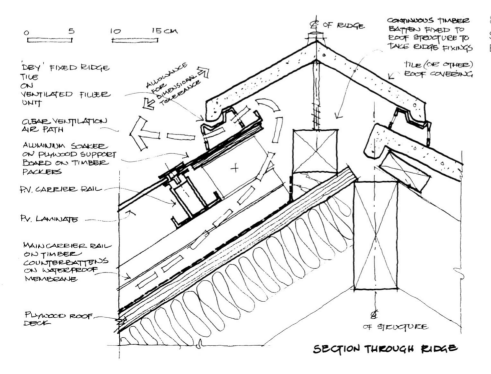

0   5   10   15 CM

'DRY' FIXED RIDGE
TILE
ON
VENTILATED FILLER
UNIT

CLEAR VENTILATION
AIR PATH

ALUMINIUM SOAKER
ON PLYWOOD SUPPORT
BOARD ON TIMBER
PACKERS

P.V. CARRIER RAIL

P.V. LAMINATE

MAIN CARRIER RAIL
ON TIMBER
COUNTERBATTENS
ON WATERPROOF
MEMBRANE

PLYWOOD ROOF
DECK

℄ OF RIDGE

ALLOWANCE FOR DIMENSIONAL TOLERANCE

CONTINUOUS TIMBER
BATTEN FIXED TO
ROOF STRUCTURE TO
TAKE RIDGE FIXINGS

TILE (OR OTHER)
ROOF COVERING

℄ OF STRUCTURE

SECTION THROUGH RIDGE

8.14.
Section through the ridge of the Oxford Ecohouse PV system (Jeremy Dain).

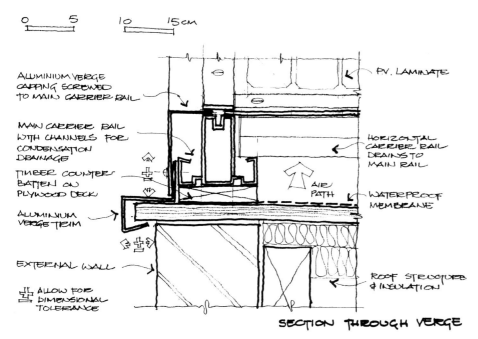

Labels on the drawing:

ALUMINIUM VERGE CAPPING SCREWED TO MAIN CARRIER RAIL

MAIN CARRIER RAIL WITH CHANNELS FOR CONDENSATION DRAINAGE

TIMBER COUNTER BATTEN ON PLYWOOD DECK

ALUMINIUM VERGE TRIM

EXTERNAL WALL

ALLOW FOR DIMENSIONAL TOLERANCE

PV. LAMINATE

HORIZONTAL CARRIER RAIL DRAINS TO MAIN RAIL

AIR PATH

WATERPROOF MEMBRANE

ROOF STRUCTURE & INSULATION

SECTION THROUGH VERGE

8.15.
Section through the verge of the Oxford Ecohouse PV system (Jeremy Dain).

Building integration

Aluminium edge frames were incorporated onto the individual PV modules. This is no longer necessary, as now the glass laminate is available as an independent unit, and can be mounted directly into the array framing lattice. To prepare the roof for the mounting of the array a layer of very flat 18 mm marine plywood was laid flat, and level over the conventional rafters of the roof. Onto this layer was laid a high quality membrane that could withstand the high temperatures that develop behind the modules. Onto this was built a grid work of EETS aluminium extruded profiles designed with a lower foot screwed to the sarking with drip channels on each side to carry any water that penetrated around the sides of the panels down the roof. Some 75 mm above this was a lateral shelf onto which the modules were laid, providing an air gap behind the array. This air gap had been chosen following measurements on a full scale mock-up by EETS in their solar test laboratory. There is now a European design guide in preparation by the EU PV Cool-Build project, to allow the effect of this type of decision to be estimated.

At each module rise a horizontal carrier bar was fixed to the vertical frames to support the lower and upper ends of the panel. Once put into position within this aluminium structure the panels were then secured with aluminium cover strips, screwed onto the centre of the extruded profiles. This is very similar to methods used to construct some conservatory glazing systems.

At the base of the vertical channels up behind the module a strip of plastic netting was placed to prevent birds, vermin and large insects from travelling up behind the modules. At the apex of the roof this ventilation channel was vented out through a row of ventilated ridge tiles from Redland Roofing Ltd, which had been tested in their UK laboratories. This ensured that air could enter the space behind the array, move up and be exhausted from the roof ridge. This is important because as the modules get hotter and rise above Standard Test Condition temperature of 25°C, they become less efficient, so moving air behind them is one way to cool them and increase their output. In more recent projects the heat from behind the panels is used as pre-heat air for the heating systems in winter. This can be seen from the OM solar house at Hamamatsu (Case Study 6), where PV heat is used to heat rocks in an interseasonal heat store.

Running between the vertical support bars were plastic conduits through which the wires from each panel were run up to the apex of the roof. The apex of the roof was chosen, rather than the eaves, as the 'higher the drier' rule seems to apply and electricity and water do not mix well. Taking the wires to the apex of the roof also shortens the wire runs from the array to the inverter.

Below the apex of the roof, holes were drilled through the roof structure and plastic conduits placed in them through which the module wires were introduced into a plastic duct beneath the ceiling of the second floor rooms. Plastic was always used for ducts as it is safer than metal for this purpose.

The modules in the array were wired together in three strings for connection to the inverter. The PV system working voltage was chosen to be nominally 300 V DC for good inverter efficiency (Dichler, 1994). This can present a hazard to installation and maintenance personnel and identifies a training requirement for installers and users.

The location of the inverter is in a closed area on the second floor at the same level as the PV modules. The area has a fire-resistant lining, a smoke detector and is vented. This location ensures that module output cables are kept relatively short with protection devices in place. Standard wiring and wiring installation protocols were used.

During the construction of the array the main building problems encountered concerned the ridge, skylight, verge and eave details. In any PV project the responsibility for the construction of the joining details, where the array meets the building, should be made clear and clarification is required early on as to which contractor should build these and supply the necessary materials. A site manager with day-to-day control of the project would be a valuable asset.

Planning and Building Regulations approval

The local utility company Southern Electric agreed to accept documentation from SMA showing that the inverter had been tested to demonstrate that, in practice under laboratory test conditions, the inverter meets the theoretical performance specified in its attached literature. This was seen as a more practical method of ensuring that the stringent and expensive European G59 requirements are met than site testing the system under variable frequency and voltage conditions.

The Planning Department of Oxford City Council was very interested and helpful during the process of gaining Planning Approval and at no time

HOW TO CATCH THE SUN

Dr Susan Roaf's house faces south so that the solar panels on the roof get the maximum sun throughout the year

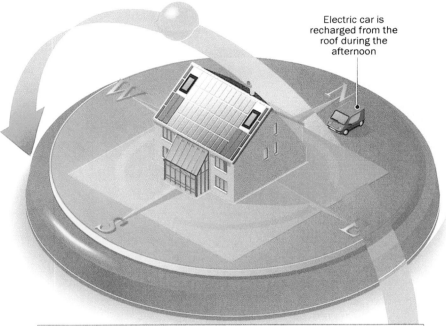

Electric car is recharged from the roof during the afternoon

THE ZERO-ENERGY EQUATION
First six months' results

Photovoltaic panels on roof produce up to 4 kw

1016 units of gas and electricity imported

Solar water-heating panels

862 units of electricity to top up supply at night

154 units of gas for boiler to top up hot water in winter

Electricity for cooking, lighting and charging the electric car

Hot water for washing and heating

1082 units of electricity exported to the National Grid

Careful use of power means that more electricity has been exported than imported in the first six months

8.16.
The excess electricity generated on sunny days is also used to power a Kewet El Set electric car (Tony Garrett @ *The Times*, 27 January, 1996).

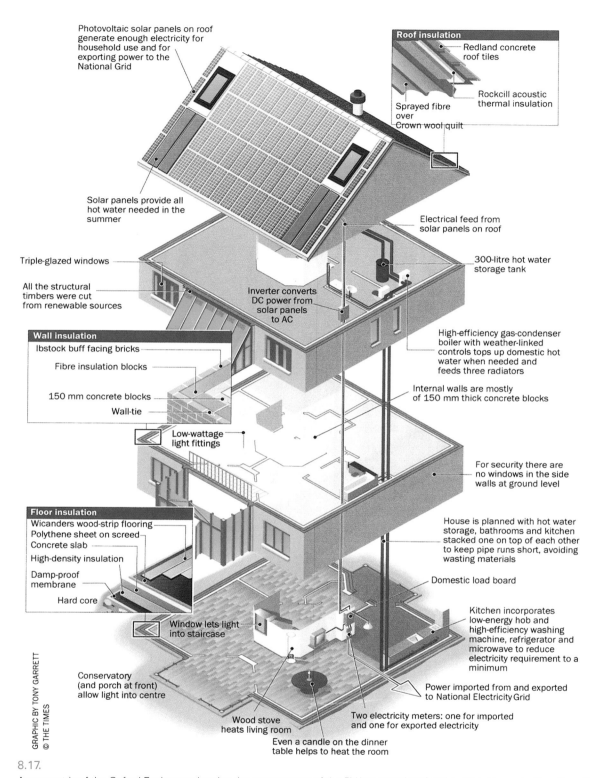

Photovoltaic solar panels on roof generate enough electricity for household use and for exporting power to the National Grid

Roof insulation
Redland concrete roof tiles

Rockcill acoustic thermal insulation

Sprayed fibre over Crown wool quilt

Solar panels provide all hot water needed in the summer

Electrical feed from solar panels on roof

Triple-glazed windows

All the structural timbers were cut from renewable sources

Inverter converts DC power from solar panels to AC

300-litre hot water storage tank

High-efficiency gas-condenser boiler with weather-linked controls tops up domestic hot water when needed and feeds three radiators

Wall insulation
Ibstock buff facing bricks

Fibre insulation blocks

150 mm concrete blocks

Wall-tie

Internal walls are mostly of 150 mm thick concrete blocks

Low-wattage light fittings

For security there are no windows in the side walls at ground level

Floor insulation
Wicanders wood-strip flooring
Polythene sheet on screed
Concrete slab
High-density insulation
Damp-proof membrane
Hard core

House is planned with hot water storage, bathrooms and kitchen stacked one on top of each other to keep pipe runs short, avoiding wasting materials

Domestic load board

Window lets light into staircase

Kitchen incorporates low-energy hob and high-efficiency washing machine, refrigerator and microwave to reduce electricity requirement to a minimum

Conservatory (and porch at front) allow light into centre

Power imported from and exported to National Electricity Grid

Wood stove heats living room

Two electricity meters: one for imported and one for exported electricity

Even a candle on the dinner table helps to heat the room

GRAPHIC BY TONY GARRETT
© THE TIMES

8.17.

Axonometric of the Oxford Ecohouse showing the arrangement of the PV integrated roof and system (drawn by Tony Garrett, and published in *The Times* newspaper, London, on 27 January 1996).

showed any bias against the use of photovoltaics on the house. This was helped by the fact that the south roof faces away from the road and would only be slightly visible from neighbouring properties. However, the willingness of the Planning Officer to accept a picture of what PVs look like, rather than a sample, demonstrated an open and constructive approach to their use.

Building Control

The Building Control Officer at Oxford City Council requested details of the construction of the photovoltaic roof and a photograph of what the panels would look like. The Officer also requested proof that the PV roof would not be too heavy and that it complied with fire regulations requirements. The BP585 monocrystalline panels weigh 7.5 kg per panel, which is 530 mm $\times$ 1138 mm in size. The north-facing roof of the house was covered in Redland Concrete tiles, which weigh 76 kg m^{-2} so the PVs weighed significantly less.

Fire rating

BP Solar had never had their panels fire rated and therefore could not supply any information on the fire rating of their array. A number of fire experts were contacted who helped us demonstrate that the roof did indeed meet the fire requirements in the following way.

Under the relevant UK Fire Test Code BS476, Part 3 (1958) the roof had to achieve an AA, AB or AC rating because the house is less than 6 m away from the adjacent buildings, so qualifying for these ratings under Table 5 of the Approved Documents B, section 14. The first A of the rating relates to fire penetration: A is a one-hour resistance to fire penetration and is mandatory. This is to mitigate against threat to life of the building inhabitants and protection of the building from burning firebrands landing on the roof. In the case of the roof of the Oxford Ecohouse, it is formed of sheer glass between aluminium glazing bars on which a brand would not rest for long enough to cause significant fire penetration. The second letter, A, B or C, relates to fire spread. the Velux windows in the roof achieve AA rating owing to their 4-mm-thick surface glass which, by dint of its thickness, is deemed to have a one-hour rating. The PV modules also meet the A rating fire spread requirement owing to their upper surface being enclosed in 3 mm toughened high-transmission glass (92 per cent), which has a higher fire rating than a single pane of glass and retains its structural integrity in temperatures of up to 1000°C, at which point it becomes friable. The key fire risk to a roof is posed by a burning firebrand from an adjacent building on fire. Wood ignites at around 400–450°C and a softwood firebrand will burn at around 200–250°C, so these temperatures will not significantly damage or ignite the toughened glass. The glass in the PV modules is held in a frame of anodised aluminium in a silicon sealant. The panel has a tedlar backing and is laid on a high-grade sarking on a marine-grade plyboard layer 18-mm-thick, above the actual structural timbers and insulation. The roof at the Oxford Ecohouse is also insulated with Thermal-Pruf Insulation, which is non-combustible conforming to the British Standard BS476 Pt.4.

The Building Control Officer was satisfied with the information supplied and the roof was deemed to meet the local Fire Regulation Requirements. The PV industry does need to provide designers and regulatory authorities with fire ratings for all products if they are to be used externally on buildings.

Agreement with local electricity company

The requirements of Southern Electricity in terms of protocols required included the following:

- connection agreement
- parallel running agreement
- tariff agreement.

CASE STUDY: GRAHAM DUNCAN'S HOUSE IN NEW ZEALAND

Brenda and Robert Vale

It is in its electrical systems that Graham Duncan's house differs substantially from convention. The house is entirely self-contained for its electricity supply, although there is mains electricity available from Mercury's lines directly outside in the road. The electricity is generated by two renewable sources, the sun and the wind. The solar contribution comes from 16 60-W Solarex poly-crystalline photovoltaic panels mounted on the north-facing roof at a slope of 42°. The panels are spaced off the roof with 50-mm-thick wooden bearers running down the slope and are carried on aluminium rails fixed across the bearers. This provides a spacing of about 75 mm between the back of the panels and the roof surface, which may help to provide some cooling to the panels that become less efficient at higher temperatures. A recent addition is a further four 50-W panels mounted on the north-facing wall below the roof. The installed capacity for solar power generation was 960 W, but the additional panels have raised this to 1.16 kW. In addition to the solar panels there are three small wind turbines. Two of these are UK-made Marlecs, with a nominal output of 70 W each. The third is an American-made Air Marine turbine, which has a quoted output of 300 W. However, this is at a higher wind speed than the output given by the manufacturers for the Marlecs, so the two different types of turbine cannot be compared directly. Graham estimates that the two Marlecs are notionally 100 W each and the Air Marine is 200 W. The turbines are all supported on galvanised steel poles with guy wires. They are not really mounted high enough in terms of obstruction to the wind from the house and surrounding trees.

The incoming electricity is stored in batteries via a regulator, a solid-state device that ensures the batteries do not become overcharged. The batteries themselves are six Trojan L16s, each with an energy storage of 350 Ah at 6 V. These are lead-acid batteries described as 'the workhorse of the alternative energy industry' (Schaeffer *et al.*, 1994: 181). They have an expected life of 10 years, and each weighs 58 kg. Together, the batteries can hold 12.6 kWh of electricity, about the same power as is provided by just over 1 litre of petrol.

However, this amount of electricity cannot be drawn from them without shortening their life. Ideally the batteries should not be discharged to more than 50 per cent of their capacity, with an absolute lower limit of 80 per cent discharge. Most renewable energy systems incorporate a cut-off that prevents

8.18.
Sketches of solar panels (either photovoltaic or solar hot water panels) demonstrating that even in the vernacular, with a little thought the panels can be very pleasingly integrated into the architecture of the house.

power being drawn from the batteries when they fall below a pre-set level of discharge. This is achieved by measuring the battery voltage, which drops as the electricity is drawn off.

Batteries store and supply electricity as direct current, but many household appliances use alternating current at 230 V, as supplied by the electricity-generating industry. To obtain AC from the batteries Graham uses a transistorised inverter. This was a Trace 1500 W model, made in the USA. Trace inverters are alleged to be highly reliable and have a good reputation, but Graham's blew up early in 1998 after only about two years of use. For a short time he then used a rotary inverter. This is a very simple mechanical device that uses a DC electric motor to turn an AC alternator. The disadvantage is that it is considerably less efficient than a solid-state inverter, which may provide at the AC output about 90 per cent of the power that goes in from the batteries. The rotary inverter has been replaced temporarily with an Australian Selectronic 350 W inverter. The wattage of the inverter determines what it can operate. Most inverters are described by the load that they can maintain continuously, so a 1500 W inverter will handle more than four times the load of a 350 W model. Most inverters can handle much

CHECKLIST – ENSURING YOUR PV SYSTEM WORKS WELL

1 Buy a system display that clearly shows the system output so you can see if the system is working well against predicted outputs per day, month and year. Make sure you have a performance warranty from your installer and, if the system is not performing as expected, call them back to determine if there are any problems.
2 Cleaning. In areas with fairly high rainfall this may not ever be necessary. In hot dusty countries modules may have to be washed every day. The angle of tilt also influences the amount of dust that will settle on a module and those that are horizontally placed will accumulate the most surface dirt. Do not forget that water will lower the panel temperature and, if over 25°C, will improve the operational efficiency of the panel. Always ensure there are no exposed electrical connections when cleaning modules as water and electricity do not mix.
3 Insurance companies do not supply standard policies for solar houses. These should have lower premiums because the insurance industry will benefit more than most from low CO_2 buildings. This is because they have to cover the costs of climate damage resulting from increased emissions from buildings that fuel global warming. The first big insurance company that produces a solar house policy for the UK will get a prize from the authors of this book but we do not accept any liability for those crushed in the stampede!
4 Make sure that the contract you sign for the installation, or the exchange of letters, clearly defines the warranty period of the system as installed. Contracts need to be developed that assign clear liability for all work done on site on the PV system and its interface with the building, and warranties need to be drawn up to cover the houseowner in case of failure of any part of the system. For instance, while a PV module company will cover the cost of replacing a panel that fails within 5 or 10 years, who pays for the scaffolding necessary to investigate and replace the module? If the problem was a sheet of glass, the insurance company would pay but what if it is because of faulty wiring on the back

of a module by the installation contractor or module manufacturer? It is advised that in the future owners should consider this issue, discuss it with their insurance companies and draw up their own contracts to be agreed and signed before a tender for work is awarded to a sub-contractor.

higher loads for short periods, which enables them to deal with the high starting currents of electric motors. In Graham's house the failure of the Trace inverter means not being able to use the vacuum cleaner or microwave, which worked off the larger inverter but not off the smaller one. The inverters all contain a shut-down mechanism if an attempt is made to draw off too much power by plugging in too large a load for too long. Inverters have other complications that have to do with the type of alternating current that they produce. True alternating current, as produced by the electricity industry or the rotary inverter, has a smooth waveform. A solid-state inverter switches the current on and off very rapidly and creates a version of AC that may be very far from smooth. The better quality inverters produce a 'modified sine wave', which is a reasonable approximation to mains electricity. The importance of all this is that some devices, such as certain computers or hi-fi equipment, need the smooth sine wave in order to work correctly and may not work at all from a modified sine wave.

Graham has wired his house to make the best use of different kinds of electricity. Since even the best inverter is only 90 per cent efficient it makes sense to use as much electricity as possible as direct current. In Graham's case this means DC lighting, using compact fluorescent lamps in special light fittings that contain the circuitry to run the lamps off DC. The water pumps are DC, as described above, and the refrigerator, which is quite small, has been rebuilt with a DC compressor. There is also a DC television and radio. Low-voltage DC wiring has to be larger in diameter than AC 230 V wiring, as electricity is transmitted more easily at higher voltage. This makes the wiring slightly more expensive. The 230 V inverter runs a larger TV, a video, stereo, computer, fax and washing machine.

GOOD PUBLICATIONS ON PVS

Arthur D. Little, Inc. (1995). *Building Integrated Photovoltaics (BIPV): Analysis and U.S. Market Potential.* NREL/TP-472-7850. National Renewable Energy Laboratory, Golden, CO.

Davidson, J. (1987). *The New Solar Electric Home: The Photovoltaics How-to Handbook.* Aatec, Ann Arbor, MI.

Derrick, A., Francis, C. and Bokalders, V. (1991). *Solar Photovoltaic Products: A Guide for Development Workers.* Intermediate Technology Publications Ltd, London.

Duffie, J. A. and Beckman, W. A. (1991). *Solar Engineering of Thermal Processes*, 2nd edn. John Wiley & Sons, New York.

First International Solar Electric Buildings Conference Proceedings, Volume 1, 4–6 March 1996, Boston, MA. Northeast Sustainable Energy Association, Greenfield. MA.

Forging PV – Building Bridges. A Joint NREL/DOE PV-DSM/PV:BONUS Workshop Proceedings; 19–20 October 1994, Newark, DE. National Renewable Energy Laboratory, Golden, CO.

Fowler, P. J. (1993). *The Solar Electric Independent Home Book*. Rev. edn. Fowler Solar Electric, Inc., Worthington, MA.

Humm, O. and Toggweiler, P. (1993). *Photovoltaics & Architecture: The Integration of Photovoltaic Cells in Building Envelopes*. Birkauser Verlag, Basel, Switzerland.

Kiss, G. and Kinkead, J. (1995). *Optimal Building – Integrated Photovoltaic Applications*. NREL/TP-473-20339. National Renewable Energy Laboratory, Golden, CO.

Kiss, G., Kinkead, J. and Raman, M. (1995). *Building – Integrated Photovoltaics: A Case Study*. NREL/TP-472-7574. National Renewable Energy Laboratory, Golden, CO.

KissCathcart Anders, Architects, P. C. (1993). *Building – Integrated Photovoltaics*. NREL/TP-472-7851. National Renewable Energy Laboratory, Golden, CO.

Lasnier, F. and Gan Ang, T. (1990). *Photovoltaic Engineering Handbook*. A. Hilger, Bristol, New York.

Mounting Technologies for Building Integrated PV Systems. Proceedings of the IEA International Workshop, 1992. Moenchaltorf, Switzerland.

Parker, B. F., ed. (1991). *Solar Energy in Agriculture*. Elsevier, Amsterdam.

Roberts, S. (1992). *Solar Electricity: A Practical Guide to Designing and Installing Small Photovoltaic Systems*. Prentice-Hall, Englewood Cliffs, NJ.

Schoen, T. J. N. (1994). *Photovoltaics in Buildings*. IEA Task 16. Ecofys Research and Development Consultancy; Utrecht, The Netherlands.

Sick, F. and Erge, T. (1996). *Photovoltaics in Buildings: A Design Handbook for Architects and Engineers*. IEA. James & James, London, UK.

Strong, S. J. and Scheller, W. G. (1993). *The Solar Electric House: Energy for the Environmentally-Responsive, Energy-Independent Home*. Sustainability Press, Still River, MA.

Thomas, R. and Grainger, G. (1999). *Photovoltaics in Buildings: A design Guide*. Produced by Max Fordham and Partners and Association with Fielden Clegg for the DTI, ETSU Report No: s/p2/00282/REP.

Warfield, G., ed. (1984). *Solar Electric Systems*. Hemisphere Publishing, Washington, DC.

Zweibel, K. and Hersch, P. (1984). *Basic Photovoltaic Principles and Methods*. Van Nostrand Reinhold, New York, NY.

Magazines

Home Power Magazine: A bi-monthly magazine that is information-central for details on working and living with PV and other renewable and sustainable technologies. P.O. Box 520, Ashland, OR 97520, USA. Tel./Fax: 916-475-3179; Subscriptions: 800-707-6585; bbs: 707-822-8640; email: hp@homepower.org; web address: http://www.homepower.com

Solar Today: American Solar Energy Society bi-monthly magazine covering all renewable energy applications, new products and new installations. ASES, 2400 Central Avenue, Suite G-I, Boulder, CO 80301, USA. Tel.: 303-443-3130; Fax: 303-443-3212; web address: http://www.ases.org/solar

Internet websites

National Renewable Energy Laboratory: http://www.nrel.gov

Sandia National Laboratories, PV: http://www.sandia.gov/pv

Solar Radiation Data Manual for Buildings: http://rredc.nrel.gov/solar/old_data/nsrdb/bluebook/atlas

DOE Office of Building Technology, State and Community Programs: http://www.eren.doe.gov/buildings

NREL Buildings and Thermal Systems Center: http://www.nrel.gov/stbt.html

Green Building Information Council: http://greenbuilding.ca

Center for Renewable Energy and Sustainable Technology (CREST): http://solstice.crest.org

Solar Energy Industries Association: http://www.seia.org

Utility PhotoVoltaic Group: http://www.ttcorp.com/upvg/index.htm

Solar Design Associates: http://www.solardesign.com/~sda

PV Power Resource Site: http://www.pvpower.com

9 SOLAR HOT WATER SYSTEMS

WHAT IS A SOLAR HOT WATER SYSTEM?

Solar hot water systems gather energy from solar radiation and turn it into heat that is then distributed in the form of hot air or water to where it is to be used or stored until needed.

An active solar water heater consists of a *solar collector*(s), a hot water *storage tank*(s), and a *pump*. In addition, a heat exchanger and expansion tank are required in freezing winter climates and an electrical generation device is needed if regular AC grid-connected power is not available. Piping, insulation, valves and fittings are considered installation materials and are normally available at hardware stores and plumbing centres.

A solar collector consists of a translucent cover, an absorption plate and a heat transfer system, involving hot water pipes or hot air.

A good liquid solar collector should have a minimum life expectancy of 20–30 years. Most of the collectors built since about 1980 are manufactured with materials that should give a 30–50 year lifespan with a small amount of periodic maintenance. Good liquid collectors typically have copper water ways (piping and tubing), a tempered glass cover and an insulated metal enclosure.

Although a little of the radiation falling on the translucent cover will be re-reflected away, most will pass through and be absorbed by the absorption plate and heat the water contained in it. As soon as the water begins to get hotter than its surroundings the absorption plate will begin to lose heat to its surroundings, which is why insulation is used under it to avoid excessive heat loss to the roof below by conduction, convection and radiation. In areas where the water is being heated to temperatures over 35°C above air temperature heat losses from the absorber plate could be very high and double glazing should be used for the translucent cover to conserve this heat. This is despite the fact that the double sheet of glass may transmit only around 70 per cent of the heat it receives onto the absorber plate. There are a large number of different configurations for collectors, which may range from a simple black hose pipe on the lawn to a very sophisticated evacuated tube collector that is more efficient than a more usual flat plate collector at absorbing

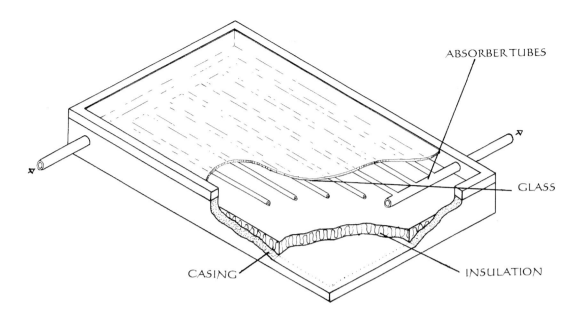

9.1.
A solar collector.

ABSORBER TUBES

GLASS

INSULATION

CASING

heat from an overcast sky. When considering which collector to use on your own building a key consideration is how efficient a particular collector is and how efficient you need it to be.

TIPS FOR CHOOSING A SOLAR COLLECTOR
1   Copper water tubes and headers in the collector are necessary if any water solution is to be used as the heat transfer liquid. A liquid solar collector under no-flow or stagnation conditions can attain boiling temperatures. Plastics other than silicone or PTFE are not suitable materials for glazed liquid collectors.
2   The absorber plate is made of copper, aluminium or steel and bonded to the waterways. The plate surface is approximately equal to the glazing surface and is painted or anodised with a black paint or selective coating. A selective (black nickel or black chrome) surface on the absorber increases the collector output by limiting re-radiated heat (emittance) from the absorber. The method used to bond the plate to the absorber is an important consideration. The better the bonding, the higher the output. Simply wiring or clamping the tubes to the plate will produce discouraging results.
3   The sides and back of the solar collector that do not face the sun should be insulated to prevent heat loss and covered in a weather-tight enclosure. Most collector enclosures manufactured today are made of aluminium owing to its outstanding weatherability. Insulation used is either fibreglass or polyisocyanurate, both of which can withstand very high temperatures. Styrofoams, by comparison, are unsuitable because they begin to degrade at temperatures well below collector stagnation temperatures.
4   International independent testing procedures now allow for comparison of collector performances and confirmation that minimum standards have been met. Such standards include ISO 9459, EN 12975 and EN 12976.

THE HEAT DISTRIBUTION SYSTEM

These are the pipes that circulate hot water from the collector to its storage tank or point of use. It is by circulating water through the solar collectors that the absorbed energy is brought to the point where it will be used. Water can be moved round the system in one of two ways: gravity circulation (thermosyphoning), and forced circulation. The decision to use or not to use a pump is one of the first steps in planning a solar system. Distribution system can be either direct or indirect.

1 **Direct system** is one where the tap water is circulated directly through the solar collector:

- these systems initially have less storage transfer loss
- long-term scaling and corrosion of components can occur with aggressive water types, possibly increasing transfer loss
- non-chemical methods of preventing damage by freezing water are required in many climates
- in many hot and sunny areas, the direct system allows for a cheap, simple method via a black painted metal tank on the roof, absorbing solar radiation to heat the water during the day for domestic use in the evening.

2 **Indirect system** is one that employs a separate fluid circuit to transfer heat from the solar collectors to the store:

- permits use of anti-corrosion inhibitors and antifreeze (food-grade polypropylene glycol) that permits a wider range of materials to be employed in the absorber and the pipework
- these systems usually have higher initial purchase costs but less risk of corrosion or bursting
- allows higher temperature collection
- reduces deposition of solids within collector during stagnation.

CIRCULATION SYSTEMS FOR HOT WATER

1 **A natural thermosyphon system:**
- warm water will rise above cooler water creating a thermosyphon pressure which can drive a fluid movement through an inclined pipe
- with solar energy, heated water can naturally rise to the top of the collector and up through the distribution pipes into the store
- cold water is drawn into the bottom of the collector from the base of the tank
- the store should be located at least 0.5 m above the collector, even for short pipe runs
- the pipe routes need careful planning to rise, not restrict fluid movement by under sizing pipes or by pipes that are too long
- requires purpose-built collector types to work well
- is a simple, low-cost system
- no parasitic or standby electrical losses
- sluggish performance in interim weather conditions
- poor control of overheating.

2 Pumped system:

The power to move heat between collector and store is derived from an electrically-driven pump which:

- allows greater choice of collector and pipe layout
- removes the heat from the collector at the optimum rate
- reduces heat loss through pipes
- allows heating multiple stores with intelligent switching of priorities
- permits overheat control and integral frost-protection
- makes it possible to accurately calculate heat flow
- costs more than a thermosyphon system and has more moving parts to wear out
- requires pump control when used with AC mains entailing standby losses
- loses some parasitic power when used with AC mains
- has option of direct PV pumps.

3 System types:

3.1 Open vent – a pipe that is open to the atmosphere and is a key safety measure. This is located at the highest and hottest part of the circuit on the flow from the collector. If the collector fluid boils it can vent out safely into a cistern header. With direct systems the header may also be the cold water store. When a pump is not running, heat is prevented from rising back into a collector, which is mounted higher than the store by means of a non-return device including a spring-loaded valve or deliberate dip in the pipe. A separate pipe usually feeds the header contents into the return to the collector. Open-vented systems, whilst simple, can allow fluid to evaporate over time and require regular attention especially if antifreeze is used.

3.2 Sealed and pressurised – in these systems the open cistern is replaced by an expansion vessel that is typically a small metal sphere about the size of a football with an internal rubber diaphragm separating the vessel into two halves. One half contains compressed gas, such as air or nitrogen, while the other half is connected to the fluid in the system. As water expands on heating, it is pushed into the vessel and this extra pressure is relieved by movement in the diaphragm. This vessel can be at any height in the system. The operating pressure of the vessel is normally sufficient to overcome the static head of fluid pressure plus an amount to raise the boiling point of the fluid, i.e. 1.5 Bar. A spring-loaded safety pressure relief valve, filling point and pressure gauge are typical features of such a system. With sealed systems, collector position is not restricted by the need for a higher header cistern.

3.3 Pumped, closed loop – often found in drain-back systems, the fluid is not necessarily above atmospheric pressure when cold. A reservoir of air is always present in a drain-back vessel to accommodate expansion. Only when the pump is engaged, is the collector filled with fluid. When off, the fluid drains back into a freeze-protected area in the dwelling. Permissible collector locations depend on the pump size and the size of the drain-back vessel. No intentional opening to atmosphere is necessary but is sometimes added in larger systems to improve drain-back.

THE HOT WATER STORE

Heat storage is a key feature of the solar hot water system. Without it the hot water would be available only when the sun is actually shining. A storage tank allows the solar system to operate whenever energy is available and to supply the energy when it is needed.

The store can either be sized to hold enough heat for 24 hours, so that the water heated during the day can be used in the evening, or in extreme cases as an inter-seasonal store where the container is of a much larger size. A larger store can be gradually heated up over hot days and retain that heat

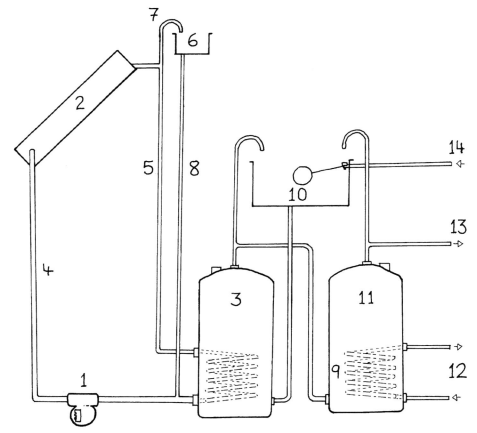

9.2.
Indirect open-vent pumped system.

1.	CIRCULATOR OR PUMP	7.	SOLAR PRIMARY VENT PIPE
2.	SOLAR COLLECTOR	8.	SOLAR PRIMARY FEED PIPE
3.	SOLAR STORAGE TANK	9.	HEAT EXCHANGER
4.	RETURN PIPE CARRYING COOLED WATER TO COLLECTOR	10.	COLD FEED TANK
		11.	HOT WATER CYLINDER
		12.	CONNECTIONS TO BOILER
5.	FLOW PIPE CARRYING HEATED WATER TO THE SOLAR TANK	13.	TO HOT WATER TAPS
		14.	MAINS WATER SUPPLY
6.	SOLAR PRIMARY CIRCUIT EXPANSION TANK		

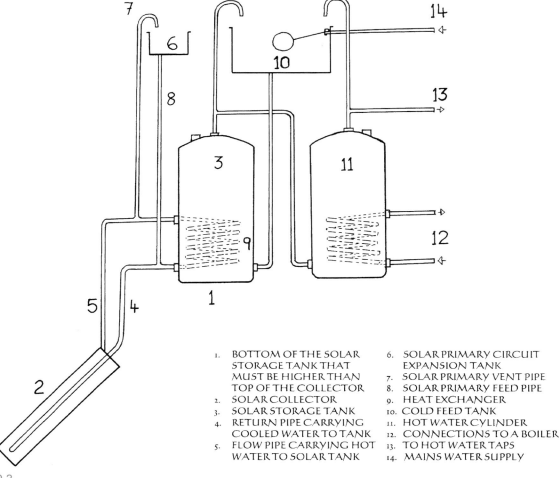

9.3.
Indirect open-vent thermosyphoning system.

1.	BOTTOM OF THE SOLAR STORAGE TANK THAT MUST BE HIGHER THAN TOP OF THE COLLECTOR	6.	SOLAR PRIMARY CIRCUIT EXPANSION TANK
2.	SOLAR COLLECTOR	7.	SOLAR PRIMARY VENT PIPE
3.	SOLAR STORAGE TANK	8.	SOLAR PRIMARY FEED PIPE
4.	RETURN PIPE CARRYING COOLED WATER TO TANK	9.	HEAT EXCHANGER
		10.	COLD FEED TANK
		11.	HOT WATER CYLINDER
5.	FLOW PIPE CARRYING HOT WATER TO SOLAR TANK	12.	CONNECTIONS TO A BOILER
		13.	TO HOT WATER TAPS
		14.	MAINS WATER SUPPLY

through the following cloudier ones. Most domestic systems just use diurnal storage. The hot water store can be used either as a single hot water supply or as a pre-heat for an existing domestic hot water system.

When an indirect system is chosen, a heat exchanger will be needed with the store. This serves to separate the fluid flowing though the collectors from the water flowing to the tap inside the house. It must allow for heat absorbed in the collectors to pass into the water in the storage tank.

STORING SOLAR ENERGY

- The solar store should be well insulated. A minimum of 50 mm of mineral fibre quilt or equivalent should be sought.
- Proper sizing of the solar storage is essential for defining the strategy for collector, heat distribution and circulation design and may be likened to the safety of the whole system.

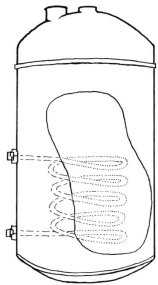

9.4.
Heat exchange coil in the bottom of a hot water cylinder.

WHY USE A SHW SYSTEM?

All ecohouses should use solar hot water (SHW) systems to heat their water if possible. This is because it is reliable, tried and tested technology which uses free, clean energy from the sun.

HOW GREEN IS A SHW SYSTEM?

The domestic sector is responsible for around 30 per cent of the carbon emissions of developed countries, mainly owing to the CO_2 emitted as a by-product of power generation and fossil fuel burning. Of this 30 per cent, 25 per cent goes to heating water for use from the taps and to provide pre heating for space heating systems.

Table 9.1. CO_2 emissions from a typical three-bedroom semi-detached house built in 1995 in the UK

	Emissions (kg CO_2 year^{-1})
Space heating	1506
Hot water	864
Cooking	125
Pumps and fans	96
Lights and appliances	1650
Total	4241

Thus domestic hot water systems are responsible for between 6 and 8 per cent of the total CO_2 emissions in developed countries such as the UK. If every house had a solar hot water system that could produce over half the entire annual domestic hot water requirement using free, clean solar energy, then we could save around 3 per cent of all emissions of greenhouse gases from the country simply by adopting a mandatory solar hot water policy. In Israel all new houses have to have SHW systems. Of course in a hot tropical country, where SHW systems can produce up to 100 per cent of the annual hot water requirement, SHW systems could save 6 per cent of greenhouse gas emissions. It is understandable that building owners should more often think about the cost of their purchases rather than the global impacts of their invisible emissions.

WHAT WILL IT COST TO USE SHW?

Clever governments, such as that in the Netherlands, have realized that a little help to an industry at the right time can have a disproportionate impact on its success. Hence, in a public–private partnership in the Netherlands the cost of SHW systems has dropped enormously. Even in Britain you can go out and buy a Dutch system now off the shelf, with tank and panels included, for as little £1200. In other parts of the world the production costs of systems are, of course, much less.

THE PROCESS OF DESIGNING A SHW SYSTEM

What follows is a step-by-step approach to designing and building a SHW system. There are many different types of SHW systems available with different features, capabilities and costs. It is important to follow the steps described here to get the optimum SHW system.

AN EXAMPLE FROM THE UK

A total solar collector area of around $5\,m^2$ is recommended for a typical domestic water heating installation. A little maths shows us that it is possible to collect 1500 kWh of energy per year. If the original heating method was an electric heater, that would have cost around £200 at today's prices. Since the $5\,m^2$ of solar collector will cost around £2000, the payback period, excluding initial labour and installation costs, would be around 10 years. Since the lifespan of solar collectors is around 20 years, one gets 9 years of free hot water. In terms of the modern economy 9 years could be a long time, but we must remember that we do not know what the cost of the energy will be in 9 years' time, though it will almost certainly be lower than today.

Step 1. Identifying the variables

Hot water usage
The greater the rate of DHW (domestic hot water) use, the more worthwhile a larger collector will be

---

Storage capacity
Relevant to hot water use of collector size

Hot water type
Can limit some choices of storage and collector

Climate/Isolation
Minimum and maximum ambient temperatures, isolation and snowfall all affect collector choices

---

Position
Physical location of the collector and store

Step 2. Sizing the system

Two key variables of the SHW system first have to be sized: the area of the solar collector and the capacity of the store.

Solar store

In industrialised countries, people use an average of 40–60 litres hot water per day per person. A family of three to four people will use 160–240 litres per day. The store size is preferably designed to provide at least the daily DHW regime of the family and store at least a day's worth of solar collection without unduly stressing components. A typical size for a family of four might be about 200 to 300 litres.

Often overlooked, but when an indirect system is used, ensure a heat exchanger is fitted with adequate surface area typically one square metre for a good household system.

Tall thin stores permit greater stratification between top and bottom and promote solar efficiency.

Collector area

Once an estimate for the amount of water that will be used and the necessary store size is determined, the area of the solar collector can be calculated. The sizing need not be exact as SHW can rarely provide 100 per cent of hot water and a back-up source should always be made available for comfort and hygiene. Collectors are usually made in modules with fixed areas in the range of $1\,m^2$ to $4\,m^2$. Hence the choice will often be made up of multiple modules.

Tips: Assuming an ideal collector position at middle latitudes for SHW heating:

- The basic rule of thumb for sizing solar collectors is to use $1\,m^2$ of them for every 50–65 litres of hot water needed a day.
- The rule of thumb for relating the solar collector area to the storage size says that 50–65 litres of water storage is needed for each square metre of solar absorber. A $5\,m^2$ solar collector area provides 60 per cent of the SHW needed for the Oxford Ecohouse in the UK. The same system provides 75 per cent of the SHW system for the Bariloche Ecohouse in Argentina.
- The easy way to measure the contribution of an SHW system to the hot water energy requirements is to look at the energy bills before and after a SHW is fitted. Computer performance predictions can be made in cases where weather data and collector performance specifications are available.

Step 3. Choosing the system

Most commercially available collectors have been shown how to operate within a band of within 20 per cent of each other's energy conversion rate.

Often higher costs reflect the higher efficiencies and durability of products. Independent testing agencies frequently publish results in order to verify manufacturer's claims. A high-efficiency collector can be restricted if the rest of the system is not of similar ilk. If the proposed collector position is not restricted in size, then a lower-efficiency collector can be extended to supply the same energy albeit at a slightly lower fluid temperature. Take care that packaged systems have not reduced quality of system components simply for the gain of initial cost or reduced installation time.

Appearance of the collector may influence choice. Some can be flushed into the building fabric, whereas some roof types only permit above the roof location.

Local conditions may restrict choice. Sparks from a nearby solid fuel appliance or aggressive rodents may obstruct use of plastic, polymer or resin components. Planning authorities or neighbours may require consultation.

Confirm if the manufacturer has designed the collector for recycling, i.e. provides a label of all materials and ensures the packaging is not excessive and consists of benign materials.

Some collector types cannot simply be switched off when the store becomes hot enough. With certain store types or with vulnerable people, it would be wise to choose a collector that is designed to repeatedly allow this upon demand.

Step 4. Protecting the system from freeze damage

Even one freezing night can destroy a collector unless precautions are taken:

Antifreeze – special non-toxic food grade chemicals are available
Pump control – recommended if freezing expected for only a few days a year. Triggered by collector temperature sensor
Drain-back – pump controlled by temperature sensor so switches off automatically, and the fluid drains from the collector
Drain-down – valve controlled by temperature sensitive lever, opens to dump fluid contents. Requires manual refill
Freeze tolerant – new pipe materials are designed to permit freezing without pipe damage
Insulation – reduces chance but never eliminates freezing risk.

Step 5. Comfort and health

Water carries bacteria which, under certain conditions, can proliferate. Although there have been no known cases connected with solar hot water, it makes sense to assess the risk to vulnerable people. The principal method of precaution requires the SHW design to permit all water to be heated above 55°C, before reaching domestic appliances. Since SHW rarely provides 100 per cent annual coverage, an auxiliary heat source should also be enabled ensuring that this thermostatically responds to solar input and does not interfere with transfer of solar heat.

The key ally to this process is the natural buoyancy of heated water above cooler water, which permits stratification of a solar store. Hence solar heat transfer should be designed below- or up-line (in a separate store) of an auxiliary heat source with indirect coils below any other indirect coils and below electric immersion elements.

SHW can, of course, also create very high temperatures, sometimes sufficient to scald. A correctly sized store can minimise this risk but so can an automatic bleeding device or mixing valve, which cools overheated water with cold water just as it leaves the store.

Step 6. How many stores?

If there is an existing hot water system in the house, solar heating can take place in the existing store or in a separate solar store, which then feeds into the existing one (pre-heating). Alternatively, a special single store can replace the existing one.

Storage tank(s)
- If the solar collectors are connected to the existing storage tank there will be saving in both spending and physical space but potentially at the expense of overall performance. The insulation levels may be inadequate and the auxiliary heat source may interfere with efficient solar heat transfer when engaged. Comfort may also be compromised.
- Additional hot water storage capacity and a simpler installation are possible if a separate solar pre-heat store is chosen. The cold feed from the existing one is diverted to the bottom of the new solar store, which then feeds from the top of the first tank. This method can be inefficient with short water draw-offs as the solar heat remains trapped in the pre-heat store. A special large single store can allow sufficient separation of multiple sources of heat and retain solar efficiency whilst allowing the hottest heat to rise for immediate draw-off. It can also allow improvements to other heat store transfer coils and permit sufficient insulation.

Step 7. Installing the solar collectors

Key considerations when placing the panels include:

Orientation
In higher latitudes it is more important to face the panels, either north or south, directly towards the sun. Forty-five degrees either side of south will make little difference. As one nears the tropics, the higher availability of sunshine makes their orientation less important and they can even face east or west and still provide adequate heated water for domestic needs if properly sized. Within the tropics they can operate well even when laid flat, due to the abundant sunshine, but of course if a thermosyphon system is used the water tank still needs to be above the collectors and the collector inclined.

Collectors may be placed:
- at ground level
- as canopies on the outside walls of buildings, above sunspaces or as sun shades above flat roofs
- on a sloping roof
- on an angled collector supports on flat roofs or walls
- flat horizontally where the collector design permits rotation of tubes
- flat vertically where the collector design permits rotation of tubes.

WARNING: Do not put the collector in a position shaded from the sun by the building or adjacent trees

---

How to get the tilt angle right for the SHW collector

The tilt angle will depend on the design concept of the SWH system. This is generally not critical. If preferred, a tracking assembly will rotate to always face the sun.

1 If the intention is to maximise the SHW output over the year, the collectors should be inclined at an angle equal to the site's latitude, from the horizontal.
2 If the intention is to maximise the SWH production during winter, the collectors have to be inclined 10 more degrees than in case 1.
3 If the intention is to extend the 'solar' season, then the collectors should be tilted 10 degrees less than in case 1.

SWH collectors together

Each SHW collector will have a cool inlet (return) and a hot outlet (flow) pipe. Sometimes this is reversible when assembling collectors. In order to optimise collector efficiency and air removal, ensure that where fluid moves up though a collector, the flow is placed at a high point, often near the collector temperature sensor (if fitted) and that an air release point is fitted.

Proportions

When deciding where a panel will be placed on a roof, remember the simple rules of proportion and design. Try and line up one or more of the sides of the collectors with an existing feature on the roof such as a roof light or a chimney. Take care to balance the form of the collector in such a way that the proportions of the roof minimise the chance of it looking out of place.

Collectors on roofs

A roof is often favoured for solar collectors as it is most likely to be free of shading, is frequently at a reasonable angle of pitch and is away from risks of breakage. Roofs are also the most dangerous of locations to work from and an assessment of risk is required. When fitting solar collectors to roofs a number of different systems can be used to fix the collectors to the structural roof's strong points. Frequently these fixings are supplied with a collector and collectors mounted above the roof covering are very common. To achieve this a bracket must hold the collector to the roof structure and the roof is therefore altered from its original design with structural and durability implications and due care is required.

The following is regarded as good practice in respect of pitched tiles or slates:

- to maintain access to roof covering below the collector
- to impart no loads (static, wind or snow) onto the roof covering
- to design loads onto substantial roof structures, i.e. rafters, purlins, trusses
- to provide sufficient lap of flashing where tiles are cut or raised
- to allow for negative pressure lifting adjoining components.

For pitched tiles or slates, existing practice has tended towards malleable aluminium or stainless steel straps under tiles and hooked over battens, the same screwed onto rafter tops or aluminium angle screwed through drilled holes in tiles. Screwed fixings tend to be stainless steel. Silicone sealant and rubber grommets are used for weathering fixings. For modern single-lap interlocking tiles, there is increased use of imported pre-formed rigid stainless steel brackets fixed to rafters under tiles, and pre-manufactured plastic tiles with integral steel mounts that replace whole tiles.

Both slates and solid stone slabs can cause difficulties due to their non-accessible fixings making location of underlying structures tricky. They are also frequently found in non-standard sizes preventing standard bracket solutions. The underlying structure can include continuous wooden decking as opposed to battens. A partial re-roof may be required to allow good practice insertion of appropriate zinc or lead flashing with custom brackets.

Double-lab small clay tiles can be exceptionally hard and yet brittle. The close spacing and thinness of battens also create problems with bracket insertion. Good practice for this type would inevitably require use of flashing.

Once the bracket method has been assessed for a pitched roof, the general procedure will normally involve:

1 temporarily marking underlying roof structure to indicate on top
2 temporarily marking the approximate overall collector dimensions
3 ensuring pipe locations will permit good plumbing practice
4 ensuring course edges (bottom of tile) do not interfere with top and bottom brackets
5 ensuring pipe and sensor cable penetrations are likely to miss roof structure
6 selecting suitable tiles for removal
7 fixing brackets and make good.

Domestic flat roofs on typical extensions do not permit examination of the underlying structure and penetrations are difficult to seal in good practice without specialised burning equipment and skills. Many existing flat roofs have a frequent replacement of felt covering (sub-fifteen years) requiring the

9.5.
Piping details of the SWH system at the
Bariloche Ecohouse (Manuel Fuentes).

solar system to be readily demountable. Most collectors on flat roofs necessitate a metallic A-frame structure for correct orientation and extra wind-loading should be considered. There is a growing trend to use ballast weights rather than structural tie-in and tables are available to calculate these, although the capacity of the whole roof still has to be considered as well as water drainage.

9.6.
Fixing the SHW system to the roof structure, at the Bariloche Ecohouse (Manuel Fuentes).

The following roof types provide substantial extra challenges to mounting solar collectors and experienced assistance should be sought. These include:

- asbestos cement
- built-up felt supported by wood-wool boards or insulation
- profiled metal supported on metal beams
- sheet metal
- conservatory or greenhouse
- wooden shingles.

Good bracket design should always seek to leave underlay intact. Where broken, adhesive tapes for repair are available for some types but others may require remedial work. Existing trade practice uses silicone sealant for small repairs.

Checklist:
- Collectors are heavy and external timber should not be used in humid climates as it is not durable enough.
- Space should be left between the collector and the roof tiles beneath to allow free passage of rainwater and melting snow and to prevent the build-up of debris around the collector that may over time cause the roof to leak.
- If the system is left empty, consider covering it to prevent excessive heat build-up.
- Do not install collectors onto the roof alone.
- Make sure ladders are firmly secured and that they are used only for personal access.
- Insulate pipes where possible, remembering stagnation temperatures, UV degradation and rodent risks.
- Fixings should be corrosion resistant, i.e. stainless steel.
- Choose good but cloudy weather for fitting the SHW system.

Controlling the system?

- A reasonable SHW system should be automatic and not require daily user intervention.
- Sensors can be used to monitor the temperatures and control pumps. A differential temperature controller (DTC) compares collector temperature with the store to pump only when there is sufficient gain.
- A high differential, above 7°C between collector and store, is appropriate where system losses in pipework are high.
- The high sensor should be located so as to best represent the temperature of the collected solar energy, i.e. immersed in the collector waterways.
- For the low sensor, the sensor should represent the temperature of the stored water, i.e. immersed inside the lower part of the store.
- The choice of heat transmission fluid has some effect on the system design, e.g. where lowering the specific heat capacity.

9.7.
The SHW system at the Bariloche Ecohouse after installed (Manuel Fuentes).

CASE STUDY: THE INTEGRATED SOLAR ROOF AT THE OXFORD ECOHOUSE

The Oxford Ecohouse has a system where the angled roof is built up with a rigid aluminium frame screwed to the roof. Onto this, over parts of the roof, photovoltaic panels are fitted and held down by a screw-fixed cover strip. Over other portions of the roof, $5\,m^2$ solar hot water panels are screwed down beneath the same cover strips. The solar thermal system consists of a flat plate solar collector manufactured by AES and mounted on the roof co-planar with it. It has two series-connected flat plate collectors with $5\,m^2$ surface, connected to a 300 litre tank. The solar hot water collectors are used to supplement the energy demand for domestic hot water (SHW) and to pre-heat the tank used for heating the three radiators in the house. At the Oxford Ecohouse the hot water collectors were manufactured to fit into the same aluminium angle grid as the photovoltaic modules and held in place with the same cover strips. This roofing construction has proved completely waterproof.

The collector feeds directly into a secondary heating coil in the hot water storage tank. The primary coil in the Yorkpark twin coil tank is connected to the gas condensing boiler.

CASE STUDY: THE MADIBA HEAT BARROW FROM SOUTH AFRICA

One of the most innovative SHW systems developed to date, the Madiba Heat Barrow has been developed by the Engineering Department of the University of Pretoria for use in the poorer communities in South Africa where every drop of water must be carried over vast distances in very primitive containers. The

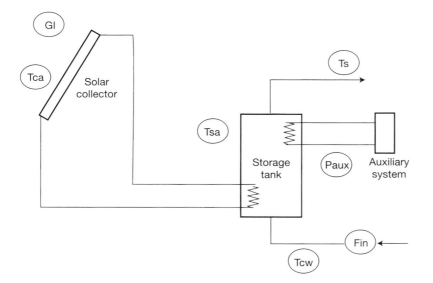

9.8.
A schematic diagram of the SHW system at the Oxford Ecohouse.

9.9.
The Madiba Heat Barrow can be pushed by children and acts not only as a solar hot water collector but also as a water carrier (Edward Matthews, Department of Engineering, Pretoria University).

water in many settlements also often contains harmful organisms that would be killed if the water could be heated to certain temperatures for certain periods of time. Wood is scarce in these regions and hot purified water a luxury. The ingenious idea behind the Madiba Heat Barrow was to combine the hot water collector with the hot water store in a movable water collector/container. An enormous amount of research, largely by Benjamin Rossouw (Rossouw, 1997), went into the development of this product that is now being tested in a number of communities. The amount and location of the insulation were important as were the materials of which it was built that have been designed for mass production and to keep the cost of the barrow below 300 Rand. The hot water wheel barrow, which also provides the distribution system for the heat, has proved that it can, on sunny winter days, heat water to over 60°C at midday and, by 20:00 h, the water is still piping hot at 40°C. The shape of the barrow and the wheel at the front have been designed for maximum manoeuvrability, for use by children and to prevent erosion furrows in the soil.

GOOD PUBLICATIONS ON SOLAR HOT WATER SYSTEM DESIGN

ANSI/ASHRAE (1987) *Methods of Testing to Determine the Thermal Performance of Solar Domestic Water Heating Systems,* ASHRAE, 95.

Duffie, J. A. and Beckman, W. A. (1980) *Solar Engineering of Thermal Processes, Wiley, New York.*

ETSU (2001) Analysis of Four Active Solar Installations.

ETSU (2001) Side by Side Testing of Eight Water Heating Systems.

European Standard Thermal Solar Heating Systems and Components (2001) Factory made systems – EN 12976.

European Standard Thermal Solar Systems and Components (2001) Solar collectors – EN 12975.

CADDET (1995) Mini Review of Active (Thermal) Solar Energy.

Centre of Alternative Technology (2000) Tapping the Sun – A Guide to Solar Water Heating.

UK Solar Trade Association (1999) Solar Energy Information Sheet.

Websites
http://www.ieatask24.org
http://www.solartradreassociation.org.uk
http://www.mysolar.com
http://www.solarenergy.ch
http://sel.me.wisc.edu
http://www.solar-rating.org
http://www.fsec.ucf.edu
http://www.soltherm.org
http://www.Solarkeymark.org
http://www.caddet.co.uk
http://wire.ises.org

10 USING WATER WISELY

WHY SHOULD WE USE WATER WISELY?

Four things are conspiring to make fresh water one of the most valuable commodities in the twenty-first century:

1 increasing world populations
2 climate change
3 man's ever increasing interference with the natural flow of water.
4 pollution.

In 1990 the World Health Organisation estimated that 1230 million people did not have access to adequate drinking water. By 2000 this figure was estimated to have risen by 900 million people. Add to this already chronic problem the devastating impacts of climate change and the results can be catastrophic, even in the most developed countries in the world. On top of these issues comes another: the increasing household demand for water around the world. In England and Wales alone household water use is predicted to increase by 10–20 per cent between 1990 and 2021 under a medium-growth scenario without climate change. Per capita demand for domestic water is predicted to rise owing to the projected increase in use of dishwashers and other domestic appliances, with a further increase of 4 per cent with climate change owing to higher use of personal showers and garden watering. Demand for spray irrigation of crops in Britain is predicted to rise by 115 per cent with climate change between 1990 and 2021, with most irrigation water taken from rivers and groundwater.

This increasing demand for water can be met either by increasing the capacity of supply (e.g. by building new reservoirs), by reducing the consumption of water or by reusing water where we can.

WATER CONSERVATION

Water conservation tends to conjure up images of scorched gardens, dirty clothes and unflushed WCs; the sort of measures that are tolerated during droughts. In practice, a wide range of measures are available for saving water and whilst some do require reduced standards or changed habits others are actually associated with a higher standard of performance.

To clarify this it can be helpful to divide measures up into the following five categories:

1 water conservation
2 water efficiency
3 water sufficiency
4 water substitution
5 water reuse, recycling and harvesting.

Water conservation – doing less with less

Particularly appropriate at times of drought, but moderate application such as washing cars less often (but keeping lights and glass clean), may have some general applicability. Standards such as hygiene and aesthetics will usually suffer. Acceptability is very culturally dependent.
   Examples:

- if it's yellow let it be mellow, if it's brown, let it go down
- don't water lawns
- don't wash the car
- take shallow baths and short showers.

Water efficiency – doing more with less

No lifestyle changes should be required and efficient fittings should do the same job with less water. Often, efficiency improvements lead to other advantages such as reduced energy consumption, lower noise and even better performance.
   Examples:

- hydraulically-efficient WC pans and cisterns (i.e. not just reduced flush volume)
- optimised water pipe dead-legs and insulation
- optimised bath shape
- tap aerators and sprays
- showerhead design
- efficient white goods
- garden design, drought tolerant plants and grasses, mulch
- fix leaks.

Water sufficiency – enough is enough

This approach is one of optimisation and, as with efficiency, there should be no loss of effectiveness. Optimising *water sufficiency* usually involves technical and user input. For example, baths can be optimised in shape and limited in size but users can still choose how deep to fill them. Similarly, dual flush WCs promise savings dependent on correct use. Conversely, habit-dependent savings such as turning off taps when brushing teeth can be influenced by technical innovations such as taps with a water-brake feature to remind the user not to turn them on more than is needed.

Examples:

- WC displacement devices and careful adjustment of flush volume
- dual flush
- 'ergonomics' – ecobutton on shower, water-brake taps
- flow regulation
- bath sizing
- control – automatic or manual, e.g. turn off tap when brushing teeth or timed taps
- careful garden watering.

Water substitution – replace water with something else, such as air
This is self-explanatory and covers technical solutions such as vacuum and compost toilets as well as simply using a broom rather than a hose to clean paths. Some alternatives to water may have a higher environmental impact than water but this may be justified in extreme environments; for example, if water is not available or disposal is limited.
Examples:

- dry toilets
- waterless urinals
- vacuum drainage (uses some water but air used for transport)
- clothes brush
- dry cleaning (not done for water saving).

Water reuse, recycling and harvesting – a potentially virtuous circle
Definitions vary but we suggest that reuse refers to direct reuse with minimal treatment, whilst *recycling* refers to a process of treatment prior to reuse.

10.1.
A leak-free 4 litre flush WC
(Courtesy of Green Building Store,
www.greenbuildingstore.co.uk).

Direct reuse is generally a low-cost option but requires a good availability and quality match between resource and sink to avoid the need for treatment and storage. Recycling introduces the need for extra energy and possibly chemicals for treatment. Other impacts should be considered if the aim is environmental improvement rather than just water saving.

Examples:

- Direct *reuse*:
  - rainwater harvest
  - water butts
  - greywater irrigation (direct)
  - shared bath water
- *Recycling* – treatment, storage reuse:
  - greywater recycling
  - blackwater recycling.

Technologies

Water conservation becomes increasingly important as demand for water increases and shortfalls in supply occur. A number of water saving measures can be used in the home with little impact on the every day lives of householders. These can involve:

1. WCs
2. dry toilets
3. showers
4. washing machines
5. taps.

WCs

WCs account for most domestic water use, typically between 30 and 40 per cent of all water used in the home. Where existing WCs have over sized cisterns modest savings can be achieved by using a displacement device, typically a plastic bottle, bag or dam. These measures are cheap but care must be taken to ensure that the volume of water is sufficient to clear the pan, otherwise double-flushing will occur leading to increased water use.

For new installations most countries now insist on a 6 litre maximum flush volume. Singapore requires a maximum of 4.5 litres and Australia 4 litres. In practice, the Australian specification has been met by 6 and 3 litre dual flush, which will theoretically average about 4 litres per flush. In Scandinavia 4 and 2 litre dual flush is standard but not required by law.

Until January 2001 all WCs installed in the UK had to use a leak-free siphon flush rather than a valve mechanism which is the norm for the rest of the world. Whilst valves are now allowed the issue of leakage remains. In the US, for instance, the American Water Works Association estimate that 20 per cent of all American toilets leak at a rate of approximately 20 000 gallons (76 m^3) per year per toilet.

The lower limit for normal gravity drains is generally thought to be about 4 litres/flush. Lower volumes can be used with devices such as flush boosters, which collect a number of flushes, and release these in one large flush to ensure good drain carry.

Vacuum and compressed air systems further reduce the volume of water required to around 1.2 litres/flush but are not currently considered appropriate for domestic installations.

Dry toilets

Dry toilets use no water for flushing. The compact type is usually electrically powered, heating the waste material to accelerate breakdown and evaporate urine or to dry the contents to form an 'ash'. The main problems with this type of toilet are the high energy use, plastic construction, large size and proximity

10.2.
The ceramic pedestal of a high quality compost toilet (Nick Grant Elemental Solutions).

of the user to fresh faeces. Proper composting, or mouldering, toilets (greater than 1.5 m³) do not usually require an external input of energy although a small (2–3 W) fan is recommended. Large composting toilets may be environmentally acceptable as they consume no water, require no drainage pipework and produce compost that can be used in the garden. However, such systems can be difficult to incorporate into standard house designs and the responsibility for sewage is put onto the householder. Enthusiasts appreciate the lack of splash, noise and smell but some people can be nervous of the dark hole under the seat. For sites with water supply or drainage limitations such toilets can provide an economic and robust solution. All composting toilets require some care: the owner must periodically add other organic material, turn compost to aerate the waste, and remove finished compost. The compost is often used around the yard for mulching ornamental plants.

Waterless urinals are becoming increasingly used in public toilets around the world. Domestic urinals appear in some continental sanitaryware catalogues but are not common. Some ecohouses use the bidet as a low-flush unisex urinal.

Showers

In the UK the average amount of water used for a conventional shower is approximately 30 litres, whilst a bath requires about 80 litres. Initially, it appears that showering is more energy- and water-efficient, but the fact is that households with showers use them more frequently than households without showers use their baths. Also, pumped and multi-head showers are not as water-efficient as conventional showers. Real savings can be made if you choose your products wisely but generalisations are difficult as user expectations and water pressure vary widely. Atomising and aerating showers offer

10.3.
Aquaflow Regulator to replace standard isolating valves. Regulators mentioned in text (Nick Grant Elemental Solutions).

power shower performance with less water but are only suitable for mains pressure and can cause a cold feet effect. Most *water saver* showers will use more water than UK electric showers or low pressure gravity fed ones.

Separate temperature and flow controls will reduce water and energy waste whilst trying to optimise flow and temperature by adjusting the hot and cold valve. They will allow the flow to be stopped to apply shampoo without losing the temperature setting. Simple flow regulators or restrictors allow a *water sufficient* flow rate to be set regardless of user awareness and water pressure variation.

Conventional shower heads can discharge water at between 0.3 to 0.5 litres/sec. Low-flow showerheads can reduce this to below 0.2 litres/sec depending on the supply pressure. Research conducted in the USA has shown that the use of low-flow showerheads can save approximately 27 litres each day per person (for a person who mainly showers rather than takes baths). This equates to an energy saving in hot water of 444 kWh per person each year for water heated by gas (or 388 kWh for water heated by electricity). The cheaper alternative to low-flow showerheads is to fit a flow restrictor to the supply to an existing shower head, although this may increase the showering time.

Washing machines

Presently, 85 per cent of households in the UK, for instance, possess a washing machine and 10 per cent a dishwasher. Together these consume about 15 per cent of domestic drinking water. The ownership of these previously luxury goods is increasing.

The water and energy efficiency of machines is improving rapidly and can be determined from Energy labels in Europe and equivalent schemes in other countries. Usually the better machines tend to be the most efficient in terms of wash performance, water and energy use.

UK water by-laws govern the maximum permissible volume of water used for a wash: between 150 and 180 litres for a washing machine (depending on drum size) and about 196 litres for an average dishwasher although European machines all use far less water than this – in most European countries new machines use less than 50 litres/cycle (5 kg). Modern high-efficiency washing machines use far less water than the older types (Figure 10.4); the AEG washing machine uses as little as 68 litres of water for a 5 kg fill and only 1.4 kWh for a hot and cold fill. This is around a third of the water used in a conventional machine. For the dishwasher the Oxford Ecohouse uses another AEG machine which uses only 15 litres of water and 1.2 kWh electricity for a 50°C biowash cycle (see Elemental Solutions, 2003).

Flow regulators should be a standard item in all mains pressure plumbing systems as they balance flow and dynamic pressure. This means that the available flow is divided appropriately between the various outlets at a *water sufficient* rate. Thus, if the WC is flushed or a kettle filled whilst someone is in the shower, the flow and temperature will remain more stable if flow regulators are fitted throughout the plumbing system. Water and energy savings are an added bonus and will be greater with less aware users who leave taps and showers running at full flow.

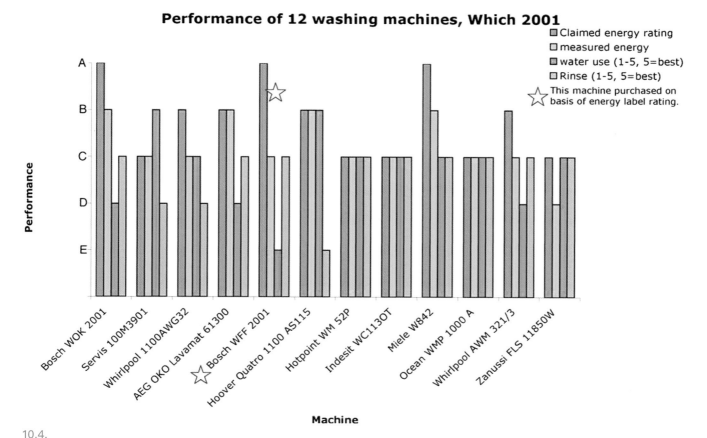

10.4.

Graph illustrating test results on washing machines to see if they live up to their Energy Label ratings. Data taken from Which? 2001.

Automatic **leak detectors** are becoming increasingly available in the UK. These devices are fitted into the incoming mains and close when a leak is detected, preventing both the waste of water and damage to property. Some operate by sensing a high or sustained flow rate and others use conductivity detectors placed where leaks might occur to activate electronic valves. Simple remote stop valves are also available at low cost, which allow the mains feed to be shut off with a flick of a switch when leaving the house. One model uses water pressure to operate the valve and so requires no battery or mains connection.

Taps

Automatic **closure taps** can produce water savings in commercial and public buildings where there is a risk of taps being left open accidentally. Spray taps are ideal for hand washing but not for filling a basin so their application is limited to commercial washrooms and small domestic hand basins. Sprays typically work best at about 1.8 litres/minute compared with a more typical 6–12 litres/minute for normal taps. In the UK a simple device is available which provides a spray at low flows but increases to full flow as the tap is opened.

Another innovation is the water-brake feature found on a few single-lever mixer taps. This limits flow to about 5 litres/minute unless extra force is applied to overcome a mechanical stop. Some of these taps also provide only cold water when the lever is in the mid position thus saving energy.

WASTEWATER SYSTEMS

Wastewater is used water. Wastewater may contain substances such as human waste, food scraps, oils, soaps and chemicals. In houses, wastewater can include the water from sinks, showers, bathtubs, toilets, washing machines and dishwashers. Businesses and industries also use water for a wide variety of other purposes.

Wastewater can include stormwater (rainfall) run-off. Although many people assume that stormwater run-off is clean, it isn't. Contaminants such as hydrocarbons wash off urban surfaces such as roadways, parking lots and rooftops and can harm our rivers, lakes and marine waters.

KEY DIFFERENCES BETWEEN GREY WATER AND BLACK WATER

1 Grey water contains only one-tenth of the nitrogen of black water. Nitrogen (as nitrite and nitrate) is the most serious and difficult-to-remove pollutant affecting our potential drinking water. As grey water contains far less nitrogen, it is unnecessary for it to undergo the same treatment process as black water.

2 The medical and health professionals view black water as the most significant source of human pathogens. Organisms that threaten human health do not grow outside of the body (unless incubated) but are capable of surviving especially if hosted in human faeces. Separating grey water from black water dramatically reduces the danger posed by such pathogens because in grey water the faeces that carry (and may encapsulate) them are largely absent. However, other bacteria are present in grey water and can cause rapid growth of any faecal contamination present in pipes and septic systems. Care must be taken to ensure that both grey and black water travel rapidly through the pipes in buildings and that there are no points in the system where they can stagnate.

3 The organic content typical of grey water decomposes much faster than the content typical of black water. The amount of oxygen required for the decomposition of the organic content in grey water during the first 5 days (Biological Oxygen Demand over 5 days or BOD5) constitutes 90 per cent of the total or Ultimate Oxygen Demand (UOD) required for complete decomposition. BOD5 for black water is only 40 per cent of the oxygen required. BOD1 for grey water is around 40 per cent of the UOD; BOD1 for black water is only 8 per cent of the UOD. This means that the decomposing matter in black water will continue to consume oxygen far longer and further away from the point of discharge than it will in grey water. This faster rate of stabilisation for grey water is advantageous for the prevention of water pollution as the impact of greywater discharge generally does not travel as far from the point of discharge when combined with wastewaters. This is especially true for sand and soil infiltration systems. As grey and black waters are so different it is better to separate them and, more specifically, to keep urine and faeces out of the water altogether and to treat them separately for the best protection of health and the environment. Doing so also has significant savings for homeowners.

When we pull the plug in the bathtub or flush the toilet, few of us give much thought to where the wastewater is going but wastewater doesn't just disappear when it leaves our homes and businesses. There are three types of sewer systems:

1 sanitary sewers carry wastewater from sinks, toilets, tubs and industry
2 storm sewers carry run-off from rainfall, called stormwater
3 combined sewers carry wastewater and stormwater through the same pipe.

Together, these form our wastewater collection system.

* In the USA each day, the average person produces about 220–450 litres of wastewater. That's enough to completely fill a bathtub two times.
* If everyone installed water-saving toilets and showerheads, we could substantially reduce domestic water consumption.
* Each day, in the USA the average person uses 260 litres of water for domestic purposes. That's about 7 million litres of water in a lifetime.
* A leaky tap will waste in excess of 90 litres of water each day.

GREY WATER REUSE SYSTEMS

Grey water systems reuse either rainwater or water that has already been used once in the home, such as shower, bath and washing machine water,

10.5.

Section through the village of Khoranaq, in the Central Persian desert north of Yazd, showing the passage of the water from an underground channel or Qanat through the village, being used from clean to dirty uses. On its path the underground stream is used to: 1. fill the drinking water cistern; and 2. the bath house or Hammam; where it emerges it is used for 3. washing of kitchen ware and clothes (without detergents); and 4. drops down a vertical chute to turn the horizontal mill wheel and emerges again to provide drinking water for the animals and water for the fields. Washing of clothes with detergent is done downstream of the animal drinking water pond and the water run to waste (Roaf).

for secondary, non-potable purposes such as flushing WCs and watering the garden. The concept of domestic water reuse is not new. People have for centuries been reusing water as they go about their daily lives, whether it be throwing the cold contents of a tea pot onto the garden or for surviving in the desert, as shown in Figure 10.5.

The reuse of grey water potentially reduces the need to use potable water for non-potable applications with the water effectively being used twice before discharge to the sewer. The major reuse potential is for WC flushing, garden watering and in some parts of the world car washing, all functions for which the use of pure potable water is unnecessary. Grey water systems can result in the conservation of water resources and reduce demand on both public water supplies and sewage collection and treatment facilities.

The UK experiences with domestic grey water systems for WC flushing have not been a success and it is difficult to see how such systems can be economic or environmentally beneficial particularly as reduced WC flush volumes make the potential savings even more marginal. For dry climates and droughts, simple direct reuse of cool grey water without treatment or storage can contribute to a green and productive garden without the need for mains water.

RAINWATER HARVESTING

In many countries traditional homes had a water cistern incorporated into them to collect rain from the roof for their entire domestic needs. As Case Study 17 in Mexico City (see page 408) shows this is still being done in modern ecohouses. Where mains water is available, efficiency measures are generally more economically and environmentally viable than collecting and pumping rainwater.

Rainwater drainage

Mains stormwater connections are not usually compulsory and in the UK some water companies offer reduced fees if it can be shown that no roof or surface water discharges into the mains sewer. Although relatively clean, stormwater can be more problematic than sewage because of the high peak flows that can overload treatment plants which receive combined sewer flows.

The use of impervious surfaces for paths, roads and car parking prevents rainwater naturally filtering into the ground and instead creates contaminated run-off containing pollutants such as animal faeces, tars and vehicle fuel and oil. The natural solution to these problem is an approach usually known as Sustainable Drainage Systems or SuDS (formerly referred to as Sustainable Urban Drainage) or Best Management Practice (BMP). SuDS aims to:

- reduce the load on sewage treatment plants
- prevent pollution
- control flooding
- recharge groundwater
- replace lost wetland habitat
- enhance amenity value.

PLANNING A NEW GREY WATER SYSTEM

1 **Make a brief inventory** of grey water sources and the number of uses that they get.

Laundry	litres per person per day
Dishwasher	litres per person per day
Bath	litres per person per day
Other sources	litres per person per day
Total grey water	litres per person per day

Try to determine how many litres per cycle your appliances use – or use the short-form sizing estimator given below.

Approximate water use of standard appliances	*Litre*
US washing machine (top-loading)	120
European washing machine (front-loading)	40
Dishwasher	10–20
Low-flow showerhead (per shower)	10–20
Other sink use (shaving, hand washing, etc.)	5–20

2 **Use the general site data and design considerations in the box below** to determine what steps are relevant for your situation. Give

---

DESIGN INFORMATION: EXISTING TREATMENT FACILITIES AND PROCESSES

- Septic tank.
- Leach-field.
- Cesspool.
- Other influent quality and quantity.
- Number of bedrooms.
- Number of persons – normal occupancy.
- Type of appliances and unit flow-rates:
  - Dishwashers
  - Washing machines
  - Bathtubs, showers.
- Evaporation rates.
- Temperature data.
- Rainfall data.
- Effluent reuse goals.

---

special consideration to the final dispersion of the effluent, making sure that the soil can accept the amount of water that will be generated, treated and discharged (your local professional engineer can do a percolation test to determine the ability of the ground to accept water). If water shortage is a particular restriction, note that grey water filtered through a

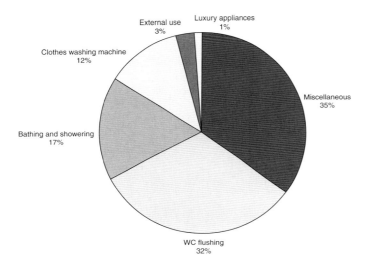

External use
3%

Luxury appliances
1%

Clothes washing machine
12%

Miscellaneous
35%

Bathing and showering
17%

WC flushing
32%

soilbed as described in this text will not become anaerobic and thus can be saved for lawn irrigation, car washing, etc.

3 **Check with your local authority** regarding any special/local concerns and regulations. Submit your application to the local board of health or consult your local professional engineer for plans and documents needed for your application (usually a topographic site drawing with pertinent information about your site and the proposed solution).

POTENTIAL PROBLEMS WITH GREY WATER

The possible problems of using grey water can be grouped into three categories including those that impact on:

- human health
- plumbing systems
- the external environment.

Human health

The first of these is of greatest concern and arises principally as a result of the risk of pathogenic micro-organisms occurring in grey water. Although by definition grey water does not contain faecal contamination, tests have shown that these contaminants can be present. For example, analysis of grey water from the washing machines, showers and bathroom sinks of different families in the USA revealed the presence of micro-organisms of faecal origin (counts were only high in grey water from families with young children, however, where faecal coliforms averaged 1.5×103 cfu per 100 ml; Rose et al., 1991). The actual risk to health posed by reusing grey water depends not just on the level of contamination but also on the degree to which humans are exposed to the water and their susceptibility to any pathogens present. Additionally, many systems incorporate a disinfection process.

Plumbing systems

These include the reuse systems themselves. Problems include corrosion, fouling and microbiological growth. These problems may be greater than in potable water supply systems owing to the materials present in grey water, both particulate and dissolved, and the fact that grey water is often warm when first collected. However, risks can be minimised through careful design of systems and the adoption of appropriate maintenance procedures.

The external environment

Problems here include, for example, a risk of groundwater contamination if grey water is used for landscape and garden irrigation and an increase in the concentration of waste discharged to sewers, which could potentially cause blockages and have implications for sewage treatment works. The risk of such effects occurring is only likely to be significant under certain circumstances. The risk might increase, for example, if there were a very high uptake and use of systems in a sensitive area. It is also important to note that in most cases both positive and negative environmental effects can be identified, and that the overall balance is usually positive.

Many countries, such as the UK, at present have no published Grey Water Standard relating to grey water reuse systems. However, depending on the particular circumstances under which the systems are to operate, a number of Regulations and Acts of Parliament may apply. In the UK perhaps the most relevant standard is The Bathing Waters (Classification) Regulations 1991, which have been suggested as possible water quality standards for grey water systems because they are less stringent than the requirements for water for potable use. Additionally they were designed for a situation where there is physical contact with water and in which there may be occasional accidental ingestion. Several by-laws also affect the use of grey water systems, particularly those related to backflow prevention and accidental cross-connection between potable and non-potable supplies.

TREATING SEWAGE ON THE SITE: SEPTIC SYSTEMS

Where a mains sewer connection is available it is generally best to be connected to it, and in most countries this is a requirement. For rural dwellings on-site treatment will usually be required and, where site conditions permit, the system of choice is the septic tank system.

All modern conventionally designed septic systems are composed of the following four basic components:

1 building sewer
2 septic tank
3 distribution box
4 drainfield (or leachfield).

In a conventionally plumbed home all these combined wastewaters flow out of the house into the septic tank through a single 12-cm-diameter pipe called a building sewer pipe (see Figure 10.7).

The septic tank, usually made of concrete, is designed to be watertight. Tank capacity ranges from $4\,m^3$ for a typical three-bedroom, single-family dwelling to $15\,m^3$, depending on the number of bedrooms in the home. Some large residential or commercial applications may require larger tanks, or more than one tank often arranged in series. Most solids entering the septic tank settle to the bottom and are partially decomposed by anaerobic bacteria to form sludge (Figure 10.8).

Some solids float and form a scum mat on top of the wastewater. Little treatment of wastewater occurs in the septic tank, it being mainly a unit for removing solids. A properly maintained septic tank keeps solids and grease from entering and clogging the drainfield, the land into which the tank over-flows drain.

The accumulation of sludge at the bottom and scum at the top of a septic tank gradually reduces the wastewater volume storage capacity of the sep-tic tank. When this happens, incoming solids are not settled out efficiently and may be flushed from the tank into the drainfield and cause clogging and premature system failure. Periodic septic tank pumping (every year) helps prevent solids from entering the drainfield.

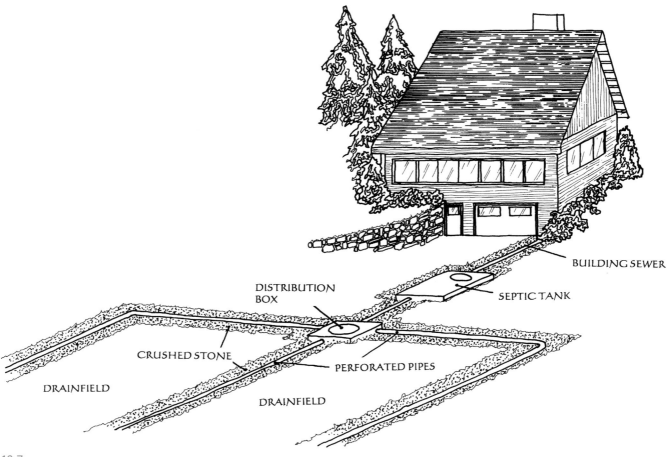

10.7.
Diagram of a house, septic tanks and drainfield.

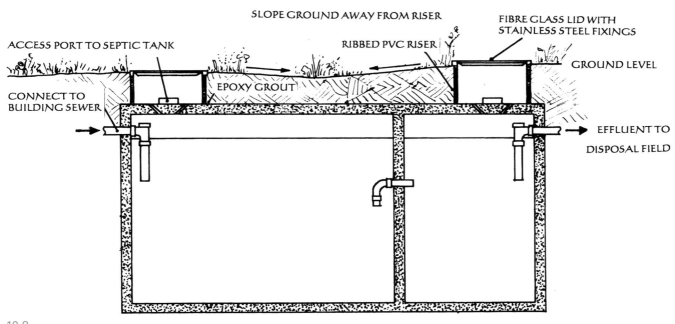

ACCESS PORT TO SEPTIC TANK

SLOPE GROUND AWAY FROM RISER

RIBBED PVC RISER

FIBRE GLASS LID WITH
STAINLESS STEEL FIXINGS

GROUND LEVEL

CONNECT TO
BUILDING SEWER

EPOXY GROUT

EFFLUENT TO
DISPOSAL FIELD

10.8.
Diagram of a conventional two-compartment septic tank.

The drainfield typically consists of perforated pipes in shallow trenches filled with gravel. Variations include gravel-less trenches, chambers, mounds and shallow pressure-dosed systems with much variation between countries. Always consult local regulations which cover design, sizing and location of drainage fields. Where the site is unsuitable for a drainfield it may be possible to use a mound system or pressure-dosed infiltration system but specialist advice must be sought.

SYSTEMS BEYOND THE SEPTIC TANK

These systems are specially engineered and, with the exception of incinerating and composting toilets, are required to discharge to a drainfield.

Nitrogen removal systems

Nitrogen inputs from septic systems can degrade coastal, pond water quality and groundwater supplies beneath densely developed areas. These septic systems are designed to remove nitrogen from the wastestream through biological denitrification. Nitrogen removal systems incorporate an aerobic treatment step, separate anaerobic tanks and carbon sources that supply energy to the bacteria responsible for removing the nitrogen in the wastestream.

Incinerating toilets

Incinerating toilets are designed to handle only the black water component of the household wastestream. In these toilets, urine and faeces combust at high temperatures to produce an inert ash by-product devoid of nutrients, bacteria, viruses and pathogens. Although black water contaminants are totally eliminated from the wastestream, a septic system must still be installed to treat the grey water generated in the household. Water conservation measures can be used to help keep the nutrient and microbial contaminant loadings associated with the grey water wastestream to an absolute minimum.

Composting toilets

In composting toilets, wastewater collects in a tank located beneath a toilet, usually in a basement. The homeowner adds organic material, either sawdust or peat moss to the tank. Microorganisms break down the mixture into 'compost'. Heat, oxygen, moisture and organic material are needed by the microbes to decompose the waste.

This technology dates as far back as the early 1930s and has recently experienced a surge in popularity. Most composting toilets need neither electricity nor heat to operate, whereas some models require minimal inputs of both.

SEPTIC TANK MAINTENANCE

Once built, periodic pumping and inspection of existing septic systems is the key to maximising the longevity and performance, and reducing the environmental impacts of the system. Tank pumping will prevent solids from overflowing into and prematurely clogging the drainfield. As a rule of thumb, septic tanks should be inspected yearly and pumped every 1–4 years.

As previously mentioned, septic system siting, design and installation are the responsibility of the site evaluator, designer and system installer.

System additives

Many septic system additives are marketed as 'cure-alls' for a variety of system problems. Products sold to 'clean' septic systems generally consist of acids, hydrogen peroxide, biological agents or chemicals containing organic solvents. There is no evidence that any of these additives can correct or prevent failure. Use of chemical cleaners can seriously damage the system, alter soil permeability and contaminate groundwater.

Some biological septic tank additives promise to completely eliminate the need for routine periodic pump outs, claiming solids are removed by enzymatic processes. It appears that biological additives function to disperse and resuspend solids in the septic tank, which are then flushed into the drainfield, exacerbating the problem of organic-matter clogging.

SEPTIC SYSTEM LONGEVITY

A septic system drainfield that is suitably located, adequately designed, carefully installed and properly maintained still has a certain lifespan. All drainfields accumulate organic slime material at the junction of the drainfield and native soil. This slime layer is referred to as a biological mat (biomat).

Biomat formation is an inevitable process, eventually sealing the whole drainfield and restricting wastewater movement into the surrounding soil. Biomats do allow some limited flow through them, but it is considerably less than the percolation rate of the native soil material. Surfacing of effluent can occur when wastewater volume to the drainfield exceeds rate of movement through the biomat and into the surrounding soil.

Biomats are slow to develop in coarse-textured sandy or gravely soils. In finer textured silty or clay soils and in dense compacted soils they develop rapidly. Biomat formation in fine textured or dense soils may produce premature system failure if drainfields are not adequately sized. In contrast, biomat formation in some coarse textured soils may actually improve wastewater treatment by providing an additional step to mechanically and biologically filter out pollutants. Dividing the drainfield into two sections and alternating them allows the biomat to break down and for infiltration capacity to be restored.

WHY IS DEPTH TO GROUNDWATER TABLE SO IMPORTANT?

The groundwater table is that elevation beneath the ground surface where the soil becomes saturated with water. Determining the depth to the groundwater table (also called water table) at a proposed development site is essential for proper design and function of a septic system. Saturated soils produce anaerobic (very low oxygen) conditions that reduce wastewater treatment and promote pollutant movement. Unsaturated soils are well aerated (aerobic conditions) and encourage wastewater treatment processes. Thick unsaturated zones of soil beneath a drainfield have better wastewater treatment potential and offer more groundwater protection than shallow unsaturated zones. The depth of the groundwater must be measured by a qualified professional in the rainy season when the water table is at its highest.

SITING A SEPTIC SYSTEM IN THE LANDSCAPE

When evaluating a site for on-site sewage disposal, landscape position can give helpful general information about:

- 'lay of the land'
- location within the watershed
- location relative to wetlands.

Low-lying areas on the natural landscape are often associated with wetlands and floodplains of rivers, streams, ponds and reservoirs. Water tables in these areas are at or near the ground surface. Soils in low-lying areas are wet for long periods of time and are often poorly drained, ponded or flooded. These soils are not suitable for on-site sewage disposal.

Areas located on the sides and tops of hills are called uplands. Upland areas normally have drier soils that are both better suited to and capable of absorbing wastewater loads. Groundwater tables tend to be deeper at hilltop positions and gradually become shallower as one moves down the landscape to low-lying areas. In some cases, however, upland positions may have depressional areas that, owing to local relief and poor soil drainage, are too wet for sewage disposal. Dense basal till soils, often found on the tops and sides of hills, have firm subsoils that restrict water movement. Some dense basal till soils may be suitable for onsite sewage disposal but require large drainfields and careful design. Septic tanks are not normally allowed close to wells, boreholes or in groundwater protection zones.

ALTERNATIVES TO SEPTIC SYSTEMS

Where a septic system is not appropriate – for example due to insufficient land, heavy clay or a high water table – then an alternative system is required. Passive systems include sand filters, trickling filters and reed beds and these are usually the preferred technologies from an environmental perspective. Powered package treatment plants are widely available with electrical consumption of about 1.2–3 kWh/day for a 4–6 person system.

CASE STUDY: THE GREY WATER SYSTEM AT LINACRE COLLEGE, OXFORD

Linacre College built a great new 'green' building as a hall of residence, gym and restaurant in 1995. Anglian Water decided to use this building as a test bed for their innovative grey water system. This consisted of a two-stage process, in which stored grey water is passed through a sand filter to remove solids, then through a hollow fibre membrane separation process, which removes soap, bacteria and some dissolved organic material. Despite the fact that these filters produced a relatively high quality of water, the design of the system as a whole had serious defects including:

- the undergound concrete grey water collection pit was acting as an anaerobic culture vessel, and very quickly rendered the grey water into a condition that was impossible to treat
- the pipe run from the building was too long and shallow, allowing time for bacterial regrowth
- the length of time the water was remaining in the tank was too long. Chlorine disinfection upstream was found not to have any effect and was environmentally undesirable
- the organic material present in grey water changed into a form that was able to pass through the membrane and be assimilated later, in the distribution network. This resulted in the fact that while the treated water was itself clear and sterile, there was sufficient organic material present to allow regrowth later in the system, as the distribution network could never be totally sterile without excessive use of chemicals.

Lessons

- Fast movement to point of treatment, rapid treatment times and avoidance of any possible areas of stagnation will all help to make grey water more readily treatable, by whatever means designers of future systems choose to use.

- Rainwater is usually low in organic material and nutrients, and can be stored in water butts in the home. However, it was found that rainwater can collect material from roofs and down pipes and, when allowed to remain undisturbed for long periods, can become septic. A large amount of black sludge had formed in the rainwater collection tank and analysis showed that anaerobic conditions had developed. Care must be taken at the design stage to allow for complete cleaning of rainwater storage tanks when necessary.

CASE STUDY: GLEDLOW VALLEY ECOHOUSES

The Gledhow Valley Ecohouses are three timber-framed dwellings that have been built to meet high environmental standards. The clients for the scheme are the owners and occupants of the houses, who undertook their own architectural design, as well as being involved in the actual house construction. An autonomous water system was developed for the houses, without a link to a mains water supply or sewage outlet. The water supply operates off a three-pipe system: drinking water is supplied from rainwater collected off the roof, which is stored and sterilised, whilst hot and cold water for washing and bathing is taken from a storage pond in the communal garden area. Wastewater, along with any rainwater run-off, is fed to a reed bed for treatment and then recycled into the storage pond. Composting toilets are used in all three houses, so the recycling system only treats grey water. Like many self-build schemes, the pace of construction was leisurely, with no fixed 'hand-over' date. Some of the clients started living on the site and using the grey water system on an experimental basis.

A reed bed was constructed in the garden adjacent to the houses, around $8\,m^2$ in size, planted in a peat/soil base over a plastic membrane. The principle of operation of a reed bed is anoxic and aerobic biological breakdown of organic components in the wastewater. This takes place around the underground stems of the reeds where large populations of common aerobic and anaerobic bacteria grow. The plants will also absorb a certain amount of chemical impurities from wastewater, such as phosphates and nitrates.

Water that has passed through the reed bed is fed to a storage pond, around $12\,m^2$ in area and $0.5\,m$ deep, which also has a plastic liner. There is no soil medium in this pond, but it does contain oxygenating weeds. The water from the pond is filtered in three stages, with a fine mesh filter at the pond outlet and with cartridge filters between the pump and the tank. The mesh filter has a large surface area and is easily accessible for cleaning, and the second filter has an automatic backwash unit using a stainless steel cartridge. The occupiers did not wish to use chlorine or chemical treatment of water, and a Teflon-coated ultraviolet unit is linked to the holding tank to give bacterial sterilisation to the incoming water. Water in the tank is recycled through the UV unit at periodic intervals to maintain sterilisation during times when little water is being used and to reduce the risk of algae growth in the tank.

Lessons

- It is important to minimise water use in designs before adopting recycling schemes. Devices such as those listed at the beginning of the chapter may provide a simpler solution to water conservation.
- Grey water can be mucky stuff! High levels of contaminants and bacteria (including faecal coliforms) can be present, and it needs treating with care. Reed beds can be a successful part of treatment but they require proper design and attention throughout their lives.
- Grey water recycling systems will generally require careful maintenance and monitoring, and control over which detergents, chemicals, etc., are put into the wastewater. This demands acceptance of a high level of responsibility by users of a system.
- Water used for washing and bathing in houses really needs to meet drinking water standards to ensure safety of the occupants. Standards for WC flushing, washing machines, watering vegetables, etc., are often unclear. If you want to put in a grey water system decide what standards you want it to meet, ensure that these standards are included in an agreement with the contractor and test that these standards are maintained over time.

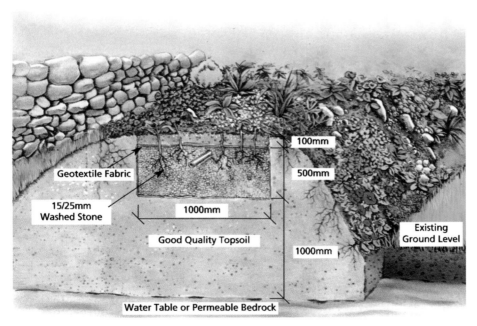

10.9.
Diagram showing how grey water can be incorporated into garden features with the construction of a sub-surface irrigation system (Biocycle Ltd: biocycle@intigo.ie).

- Collection and use of rainwater may often be a more appropriate solution to a water conservation problem than grey water recycling.
- The results for control of bacteria were more disappointing. The main reason for this seems to be the failure of the UV treatment, partly caused by a build-up of sediment in the UV unit. As UV does not have a residual sterilisation effect it was also possible for bacteria to multiply in the pipework.

- Electrical energy use for the whole water system has been monitored over a three-month period, and showed a total consumption of around 100 kWh (equivalent to a cost of 70 pence). This roughly equates to energy use of 2 kWh per 1000 litres of water used.
- The technology of grey water recycling involves a wide spread of disciplines, from microbiology to building services engineering. In these circumstances it is often much more difficult to offer a straightforward 'technical fix' to design problems.

RECOMMENDED READING

Jeppesen, B. (1996) Model Guidelines for Domestic Grey water Reuse for Australia. Urban Water Research Association of Australia, Research Report No 107, Melbourne, Vic.

Jeppesen, B. and Solley, D. (1994) Domestic Grey water Reuse: Overseas Practice and its Applicability to Australia. Urban Water Research Association of Australia, Research Report No 73, Melbourne, Vic.

Methods for the Examination of Waters and Associated Materials. Series of monographs, HMSO, London.

Mustow, S., Grey, R., Smerdon, T., Pinney, C. and Waggett, R. (1997). Implications of Using Recycled Grey water and Stored Rainwater in the UK. Report 13034/1, BSRIA, Bracknell.

National Sanitation Foundation Joint Committee on Wastewater Technology (1983) Standard 41: Wastewater Recycle/Reuse and Water Conservation Devices. NSF, Ann Arbor, MI.

The Microbiology of Water 1994 – Part 1 – Drinking Water. HMSO, London.

US Environmental Protection Agency (1992) Guidelines for Water Reuse. EPA/625/R-92/004, US EPA Center for Environmental Research Information, Cincinnati, OH.

Water Supply (Water Quality) Regulations 1989 (SI 1989/1147), HMSO, London.

Water Supply (Water Quality) (Amendments) Regulations 1991 (SI 1991/1837), HSMO, London.

World Health Organisation (1989) Health Guidelines for the Use of Wastewater in Agriculture and Aquaculture. WHO Technical Report Series 778, Geneva.

LCA

Brix, H. (1999) How 'green' are aquaculture, constructed wetlands and conventional treatment systems? *Water Science and Technology* 40(3).

Crettaz, P., Jolliet, O., Cuanillon, J.-M. and Orlando, S. (1999) Life cycle assessment of drinking water and rain water for toilet flushing. *Aqua* 48(3), 73–83.

Dixon, A. (2001) Watersave Network.

Grant, N. and Morgan, C. (1999) Ecological Wastewater Management: Challenging Assumptions and Developing Contextual Design Solutions. CIBSE National Conference Proceedings, October 1999.

Demand forecasting

Environment Agency (2001) A Scenario Approach to Water Demand Forecasting. Environment Agency, Worthing.

Environment Agency (2001) Water Resources for the Future: a Strategy for England and Wales. March 2001. This document and the associated regional ones give an excellent analysis of the problems of water supply in the UK.

Water conservation

Environment Agency (2001) Conserving Water in Buildings, 'Fact Cards'. Environment Agency, Worthing.

Environment Agency. Demand Management Bulletin; water efficiency newsletter free from the EA Water Demand Management Centre.

Envirowise, Environment and Energy Helpline. Tel: 0800 585794, e.g. GG67; Cost-Effective Water Saving Devices and Practices.

Fiskum, L. E. (1993) Shower Test. BYGGFORSK, The Norwegian Building Research Institute, Oslo.

Harper, P. and Halestrap, L. (1999) Lifting the Lid. Centre for Alternative Technology, Machynlleth. The definitive UK dry toilet book, also covers household nutrient recovery and composting.

Keating, T. and Lawson, R. (2000) The Water Efficiency of Dual Flush Toilets, Southern Water.

Water Conservation: IP 2/00, Low Flow Showers and Flow Restrictors. BRE Water Centre. Available from CRC. Tel: 020 7505 6622.

Reuse

Brewer, D., Brown, R. and Stanfield, G. Rainwater and Greywater in Buildings: Project report and case studies, Technical Note TN 7/2001, BSRIA.

Grant, G. Nutrient Cycling. *Eco Design*, Vol VI, No. 3. The Journal of the Ecological Design Association.

Lens, P., Zeeman, G. and Lettinga, G. (eds) (2001) *Decentralised Sanitation and Reuse*. IWA Publishing.

Marking and Identification of Pipework for Reclaimed (Greywater) Systems, WRAS IGN No 9-02-05, 1999.

Sayers, D. (1999) Rainwater Recycling in Germany. Proceedings from a visit to WISY, Frankfurt, 17–19 August 1998, National Water Demand Management Centre.

Sewage treatment

Grant, N. and Moodie, M. (1997) *Septic Tanks: an overview*. Centre for Alternative Technology, Machynlleth.

Grant, N. and Griggs, J. (2000) BRE Good Building Guide GB42 Part 1, Reed beds: application and specification: Part 2, Reed beds; design, construction and maintenance. CRC Ltd, Tel: 020 7505 6622.

Grant, N., Moodie, M. and Weedon, C. (2000) Sewage Solutions; answering the call of nature. Centre for Alternative Technology, Machynlleth. Introduction to sewage treatment, conventional and alternative.

Metcalf and Eddy Inc. Tchobanoglous G. (1991) *Wastewater Engineering: Treatment Disposal Reuse*. McGraw-Hill.

Private water supply

Brassington, R. (1995) Finding Water: a Guide to the Construction and Maintenance of Private Water Supplies. Wiley.

Regulations

Water Regulations Guide (2000) Water Regulation Advisory Scheme.

Water Supply (Water Fittings) Regulations (1999) SI 1999 No 1148, No 1506 Water Industry, England and Wales.

SuDS

Environment Agency. Designs that Hold Water, Video.

Martin, P. *et al.* (2000) *Sustainable Drainage Systems – Design Manual for Scotland and Northern Ireland*, CIRIA, Publication Code: C521.

Scottish Environment Protection Agency, Environment Agency. *Sustainable Urban Drainage Systems: an introduction*. Free from EA or SEPA.

11 SMALL-SCALE WIND SYSTEMS

MATTHEW RHODES

INTRODUCTION

So great is the tremendous energy in the wind that it can lay waste whole buildings, settlements and forests as it passes over the face of landscapes in the form of hurricanes, tornadoes, cyclones and their modest cousins, gales. The wind has been harnessed since antiquity to power windmills, pump water, generate electricity and cool buildings and people. The wind gains its power ultimately from the sun and wind power is essentially solar energy in another form, as it is the sun which warms air and creates the variations in pressure that drive the wind.

The challenge for wind system designers is the variability of wind. The power generated from any wind turbine varies with the cube of wind speed and this means that small variations in wind speed from one site to another, or from one day to the next, can have a significant impact on the performance and payback of a turbine. Local obstacles, like trees or buildings, can lead to highly variable local wind patterns and these differences make it difficult to generalise about wind turbines because the same sized systems on two different sites – perhaps very close to each other – can have radically different performances.

However, there are some general guidelines and rules of thumb for incorporating wind power in projects. This chapter summarises these, and also provides a common sense approach to developing small wind projects.

PRINCIPLES OF WIND GENERATION

Wind turbines can be divided broadly into two types:

Large systems, from 100 kW upwards. These include 2–5 MW systems used offshore and on commercial wind farms. The largest turbines often have towers well over 100 m tall and rotor diameters exceeding 50 m. Some systems in the 300–100 kW range are suitable for community use (e.g. one or two turbines to run a small group of buildings or village), but in general installing this type of turbine requires a substantial engineering project, costing in excess of £150 000 and involving a diverse range of professionals to do environmental impact assessments, electrical systems studies and design.

Small systems, rated at less than 100 kW. These can be as small as 25 W (roughly 25 cm diameter) and easily handled by one person. Below about 1.5 kW it is possible to mount some of these directly on buildings, although this reduces their effectiveness considerably.

As a very rough rule of thumb at the small scale, the rotor diameter of a turbine in metres will be fairly similar to its rating in kW. Thus a common 1 kW turbine has a rotor diameter of 1.75 m, a 2.5 kW turbine has a diameter of 3.4 m, and a 6 kW turbine 5.6 m. This rule of thumb breaks down quickly as power ratings rise: 25 kW turbines typically have rotor diameters in the region of 10 m, and 200 kW turbines 30 m.

11.1.
A 1 kW building-mounted turbine working in conjunction with solar PV and solar thermal systems at Daventry Country Park (Source: Encraft Ltd).

At small scale wind turbines are essentially electric motors running backwards, rather like the alternator in most cars. An electric current is generated by moving a coil through a magnetic field. Most small wind generators use permanent magnet generators, where the magnet rotates inside a static coil.

Small wind systems are direct drive, with the moving blades of the turbine turning the generator directly. This is an important difference between small wind and the larger commercial wind generators. The commercial systems usually have gearboxes, adding to the noise impact considerably, and it can be helpful to point out this difference when dealing with planning authorities and neighbours.

Small wind turbines generally generate DC electricity at 12 V or 24 V. This can either be used directly, with batteries and a charge controller in exactly the same way as PV systems, or it can be converted into AC with an inverter, again, in exactly the same way as PV systems. Wind systems use similar inverters to solar PV systems, often the same hardware but with different software packages.

WHAT DO WIND TURBINE RATINGS MEAN?

The rating of wind turbines needs to be handled with care. As the power output of a wind turbine varies with wind speed, most turbines are rated at a laboratory wind speed of 12 m/s (metres per second). This means ratings are helpful to compare turbines to each other, i.e. a 6 kW turbine will generally be twice as powerful as a 3 kW turbine at high wind speeds, but they are meaningless for design purposes and to calculate energy outputs directly (a subject covered below).

It is also worth bearing in mind that 12 m/s is around 30 mph, and this should be put in context against an average UK wind speed of 5.6 m/s. This means that most wind turbines rarely achieve their rated power output, a term that simply relates to this standard reference used across the industry and, of course, like much in technical sales, tends to give the impression that machines are more powerful than they actually are.

WHY USE WIND POWER?

The short answer is that on good sites wind turbines are amongst the most economical of all renewable power options. Pound for pound, the costs of a kWh of electricity generated from tower-mounted wind systems, not building-mounted, will be a sixth to a third the cost of PV electricity on sites with UK average wind resources. It is generally feasible to get paybacks of under 20 years, before any grants, and the larger your system the faster the payback, so community-scale systems of 300 kW upwards can often pay for themselves in five to six years or less. For a 2.5–6 kW system on a reasonable site, you should look to recover the costs of the installation in around 12 to 15 years, and this is using 2006 prices at a time of rising conventional electricity prices.

Another virtue of wind is that it is sometimes feasible to generate all the electricity for a building from a single wind installation, without dwarfing the rest of the project budget in the process. As discussed under the section on costs below, tower-mounted domestic UK wind systems should come in between £6 000 and £20 000, and for this cost the total output will substantially exceed the electrical energy requirements of a well-designed ecohouse.

Like PV, 100 per cent of electricity generated from wind turbines is renewable, and because the systems are generally made from steel and composite materials, the carbon emissions associated with the energy used in manufacturing the system are generally recovered in the first nine to twelve months of operation.

11.2.
An Iskra 5.3 kW wind turbine outside
'The Turbine' innovation centre in
Nottinghamshire. (Image courtesy of
Martine Hamilton Knight and
Nottinghamshire County Council.)

ADVANTAGES AND DISADVANTAGES OF WIND POWER COMPARED TO PV

Well-designed wind turbines share the advantages of PV in generating clean green power, minimising transmission losses and providing local independent electricity supplies.

The advantage of wind power compared to PV is its cost per unit of green electricity generated, the potential to generate larger amounts of electricity for a home with limited roof size and its flexibility. Turbines can be mounted anywhere where there is a clear wind stream, and are a reliable and established technology.

On the downside, it is much harder accurately to predict the output from a wind system as part of a building project than it is PV, because typically the impact of local wind patterns will be impossible to determine before installation without extensive monitoring, which could easily exceed the cost of the actual turbine. You have to take educated guesses in the design process, which can sometimes be uncomfortable.

Wind systems do also require maintenance, although this shouldn't be much more than oiling them once a year, and most have design lifetimes of around 15 years, which is considerably lower than PV. Unlike PV, they are not really at home on buildings, and building-mounted turbines are really only valid as the icing on an eco-cake: they are rarely likely to be an integral part of an eco-design and energy supply system. The wind turbine is not a natural feature of an urban or suburban landscape unlike PV systems.

Noise and visual impact are sometimes perceived as disadvantages, but in practice are more issues of perception and politics than science. Most small wind turbines have measured noise outputs at or close to the hub in the region of 55 dB(A) or less. This should be put in context: normal conversation is around 60 dB(A) and the commercial wind turbines, with gearboxes, which you can hear at a distance, often have hub noise levels exceeding 100 dB(A).

A useful UK noise benchmark is 35 dB(A) which is used as the standard for normal night-time background noise in rural areas. A source of noise at 55 dB(A) will be audible above background noise only within 3 m or less, assuming no intervening obstacles such as walls, windows or trees.

Noise tends to be used as an objection to wind turbines by people who have read about planning enquiries into large wind farms, and who assume that systems between 1 and 10 per cent of the size of commercial wind turbines must have the same characteristics as the large systems. This is a fallacy that most planning authorities and environmental health officers have now understood. A better way for people to think about small wind in relation to large wind is to use the analogy of bicycles and juggernaughts: both have wheels and transport things, so they are both transport technologies, but this does not mean that they are equally dangerous or should be subject to identical technical regulations.

BUILDING-MOUNTED TURBINES

Rooftop wind turbines became available in the UK during 2006, and created considerable media and public attention. They have special mountings to minimise potential vibration issues, and can be mounted on structurally sound gable end walls above the roofline (but not above chimneys). Systems are available from half a dozen suppliers in the range of 400 W to 1.5 kW.

No long-term performance data is yet available, but most experts confidently predict that the maximum likely output from building-mounted systems will be in the region of 300–800 kWh a year on most UK sites. This is because turbulence around buildings effectively reduces local wind speed by at least 25 per cent, and at these lower wind speeds the power output of the larger machines will not be much greater than that from the smaller ones.

At this level of output the cost per unit of electricity generated over the lifetime of the turbines is comparable to PV generation.

On the plus side, rooftop wind turbines are being marketed as mass market products. They are generally designed to 'plug-and-play' and can be wired into a normal domestic ring main. This has made them popular, and an effective way of offsetting the carbon emissions caused by standby lighting and appliances in many UK homes.

VERTICAL AXIS WIND TURBINES

As well as the traditional horizontal axis wind turbines, it is also possible to buy vertical axis machines. These generally have a lower power output than the horizontal axis machines, which is why you don't see them very much, but they can offer interesting architectural possibilities.

There are two basic designs: Savonius and Darrieus. Savonius machines are S-shaped in plan view, and Darrieus systems are basket shaped (Figure 11.4).

Vertical axis machines are virtually silent, and are less affected by turbulence than horizontal axis machines because they don't need to turn into the

11.3.
Details of typical mounting arrangements for a 1 kW building-mounted turbine. At present most manufacturers will only mount systems on strong gable end walls like this one, which they test before installation. (Source: Encraft.)

wind continuously. They generally need slightly higher wind speeds to work well and they need more power from the wind to get moving.

On the negative side, small systems are not very powerful as power is proportional to the swept area. Thus, for example, a 1 m tall 30 cm diameter Savonius machine might generate around 40–100 kWh per year of electricity, or sufficient to power a single light bulb.

Maintenance of vertical axis machines is also potentially more complex than horizontal systems as you need to dismantle the whole system to get at the main bearings. However, for all types of turbines, maintenance requirements for well-built systems should be relatively simple, so this isn't a major issue.

There are, however, some interesting helical (DNA-like) designs of turbine, such as the Quiet Revolution (Figure 11.4) and Turby machines. These are typically 5 m tall and 3 m in diameter, so suited only to larger projects. A system of this size will cost around £30 000 installed.

11.4.
Free-standing Darrieus turbine. These systems can also be incorporated in large building projects (e.g. on the roof of office developments), although there are no examples yet in the UK. (Source: Quiet Revolution Ltd, www.quietrevolution.co.uk).

HOW MUCH DO WIND TURBINES COST?

Table 11.1 below gives an indication of the installed cost and likely output at three different wind speeds for various different horizontal axis wind turbines available in the UK. Unlike PV, where much of the cost is the materials and there is significant potential for economies of scale in manufacturing (leading to expectations that prices will fall in the next few years), wind power is a mature technology and there is limited potential for cost reduction as the market grows.

Table 11.1.

Turbine	Installed cost (£)	Theoretical annual output (kWh) at sites with an average annual wind speed of		
		4 m/s	5 m/s	6 m/s
Eoltec 25 kW	40 000	17 000	32 000	51 000
Proven 6 kW	22 000	6 700	11 600	16 900
Iskra 5.3 kW	21 000	5 000	8 700	13 100
Proven 2.5 kW	12 000	2 400	4 200	6 300
Windsave WS1 000*	1 500	120	370	740

*building-mounted

From this table you can see that the payback from the same wind system could vary by a factor of three to six depending on the wind speed. It is quite normal for average wind speed on the same site to go up and down by 25 per cent from year to year.

A typical wind turbine installation will involve a number of elements, and the table below shows a typical breakdown for a 2.5 kW system.

Table 11.2. Typical breakdown for a 2.5 kW system

Turbine	£3 500
Mast	£2 400
Inverter	£1 600
Controllers, switches, meters	£500
Foundation/ground works	£2 000
Installation	£2 000
Total	**£12 000**

All these costs are for grid-connected systems. For off-grid systems you should budget 25 per cent extra for batteries.

Grants are often available and worth looking for, although off-grid systems are generally not eligible.

SIZING AND SPECIFYING YOUR WIND SYSTEM

As with all renewable generation projects connected with buildings, the most important starting point in specifying a wind system is to minimise the total electricity demand that the wind system will have to meet. This is covered in detail in Chapter 8 and the process is the same if you are designing a wind system.

Here is a straightforward checklist to follow in designing a wind system.

1 Identify the total electrical demand your system will have to meet.

For wind, this is best done for a full year. You can take your total electrical demand from an electricity bill, if your project is for an existing building, or you can make an estimate by multiplying the power of each of your electrical appliances (in kW) by the time it is on each year (in hours). Round these figures upwards, because you don't want to under-design.

So, for example, if you have a computer you use to work on at home and it is rated at 60 W (i.e. 0.06 kW), and is on for an average of 2 hours each day, the total annual electricity demand from your computer would be:

$$0.06 \times 2 \times 365 = 438 \text{ kWh (remember to divide Watts by 1000 to get kW)}$$

You should get an answer, for a family of four, broadly in the range 1000 kWh to 10 000 kWh, and only in the higher range if you are using electricity for heating (for example with a ground source heat pump). The average UK (non-eco) home typically uses between 3500 and 6000 kWh electricity per year excluding heating.

2 Decide whether you want an off-grid or on-grid system.

If your house is already connected to the grid, it is generally best to opt for a grid-connected wind system. This enables you to export excess power (and usually to get paid for it, which makes your project cost–benefit better) and to use the grid to balance out peaks and troughs in your own generation. It also means you don't have to pay for and design a battery system, which can be expensive and involves making difficult trade-offs between cost and the risk of running out of power.

Off-grid systems are sometimes necessary because the house is not connected to the national grid at all, or you may opt to try and power a defined group of appliances from a system that is somehow distinct from your main electrical circuits, for example garden lighting, a barn or shed. In this case it may also be worth opting for a full DC system, eliminating the cost of the inverter, provided you are willing to seek out a suitable range of DC appliances.

3 Pick the most exposed location you can on your land or site for the proposed turbine.

Some wind purists would advocate siting any turbine at least 10 m higher than any obstructions within 175 m, but this is to secure perfect conditions, and you can usually apply common sense, avoiding trees or buildings and trying to get the turbine well above nearby obstructions.

In siting the turbine you should also bear in mind that the low voltage DC most small wind systems generate is not a very efficient way to transmit power, and DC systems incur heavy losses with distance from the generator. This means that you should try to site the inverter and control electronics as close as possible to the turbine itself, which may mean building a small weatherproof enclosure close to the turbine site. Once power is converted to 240 V AC you can treat it like any other electrical system.

Small wind systems are generally mounted on masts between 9 m and 15 m tall, similar to large telegraph poles, and these are supplied 'off-the-shelf' by the manufacturers.

4   Obtain an estimate of the wind speed at your site.

For a preliminary design, the best way to do this is to use the (free) national database of wind speeds by location, called NOABL. This is published by the DTI and available from the British Wind Energy Association website at http://www.bwea.com/noabl/index.html. The database is a mathematical model of wind flow over the UK landmass, ignoring vegetation and buildings. This is far from perfect but is nevertheless the best data available. You can use your postcode to get the ordnance survey grid reference for your proposed location, and the database will give you an estimated annual average wind speed at 10 m above ground level for each square kilometre in the country.

5   Use this wind speed and your annual demand figure from step 1 above to make a very tentative first estimate of the size of system you'll need (use Table 11.1 above to do this).

You can now start making some judgements as to how much of your electricity you want to generate from the wind, and roughly what size of system and budget you'll be looking at. This should give you sufficient information to approach specialist suppliers with confidence, and get more detailed technical data on their machines and the likely costs and performance.

6   Calculate the actual likely output of the proposed machines for your site.

Now you have narrowed down your choice of turbines, you are in a position to do some more precise calculations as to likely outputs and performance on your site. Be warned, however, that this section is optional, and really only for those of a mathematical inclination! So you don't have to do this – you can rely on your installer or supplier and their analysis instead. But for those who really want to know, here is the normal method used in the wind industry to predict the electrical energy generation from a wind turbine.

As already mentioned, all wind turbines have power outputs that vary significantly with wind speed, and if you plot these on a graph you get a curve that is unique for every design of wind turbine, called a power curve (see Example 1). This plots kW output against wind speed, so you can look up, say, the output of the turbine at 6 m/s by reading along the horizontal axis until you get to 6 m/s and then going vertically upwards until you meet the curve, then reading across to the vertical axis to get the power output (see example again).

Of course the wind doesn't blow at 6 m/s all the time, and simply multiplying the average wind speed for the site by the power output at that wind speed is meaningless, because you really need to know how long the wind blew at 1 m/s, 2 /s, 3 m/s, etc. as well (i.e. how the average was made up).

So to get a more accurate figure for expected energy generation on your site what you have to do is multiply the whole power curve by another curve showing the distribution of wind speeds on the site (see Example 2).

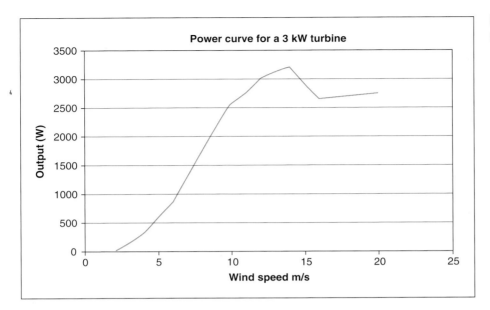

Example 1
Power curve for a typical 3 kW turbine.

A wind speed distribution curve plots all possible wind speeds from 0 to hurricane force gale, and shows for how many hours each year the wind blows at that particular speed.

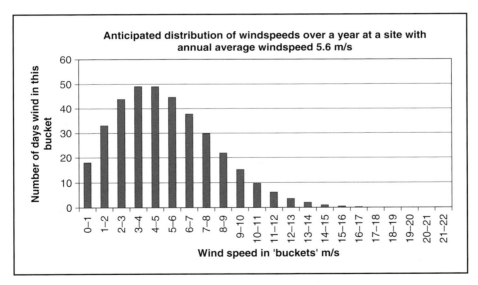

Example 2
Distribution of wind speeds for a typical exposed UK inland site.

You can multiply the two curves for a given turbine and site using a computer, and, hey presto, you'll get a predicted output in kWh.

However, at domestic scale you'd be wise then to add in a few safety factors, particularly if you are designing an off-grid system you will rely on. Average annual wind speed varies considerably from NOABL predictions on many sites, and in any case NOABL gives long-term averages: the actual figure can easily vary by +/−25 per cent from year to year.

You would be wise, therefore, also to examine best and worse case scenarios where the wind speed might be 25 per cent lower than the prediction, and also 25 per cent higher, and to think through the impact on your overall design should these events occur.

7 Make a final selection and engage with a competent installer.

Once you get this far you should have a pretty clear idea of which turbine you want and how much of your electricity and net carbon savings a wind system might contribute to your design each year. For anything above 1 kW you will need a specialist installer, in particular to do the foundations and mounting of the systems, but there are an increasing number of good companies you can use. Look for companies accredited by current government grant schemes, or by the Renewable Energy Association.

DEVELOPING YOUR WIND PROJECT

All wind systems currently require planning permission in the UK, although the government is consulting on making the building-mounted versions permitted-developments in non-conservation areas.

In general, local authorities and planning officers are increasingly support-ive of small wind, and often have policies in place expressing positive sup-port for applicants with appropriate on-site renewable generation. However, most also still lack confidence in resisting concerted campaigns of oppos-ition by neighbours or opponents of wind power, despite the reality that this is often based more on misunderstanding (usually the assumption that 1–6 kW wind systems are similar in character to 1–5 MW systems).

This means that if you are planning to make wind an element of your pro-ject, you would be advised to consult with your neighbours before approach-ing the planning authorities. The flip side of this is that if you have supportive neighbours you should find the application relatively straightforward.

In general, surveys are increasingly showing popular support for small wind – typically with between 50 and 80 per cent of respondents expressing willingness to see installations in their community. Most people who have developed projects successfully find that they meet initial wariness from neighbours, but that this can also be overcome by taking a straightforward factual approach. The reality is that small wind systems are a benign technol-ogy, and their development in the UK has unfortunately suffered from asso-ciation with their larger and more controversial cousins. Other countries have approached wind power development from home scale upwards, and have not experienced the kind of misunderstandings and resistance that has blighted the UK.

12 HYDRO POWER

JAIR HARDER AND MANUEL FUENTES

INTRODUCTION

Hydro power has been used for centuries to turn wheels to grind grain, raise water to irrigate fields and gardens, and to drive large mechanical devices. One of the most widespread of the water power devices is the waterwheel. It has been used since at least 1000 BC by the Assyrians on the banks of the Euphrates[1] and is found in countries around the world from China to Britain and from Canada and Australia to Nepal in the Himalayas.

The generation of electricity for households began in nineteenth-century England with a system built between 1878–84 in the stately home of Cragside near Rothbury in Northumberland using hydro power to run big labour saving machines such as laundry appliances, the rotisserie and a hydraulic lift. The surplus electricity supplied power for a large arc lamp. Now, a century and a half later, the generators and turbines at Cragside, improved and developed over time, are still working.[2]

This chapter is written for people interested in using 'small-scale hydro power generators' to run their ecohouses, a phrase used to denote generators with power outputs ranging from a few hundred watts up to 5 kW.

HYDRO POWER

Every body of water contains energy that can be used to produce electricity, and most rivers or lakes, along or across which there is a difference of altitude or height, could possibly be used to generate electricity. In order to convert the energy in the water into electricity one technically needs to 'transpose the gravitational potential of this energy into electrical energy' and this is done in a *turbine*. In Figure 12.1 a *pico*-hydro system (very small) is shown with all the components that are needed to accomplish this transposing process. Every step of the process of generating hydro power is summarised in the figure with the whole process briefly described.

The sequence of the letters follows the way the water travels through such a system. There are several different ways of generating hydro power but every system includes the following common components.

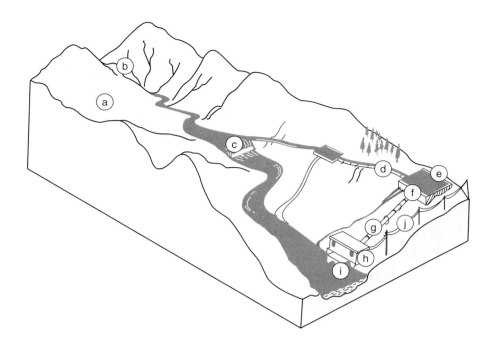

a) Catchment area
b) Run-off
c) Water intake diversion weir
d) Channel
e) Settling tank
f) Trash rack
g) Pen stock
h) Powerhouse
i) Tail race
j) Transmission cable

a) Catchment area

All the rain that falls on this specific area of land will find its way down the *catchment* run-off paths except the water that evaporates, gets lost by transpiration from trees and plants or percolates down to the underground aquifers or water stores where it is stored until it drains away via subterranean water courses or is drawn to the surface again for reuse. The catchment area is bound by the contour lines of the hills or mountains that delineate its slope systems. The size of the catchment area is important, because the larger the area, the more water it can harvest and the more constant the flow of its rivers is likely to be throughout the year.

b) Run-off

Run-off is a term used to describe water moving down a slope system within a catchment area but is perhaps more simply described by terms like *river* or *water course*. The volume of water passing through a river during a given time period is known as the *flow* of the river. When the flow increases by 100 per cent, the power output of a hydro power system will increase by 100 per cent as well. The *velocity*, or speed of flow, of the river depends on the gradient of the slope and the depth of the river.

c) Water intake diversion weir

A *weir* is a dam that is used to raise the river to a constant level to ensure that water flows into the turbine intake throughout the year. Furthermore, the weir slows the water down before entering the intake. Diversion dams for small streams are easy to build to a height of 1 m. Stones, logs or other material

12.1.

A pico-hydro system with all the components that are needed to generate energy. The sequence of the letters follows the way the water travels through such a system (Source: Langley and Curtis. (2004). *Going with the Flow – small-scale water power*. CAT Publications. Available from CAT Mail Order, telephone 01654 705959 or at www.ecobooks.co.uk).

located near the site can be used as long as there is a small pool that supplies the intake of water. When a larger dam is required, experienced advice is recommended.

d) Channel

An open channel is typically used to carry water from the weir to the settling tank. This channel transports the water to a place where the watercourse will have the highest head and the shortest fall. The velocity of the water in this channel depends on the material it is built of and the resistance of its sides, and the size and slope of the channel. It is recommended to keep the velocity as slow as possible to prevent erosion of the channel sides and because a high velocity will result in head loss.

e) Settling tank

A *settling tank*, at the end of the channel, slows the water down before it enters the penstock. In this tank the debris and silt is settled on the channel bed to prevent damage to the turbine.

f) Trash rack

The *trash rack,* or screen, is a very important part in the system. Without a trash rack many turbines would not work for long because debris carried by the stream would cause damage to the turbine. The screens are made from flat bars and come in all kinds of shapes and sizes. The type of rack needed depends on the site conditions and the type of turbine in use. Metal is the most common material used and this has to be zinced to prevent oxidation and decay. Plastic could be used in environments where there is a higher chance of freezing.

Often two trash racks are used to filter the trash in a two-step procedure. Furthermore, screens often require daily maintenance to prevent the extra head loss that occurs when the screen gets full of rubbish. On ultra low head schemes trash is a big problem, especially in autumn. Leaf fall can rapidly block the screens and such considerations may influence the use of the more robust water wheels over the more delicate high-tech turbine devices.

g) Penstock

The *penstock* is a closed pipe through which water flows towards the turbine. The pressure in the pipe depends on the total head distance that the water falls. The higher the drop, the higher the pressure of the water in the penstock and thus its gravitational potential energy. In fact, the head is proportional to the potential power just like the flow. The wall thickness of the pipe is determined by the pressure in it. A pipe with fewer bends and changes in diameter will result in the lowest head loss, thus making it the most efficient construction. The surface roughness inside the pipe causes friction. One rule of thumb states that the bigger the diameter, the lower the frictional resistance of this pipe; however, the larger its diameter the more expensive the pipe will be. The challenge is to find the most economic solution.

One hazard to beware of in designing the penstock is the *water hammer effect*. Water is slightly compressible and because of this characteristic, shock waves can occur and propagate through confined water systems. Shock waves in pipe systems can result from sudden changes in flow such as:

- rapid opening or closing of control valves
- starting and stopping of pumps
- the recombination of water after water column separation, or
- the rapid exhaustion of all air from the system.

When sudden changes in flow occur, the energy associated with the flowing water is suddenly transformed into pressure at that location. This excess pressure is known as surge pressure and is greater with large changes in velocity and can be over 50 per cent more than the normal head pressure. Characteristics of the pipe such as the materials used in construction, the wall thickness, and the temperature of the pipe all affect the elastic properties of the pipe and how it will respond to such surge pressures.[3]

h) Powerhouse

The *powerhouse* is the building where the kinetic energy or gravitational potential energy will be transposed, or changed, into electric energy. In this building the hydro turbine and the generator are stalled. The electric system (the battery bank, inverter and a charge controller) may also be placed in the powerhouse. The electric system is usually located as closely as possible to where the loads occur to improve the efficiency of the transmission of electricity. The size of a powerhouse for domestic use would not be bigger than $2 \times 2 \times 2\,\text{m}$.

i) Tailrace

The *tailrace* leads the water back into the main river. This can be a concrete or brick structure or a pipe.

PLANNING A HYDRO SCHEME

As mentioned above almost every body of water contains energy that can be used to produce electricity, so if there is a river or stream close to your eco-house it is worth investigating whether this watercourse has got enough potential power to run your home. Hydro schemes are most viable when all the needs of the household loads can be met by the system.

Listed below is the basic sequence of what you need to do to develop a hydro scheme:

1 Site assessment
2 Legal agreements
3 Power requirements
4 Turbine design
5 Diversion system design
6 Electrical system design
7 Economics – can you afford it!

The development of a hydro scheme, especially for non-technical people, can be complicated. Also a hydro system can be expensive, especially when the system is poorly designed, but you may feel this is a good investment to generate your own electricity in a market of rising energy prices, or there may simply be no other adequate supply for your ecohouse. Watercourses follow the bottom of valleys where the wind potential is likely to be low!

For these reasons it is recommended that you get in touch with a local hydro specialist who can help you design the technical system (turbine design, diversion system and electrical system) and install it afterwards. If you really want to do it all yourself, then follow up the references at the end of the chapter that will be useful during the design stages. Special attention is given in the following paragraphs to the site assessment, the legal agreements you will need, and the economic assessment on which you will base your decision to proceed with the design. For an insight into how much energy you are going to need your system to generate, i.e. your domestic load and how to configure the electrical system, see Chapter 8 on photovoltaics.

Site assessment

The site assessment starts with a rough assessment of the hydro energy potential of the site. If this shows that there is enough potential to generate an interesting amount of electricity, a more thorough hydrological study can be made. This second study provides a prediction of the behaviour of the river throughout the year. Naturally, the prediction alone is not sufficient to base a final decision on and it has to be checked with actual site measurements. During the site measurements the head and the flow of the river would have to be measured, which can be done by several methods.

Step 1: *Head approximation*
The *head* is the vertical distance over which the water will fall. It can also be explained as the difference in altitude between the intake water level and the turbine position, measured off the map contours. With low head schemes (less than 5 m), the head cannot be determined from the map. On such occasions the head has to be measured at the site.

Step 2: *Flow approximation*
The *flow* changes all the time throughout the year therefore the average daily flow, Q_{AD}, is used to represent the flow. The annual average daily flow can be approximated with the following equation:

$$Q_{AD} = \frac{a \times (r - e)}{s}$$

Q_{AD} = Average daily flow [m^3/s]

a = the catchment area [m^2],

r = annual rainfall [m],

e = annual evaporation [m]

s = number of seconds in the year [32×10^6 sec]

The catchment area can be determined from the contour lines on the scaled map and a knowledge of the directions of the run-off. The annual run-off is the amount of water which runs down the slope throughout the year. This is expressed above as a depth which is equal to the annual rainfall over that specific area minus the water which evaporates before it ends up in the stream.

Step 3: *Approximation power output*
The above calculation gives you an approximation of how the power output can be calculated. This result has to be multiplied by an efficiency factor. A well-accepted efficiency value for a small hydro system is 50 per cent. With the flow data and the head of the scheme known, the power output can be calculated and from these results it can be concluded whether or not the site has got enough potential to power your house.

$$P_{approx} = Q_{Design} \times H_{Gross} \times \gamma \times e$$

P_{approx} = Approximated power output [kW]

Q_{Desigr} = Design flow [m^3/s]

H_{Gross} = Gross-Head [m]

γ = Specific weight of water [9.81 kN/m^3]

e = efficiency [1]

Flow prediction
In the previous paragraphs one flow prediction method is explained. Two other prediction methods can also be used:

1 Flow assessment using catchment data.
2 Flow assessment using stream correlation.

1. Flow assessment using catchment data

This method can only be used when a gauge station is located further down stream of the river. With the data from a gauge station,[3] an estimate can be made of the average flow rate at the specific scheme. The rainfall will hardly vary over a small catchment area and therefore the flow rate will be proportional to the catchment area.

The average flow rate at the gauge station has to be taken into account to calculate the average flow rate at the site. The following equation can be used:

$$Q_{mean} = \frac{\text{Catchment area site}}{\text{Catchment area station}} \times \frac{\text{average flow rate gauge}}{\text{station [}m^3\text{/s]}}$$

2. Flow assessment using stream correlation

Another method that can be used for flow prediction is *stream correlation*. This method is handy when there is no existing flow data from the stream or when only very limited data has been measured. This method is based on data from the analysis of flow patterns of a neighbouring stream or river for which the flow has been measured by a gauge station. The first step is to obtain the flow data is available. Where the correlation has to be made with no flow data from the target stream whatsoever, then the data should be computed in tabular form.

The information needed to accomplish this correlation is the annual rainfall figures of the target stream and the gauged stream as well as the catchment areas of both sites. The information can be obtained by the same process as discussed above. To determine the correlation an adjustment factor has to be found. Hence by first multiplying the annual rainfall by the catchment area of the target stream and, secondly, by dividing this result by the annual rainfall multiplied by the catchment area of the gauged stream this can be arrived at. By multiplying the flow of the gauged stream by the adjustment factor, an estimation of the flow at the target stream can be calculated.

Legal and environmental considerations

The impact of a hydro scheme on the environment depends on its scale. The impact of a large commercial scheme is not comparable with the impact of a *pico*, or very small, hydro scheme, but there are still a large number of legal and environmental considerations to be taken into account when developing a *pico-hydro* scheme.

For a start there are often several kind of licences required from different organisations, several of which will have the responsibility of protecting the rivers, nature and the culture of the countyside from adverse impacts. In England and Wales, for example, these are the responsibilities of the Environment Agency and local Planning Authorities. The Environment Agency is concerned with several aspects of the impacts caused by hydro power schemes on river systems and the Planning Authorities are responsible for granting planning permission for them to be built.

These organisations are very important to the project development process and working closely together with them, particularly at the planning stage, is a very good idea. It is recommended that you approach these stakeholders early on in the development and work with them for your mutual advantage. Other kinds of stakeholders to take into account could be neighbours and National Park Authorities.

Abstraction licence

Hydro power can require a high percentage of the flow of a watercourse to be diverted from a stream or river. For such a diversion, water will be abstracted from the mean flow to the diversion system. To abstract water from a river an *abstraction licence* is needed and can be obtained from the relevant agency that is responsible for river flows. In the UK this is the Environment Agency. If the flow of water to operate the turbine is through the structure, and not via a diverted stream, a licence is not required. Moreover, when the abstraction concerns an amount of water lower than 20 cubic metres per day (0.23l/s) then a licence is not required either.

One of the key restrictions imposed by such a licence is that the water will continually flow in the stream between the intake and the tail water level. There has to be a minimum of 95 per cent flow rate available throughout the year, also known as the 95 percentile flow. This restriction is imposed so that watercourses do not dry up and can continue to feed an adjacent weir.

Impounding licence

The installation of a hydro power device that is built causing the flow of the river to be obstructed or impeded during its construction or alteration will require an *impounding licence*.

Works agreements

Works agreements are needed to cover conditions which are not controllable with an abstraction or impoundment licence. This is when generation is not taking place and after completion of construction of impoundments work. Hydro power schemes can have a big influence on the flow of the river. For instance, when the scheme is not in operation due to maintenance, breakdown or flooding the Environment Agency has to be sure that flow further down stream will be contained and hazards are being safeguarded against.

Turbine design

Turbine and generator

The turbine, along with the generator, is the heart of a hydro system. The turbine and the generator are responsible for the conversion of the energy contained in the water into other forms. The turbine converts potential or kinetic energy into mechanical movement and the generator converts the mechanical movement into electrical energy. The turbines, especially for domestic use, that can be bought on the commercial market are often supplied with a generator, and the electricity produced by the generator is in the form of AC, or alternating current.

In this part of the process the gravitational potential energy of the system is converted into mechanical energy. Turbines can be divided into two groups. In the first group potential energy is converted directly into shaft power. This kind of turbine is known as the reaction turbine and is often submerged in the water as shown in Figure 12.2. When the flow goes through the turbine the weight of the water gives a push to the blades of the runner with shaft rotation as the reaction. The principle is based on the third law of Newton: for every action there must be an equal and opposite reaction. A simple example of a reaction turbine, to explain the principle, is the historical water-wheel. The water flows into buckets and the gravity that works on the mass of the water makes the wheel turn. A typical feature of a reaction turbine is a *draught tube* which is a tube that extends underneath the turbine into the tailrace. The draught tube increases the head. During the operation the tube is filled with water, providing a suction head which adds to the head above the turbine. Reaction turbines are efficient on low-headed schemes and a high flow of water through them is required. The head has to be lower than 7 m, and a reaction turbine for pico-hydro systems can be used with flows of 0.04 m^3/s and over.

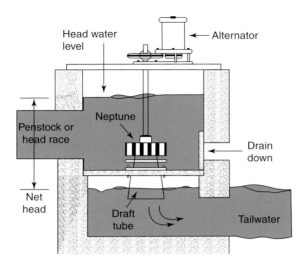

12.2.

Section through a reaction turbine. The water is supplied by the penstock into a chamber in the reaction turbine. The head is equal to the difference between the top of the head water level and the base of the tail water level. As seen the turbine is totally submerged (Source: ABS Alaskan, Inc. http://www.absak.com/).

In the second group of turbines the gravitational potential energy is first converted into kinetic energy before entering the turbine and then the kinetic energy is converted into shaft power. This type of device is known as an impulse turbine, as shown in Figure 12.3. The first conversion is done by one or more nozzle which creates a jet of water that strikes the buckets mounted on the periphery of the runner. The momentum which is caused by the water jet will make the shaft rotate. After contact with the runner the water loses its kinetic energy and drops down into the tailrace. These kinds of turbines are highly efficient on high-headed schemes, typically with heads of over 7 m. The advantage of an impulse turbine is that no high flow is required, and with a flow of only 0.007 m³/s an interesting amount of electricity can be generated, which explains why these types of water turbines have been used in the arid lands of the Middle East and China to grind grain for millennia.[4]

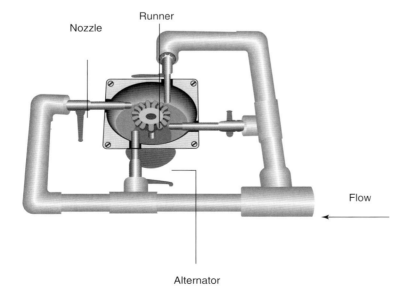

12.3.

An impulse turbine. This impulse turbine is driven by four water jets. Each impulse turbine has its own optimal speed. With several nozzles a higher flow can be used which will result in a higher power output (Source: ABS Alaskan, Inc. http://www.absak.com/).

The optimal type and size of turbine to use depends on site conditions. Reaction turbines are most efficient for low-headed schemes and impulse turbines are highly useful at sites with high heads. Table 12.1 summarises the best types of turbines to use depending on the local site conditions and the attributes of each turbine.

Table 12.1. Summary of turbine operating conditions for pico-hydro systems. For more information on the different turbine types see for instance: http://www.absak.com/

Hydro power – local site characteristics	Impulse turbine	Reaction turbine
High head Above 10 m	Pelton Turgo Multi-jet pelton Cross flow	
Medium head 3–10 m	Cross flow Turgo Multi-jet pelton	Francis Watewheel
Low head 1–3 m	Cross flow	Propeller Francis Kaplan Waterwheel
Turbine requirements	Low flow – less than 0.1 m³/s	High flow – more than 0.03 m³/s

Electric system

When electricity is produced it has to either be transported to a battery bank or directly to the loads. The transmission provisions for a hydro power system are very important and have a real impact on the balance of system efficiency. For instance when the electricity is held up because the system has no diversion load, and there is nowhere for the generated electricity to go, the alternator will get too warm, which results in wear and tear. The diameter of the cable leading from the generator depends on the length of the transmission line. For example, with a long transmission distance, a larger diameter is needed. A larger diameter will cause less energy loss en route, in a similar way that the water in the penstock flowed more efficiently in a larger diameter pipe.

Electricity is also a kind of flow and can be understood using the same principles as those that apply to the flow of water. The diameter of the cable depends also on the current in the produced electricity. The current is similar to the flow in a river only for electricity. The process of transmission will always cause a voltage drop from its beginning to end as energy is lost in transportation, which means that the power output when it reaches the house will be less than is converted in the generator.

The Alternating Current (AC) can be converted into a Direct Current (DC) using a *rectifier* that enables the power arriving to the electric system of the house to be directly stored in batteries (that require a DC supply) or to be used in the DC circuit in the house. If the loads in the house, as is typical, require an AC supply then the DC conversion is not needed, which means that the electricity generated can be connected directly into the main electricity board of the house. This is very important when a system is grid connected. When not all the generated electricity is used in the household loads the electricity needs to be diverted to a *diversion load*. This kind of electricity is called surplus electricity. Grid connection, as explained in Chapter 8, is an example of a diversion load. The surplus power will be delivered into the grid either through a two-way meter or via an import and an export meter.

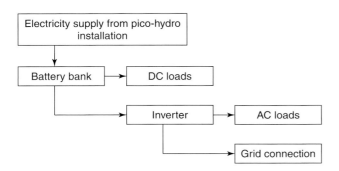

12.4.
Electric system of a pico-hydro scheme
(Source: Manuel Fuentes).

Economics

Capital cost

The most expensive part of the development of a small hydro system is the capital costs of the hardware, excluding the running costs of the system. It is advised that for the ecohouse builder hydro systems are not like wind or PV, and it is not viable with hydro systems to generate less electricity than you need and plan to build a bigger turbine in the future when you can afford it. It is recommended to generate an amount of electricity equal to the power requirements of your house from day 1. To give you an idea of the cost differences of different sizes of systems, a 2 kW hydro system is around 50 per cent less expensive than a 5 kW scheme. The greater the kW installed, the greater the viability of the scheme for hydro. This is because the civil engineering works for both types of schemes are pretty similar.

The cost of a hydro scheme also depends on the kind of scheme; low head or high head. A turbine for a high-head application is less expensive, with only the penstock costing more, according to the increased length and pressure of the pipe. A low-head scheme requires a more expensive turbine and often more complicated civil works. This is of course different when an old scheme is refurbished. Usually a high-head scheme is more cost-effective.

Operation and maintenance costs

The operation and maintenance costs of a hydro system are not very high. When a system isn't working, in other words when the installation doesn't produce electricity, this is called downtime and can be caused by blockage of the diversion system, flooding or equipment failure. A weekly check of the diversion system is recommended. Bearings have to be replaced once every four to seven years but have to be greased every six months. When the system uses a belt to drive the generator it is advisable to have a spare one on the site. The annual cost is around £20–50 per kW.

Funding

Climate change is now an acknowledged fact and people in all walks of life are beginning to understand that if we are to survive with our comfortable lifestyles intact our first energy of choice must be renewable energy, from today. Even governments now acknowledge this and in the UK a range of climate-change-related incentive schemes has been introduced, including schemes supporting the uptake of renewable energy technologies.

One such scheme in the UK is the *Clear Skies* funding programme, which gives grants for all kinds of renewable systems and energy-efficiency schemes. You may be eligible for such a grant for your own home, and more information on the funding available for such schemes is available on the Clear Skies website (www.clearskies.co.uk). The grant for a 0.5–5 kW installed micro-hydro system is around £1000 per kW installed with a maximum grant of £5000. Grants are available for micro-hydro systems for domestic use only, so you may be in with a chance there!

REFERENCES

Books

1 Roaf, S. (1982). The Water Wheels of Ana, *UR*, nos. 2/3, pp. 84–9.

2 http://www.northeastengland.talktalk.net/page82.htm

3 Clark, G. A., Smajstrla, A. G. and Haman, D. Z. *Water Hammer In Irrigation Systems*, University of Florida IFAS Extension papers, available on: http://edis.ifas.ufl.edu/AE066

   Penche, C., de Minas, I. Dr, *Layman's Handbook on how to develop a small hydro site*. Commission of European Communities, ESHA, June 1998.

   Ir. A. J. M. van Kimmenaede, *Warmteleer voor technici*. Wolters Noordhoff, Haarlem, March 1995.

   Curtis, D. *Going with the Flow*, The Centre for Alternative Technology, April 1999.

4 Roaf, S. (2000). Mills and Bunds of the Baqaq: Some aspects of the ancient and modern use of water in Iraq, SUMER, Baghdad, vol. 50, 30–41.

Websites

http://www.nwl.ac.uk/ih/nwa/index.htm (National Water archive)

www.environment-agency.gov.uk (Environment Agency)

www.waterturbine.com (Turbines)

www.absak.com

http://www.met-office.gov.uk (Meteorological office)

www.cat.org.uk

www.britisch.hydro.org

http://www.qub.ac.uk/civeng/research/hy/researchpages/subpages/
waterwheels.htm

13 GROUND SOURCE HEAT PUMPS (GSHP)

JOHN PEAPELL

INTRODUCTION

A GSHP is an extremely effective device for reducing the carbon emissions from a building's heating system in most circumstances. In a GSHP, underground pipes are used to harvest the sun's warmth, which has been captured and stored in the earth, and move it into a building. Where the conditions are suitable GSHPs can capture enough solar energy to provide all of the water and space heating requirements of a small or large house, and in some projects they can do the same for massive offices and retail stores.

Of course, as for any renewable energy system, it is important to reduce the initial energy requirement for the building by including appropriate insulation, reducing air infiltration, and utilising passive solar gain. Every different renewable energy system will have its own limitations of its use. It is very difficult to use most wind generators in cities. Solar systems don't work on shaded sites. Biofuels inherently produce very low carbon emissions but there are many buildings where it is implausible to arrange for the delivery and management of a biofuel heating system. Heat pumps are usually powered conveniently by mains electricity, are managed in identical ways to conventional domestic boilers and are very low maintenance. It is difficult however to install GSHPs in tight urban locations where access to lay pipes in the earth is impossible to arrange.

While they are called GSHPs in this chapter they may also be used to cool buildings, although a good passive building in many parts of the world, including the UK, should not need cooling. GSHPs can be characterised as being inherently reliable, having high capital costs, low running costs and being able to usually pay for themselves within four to eight years compared with oil or mains gas heating systems. GSHPs typically emit a fraction of the CO_2 produced by more conventional heating systems and their energy costs range between 30–50 per cent of a conventional fuel system per year to run.

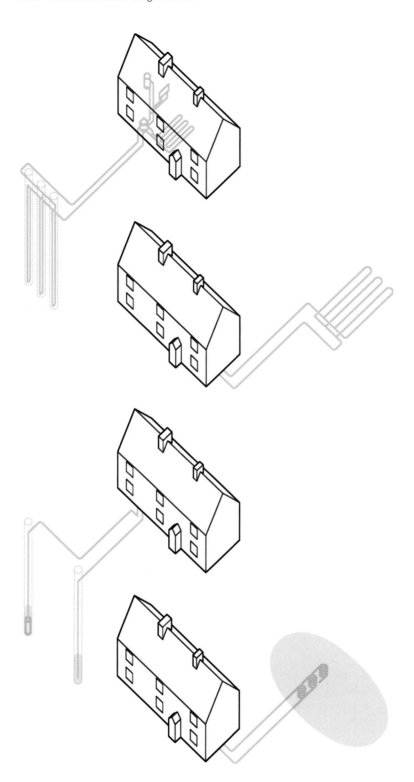

13.1.
Various underground pipe layouts.
Ground source heating systems
illustrated in this chapter are designed
and installed by Geothermal International
Ltd (www.geoheat.co.uk).

HOW HEAT PUMPS WORK
Clark Brundin

A heat pump is like a refrigerator. Both are in effect heat engines that are running backwards. A heat engine takes in thermal energy at a high temperature, and produces work (mechanical energy) by reducing the temperature and rejecting the thermal energy (heat) at a lower temperature. Examples of heat engines are internal combustion engines (as in a vehicle) and external combustion engines (as in an electric power station).

Electricity is a form of mechanical energy since it can be used immediately to produce an equal amount of work. The efficiency of heat engines is determined by the temperature at which heat is absorbed and rejected. Because the upper temperature is limited by the materials of which the engine is constructed, and the lower temperature is limited by the environment into which the heat is rejected, the maximum efficiency achievable is less than 50 per cent, and normal engines are less than 40 per cent. The best power stations approach 40 per cent efficiency.

Work (of which electric energy is a form) can be used to produce heat in two ways. It can be converted directly into heat in a resistance heater. When compared with the alternative of simply using the fuel used at the power station

How The Units Work

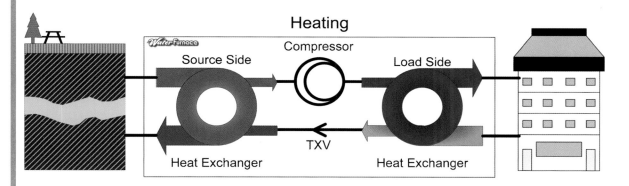

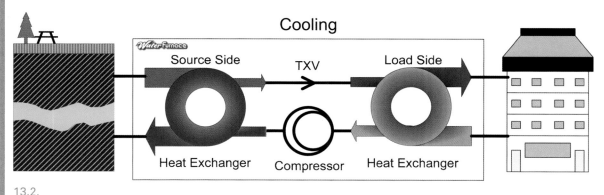

13.2.
How heat pumps work.

to heat the house with a boiler, this results in the loss of 60–70 per cent of the thermal energy at the power station generating the electricity.

Alternatively, the electricity (work) can be used in a heat pump (a reversed heat engine) to raise the temperature of thermal energy from the surroundings to a higher temperature in order to heat the house. The smaller the temperature rise required, the more effective is the heat pump. Thus one locates the heat source below ground level, where the temperature is higher in winter and more constant than on the surface. A good heat pump can produce four units of heat for every unit of work put in, thus in the end being more efficient than the boiler. Heat pumps are particularly widely used where cheap electricity from renewable sources (mainly hydroelectric power) is available. If the electricity is cheap, the additional capital cost of installing and maintaining a heat pump is more justifiable and this is why a good combination is to use a GSHP with a wind turbine to produce the cheap electricity needed to run the heat pump.

The difference between a heat pump and a refrigerator lies simply in which end of the process is of interest. A refrigerator pumps heat out of the box and rejects it to the environment at a higher temperature because in a fridge it is the lower temperature which is of interest. A heat pump pumps heat out of the ground and rejects it at a higher temperature to heat the house. Here we are interested in the higher temperature, and do not mind that the ground is being cooled in the process. In some parts of the world the same system can be used to heat the house in the winter and cool it in the summer, simply by reversing the roles of the heat source and heat sink.

HOW IS A GSHP DESIGNED?

As stated in the box, GSHPs basically warm (or cool) a building by transferring heat from a relatively low-temperature reservoir to one at a higher temperature. In this case the pipes of a GSHP can draw enough warmth to heat a house from the lower temperature reservoirs of the soil, rocks, lakes, rivers or the sea, which were all heated originally by the sun. The GSHP system then converts these lower temperatures in the 'heat pump' to the higher temperature needed for the hot water in the conventional central heating and domestic water systems. The only fossil fuel that is burnt in this process is that needed to provide power for the heat pump unit.

In the simplest GSHP system, a loop of pipe is buried in the ground with the flow and return connected to a heat pump. A *brine* – a mixture of water and an organic antifreeze – is pumped from the unit around the loop and returns several degrees warmer from its journey through the ground. The heat pump extracts this energy from the large volume of liquid at a slightly raised temperature and converts it into a much higher temperature for the small volume used in the heating system. The ground loop continues to convey the energy into the heating system until demand is satisfied when the building, and the water tank, reaches the set temperatures.

System choices:

- Horizontal ground loop
- Closed loop borehole

- Open loop borehole
- Lakes, rivers or sea.

Horizontal ground loop

Long lifetime plastic pipes of about 50 mm diameter are buried beneath the surface of the ground. The length of this pipe must be calculated to provide enough heat for all the heating requirements of the building over the winter months, and over the following summer the sun's warmth must replace the energy extracted in the previous heating season so that the soil temperature around the pipe returns to the temperature it held at the start of the last heating season, before the next one starts. Thus it is a good idea to have the soil surface above the pipe loops exposed to the summer sun if possible as the ground is not actually a very good conductor of heat.

13.3.
Horizontal ground loops.

Different suppliers use a variety of layouts. One of the most common layouts used is that of a pipe laid 1 m deep and 1 m apart in loops, in a pattern similar to that of an under floor heating system. Some designers use more complicated heat capture systems with pipes at several depths in deeper trenches where the brine is induced into turbulent flow so that more heat is drawn quickly from the ground. Wetter ground is more effective for coupling to the pipe and giving better heat transfer from the ground into the pipes. Clays tend to be better than sandy soils and need less length of pipe in the ground from which to get the same levels of heat.

Closed loop borehole

In this system a similar pipe is formed into a 'U' tube and lowered into a 125–150 mm diameter borehole. These boreholes are usually drilled by small rigs to depths of up to 100 m. Cool brine is warmed on its journey through the tube and the heat extracted from the brine by the heat pump. The type of rock affects the heat transfer rate to the pipe and also the ease of drilling the borehole. In general, and rather surprisingly, the hard rock areas to the west of Britain are easier to drill than softer rocks.

13.4.
Closed loop boreholes completed at Hollybush Row, Oxford (Source: Dave Lenhardt, Knowles and Son).

Open loop borehole

If a borehole can access a natural aquifer and enough water is available, the water can be pumped through the heat pump and the cooler return flow put back into the aquifer via a second borehole.

Lakes, rivers and the sea

Collector pipes laid in water are more efficient at transferring heat to the loop than those laid in the ground. This is because water is a better conductor of heat than soil. To be used in GSHP systems, lakes and rivers have to be large enough to be unaffected by the energy extracted to heat your building. A pond could be turned to ice if a GSHP in it was wrongly sized! This is where the 'renewable' energy in the systems comes from, being annually recharged by the sun. It is also possible to use open loops where a local body of water is conveniently placed near the building.

How are systems sized for a house?

Initially the heat loss for a building is calculated in order to size the heat source needed to maintain reasonable internal temperatures at around, say, 20°C,

"Slim Jims"

13.5.
Under water heat exchanger.

throughout the year. The heat loss from the building will be highly dependent on a range of features of that building including insulation, windows, airtightness and location. This heat loss calculation defines the power (in kilowatts or kW) that the boiler, or heat pump, needs to provide enough heat on the coldest day to maintain 20°C, with an assumption made on what the minimum temperature is likely to be based upon location. A machine, either a boiler or a heat pump, is chosen which is rated to provide this power.

The amount of heat energy used in the house (in kilowatt-hours or kWh) will depend on weather conditions, the length of the heating season and the amount of hot water used. The length of the ground loop or borehole will be proportionate to the kWh used. If this is undersized the danger is that a gradual cooling of the ground around the loop will take place over time, which reduces the efficiency of the system. The thermal conductivity of the ground is an important design factor. More ground loop is needed in dry sandy soil than in an area of wet clay soil. Open loop borehole, lake and river systems should be the most efficient because thermal conductivity between the water and the heat pump loop is higher than ground coupling.

Conclusion

A heat pump is sized to heat a house on the coldest day (power – kW).

The loop length, or number and depth of boreholes, is sized to provide enough heat for space heating and hot water (energy – kWh).

WFI Global Products

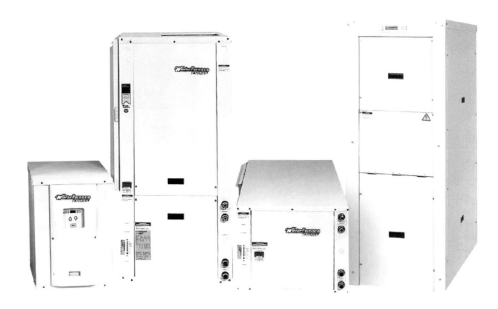

A typical modern house of 200 m² might need an 8 kW heat pump and 400 m of ground loop. A carefully designed and built house of this size could easily halve each of these elements.

RETROFITTING GSHPs

When retrofitting a GSHP the two main considerations are:

* Is sufficient land available?
* Is the existing heat distribution system appropriate?

A heat loss calculation will determine the amount of land needed. Heat distribution is, most commonly, by radiators or by under floor pipework. Heat pumps work most efficiently when they raise the input temperature of the brine by the lowest practical amount. A large low temperature radiator will be more efficient than a smaller higher temperature radiator. This was one of the factors which drove the development of under floor heating systems.

Gas or oil systems might run at 70–80°C; heat pumps systems will be designed, optimally, to 35–40°C and on spring or autumn days a radiator may not feel hot but the system will be maintaining the house to its set temperature. Radiators designed for gas or oil boilers would be too small for heat pumps and may need to be changed for 'double' or 'triple' units to provide enough area at the lower operating temperatures. In fact many plumbers will have used oversized radiators which will work perfectly well without changing them. There are two choices:

* Calculate the radiator sizes for the new output temperature and check if the existing ones need changing.

- Go with the existing system and see if any rooms do not reach the required temperature in really cold weather. Change the radiators where required.

Under floor systems are more complicated to retrofit. The high temperature output from the gas or oil system is usually mixed with cold water to provide a lower circulating temperature, but one which is higher than the output from a heat pump. As a result the pipes are positioned further apart than required to deliver enough heat. If so, supplementary radiators would have to be fitted.

Some heat pumps suppliers will use an alternative refrigerant that allows a slightly higher output temperature, which may help get around some of these issues. The penalty is a slightly reduced efficiency.

The coefficient of performance (COP) of a heat pump is not fixed and it varies according to the difference between the temperature at which the pump takes in heat from the outside world and the temperature at which it puts the heat out into the building. This difference is known as the 'thermodynamic lift'. For any given lift, the actual incoming and outgoing temperatures do not make a lot of difference but to get the most from any heat pump, one needs to maximise the temperature at which it takes in heat and minimise that at which it goes out, and vice versa for cooling. This makes the way a heat pump is used very important. A GSHP can contribute added value, for instance, by being coupled with an under-floor heating system in which a lower circulating temperature of around 35° is used rather than wasting it on trying to boost hot water to a tap temperature of around 65°, for which the COP falls to 3.3.

		Typical Performance of Modern scroll Compressor							
		Refrigerant R470c							
Evaporating Temp (°C)		−25	−20	−15	−10	−5	0	5	10
		Heating Coefficient of Performance							
Condensing Temp (°C)									
15		4.62	5.59	6.74	8.01	9.27	10.29		
20		3.96	4.36	5.72	6.83	8.05	9.22		
25		3.43	4.08	4.87	5.82	6.9	8.06	9.15	
30		3	3.53	4.19	4.97	5.9	6.94	5.04	9.05
35		2.65	3.09	3.62	4.27	5.05	5.95	6.95	7.99
40		2.36	2.72	3.17	3.7	4.34	5.1	5.98	6.94
45			2.42	2.79	3.23	3.76	4.39	5.13	5.98
50				2.47	2.84	1.27	3.8	4.42	5.14
55					2.51	2.87	3.3	3.82	4.43
60						2.53	2.89	3.31	3.82
65							2.53	2.89	3.3
		Thermodynamic Lift (kelvin)							65
15	20	25	30	35	40	45	50	55	60

13.7.

The number of kWh of heat a heat pump can put out for each kWh of electricity it uses is largely determined by the difference between the temperature of its heat source and that of its output. In this chart, the temperature of the heat source is described as the evaporating temperature and the temperature of the output is called the condensing temperature. Thus, if the fluid in the underground coil of a ground source heat pump enters the pump at 10° and the pump is putting hotter water into an underfloor heating system at 35°, the chart shows that it should be giving 7.99 times more heat out than came from the electricity alone. (Source: Paul Sikora of Dunstar from an article on Geo Dynamics in Construct Ireland, http://www.constructireland.ie/articles/0218geodynamics.php).

14 LIME AND LOW-ENERGY MASONRY

IAN PRITCHETT

INTRODUCTION

Over recent years there has been a growing appreciation of the need to use materials with as little embodied energy as possible. This includes energy used not only in extraction and manufacture but also the energy needed to transport materials to their point of use, a factor that favours the more local sourcing of materials. Issues of energy use over the life cycle of a building are also increasingly considered at the point of design including the fundamental questions of 'what type of building will it be?' and following on from that 'what materials will it be made of?' At the early design stage you may ask yourself questions like:

- Will it be a heavyweight building with high levels of thermal mass that can store free energy and shift temperature peaks, so lowering heating and cooling costs for a building?
- Will it be a lightweight structure with low embodied energy in which limited amounts of mass are strategically located to store as much energy as possible in the floors or walls?
- How long do I want the building to stand and can we design the building so that the materials can be reused when the building is eventually demolished?
- How can we make sure that as little material waste is generated as possible during construction and so reduce our materials costs by efficient design?

Traditionally, builders would have known the answers to such questions automatically, being profoundly familiar with their own local materials. Today many designers do not ask such questions in an industry that is largely dominated by issues of first cost of materials. However, with the emerging emphasis on using 'green' materials there is a growing interest in using low-tech local materials that have a low impact over their entire life cycle, and it is these issues that are covered in this chapter, with reference to the use of one main material – lime.

LIME

Lime is produced by heating calcium carbonate (limestone, chalk, shells, coral, etc.) in a kiln to a temperature of approx. 900°C. At this temperature carbon dioxide gas is given off and the calcium carbonate is chemically changed, or calcined, to form calcium oxide (known as quick lime or lump lime).

The raw material – calcium carbonate – will vary according to its point of origin and will contain impurities of various types and in varying quantities. It is these impurities that give us the range of different building limes (lime can be used in different forms, but all originate from quicklime). In the past it would have been commonplace for quicklime to be delivered to sites, but today we tend to process it beforehand. Water and quicklime are combined in a process known as hydration to produce hydrated lime. If only an exact amount of water is added the end product is a dry powder, which is sold in bags and generally known as hydrated lime or lime hydrate. If an excess of water is used (always putting the quicklime into the water for safety's sake) the process is normally referred to as slaking or slacking and the end product is a colloidal gel, often sold in plastic tubs and known as lime putty.

The properties of the dry hydrate or putty will depend mainly upon the source of calcium carbonate burned and in particular the impurities it contained. Very pure sources of calcium carbonate, e.g. Buxton limestone, will produce pure quicklime and hence pure putties or hydrates. Pure lime putty (calcium hydroxide) is known as fat lime and will not set under water. For this reason, we store it with a layer of water over the top. Mortars and plasters made from fat lime will not set under water and thus can be kept indefinitely if kept away from the air.

These pure limes set by a two-stage process. The first part (the initial set) is simply the excess moisture leaving the mortar either by evaporation or migration into the surrounding masonry. The mortar is then firm to the touch but can still be marked with a fingernail. The second stage (carbonation) is a chemical reaction, caused by carbon dioxide from the atmosphere entering the damp mortar in solution and reacting with the lime (calcium hydroxide) to convert it back to calcium carbonate. This stage can be very slow – it will depend on the temperature, the pore structure and the moisture within the mortar and can take many years to complete.

Limestones that contain clay produce building limes that are known as hydraulic, because they have the ability to set under water. The clay impurities contain silica, alumina and iron that give the limes a more complicated chemistry. The calcium ions react with the silica, alumina and iron to form complex calcium compounds. This reaction can take place under water and thus hydraulic limes cannot be stored for any length of time as putties or wet mortars because they will start to set. For this reason they are sold as dry powders.

The formation of the above compounds will take place relatively quickly, but will then be followed by the slower carbonation process, whereby the remaining free lime (calcium hydroxide) within the mortar will react with atmospheric carbon dioxide (as with fat lime).

The properties of hydraulic limes are a direct consequence of the amount of clay impurity in the burned limestone (raw material) and of the burning temperature. The more clay impurity the faster the set and the harder the mortar, if the limestone is burned at the appropriate temperature. Thus, historically, we have had a whole spectrum of building limes available ranging from natural cements like Roman cement (with a setting time of 20–30 minutes) to fat lime that will keep indefinitely under water.

In general, lime is used mixed with an aggregate or mixture of aggregates. The aggregate provides the bulk and dimensional stability of the mix and the lime performs the role of the binder, i.e. it sticks the mix together. In order for it to do this it must coat all of the particles of aggregate. Hence the minimum amount of lime needed within a mix is that which will fill all of the voids in the aggregate. The addition of more lime will help the workability of the mix, but may lead to shrinkage and cracking. The volume of voids will vary from one aggregate to another, but in general for a well-graded sand they will be about 30 per cent, hence a 1:3 (lime:sand) mix is commonly used. However, it may not be good enough to simply specify a ratio without knowing which aggregate and which lime is to be used, e.g. hydraulic limes usually have to be used in richer mixes than fat limes and historically mixes can be seen to vary enormously from very rich to quite lean.

Aggregates commonly used in this country were naturally occurring silica sand, other mineral-based sands and crushed stone, although others include crushed chalk, crushed shell, earth, crushed brick or tile. Other ingredients that were added to mortars and plasters were blood, urine, fat, tallow, oil and hair. These secondary ingredients may have been added simply because they were available in abundance and cheap, e.g. earth, but were more likely added because they modify the properties of the mix.

The Romans found that by adding volcanic dust from Pozzouli (near Naples) to non-hydraulic lime, it became artificially hydraulic. They also found that crushed brick or tile had a similar effect and, consequently, this type of additive is known as a pozzolan. Bricks and tiles are made from clay and when fired, crushed and mixed with lime, they give it similar properties to a lime with a natural clay impurity. Research has shown that the type of clay, the firing temperature and the particle size of pozzolans are all important factors and that clay as an additive or impurity without being fired does not have a significant pozzolanic effect on a mortar.

Lime is the traditional binder that has been used for centuries to make mortars, plasters and renders. The Romans brought the technology to the UK and we have a history of using it for the last 2000 years. However, over the last 100 years Portland cement has become the modern choice as a binder for most mortars, plasters and renders. It is important to appreciate that they are not like for like alternatives. Lime is soft, permeable, flexible and has a high capillarity. Cement on the other hand is hard, impermeable, rigid and has a low capillarity. This means that lime-based and cement-based materials can perform quite differently.

Lime is relatively weak in both compression and tension, and this gives masonry walls constructed with lime mortar a certain amount of flexibility. Each mortar joint, although well bonded to the masonry, has the ability to act as a tiny expansion joint. Where cracks do appear they are normally invisible (referred to as micro-cracking) and self-healing (a property called autogeneous healing). Lime is minutely soluble in rainwater and so when it rains, a weak lime solution is formed, collecting small particles of dirt and dust before running into any micro-cracks. Within these cracks the water is conducted away, leaving the mineral content to fill the gaps. In this way it is possible for walls constructed with lime mortar to expand, contract and flex, healing themselves as the micro-cracking occurs.

Cement by contrast is quite strong in tension and will try to resist movement. The tensile forces within a wall build up and are transmitted by the cement mortar from one masonry unit to the next until they become too great to withstand. At this point if there is not an expansion joint, a crack will form. The crack is likely to be quite major and will run right through the masonry and the mortar joints, finding the line of least resistance. This type of crack does not have the ability to heal itself and may become a structural defect (certainly a point for water ingress). The same property can be observed in cement-based renders, where cracking is quite typical and very troublesome.

When lime mortars are used to bed bricks or stones we find that the capillarity and the permeability of the mortar help to cushion the masonry units from the natural decay mechanisms. This is because any moisture is generally drawn into the mortar joints and evaporates from these joints rather than the masonry units. Since most of the natural decay mechanisms are associated with moisture, i.e. frost damage or salt crystallisation, we find that the lime mortar acts sacrificially to protect the masonry. Hence masonry constructed with lime mortar can last for centuries, although the mortar may need re-pointing every hundred years or so.

Cement mortar is normally less permeable than the surrounding masonry and hence most of the evaporation takes place from the surface of the masonry rather than the mortar joints. This tends to reduce the life of the masonry, which suffers the full effects of frost and salt damage.

The same properties of permeability and capillarity are vital when lime mortar is used in conjunction with timber. The ability to draw moisture away from the timber and allow it to evaporate safely is essential to keeping timber in good condition. If we look at historic buildings we can often see where the change from the lime-based materials to modern cement-based materials has caused water to be trapped leading to severe decay and loss of structural integrity.

Modern construction philosophy seems to be based on the idea of ensuring water never gets into the structure. Although this principle appears sound, it is unrealistic to assume that water will never get in. It is important to remember that the inhabitants and their way of life (breathing, cooking, washing, etc.) are some of the main sources of moisture within a building's fabric. In addition the forces of nature always seem to overcome and water inevitably gets in. It is far more important to ensure that buildings are properly designed/detailed and that particular attention is paid to materials used that allow water to escape safely from the building.

From the above description, one may deduce that cement is not a good material and that lime is a good material. This would be wrong and certainly an oversimplification. When Portland cement was invented in 1824 it was an artificial hydraulic lime, with many of the desirable properties a lime advocate would appreciate today. However, its production techniques have been continually improved to increase its strength and the properties of ordinary

Portland cement are now dictated by the demands of the Ready Mixed Concrete Industry. It may be an ideal material for structural concrete but it is less ideal when used in mortars, plasters and renders in a sustainable construction industry.

Lime and cement are very similar in their production methods and raw materials. Both are derived from limestone (calcium carbonate) with impurities (normally silica, alumina and iron). In the case of pure (air or fat) limes, the quantity of impurities is very low (typically less than 5 per cent). Natural hydraulic limes have impurity levels of (typically) 5–25 per cent occurring naturally in the raw limestone. Cement production artificially combines these materials (normally limestone and clay) to give the required chemistry.

The main difference is in the firing temperature. Limes are fired at 900–1100°C, whereas cement production takes place at 1200–1500°C. The higher temperature forms chemical compounds that set harder and faster when mixed with water. Until recently, the modern construction industry has favoured these harder faster materials; however we now need to take a closer look at what is really required to construct sustainable buildings for the future. We need to look objectively at the issue. There are too many people with closed minds, in one camp or the other. They think that *either* lime or cement is the answer. As with so many issues, the truth lies somewhere in the middle.

What the industry requires for most domestic/low-rise buildings is a low-energy binder that sets hard enough and fast enough to allow building to proceed at an economic pace, but that has the flexibility, self-healing and vapour permeability necessary to provide the qualities we need. This may be summed up as a high performance, low-energy binder. Within the spectrum of binders, this is the area occupied by the hydraulic limes. The term hydraulic lime in this chapter is used without specific reference to whether the limes are natural or artificial.

If we were to generalise, we would say that the air limes and the weaker hydraulic limes are most suitable for the conservation and repair of historic buildings. The hydraulic limes are ideal for most normal low-rise, domestic/commercial buildings. Portland cement is particularly appropriate for high-rise buildings and civil engineering (structural concrete) work and for providing high levels of thermal mass inside a building within the building's structure and envelope, as in cast concrete floor slabs.

Lime steadily went out of use in virtually all sectors of the construction industry after the Second World War. However, its use in the repair of historic buildings has undergone a revival over the last 30 years. It is now generally accepted that lime must be used to repair old buildings. Recently it has been possible to show that it can also be viable for the ongoing construction of new buildings. This is nothing new; lime has been used for virtually all new building work for thousands of years!

For any product to survive or increase, its market share it must be better, faster, cheaper or easier than the alternatives. Since lime is normally used in the historic building sector, its cause is championed by advocates from this sector. The historic building sector of the construction industry has different priorities to the rest of the industry. If a product is better this is often justification enough to use it. However, the mainstream construction industry is far more commercial and the issues of *faster*, *cheaper* or *easier* tend to carry more weight, and speed of construction is a real concern for many designers, developers and project managers.

However, it is worth recapping on the wider range of properties of this one material – lime – to demonstrate the issues that might be considered when choosing which materials to use in construction.

- **Using lime mortars can avoid having to use expansion/movement joints**

Traditional masonry did not use expansion joints. There are numerous examples of long walls (particularly around old country parks) where hundreds of metres of wall have been constructed without breaks. The difference in modern masonry is not just the choice of mortar, but also the ratio of the width of the wall to its height.

Traditional walls were normally solid (rather than cavity) and much thicker than modern walls. There is no doubt that constructing new buildings with thick solid walls would avoid the need for expansion/movement joints, however a more relevant question is 'can we avoid them just by using lime mortar?' Expansion/movement joints were not used in construction until the 1960s. It was not until ordinary Portland cement started to get very strong, in the 1960s, that expansion joints became necessary. Before this time many cavity structures were built with weaker cement mortars. Thus it is perfectly reasonable to conclude that the use of lime-based mortars will normally avoid the use of expansion/movement joints.[1]

14.1.
The new Oxford University Sports Club used hydraulic lime mortar to avoid expansion joints (Source: Simone Pritchett).

- **Lime is flexible**

  Its autogenous healing qualities dramatically reduce cracks; this is one of the major factors that allows the omission of expansion/movement joints. It is also one of the factors that makes lime-based plasters and renders perform much better than cement-based ones.[2]

- **Lime-based materials have a lower embodied energy**

  A typical lime based mortar will have a lower embodied energy than equivalent cement-based mortar. In addition it will reabsorb some of the CO_2 that was emitted during the manufacturing process on setting.[3]

- **The use of lime allows masonry (bricks and stones) to be recycled**

  We have an industry in the UK that demolishes buildings, cleans the bricks and then sells them onto a new use (often at a premium price). This is possible because buildings built before the First World War were generally constructed with lime mortars. Most buildings constructed after the First World War have been built with cement-based mortars and so their bricks cannot be recycled except for hardcore. The UK brick industry produces nearly 3 billion bricks each year. Virtually all of these bricks are laid in cement mortar and thus will never be recycled. History shows us that brick is a very durable material that if laid in lime mortar can be recycled several times and thus can be considered very sustainable. However the use of cement-based mortars can turn brick into an unreusable material.[4]

- **Lime enables low energy sustainable materials to be used**

  Materials such as water reeds, straw, timber, hemp and clay can be used as construction materials, as demonstrated in many historic buildings.

- **Moisture can easily evaporate from the surface of lime-based materials**

  This protects the surrounding masonry units. As stated earlier the lime mortar acts sacrificially to protect the masonry. Hence masonry constructed with lime mortar can last for centuries.

- **Lime-based materials can create healthier living environments**

  This is because they are hygroscopic and permeable, allowing for the transfer of moisture from the internal to the external environment. The quality of air in our houses and offices is deteriorating. This is partly due to the way water vapour behaves in buildings. We produce far more water vapour today than we did 50 years ago. Most families have ovens, kettles, baths, showers, washing machines, tumble driers, etc. All of these produce water vapour. Our centrally heated houses allow the warm air to carry more vapour and increasingly airtight buildings give it less chance to escape. Ultimately we find that the vapour condenses in areas we wouldn't choose, such as in carpets on solid floors, in cavities/voids and in other poorly ventilated areas. This can lead to mould, fungi and insects, some of which can be damaging to human health (and also damaging to the building structure). This is one significant factor in the increase of asthma, allergies and other respiratory complaints.

- **There is less waste when using lime-based materials**

  Hydraulic lime can be typically reworked for up to 24 hours after it has been mixed with water.[5] Cement-based materials normally have to be thrown away after a couple of hours. This means that if work stops for any reason (rain, or the end of the working day) any cement mortar that is left will be wasted, whereas any lime mortar will be useable the following day.[6] Recent EU legislation on chrome VI levels in cement has necessitated the addition of iron sulphate to OPC in order to counteract the effects of the chrome VI. This has reduced the shelf life of OPC to two months. This will surely lead to more waste in cement and cement-based materials. Hydraulic limes on the other hand have a typical shelf life of 12 months.

- **Lime can bring out the beauty of the masonry**
  Between 20–25 per cent of the surface of a brick wall is made up of mortar. The choice of the mortar colour and texture can have a significant impact on the appearance of the wall, and the even a mediocre brick can look like a high quality brick when laid in lime mortar.

- **Lime mortars have a proven durability**
  There are plenty of examples of buildings constructed with lime that have lasted hundreds (even thousands) of years. Recent tests have shown that hydraulic lime mortars are more resistant to the decay mechanisms of frost and salt crystallisation than equivalent cement-based mortars.[7]

Creative ways are being found to make the use of lime faster, cheaper and easier including:

- **Pre-mixed dry mortars**
  The continental model for factories blending dry sand with the lime or cement is beginning to catch on in the UK. This leads to accurately blended mortars, plasters and renders. Site-batched material has been quoted as accurate to plus, or minus, 40 per cent whereas factory batching is typically accurate to within 1 per cent. This approach allows manufacturers to get the best out of cement and soft sand, but when combined with hydraulic lime and good quality, well-graded, sharp sand offers great potential for the continuing development of hydraulic lime mortars. In Germany 85 per cent of all mortars, plasters and renders are factory batched. The concept of 'just add water' could not be simpler.

- **Quality control reduces risk**
  The quality control processes involved in the factory batching greatly reduce the risk of something going wrong. This may allow a structural engineer to apply a lower (more sensible) safety factor. There is also a financial benefit in reducing risk. It is not uncommon in the field of mass house-building to have to dismantle a house and start again (or re-point it) where the brickwork contractor has mixed the wrong mortar.

- **Storage silos and high shear mixers**
  Pre-mixed dry mortars can be supplied to sites in 25 kg bags, however additional advantages are gained when the material is delivered to site in a reuseable steel storage silo with a highly efficient high sheer mixer on the bottom. This simply requires a connection to electricity and water to enable it to produce perfect, quality controlled lime mortar at the touch of a button. A typical mixer will produce one tonne every 10 minutes.

- **Spray application saves time and money**
  This is an area where lime can compete on all levels. Hydraulic limes produce excellent plasters and renders and when applied with European spray technology, it is possible to get high quality materials and substantial savings when compared to hand applying almost any other material.[8]
- **Selecting the right mortar can save time**
  It sounds obvious, but making sure that the mortar suits the brick (or stone) can affect the build speed. It has been found that the right hydraulic lime mortar can give a higher build speed than would be possible with cement, particularly where difficult bricks such as dense engineering bricks are concerned.

It is important to look at the whole picture when considering the design, construction methods and materials of a new building. If lime mortar is simply substituted for cement mortar at the last moment to avoid expansion joints, the results may only be superficial. In order to get the most out of the material and obtain real environmental/performance benefits a holistic view should be adopted from the start to optimise the value of the material in the life cycle of the building.

14.2.
The new National Trust Headquarters in Swindon. Appropriately selected mortar allowed the engineering bricks to be laid in a fast and efficient manner (Source: Simone Pritchett).

The other major benefit of using lime is that it offers the potential to significantly reduce the embodied carbon emissions from a building at a time when there is growing concern about the impact of buildings on the global climate.

It seems likely that the government will demand environmental audits and set targets for recyclability of building materials in the near future. These measures may be separate or they may be contained within a rating system such as the Building Research Establishment's BREEAM and Ecohomes assessment methods. This scheme looks at numerous separate environmental impacts and normalises/weights the data into one single 'eco-point' score. As this becomes more widely adopted, it seems likely that lime mortars will be preferred to cement mortars because of their environmental benefit.

LOW-ENERGY MASONRY

Historically we find that earth and vegetable (and animal) materials were used combined, or independently, to make very low embodied energy buildings, typically made on or near the site by local labourers. Some examples are:

- **Cob (including wytchert)**
  Sub-soil mixed with straw and water to form thick, monolithic walls.
- **Timber frame with wattle and daub (including mud and stud)**
  A structural timber frame to support the roof and floors. The panels would then be filled with split timber or twigs woven, or tied, to form a matrix onto which mud and straw was daubed.
- **Unfired earth blocks (Clay lump or adobe)**
  Sub-soil mixed with straw and water to make blocks for construction.
- **Rammed earth or pise**
  Moist sub-soil rammed between shutters to form solid monolithic walls.
- **Timber baulk or log building**
  Large logs jointed together to form solid walls with the gaps plugged using clay.

Although all of these have worked historically and are low energy in their construction, they typically do not perform in a way that would be considered satisfactory for new buildings today. However, they are often used to perform a bespoke function in a building such as acting as a thermal store within an external building envelope. Materials that do also provide the opportunity to use and combine traditional materials in new ways and locations within a buildings include:

- Cob[9]
- Unfired earth block[10]
- Monolithic lime hemp walls
- Lime hemp blocks[11]
- Solid timber walls.

All of these options have significant thermal mass and/or insulating properties with a degree of hygroscopicity that can help to create healthy living environments with the ability to passively regulate internal temperature and humidity. Not all of these are appropriate everywhere and some may have limitations on design, but all are possible to use in the right place.

The UK construction industry has shown that it is slow to embrace change and consequently the materials that can be made into blocks and used in the conventional way will stand more chance of improving our sustainable building practices in the short term. It is to be hoped that familiarity with these materials will lead to adoption of even better practices in a step-by-step way.

Unfired earth blocks have been used for centuries and many people live in houses with brick facings, not knowing there is unfired earth behind. Unfired earth can provide additional insulation when mixed with material such as straw. It can perform adequately from the structural point of view providing the ratio between the height and thickness of the wall is correct. Houses constructed in this way are comfortable to live in (cool in summer and warm in winter). The extraction of earth and manufacture into blocks requires very little energy and no firing, so the carbon dioxide emissions are very low. This is all possible using unfired earth, so long as it is kept dry. This means protecting it from the weather and allowing it to breathe. Lime offers the answer in these areas. The external walls can be faced in masonry laid in lime mortar, or rendered.

The technology of using unfired earth is well established in the USA, where it is possible to buy mobile machines to make compressed earth blocks. These block presses can convert waste sub-soil into structural blocks at very economic rates. These blocks are quite strong (5 to 7 N/mm^2) and very dense. They offer great potential for introducing thermal mass into buildings, but require additional insulation to comply with current thermal regulations.

Up until the eighteenth century most buildings in the UK were rendered in one way or another. In parts of the country where the weather is more severe, this tradition has continued, but in areas with more moderate weather this has become less fashionable. Most countries in Europe still have a tradition for render and this is an important factor contributing to the longevity of their buildings. In the UK we are going to see render used more because the effects of climate change are causing a reclassification of the exposure maps and render will start to be a requirement on more walls in more areas, under revisions to building regulations. A return to render in the future will allow us to use more sustainable materials and, providing breathable lime renders are used, this will make an important contribution to the sustainable building issues we face.

It is easy to believe that unfired earth is as low as we can go when considering embodied energy, but nature can give us a helping hand. Plants take in carbon dioxide and break it down. The oxygen is given off, back to the atmosphere and the carbon is converted into plant material. One kg of dry plant material typically uses 1.8 kg of carbon dioxide in its production. So the more plant material we can use in the construction of our buildings, the more atmospheric carbon dioxide we can lock up. This is called carbon sequestration. This has been well known for sometime. In fact planting trees to absorb carbon dioxide has been seen as one of the weapons against global warming for some years. Using additional timber in the structure of buildings would lock up carbon dioxide, but this will only make a significant contribution if lots more trees are planted as well.

Another way to use this to our advantage is to use plant material in as many other ways as possible. Hemp and flax fibres can be made into very efficient insulation materials, as can sheep's wool. Probably the most important way plant materials can be used is in composites as either aggregates, fillers or fibre reinforcement. For example when hemp is mixed with lime it produces a composite similar to concrete, but with a good insulation value, hygroscopic properties and good vapor permeability. This is similar to materials that have been used for centuries, but has only been used in this form for less than 20 years, mainly in France.

Construction using lime hemp composites offers the potential for up to 30 per cent carbon sequestration, i.e. up to 30 per cent of the mass of the wall is locked in atmospheric carbon dioxide. This could be 10 tonnes in a typical house. So far most of the lime hemp buildings that have been constructed have been non load-bearing, with a separate timber frame. Research work is now going on to develop lime hemp composites that can be used in a load-bearing capacity. Again uptake within the mainstream is likely to be faster with pre-formed blocks rather than monolithic construction.

The French technique of spray applying lime hemp materials to construct new houses offers a very fast and efficient way forward. The spray-applied lime hemp is highly insulating and gives high levels of airtightness.

14.3.
Spray application of Hemcrete® at the Lime Technology office. This is the first project in the UK to use spray-applied Hemcrete® (Source: Simone Pritchett).

The idea of locking up CO_2 within the structure of walls offers a 'win–win' result. The thicker we make the walls, the more CO_2 gets locked up and the better the insulation levels and thermal mass of the building will be. Lime hemp walls offer good insulation and thermal mass to achieve excellent performance. The lime hemp walls can be solid with no need for a cavity and consequently the constructional details are simple and robust. History shows us that buildings like this are comfortable to live in (warm in the winter and cool in the summer) and can last for centuries. In addition using hemp in this way will help reduce the demand for aggregates and offer new opportunities to farmers.

Hemp used to be grown all over England because its fibre was used to make ropes and sails for the Navy as well as clothing. Hemp fibre is the strongest natural fibre known to man and is reputedly stronger, weight for weight, than steel. Hemp grows very fast, from nothing to 4 m high in four months and is virtually disease resistant. It can be used in rotation with other crops and helps improve the soil. Hemp got a bad name in the 1930s after publicity campaigns by the petrochemical industry linking it to its narcotic derivative, cannabis, got it banned (in order to promote oil-based materials). Nowadays industrial hemp has virtually no narcotic content, but still needs to be grown under licence.

The automotive industry, particularly in Germany, is using an increasing quantity of hemp fibre in the manufacture of car interior panels, in order to meet sustainability targets. After the fibre has been removed the woody core that is left can be chopped and used to make lime hemp buildings. The

14.4.

The new Adnams Brewery Distribution Centre used hydraulic lime mortars, plasters and renders together with 100 000 Hemcrete® blocks and 1000 m^3 of Hemcrete®.

potential increase in the demand for plant material in the construction industry could help give a boost to farming.

Using low-energy natural materials must not undermine the need for airtightness and high thermal performance, however, if we can make immediate savings in the embodied energy/emissions and then follow up with on-going savings this has to be the best of both worlds. Several recent pioneering projects have now taken these ideas forward using natural materials and combining thick lime hemp walls with high levels of thermal mass have an increasingly important role to play in constructing the ecohomes of the future.

We are now at a crossroads – there is a need to build millions of new homes over the coming decades, but environmental issues are becoming more important. Some people think that lime will never take off again in mainstream building, but small subtle changes in the market conditions will change the future. The combination of lime with modern technology and higher demand will bring the cost down. Hydraulic lime will then be the natural choice.

NOTES

1 Masonry should always be designed from first principles by an engineer with experience in this area. Simply swapping cement mortar for lime mortar may not be sufficient. The use of lime mortar is currently outside the Masonry Code of Practice (BS 5628), however, building regulations allow the design of masonry to be proven by testing, calculation or other means. There is now sufficient knowledge within the lime world to easily get through building regulations.

2 Lime-based plasters and renders tend to perform better than cement-based ones providing they are properly applied. Generally lime-based materials require a higher level of skill and do not mask poor workmanship, whereas cement-based materials can mask poor workmanship in the short term.

3 The subject of embodied energy and CO_2 emissions is complicated. There seems to be a shortage of data, and the environmental benefits of lime (lower embodied energy) are contested by the cement industry. In addition the way of measuring embodied energy may be misleading.

   ○ CO_2 emission figures for cement and lime production vary quite considerably from source to source, however, when sensible figures are used they show that CO_2 emissions from either cement or lime mortar are greatly outweighed by the CO_2 emissions from the production of the masonry. The main benefits of lime come from allowing the masonry to be recycled, or from carbon sequestration when used with hemp.

   ○ Typical brick and block cavity walls used in normal house construction are responsible for around 100 kg of CO_2 emissions per square metre of wall area.

   ○ A lime hemp wall 500 mm thick can lock up the carbon equivalent of 50 kg of CO_2/m^2 of wall area. This shows us that the difference between best and worst practice can be up to 150 kg of CO_2/m^2 of wall area. For a house with 200 m^2 of walls this is 30 T.

   ○ Using low-energy natural materials must not undermine the need for air tightness and high thermal performance, however, if we can make immediate savings in the embodied energy/emissions and then follow up with on-going savings this has to be the best of both worlds.

○ As ever, it is a generalisation to say that using lime allows bricks to be recycled and using cement does not. Weak cement mortars will allow bricks to be recycled and very strong lime mortars may make it very difficult to recycle bricks.

4 Fat lime mortars will keep indefinitely as long as they are kept away from the air (under water, or in a sealed container), but are not generally suitable for new-build work unless the walls are quite thick.

5 A simple study on one housing development (at Poundbury in Dorset) showed that there was up to 25 per cent waste in site-mixed cement mortar when compared to silo-batched lime mortar.

6 The EPSRC funded Foresight research project carried out testing of hydraulic lime mortar samples at 91 days old and found them to be more resistant to attack by crystallisation of sulphates and the action of freeze thaw cycles. CERAM Building Technologies carried out tests for Lime Technology Ltd and found that engineering brick panels cured for 28 days and then immersed in water for seven days withstood 100 freezing, thawing, wetting, freezing… cycles without damage.

7 Allen, G., Allen, J., Elton, N., Farey, M., Holmes, S., Livesey, P. and Radonjic, M. (2003). *Hydraulic Lime Mortar for Stone, Brick and Block Masonry.* Donhead.

8 Spray applying cement-based materials can offer the cost savings, but does not bring the same environmental or performance benefits.

9 Weismann, A. and Bryce, K. (2006). *Building with Cob: A Step-by-Step Guide.* Green Books, ISBN: 1903998727.

10 King, B. (1997). *Buildings of Earth and Straw: Structural Design for Rammed Earth and Straw Bale Architecture.* Ecological Design Press, USA, ISBN: 0964471817.

11 Allin, S. (2005). *Building with Hemp.* Seed Press, ISBN: 0955110904.

CASE STUDY INTRODUCTION: TOWARDS THE NEW VERNACULAR

The following 25 case studies have been collected from friends and colleagues around the world. At the beginning of each case study, a Nicol graph shows the climate at the site. On it are drawn the mean maximum, mean minimum and comfort temperatures for a local adapted population. The comfort temperatures are for naturally ventilated buildings and for indigenous people. They tend to be more accurate for the summer temperatures. Here in the UK, we tend to think that any comfort temperature line below around 17°C can be levelled off, which indicates that if people find themselves in an environment below that temperature they get too cold and turn the heat up in their houses to a more acceptable temperature. However, this is not necessarily true for people in other parts of the world – it simply does not work that way because people, wherever they live, typically seek out temperatures they find acceptable or adjust these until they are. The mean solar radiation levels for each month are, in many cases, also given in Wm^2. The mean solar radiation levels for each month are also given (Wm^{-2}). Note that there is often a time lag between the maximum levels of solar radiation and the hottest months, which is caused by the slow heating of the Earth; this also happens in a house. Although the radiation levels are lower at around 3 p.m. than at 12 noon, the air temperature is higher because it is affected not only by radiation but also by the increased temperature of the structure of the building that has been heated earlier in the day. The Nicol graph is included to give a rough idea of what the climate locally is like and so how much work the building itself will have to do to provide indoor comfort temperatures for local people. In 'Tools for Understanding the Case Studies' (page 320) we show you how to make your own Nicol graph to use as a comparison of various temperatures in different countries around the world. We have also included a section on 'Ecofootprints' to enable people to compare the environmental performance of one house against the other, bearing in mind that where you live and how you live also matter.

Each house is briefly described, its key features listed and elaborated on where appropriate. The key lessons learnt are included to enable the reader to benefit from them regarding what to do and what not to do, if they wish to emulate the design ideas described in the case studies. The case studies as a whole do show four things clearly.

1 **Time passes.** Solar and ecohouse design has progressed steadily from the 1970s until today. We can see the progression from the Matsuoka house in Tokyo built in 1978 to the sophisticated Misawa homes built in Japan today. In the later house the solar overheating problem has been solved and the solar technologies appear to be part of the whole building form and appearance, rather than as in the earlier house where the technology dominated the house form.

2 **New technologies and issues emerge.** The solar house has evolved into the ecohouse as new issues come to the fore and new technologies are devised to deal with them. Materials and their impacts have been the dominant issue of the 1990s. We have now learnt how to count the total energy impacts of buildings, including their embodied energy and energy-in-use costs over the life of the house. These new abilities will be vital as we face the challenges of this century. The next decade will see the rise of real concern about climate change. In the decade following that, society will become obsessed with dwindling fossil fuel reserves and the cost of oil and gas. The pioneering role being played by ecohouses in experimenting with and developing emerging technologies will begin to pay dividends in the near future as they set the agenda for all house design in the following decades. Where the 1970s houses tested the limits of solar hot water technologies, the latest ecohouses are pivotal in establishing photovoltaics in the market place. Architects who cannot incorporate energy and water conservation, reuse, and renewable energy into their buildings will become dinosaurs, as will their white elephant buildings. Architecture is changing fast.

3 **Human beings around the world are ingenious.** These case studies are largely about the houses that architects build for themselves. The ingenuity, thought and affection lavished on many of them is apparent. From Bjorn Berge's demountable building to Christopher Day's beautifully sculptured window making a work of art out of a view. Just when one thought there was nothing new to learn about passive buildings a crop of new ideas arises from these examples that will spawn new generations of building forms in the years to come. The use of a hanging radiator in the centre of a space by Ashok Lall, or a cool-core building in the Malaysian vernacular by Jimmy Lim are great ideas. The courage and persistence of individuals is remarkable, as we can see with the house of David Morrison on the island of St Maarten. He displays a Robert the Bruce attitude as he try, try, tries again and again to protect his home from cyclones. Each year the house gets stronger and he learns more about how to grapple with the forces of nature in his search for shelter. Out of that search comes the wisdom that will result in new building forms, new technologies and better buildings.

4 **The importance of climate in design.** No longer should any client accept a building from an architect that does not deal well with the relationship between the indoor and outdoor climate. The following case

studies demonstrate the importance of climate in shaping buildings and, regardless of money, energy or the environment, in creating that most sought after quality of a building – thermal delight. Comfort can be seen simply as the absence of discomfort but thermal delight makes people happier. Look at the case study buildings and try to imagine what sensations they would create in you as you walked through them: the smells, the warmth, the light. These are the gifts of a good designer who can work the three key ingredients of architecture: the climate, the building and the people who occupy it.

TOWARDS THE NEW VERNACULAR

The analogy of the building as 'a machine for living in' that began this book, was a twentieth-century dream.

By the middle of this century we will probably all have to live in zero fossil fuel energy homes. The seeds of the ideas sown in this book by then will have grown into the New Vernacular of housing for the twenty-first century and beyond. These ecobuildings represent the developing foundations of the New Vernacular movement. Their designers take the best of the old wisdom and combine it with the best of the new technologies. They speak of soul and place. They experiment and they make mistakes, and they evaluate the strengths and weaknesses of each design feature because they want to learn, to change, to make a difference, to lay the foundations for the better houses we urgently need for the twenty-first century. They are the pioneers of the New Vernacular.

TOOLS FOR UNDERSTANDING
THE CASE STUDIES

THE ECOLOGICAL FOOTPRINT OF HOUSEHOLDS

One of the motivations for designing the Oxford Ecohouse was to put paid to the notion that pursuing a high quality of life necessarily entailed irreparable damage to the environment. The challenge was to prove that those in richer countries could maintain an acceptably high standard of living without polluting the planet at the cost to those in poorer countries. To help better understand the relationship between individual behaviours and the built environment it is necessary to look beyond the form and construction of a building to the consumption patterns of its inhabitants irrespective of culture, geography or economy. Environmental accounting methodologies, such as ecological footprinting, can provide a very useful insight into those factors which are most important in minimising environmental impacts.

Nicky Chambers and Craig Simmons, who both live in Oxford, UK, are co-founders of Queen's Award-winning sustainability consultancy Best Foot Forward, and were the first people to calculate the overall environmental impact of British lifestyles using a sustainability indicator known as the ecological footprint. They are well known as international experts in the methodology and co-authored, with Mathis Wackernagel, *Sharing Nature's Interest* – the pre-eminent textbook on ecological footprint analysis. Here they describe the foundations of the footprint and its application to households.

The ecological footprint was first developed as a concept in the early 90s by Dr Mathis Wackernagel while working on his doctoral thesis under Professor William Rees at the University of British Columbia in Canada.

In essence, the ecological footprint is a method of accounting for natural resource consumption in a way that is consistent with thermodynamic and ecological principles. Footprint analysis measures the use of nature in as far as it impacts on the regenerative capacity of the biosphere. It expresses the use of these ecological services in area-based units using a standardised metric known as the global hectare (or gha). In other words, the footprint measures how much nature is used exclusively for producing all the resources a given person consumes, and absorbing the waste they produce, using prevailing technology.[1]

The three key benefits of the footprint are that it provides an aggregated indicator of environmental impact; it is easily communicated and readily understood; and it allows for sustainability benchmarking. The latter is accomplished by comparison with the 'earth share' – the average amount of productive area available per capita. This is calculated with reference to global land supply data and is around 1.8 hectares per person (Chambers et al., 2000).

Footprint data for different countries is published by WWF as part of their Living Planet Report (WWF, 2006). Many richer nations, the UK included, operate at an ecological deficit. That is, they do not have the ecological capacity to meet the lifestyle demands of their populations. For example, the average UK footprint is 5.6 ha whereas the average UK supply is only 1.6 ha. This is only slightly less than the 'earth share'. If everyone in the world lived like the average Briton we would need three planets to support global consumption.

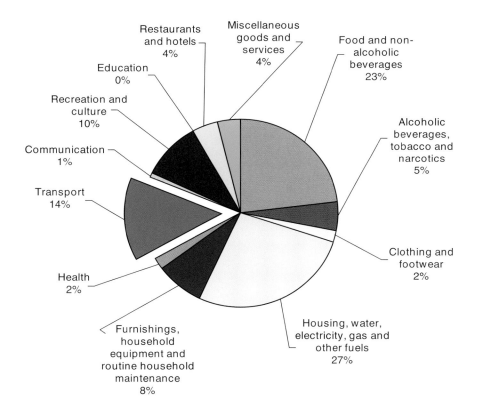

1.

Breakdown of ecological footprint by consumption category. Data covers 31 countries.

Recent research covering 31 countries relating industrial production to consumer spending (Simmons et al., 2006), assessed the relative impact of various categories of consumption (see Figure 1). It found that housing-related impacts and food had the largest footprint, followed by personal transport.

The 'EcoCal' lifestyle calculator, developed in 1996 by Best Foot Forward, combined a footprint-based measurement scheme with a package of facts, hints, tips and contact details aimed at bringing about more environmentally-responsible behaviour. Designed for use by the general public, EcoCal was produced in both software and paper-based formats.[2]

Now superseded by a more up-to-date version – known as Personal Stepwise[3] – these calculators enable an individual or household to measure, what the authors have termed, their 'ecological garden' – the amount of bio-productive space required to support the lifestyles of the residents of a dwelling. The EcoCal questionnaire comprised 45 questions – this has been reduced further in Personal Stepwise to allow for a more rapid assessment.

Questions cover five consumption categories: nourishment (food and drink); shelter (housing); mobility (personal transport); goods (including waste); and services. Examples of the information gathered in each category are given in Table 1.

Table 1 Overview of information gathered by Personal Stepwise

Category	Information gathered
Mobility	Distance travelled by car; distance travelled by bus/train
Shelter	Domestic gas and electricity consumption; size of property
Goods	Volume of domestic waste arising; recycling rate
Nourishment	Percentage of animal and plant-based foods in diet; percentage of food which is fresh and local (as opposed to processed and packaged)
Services	Spending on services such as telecommunications, leisure, etc.

Questions are determined on the basis of availability of data, significance of the impact, and the ability of households to 'make a difference' by acting to reduce their score.

The questions do not address all impacts but together can be used to estimate the total ecological footprint. As part of the original EcoCal study, 40 households were surveyed and the responses converted to their ecological footprint equivalents using pre-calculated conversion factors. The range of footprint values was large – from less than 0.5 ha (c. 10 per cent of the UK per capita average) to more than 40 ha per household (about seven times the UK average) – suggesting ample scope for improvement. The high values were typically the result of large families with energy-inefficient homes taking one, or more, long-haul holidays abroad, coupled with one-off 'high impact' purchases (such as hardwood furniture, the impacts of which should probably have been accounted for over a longer period of time to reflect durability).

These findings are comparable with other work on the urban density of households undertaken by Walker in Canada, where a restricted range of impacts (transport, energy and land use footprints) was calculated for five dwelling types.

The Oxford Ecohouse presented an ideal opportunity to benchmark the EcoCal study findings and determine the benefits offered by this innovative low-impact dwelling. The house was designed to consume the minimum amount of energy while providing a high quality living space. By most standards the ecohouse would be considered a luxury dwelling: it has all modern conveniences (washing machine, dishwasher, microwave, computer and security system for example), is set on three floors with four bedrooms, and comprises of a total living space of around 250 m^2.

The house uses solar energy in three ways: photovoltaics (PV) generate electricity; there is a solar water heating system; and the house is designed to benefit from passive solar heating, even in the winter. The passive solar heating occurs either radiantly, as the sun enters through windows and heats the thermal mass of the house, or convectively as warm air is taken in from a sunspace through floor- and ceiling-level vents.

Gas-fired appliances are used for cooking and, in winter, for evening heating. At ground level, a wood-burning stove is the main source of heat. Triple-glazed windows are used throughout. The fixed household lighting requirements have been met using low-energy fluorescent and halogen bulbs. The 'open' design of the house allows the maximum use to be made of natural daylight.

The occupants also make an effort to live a more environmentally sustainable lifestyle. They seek to reduce or recycle their waste, try to avoid air-freighted food products and, perhaps most significantly, run a small electric car charged from the PV system. The house is not totally self-sufficient in electricity although it sometimes produces a surplus. Electricity is bought and sold via a metering system, drawing power when necessary from the national grid.

Limiting their analysis to the same set of questions and categories of impact as in the original EcoCal study (and using the same basic assumptions), Chambers and Simmons calculated the footprint of the Oxford Ecohouse to be about two-thirds (65 per cent) less than the average obtained in the EcoCal study and considerably lower than one would expect given the type and standard of the property.

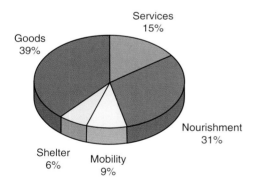

Total ecological footprint: 3.3 gha

2.
Typical breakdown of ecological footprint of a BedZED resident.

Low eco-footprint is also demonstrated in the BedZED zero-emission development in the London Borough of Sutton.[4] This demonstrated how living in BedZED would typically reduce an individual's ecological footprint by about half (see Figure 2).

Thus the eco-design of housing, along with the more environmentally friendly behaviour this encourages, would appear to have potential for substantially reducing an individual's overall ecological footprint and moving them closer to achieving a sustainable lifestyle.

NOTES

1 For more information about ecological footprints, go to www.bestfoot forward.com

2 A more up-to-date interactive lifestyle calculator is now available at www.ecologicalfootprint.com

3 See www.bestfootforward.com for more details of Personal Stepwise.

4 The architects for BedZED were Bill Dunster Associates ZEDfactory (www.zedfactory.com). Research on BedZED carried out by Best Foot Forward.

REFERENCES

Chambers, N., Simmons, C. and Wackernagel, M. (2000) *Sharing Nature's Interest: ecological footprints as an indicator of sustainability*. Earthscan Publications, London.

Simmons, C. and Chambers, N. (1998) Footprinting UK households: how big is your ecological garden? *Local Environment*, 3(3), 355–362.

Simmons, C., Gonzalez, I. and Lewis, K. (2006). *One Planet Business*. Research commissioned and funded by WWF UK. Report available at: www.bestfootforward.com/opb.html

Wackernagel, M. et al. (1999) National Natural Capital Accounting with the Ecological Footprint Concept. *Ecological Economics*, 29(3), 375–390.

Wackernagel, M. and Rees, W. (1996) *Our Ecological Footprint: reducing human impact upon the Earth*. New Society Publishers, Gabriola Island, BC, Canada.

Walker (1995) The influence of dwelling type and residential density on the appropriated carrying capacity of Canadian households. Unpublished Masters Thesis.

WWF (2006) Living Planet Report, 2006. http://www.panda.org/livingplanet/pr02/

THE NICOL GRAPH

The Nicol graph (Nicol et al., 1994) starts from the findings, by Humphreys and others, that the temperature which people find comfortable indoors varies with the mean outdoor temperature. This is especially true for people in buildings which are 'free-running' (i.e. not mechanically heated or cooled). Figure 3 (from Humphreys, 1978) illustrates the relationships.

The 'comfort temperature' is the temperature which people in a given situation will find comfortable. Each point in Figure 3 is the value of the comfort temperature determined from a survey of thermal comfort plotted against the

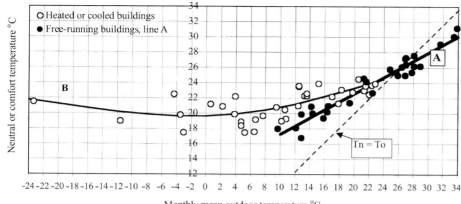

3.
The change in comfort temperature with monthly mean outdoor temperature. Each point represents the mean value for one survey. This graph is from Humphreys, 1978. The buildings are divided between those which are heated or cooled at the time of the survey (line B) and those which are free-running (line A). Subsequent analysis of the results of more recent surveys (Humphreys and Nicol, 2000) showed similar results.

mean outdoor temperature at the time of the survey. People are assumed to be familiar with the conditions they encounter culturally and climatically. In Figure 3 the outdoor temperature is taken from meteorological records as:

$$T_{mean} = (T_{max} + T_{min})/2 \qquad (1)$$

Where T_{max} is the monthly mean of the daily maximum outdoor temperature and T_{min} is the monthly mean of the daily minimum outdoor temperature at the time of the survey (T_{max} and T_{min} are usually available in meteorological records).

The most likely comfort temperature

Free-running buildings
In free-running buildings the comfort temperature varies linearly with the outdoor temperature as shown in Figure 3. Humphreys and Nicol (2000) give an equation for comfort temperature T_c as:

$$T_c = 0.534 \, (T_{mean}) + 11.9 \qquad (2)$$

Using this equation a comfort temperature can be calculated for each month of the year.

Using the relationship to help design buildings
The relationship between comfort temperature and the outdoor temperature can be used to help design comfortable free-running buildings. An example for a climate in which buildings are generally free-running throughout the year is shown in Figure 4. Here the indoor comfort temperature T_c is calculated from the monthly value of T_o (Equation 2) and plotted month by month together with T_o, T_{ommax} and T_{ommin}. Such a diagram helps the designer to judge whether passive heating and/or cooling is a possibility in the climate under consideration. The relationship between the desired indoor temperature and the range of outdoor temperatures shows whether, for instance, night cooling is likely to be a viable way to keep the building comfortable in summer, or to calculate whether passive solar heating will be enough in winter.

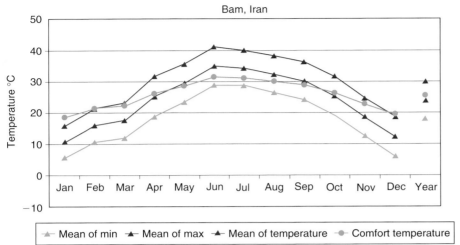

4

The Nicol graph showing the seasonal changes in mean comfort temperature T_c (green line) in free-running buildings in the city of Bam in Iran and its relation to the average daily maximum, minimum and outdoor temperatures T_o. The relationships used to calculate T_o and T_c are given in Equations 1 and 2 in the text.

This method has been extended by Roaf et al. (2001) to include the mean solar intensity to help identify passive heating options.

Buildings which are heated or cooled

Buildings that are free-running for some, or even most, of the year may need to be heated or cooled in particularly cold or hot weather. Although in theory people are able to 'wrap up warm' there is a limit to the amount of clothing which they will find acceptable and therefore to how low the indoor temperature can fall. Because the indoor temperature has been decoupled from the outdoor temperature, the comfort temperature in heated or cooled buildings is a matter of custom and preference. As long as the rate of change is sufficiently slow, people can accept a range of indoor temperatures but the customary indoor comfort temperature may be decided on local factors and may also change with the seasons as people adjust their clothing with the weather. Thus the lowest temperature considered comfortable might be anywhere from 19°C or 23°C in buildings in the same climate, depending on their purpose, the attitudes of occupants or the person who pays the bills!

The decision about which indoor temperature to specify in periods of heating or cooling will have a big effect on the energy used by the building. For instance, in the UK approximately 10 per cent of heating energy is saved for every one degree reduction in indoor temperature. It is worth making this clear to occupants and encouraging them to accept a free-running building for as long as possible and to accept a variable indoor temperature to save energy. It also emphasises the importance of using passive heating and cooling wherever possible.

The 'free-running' Nicol graph shown in Figure 4 should therefore be modified to take account of the customary temperatures of the building occupants in heated or cooled buildings. Thus if the customary temperature in the heating season is 19°C (not unusual in a house) the indoor comfort temperature should not fall below this. The Nicol graph therefore has to take the form shown in Figure 5.

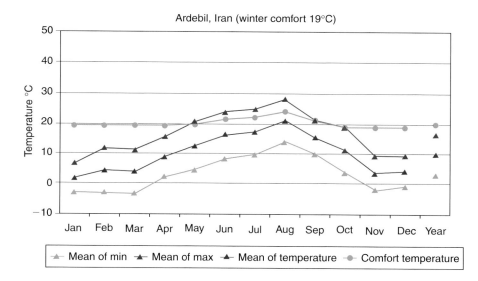

Ardebil, Iran (winter comfort 19°C)

Legend: Mean of min — Mean of max — Mean of temperature — Comfort temperature

5.
Nicol graph for buildings in a climate in which heating is necessary in the colder months of the year. The customary indoor comfort temperature in the heated building has been taken as 19°C – typical for residential buildings but probably lower than is normal in offices.

OTHER CONSIDERATIONS

The Nicol graph gives the optimum temperature which a building designer should aim to achieve. This is not the end of the story; other things need to be considered:

1 How far can we range from the optimum without causing discomfort?
2 Are there limits to the comfort temperature?
3 How quickly does the comfort temperature change?

The range of comfortable conditions

It is difficult to define the range of conditions which will be found comfortable around the comfort temperature. Change in indoor temperatures can be caused by actions taken to reduce discomfort, as well as those which are uncontrolled and therefore likely to cause discomfort. Achieving thermal comfort is therefore a function of the possibilities for change as well as the actual temperature. The width of the comfort 'zone' if measured purely in physical terms will therefore depend on the balance between these two types of action. In a situation where there was no possibility of changing clothing or activity and where air movement cannot be used, the comfort zone may be as narrow as ±2°C. In situations where these adaptive opportunities are available and appropriate the comfort zone may be considerably wider.

HOW TO MAKE A NICOL GRAPH
1 From the nearest met station (or library) get for each month of the year:
   • the mean daily maximum of the outdoor air temperature (T_{max})
   • the mean daily minimum of the outdoor air temperature (T_{min})
   • the mean daily solar radiation on the horizontal (optional).
   • (Preferably these should be averages for several years, but use the best you can find.)

2 Determine from local people (either from experience or by conducting a survey) what are the customary temperature limits in the type of building you are designing.

3 Calculate the value of the mean outdoor temperature T_{mean} for each month: $T_{mean} = T_{max} + T_{min})/2$.

4 Use the Humphreys formula to find the comfort temperature T_c: $Tc = 0.534 (T_{mean}) + 11.9$

5 If T_c falls below customary comfort limits, for instance indicating that people will be comfortable at temperatures lower than we would intuitively expect, particularly in winter, then we often flatten off the winter comfort line at a point at which we know that people, well-clothed in a good passive building, would be comfortable. We have chosen 17°C for the flat winter temperature, based on our experience of indoor winter comfort temperatures in the Oxford Ecohouse. In reality, we have measured considerably lower indoor comfort temperatures in areas, for instance, such as in the city of Swat, in the North West Frontier Province of Pakistan where we have done annual thermal comfort field studies in homes and offices.

6 Plot T_{max}, T_{min}, T_{mean} and T_c for each month of the year.

7 Where it is available, show the solar irradiation as a monthly bar as a guide to the possibilities for passive solar heating (the Roaf extension).

Limits to the comfort temperature

Clearly there are limits to the range of temperatures which are acceptable. Indoor temperatures which require us to wear a thick coat will be incompatible with many indoor activities such as office work. Temperatures which require high rates of sweating to maintain thermal balance may cause physiological strain on the body, even if it is considered acceptable in terms of comfort. It would be difficult to put absolute limits as they would depend on the local custom as well as physiology and acclimatisation, but these should be borne in mind.

Time and the Nicol graph

The Nicol graph is based on the idea that people's comfort temperature changes from time to time. The assumption behind the way the graph is constructed (using monthly data) is that the comfort temperature only changes from month to month. In fact, the rate of change can be much higher. Research has shown that the characteristic rate of change is more like a week. This means that if the weather changes from week to week, the comfort temperature will also change. Thus the Nicol graph does not say what the comfort temperature will actually be at any given time, but merely suggests its average value in that particular climate.

FURTHER READING

GBSE Guide A (2006). Chapter 1: Environmental criteria for design. Chartered Institution of Building Services Engineers.

Humphreys, M.A. (1976). Field Studies of thermal comfort compared and applied. *J. Inst. Heat. & Vent. Eng.* 44, 5–27.

Humphreys, M.A. and Nicol, J.F. (2000) Outdoor temperature and indoor thermal comfort: raising the precision of the relationship for the 1998 ASHRAE database of field studies *ASHRAE Transactions* 206(2), 485–492.

Nicol, J.F., Jamy, G.N., Sykes, O., Humphreys, M.A., Roaf, S.C. and Harncock, M. (1994) *A Survey of Thermal Comfort in Pakistan toward New Indoor Temperature Standards*. Oxford Brookes University, Oxford, UK.

1 OXFORD ECOHOUSE

Architects:
Sue Roaf and David Woods

PV:
Energy Equipment Testing: Cardiff with Jeremy Dain, Inscape Architects, Bristol

Solar hot water:
George Goudsmit, AES Findhorn

Owner:
Susan Roaf

Location:
Oxford, UK, 51°N, 1°W, 40 m above sea level

Climate:
Temperate

Area:
232 m², 250 m² including porch and sun space

CS 1.1.
The Oxford Ecohouse.

CS 1.2.
Nicol graph for Oxford.

ECOFEATURES

• High levels of insulation • High thermal mass • Passive solar sunspace with solar shading • Natural lighting • High security form • Airtight construction • Triple glazing • 4 kW PV roof • 5 m² solar hot water • Energy-efficient appliances • Wood-burning Kakkleoven • Energy-efficient lighting • Low embodied energy construction

DESCRIPTION/BRIEF

The Oxford Ecohouse is a three-storey suburban detached house on a north–south alignment. It was built of traditional cavity wall construction. The key elements of the design brief were to have a quiet and healthy house with minimal CO_2 emissions. This was achieved with heavy construction, natural finishes, no carpets and, very importantly, buffer spaces to the front and back of the house in which damp clothes can be kept.

LOW CO_2 EMISSIONS AND FUTURE ASSET PROTECTION

This house has demonstrated that the performance of an ordinary suburban house can be improved substantially yet still be built in the traditional manner. The Oxford Ecohouse produces only around 148 kg CO_2 per annum, compared with the 6500 kg CO_2 produced by similar houses of the same size. On a number of occasions choices had to be made between putting money into building performance or appearance; the kitchen had only £250 spent on kitchen units initially. In addition, when Susan retires, it will be possible to run the house on a state pension, so early investment has protected her interests over time.

MATERIALS SELECTION

At the time the house was built there was beginning to be much debate about the materials issues and the manufacturers of products helped greatly in choosing the best energy products. Ibstock wisely suggested Bradgate bricks for the house. Jeffrey Walker and Co. were chosen to supply the timber, at the suggestion of Jewsons, because of the new low-energy timber-drying plant they have and their use of timber only from well-managed sustainable British forests, such as Sherwood Forest. Hepworth Drainage had recently completed a study on the embodied energy of their drainage products. All drainage pipes, WCs, basins and shower trays were of clay or porcelain, with a steel bath for durability, by Armitage Shanks. The tiles for the house came from the award-winning low-energy production line at Marlborough Tiles. Mr Howland ran special tests in the Potterton Myson Laboratories to test the impact of placing an ordinary long radiator vertically on the wall to save wall space; he found it was 25 per cent less efficient but this is of no consequence in a low-energy house. Gordon Grant at Velux developed special roof profiles for the integration of the Velux windows into the PV roof. Chris Thomas at Redland Roof Tiles built a mock-up of the ventilated ridge section to see how it would work with the integrated PV roof. Ian Windwood carried out tests to see which adhesive was most appropriate on sunspace balconies for Wicanders floors. From the many people involved in this project came an enormous amount of real, old-fashioned building wisdom, and leading-edge scientific results. A true lesson from this house is that you should ask the company concerned about the product you want to use; they will know more about its performance than anyone else. A final aim for the house was that it should last at least 500 years.

CONSTRUCTION

The roof is constructed of concrete tiles on battens on 50 mm continuous expanded polystyrene over 200-mm-deep cellulose insulation between rafters, with 6 mm ply below. The U-value of the roof's components collectively is $U = 0.19$ W m^{-2} C. In addition the timber attic floor is insulated with 200 mm of mineral wool fibre between joists ($U = 0.24$ w m^{-2} C). The external walls have handmade bricks facing to the outside, 150 mm fill of mineral wool fibre with nylon wall ties behind the brick and 150 mm dense concrete block inner leaf with two coats of plaster finish internally. The U-value of the wall system is 0.22 W m^{-2} C. The ground floor is a 15 mm floating timber flooring on 60 mm screed, over 150 mm concrete slab, on 150 mm polystyrene floor insulation with a U-value of 0.19 W m^{-2} C. The Nor-Dan triple-glazed timber windows have a total U-value of 1.3 W m^{-2} C. In the buffer porch and sunspace there are two walls of double-glazed windows, with whole-window U-values of $2.9\,W\,m^{-2}\,C$ for each glazed wall.

Materials/element	U value (w m^{-2})	Description
Walls	0.22	Brick/block
Floor	0.19	150 mm insulation
Roof	0.14	250 mm insulation
Windows	1.30	Triple-glazed

PERFORMANCE SUMMARISED

Type	Kwh per m^2 imported per year	Electric cost (£) per year	Gas cost (£) per year	Total cost (£) per year	CO$_2$ emissions (kg per year)	Construction cost (£) (per m^2)*
Oxford Ecohouse	27	160	235	395	721	720
Typical house	90	400	844	1244	6776	720
Savings	63	240	609	849	6055	0 extra

*The construction cost was compared to a similar architect-designed house of the same size. The Ecohouse was finished internally to a basic standard only. It is now saving over 6 tonnes of CO$_2$ and getting upto £1000 running costs per year.

LESSONS LEARNED/PITFALLS

Lessons learned: Sue Roaf

Many of the lessons learned in building the house are included in various chapters of this book. Key lessons learned include:

1 the success of the solution is not dependent on a single grand idea but the aggregation of interacting and correct choices;
2 the use of small vents into the buffer porch and sunspace provide a very good quality of natural ventilation even in the coldest periods in the Oxford climate;
3 the stabilisation of the indoor climate through the use of high levels of thermal mass provides a safe and comfortable climate throughout the year;
4 the choice of good triple-glazed Nor-Dan windows was very important in the overall building performance, as was the elimination of all cold bridges in the structure with careful detailing by David Woods;
5 the buffer spaces make a huge impact on the performance of the house – every house should have a good porch in a temperate or cold climate;
6 over time you learn how best to use the different systems in a house. When I sell I will pass on a guide to 'how to get the best out of the house';
7 passive design looks really well;
8 it is possible to get really fond of a building!

Lesson learned: David Woods

It is not difficult to construct a low-energy house. It requires careful site work. Two important strategies for temperate climate are the reduction of air infiltration and elimination of cold bridges, along with increased passive solar gain and insulation. Having adopted those strategies the design of each individual element in the building takes on more meaning, especially in how each fits into the envelope.

2 HARPER ECOHOUSE

Owner/Eco-designer:
Sally Harper

Solar hot water:
George Goudsmit, AES Findhorn

Wood Stove with back boiler
The Barnatt-Millns Group

Location:
Oxford, UK 51°N, 1°W, 40 m above sea level

Climate:
Temperate

Area:
126 m²
Nicol graph – for Oxford (see CS 1.2)

CS 2.1.
2 Piccadilly, Oxfordshire, with solar thermal panels.

ECOFEATURES

• Natural and/or renewable insulation materials: sheep's wool, recycled woodwool boards, hemp, pumice and LECA • Reclaimed or renewable structural repair: green oak • Renewable energy: solar thermal and wood-burning stove with back boiler • Efficient under floor heating system • Energy-efficient lighting and appliances • On-site well water and cesspit • Thermal mass walls and floors

DESCRIPTION/CONCEPT

This ecohouse is an example of a solid stone walled traditional cottage renovated to meet the UK's 2006 thermal standards according to ecological principles. Reclaimed and organic materials are used alongside new renewable energy technology leading to a practical low carbon refurbishment, which reduced carbon emissions at 2 Piccadilly to less than 1 tonne of CO_2 per year.

Careful choice and detailing of vapour permeable insulation in floors, walls and roof ensures both a low in-use energy demand, which is not harmful to the historic fabric of the building and creates a healthy indoor environment free from mould.

The insulation solution presents an exemplar selection of materials that can be used in solid wall homes, of which there are 7–9 million in the UK, and which effectively saves energy, reduces CO_2 emissions and addresses the issues of climate change and wider environmental concerns.

Key energy conservation strategies include:

• reduced energy loss from the building fabric using natural insulation
• installed renewable or carbon neutral energy sources

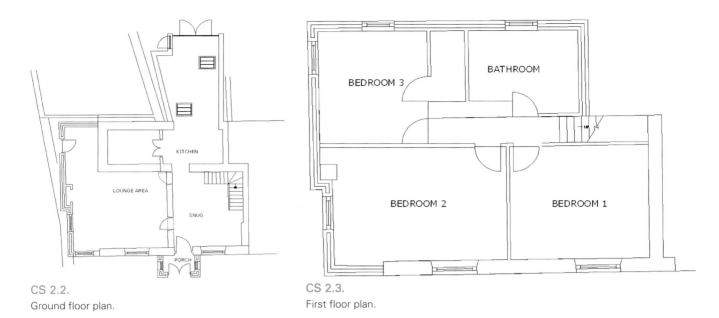

CS 2.2.
Ground floor plan.

CS 2.3.
First floor plan.

- installed efficient heating, lighting and appliances
- reuse and reclaim existing materials.

ECOFEATURES EXPLAINED

The UK's 24 million existing households account for 30 per cent of the UK's CO_2 emissions and require substantial transformation if emissions reductions are to be secured and the worst of the impacts of climate change avoided. The refurbishment and choice of ecofeatures at 2 Piccadilly were undertaken to effectively make significant CO_2 reductions through a dual approach:

- to reduce energy demand, and
- to switch to renewable or low-carbon fuel.

These refurbishment choices were based on the desire to refurbish this house in a way that uses fewer resources, or resources that can be reused or have a less toxic or energy expensive demolition impact at the end of their lives.

Natural insulation in walls, floors and roof

Internally insulating 2 Piccadilly saved approximately 4 tonnes of CO_2/year or 20 000 kWh/year. Due to concerns about resource scarcity, the reusability of materials and the health of the building and occupant's, natural insulation materials were chosen. The natural materials chosen are quick drying and vapour permeable, thus creating 'breathable' insulation in which moisture vapour passes through the layers of natural insulation materials and through to the outside. This reduces surface condensation, stabilises indoor humidity and removes the need to use a sequence of remedial silicon-injected damp course treatments as carried out in neighbouring cottages.

Sheep's wool has been used as insulation in one or another form for hundreds of years and was the first choice ecological insulation for the existing walls and roof at 2 Piccadilly. Thermafleece has a thermal performance comparable to other man-made fibrous insulants and a very low embodied energy as shown in CS 2.4 below.

The wool is 'friction fitted' between rafters or new studwork that is internally fitted to the original stonewalls. This is a quick and easy process and a definite advantage over solid insulants that require accurate cutting. The wool is protected on the cold side of the thermal insulation by a breather membrane to prevent the infiltration of

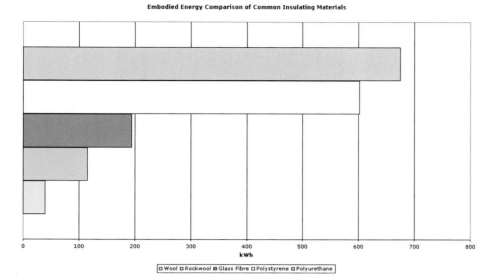

Embodied Energy Comparison of Common Insulating Materials

kWh

□ Wool □ Rockwool ▣ Glass Fibre □ Polystyrene □ Polyurethane

CS 2.4.

The Embodied Energy Comparison of common insulating materials with sheep's wool adapted from Report EC Ecoplanning Board Denmark January 1993 (http://www.greenbuildingstore. co.uk/ins-environ.php).

cold air, which could otherwise move across the surface of the wool and increase heat loss by convection. Wool is supplied in batts 1200 mm long by widths of 400 mm or 600 mm and in thicknesses of 50 mm, 75 mm and 100 mm, which can be combined to achieve different U-values.

The sheep's wool is faced with a *wood wool board* called Heraklith, which provides an 'open' surface for the application of *traditional lime plaster* and *lime wash*, which completes the 'breathable' insulating internal skin. Sheep's wool, wood wool board and lime plasters all absorb and desorb moisture quickly, which dramatically reduces the possibility of surface condensation and moulds, especially in bathrooms and kitchens. Collectively the system has excellent acoustic qualities.

The installation steps are shown in CS 2.5–2.7 and cross-section details for the roof and existing wall are shown in CS 2.8 and 2.9.)

The limecrete floor is the ecological alternative to concrete floors and provides a draught-proof, insulated solid floor that requires no damp course membrane and uses approximately half the embodied energy of a concrete floor. (Limecrete floors represent 157 kWh/m^2 and concrete floors represent 278 kWh/m^2). These floors also add thermal mass to the house, which can absorb heat during the day, moderating internal peak temperatures and ensuring wonderfully cool rooms in the summer. This offsets the loss of the thermal mass of the original walls, which occurs with internal insulation. These floors have proven to create a comfortable environment in the summer and winter at 2 Piccadilly – a delight to live with.

The limecrete floor is made up of a dry loose layer of LECA (a lightweight marine aggregate) or recycled foamed glass; the main insulant is then topped by a pumice slab (a mixture of graded pumices and lime mixed in a concrete mixer), which is laid wet. The under floor heating pipes can be fixed onto the slab when dry. The screed is edge insulated from the external walls using the pummicecrete, which maintains the 'breathability' of the system. This 200 mm channel around the edge of the rooms allows other services to be installed. Once heated at the beginning of the winter the lime screed maintains a consistent temperature throughout an 18-hour period and requires once a day 'top up' heating. The heat retention capability makes it possible to use a wood-burning stove with back boiler as the sole heating source for the UFH.

CS 2.5.
Installing natural 'vapour permeable insulation: designed to avoid a damaging build-up of moisture by allowing water vapour to migrate through the structure. 75 mm of wool is fitted in the frame.

CS 2.6.
50 mm of wool is fitted over the bracing and the wood wool board (Heraklith) is screwed to the batterns.

CS 2.7.
Cotton scrim tape is placed over the joins between the wood wool boards and held in place with a thin layer of lime plaster, before the two coats of lime plaster are applied.

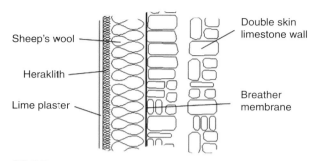

CS 2.8.
Cross-section of natural 'vapour permeable' insulation of solid stone wall.

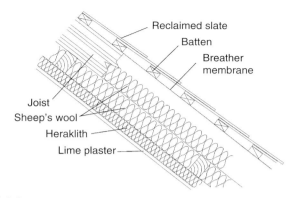

CS 2.9.
Cross-section of natural 'vapour permeable' insulation into an existing roof.

CS 2.10.
Cutting thermafleece with a serrated knife. The wool is held firm between two boards, in this case Heraklith since there was plenty to hand.

A comfortable temperature is maintained at 2 Piccadilly if the wood stove is only lit once a day for a few hours. The finished floor surface is a layer of 25 mm English limestone. (The constructional details for the limecrete floors are shown in CS 2.11 ground floors.)

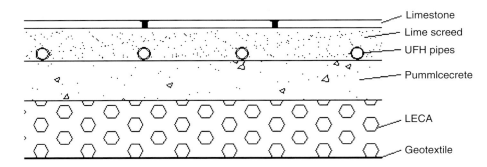

CS 2.11.
Cross-section of limecrete floors: earth blinded with sand, Geotextile, 150 mm foamed glass or 300 mm of LECA, 125 mm pumicecrete, UFH pipes, 75 mm of limecrete, 25 mm of limestone tiles.

Hemp and green oak extension

The constructional simplicity of using the cellouse fibres of the hemp plant to create a solid insulated and permeable 'infill' between timber stud walls makes it a perfect material for self-build extensions. Building with hemp highlights the exciting potential for non-food crop construction materials in the UK, and has been shown to have similar thermal performance to modern brick buildings and similar energy consumption.

The low embodied energy of the hemp and timber stud walls is 74 per cent less than a standard concrete thermalite block and polyurethane insulated wall. Hemp's non-toxic hygroscopic properties are compatible with the other vapour permeable systems used in this ecohouse.

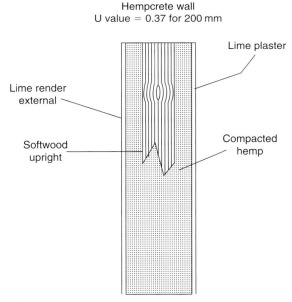

CS 2.12.
Hempcrete wall cross-section.

At 2 Piccadilly, the 200 mm hemp wall is supported by a softwood and oak frame using 500 mm upright centres without horizontal 'noggins'. Temporary shuttering using plywood sheets is used to 'cast' the walls in situ. The hemp, water and lime is mixed in a cement mixer and tipped into a wheelbarrow and then spread evenly within the shuttering in lifts of 150 mm. Each layer should be lightly tamped within the shuttering. The floor and roof of this extension are extremely well insulated.

All the windows and doors at 2 Piccadilly are oak framed and double-glazed.

CS 2.13.
Hempcrete wall ready to be plastered. The lines show the depth of each of the hemp 'lifts'.

CS 2.14.
Hemp wall materials used at 2 Piccadilly – 3 parts hemp to 1 of lime and 1 of water.

Renewable heating and solar hot water system

Finding an affordable 'green' and renewable heating and domestic hot water (DHW) system was a difficult challenge. The final installed system, integrating solar thermal and a wood-burning stove with back boiler, saved 8 tonnes of CO_2/year or 7000 kWh/year. The costs were comparable with a 'conventional' heating system although without the automated controls.

The primary heat source for the house is a wood stove with a back boiler. This stove is designed to operate as a wood boiler, which provides space heating via radiators on the first floor and under floor heating (UFH) on the ground floor and the domestic hot water (DHW). This system is 85 per cent efficient due to a unique secondary water jacket, which is heated by the flue gases. Throughout the winter, the stove is lit once a day to top up the heat in the limecrete slab and to heat the DHW. This has proved to be a simple, effective and affordable heating system.

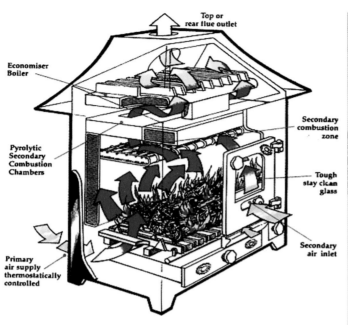

CS 2.15a and b
Wood boiler – wood stove with back boiler (Super Demon – Hellfire Combustion Co).

Four metres sq. of solar thermal (AES flat plate array) is mounted under 'fake' glass windows, an innovative solution to win approval for solar thermal in a conservation area and enabling full use to be made of a south-facing 35 degree pitched roof. The solar thermal panels heat water during summer months when there is no requirement for heat and the wood stove is not used. During the winter the solar thermal panels pre-heat the hot water cylinder (250 litre twin coil Oso cylinder). The pumps are set to operate when the solar collectors are 6°C above the water temperature in the DHW cylinder to ensure an efficient use of energy required to run the pumps. On clear winter days temperatures in the solar collectors reach up to 50°C and on average reach 30°C.

CS 2.16.
Solar thermal panel mounted under a 'fake' glass window to achieve planning permission in a conservation area.

The amortised capital costs over the lifetime energy production for the 'green' energy installed at 2 Piccadilly reveals solar thermal energy costs of 7 p/kWh, which is comparable to the cost of conventional electrically heated water, and 3 p/kWh for energy generated by the wood stove with back boiler, which is comparable to the cost of gas and oil.

Reclaimed materials and low embodied energy structural repairs

Existing materials were reused wherever possible and any replacement items were renewable and/or low embodied materials. For example the existing first floor elm joists were de-nailed, sanded and reinstalled. The failed main structural beams were replaced with green oak beams because they were only 7 per cent of the embodied energy of the equivalent steel beams. At 2 Piccadilly, the choice of oak structural beams over steel saved 4500 kWh.

CS 2.17.
Reused elm joists, de-nailed and hand sanded. The oak beam was a low embodied structural repair.

Reclaimed timbers from other demolished buildings were used to create new joists. Replacement cills, slates and quoins were bought from local reclamation yards.

Other energy reduction action.
Compact fluorescent spot lights (7 watt) have been installed in the kitchen, and all rooms have a single main light and a choice of direct task lighting; lights are fitted with low-energy light bulbs. Appliances are being updated to A+++ wherever possible.

LESSIONS LEARNED

1 Identify heat losses since insulation has the highest impact on reducing energy demand. Prioritising insulation in 2 Piccadilly reduced energy use by 58 per cent. It is especially important to reduce energy demand if the heating source is a finite resource, such as wood.
2 Integrating primary and secondary heat sources such as the wood boiler and solar thermal requires expert installers. If possible go and see the system working elsewhere. Ensure that pumps are carefully controlled by temperature sensors and are not on all the time.
3 Use the internet to source materials directly from manufacturers and to search reclamation yards.
4 Plan the project around a series of steps, the cumulative effect and design of which are effective and compatible.

3 REUSABLE BUILDING

Architect:
Bjørn Berge, Gaia, Lista AS

Owner:
Økologiske Hus AS, Norges Forskningstråd, statens Forurensningstilsyn

Location:
Marnardal, Norway, 58°N, 8°W

Climate:
Inland, cold and medium dry

Area:
132 m²

CS 3.1.
Reusable building. Økologiske Hus.

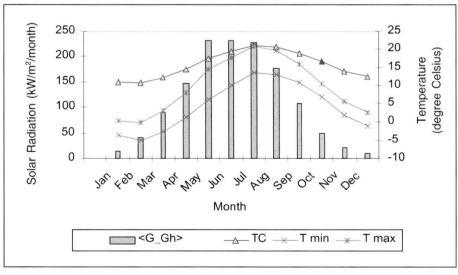

CS 3.2.
Nicol graph for Norway.

ECOFEATURES

• Reusable building materials • Low energy consumption • Excellent indoor air quality • Avoided use of poisonous substances during construction, use or demolition stage

DESCRIPTION/BRIEF

The house is located in a valley 30 miles (48.3 km) from Kristiansand. It is a one-family dwelling that can easily be extended or divided into a two-family building (two flats), a kindergarten, a workshop, small office or similar. The one-family dwelling consists of three bedrooms, one bathroom, kitchen, sitting room and storage for food and others. The interior walls can easily be moved to form other plans.

MATERIALS

The house uses an ADISA (Assembly for Disassembly) building system developed by Gaia. The house is erected on a 3.6 m grid system of concrete pad/pile foundations onto which the timber frame is fixed. The building system consists of 80 different standardised cladding and structural components that are manufactured using a minimum amount of machinery. All components are easy to dismantle. Since the components are prefabricated there is little waste in the building phase, about 0.3 per cent by weight, while for conventionally erected buildings the figure varies from 3 to 5 per cent. The building can be changed, extended or reduced with simple hand tools. Dismantled components and extra parts can be returned to local manufacturers for quality control, and redistributed to new building projects.

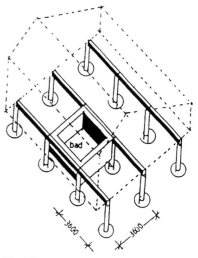

CS 3.3.
3.6 m grid system.

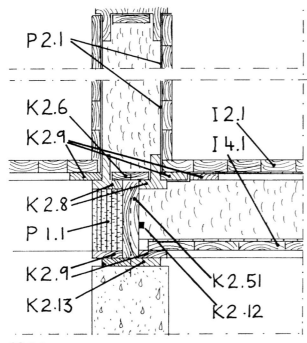

CS 3.4.
Details showing the number of reusable lumber components in the reusable building: ground floor section.

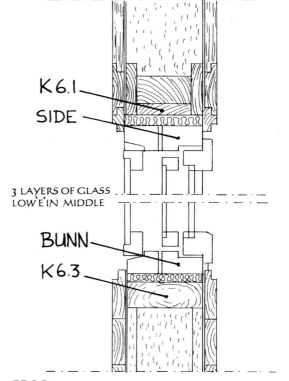

CS 3.5.
Details showing the number of reusable lumber components in the reusable building: window section.

Where only 5 per cent of the materials used in conventional wooden buildings can be reused, the Gaia Lista system achieves a reuse rate of 80 per cent. Of the remaining materials, approximately 13 per cent can be used for material or energy recycling while approximately 8 per cent is inert and can be used in filling purposes. Only 0.8 per cent has to go to a controlled waste deposit.

Thanks to careful selection of materials and production processes, the components in the ADISA system have a considerably longer lifespan than in other wooden buildings in Scandinavia. Account is taken of such aspects as where the tree comes from, when it was felled, which parts of the trunk are used in which part of the construction, and how they are used. Heavy metal impregnation fluids are not used.

EFFICIENT INSULATION

Dwellings built using this system have high insulation values, keeping the indoor temperature at a comfortable level during even the harshest winters.

Materials/element GL	U value (W m^{-2}K)	Description
Floors	0.176	200 mm cellulose fibre
Walls	0.232	150 mm cellulose fibre
Roof	0.126	350 mm cellulose fibre
Windows	0.16	three layers of glass in a coupled window, low 'E' glass in middle

The supposed distribution of materials in a demolition phase

	Kg	%
Reusable components	38.053	78.4
Recycling materials	987.00	2.0
Recycling energy	5.4	11.1

VENTILATION

Natural basis ventilation: A part of the natural ventilation system is its interior surfaces of wood. These are hygroscopic and form a buffer for humidity in the same way that heavy materials are a buffer for temperature, and this exerts a positive influence on the internal climate. A moderate and stable moisture situation will reduce the chances of mites and micro-organisms growing. The disposition and emission cycles of dust on the inside surfaces will also be reduced.

LESSONS LEARNED/PITFALLS

The house is a prototype. The design has to be improved to fit with a broader market. Gaia is currently researching a means of reducing the number of different components from 80 to preferably around 50.

ACKNOWLEDGEMENTS

siv.ark.Dag Roalkvam; Gaia Lista -siv. Ark. Ola Brattset; SINTEF – proff. Hans Granum; SINTEF – proff. Petter Aune; NTNU – siv.ing. Ida Bryn.

4 ECOHOUSE WIBERG

Architect:
Krister Wiberg, 1993

Owner:
Krister Wiberg

Location:
Lund, Sweden; 55°N, 13°W; <74 m above sea level

Climiate:
Temperate in south with cold, cloudy winters and cool, partly cloudy summers

Area:
180 m²

CS 4.1.
Ecohouse Wiberg.

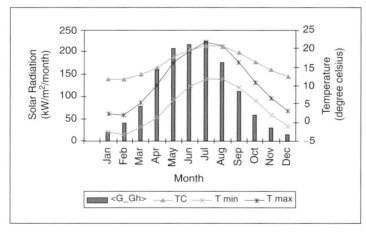

CS 4.2.
Nicol graph for Lund, Sweden.

ECOFEATURES

• Environmentally friendly building materials • Exterior and interior painted with Tempura paints • 250 mm cellulose fibre insulation between two stone walls open to diffusion • Floors of ceramic tiles or solid wood treated with natural oils • Self ventilation • Heating system: active solar heating, bio fuels and gas • Heavy frame for heat conservation • Greenhouse • Earth cellar • Composting toilets • Solid wood kitchen fixtures

FEATURES BRIEFLY EXPLAINED

Ecohouse Wiberg, located in southern Sweden, is built according to ecological principles. It includes a passive system and a ventilated and easily inspected under floor creepway. The walls are of lightweight concrete blocks with an intermediate layer of cellulose fibre sheeting, which give the house a heavy, heat-storing frame. The ventilation works on the self-draught system, the heating through a water mantled tile stove and gas. All materials are non-toxic and natural.

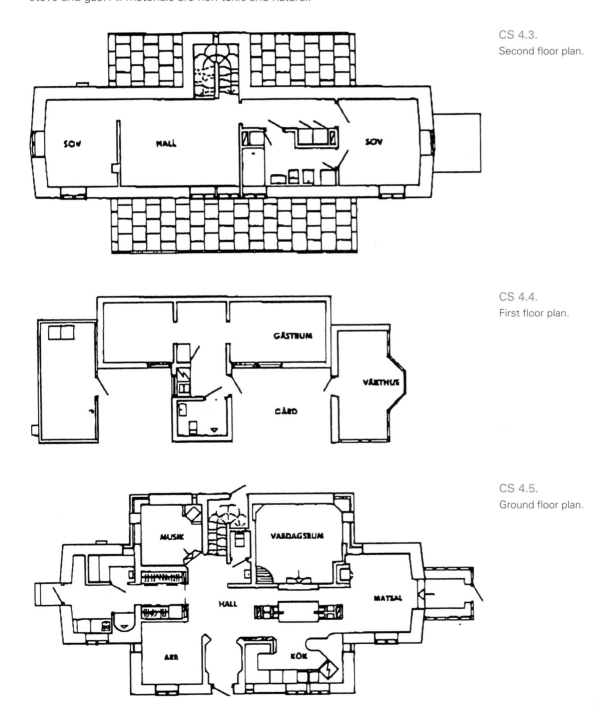

CS 4.3.
Second floor plan.

CS 4.4.
First floor plan.

CS 4.5.
Ground floor plan.

5 MONAMA

Designers:
Prashant Kapoor, Saleem Akhtar

Local Architect:
Arun Prasad

Renewable energy consultant:
Manuel Fuentes

Owners:
Dr and Mrs Ramlal

Location:
Hyderabad, Andra Pradesh, India; 17°N,
78°E; 530 m above sea level

Climate:
Inland composite

Area:
234 m^2

CS 5.1.
Ventilation shaft.

CS 5.2.
Monama entrance.

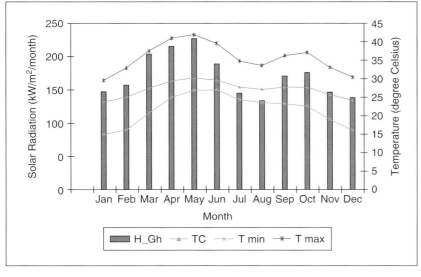

CS 5.3.
Nicol graph for Monama.

ECOFEATURES

• Low environmental impact materials • Buried pipes and evaporative cooling • Rainwater harvesting • Renewable energy

DESCRIPTION/BRIEF

Monoma, named after the clients' late daughter, is in the city of Hyderabad. Hyderabad has a history of Moghul invasion and an Islamic character as far as its historical architecture is concerned. It is among the fastest growing cities of India and is becoming extremely attractive to industrial investors. Although there has been a significant increase in the industrial activity of the region, the rate of growth of infrastructure has not been sufficiently significant to keep up with requirements. Hyderabad has deficient

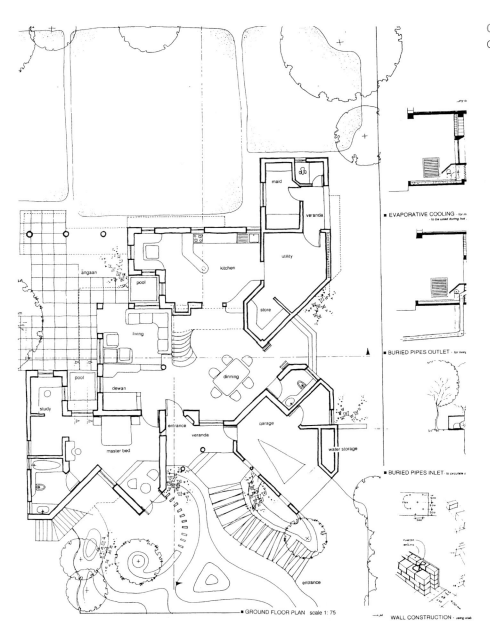

CS 5.4.
Ground floor plan.

power supply, resulting in breakdowns and power cuts almost every day. One of the main objectives for this design was not to rely entirely on the national grid for energy. The house of Dr and Mrs Ramlal relies on energy-efficient design to reduce loads and, where possible, reverts to renewable energy to meet them. Although flexible, the clients require that the master bedroom be located on the ground floor and near the road, that the garage be enclosed, that two bedrooms and a future rental space be located on the first floor with a separate entry from the main entrance to the house.

LOW ENVIRONMENTAL IMPACT

The underlying ideology behind the building design was to generate as low an environmental impact as possible, within the limits of site and budget. Environmental impact resulting from both embodied (from materials) and operational (in-use) considerations was assessed.

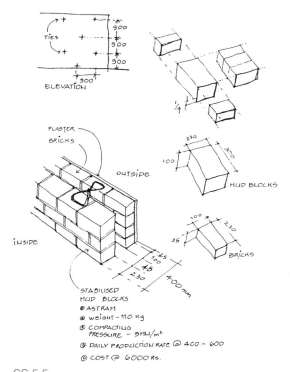

CS 5.6.
Stairs under construction (master bedroom beyond).

CS 5.5.
Wall construction, using stabilised mud blocks (country bricks).

Construction materials

Although the original idea was to use compressed earth blocks, on further investigation the soil quality in the area was found to be unsuitable. It was realised that soil would have to be transported from approximately 400 km away and country bricks that were made within a couple of kilometres of the site would be a better alternative. Country bricks tend to require plaster on the external side as they are not of a quality that can withstand the extreme climate. The solution was to make cavity walls with country bricks on the inside and first-class, wire-cut bricks on the external façade. As a result, the need to use plaster was eliminated. This strategy also provides high thermal mass, which suits the prevailing climatic conditions. The upper floor and roof structure is made with reinforced concrete, which has low environmental impact. Natural materials have been chosen for most internal finishes. Simulations showed that the ground floor would require a high thermal mass to prevent overheating of interior spaces, whereas a high thermal mass had less influence on the top floor indoor temperature.

WALL ORIENTATION AND FORM

Orientation of the wall openings, combined with their size and angle, modulate solar gains passing through. The south wall orients openings to accept low solar gains in the winter and can easily be shaded in the summer, owing to the sun's high position in the sky. Shading of the west and east windows presents difficulties because of the low position of the sun and, additionally, west-oriented openings are associated with external conditions of high solar radiation and ambient temperature during the summer. Thus, the windows in this orientation were minimised or replaced with

CS 5.7.
Living room.

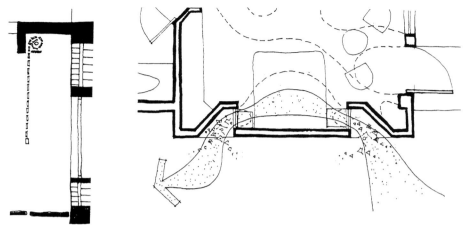

CS 5.8.
South and west windows, designed to avoid direct solar gain.

other design solutions. Depending on the time of the day, high or low pressure zones form in either east or west directions. This induces air movement from the zone of high pressure to that of low pressure. The windows of the house have been specially oriented such that these pressure differences, in combination with the prevailing wind direction, may be utilised for continuous ventilation. There is also a ventilation shaft to exhaust hot air located in the central part of the house which is based on the principles of buoyancy and venturi's effect. The difference in pressure between the outside and the inside air results in the drawing up of air through the shaft and inducing further movement through openings such as windows. The open plan design supports this process by eliminating any internal resistance to the full movement of air.

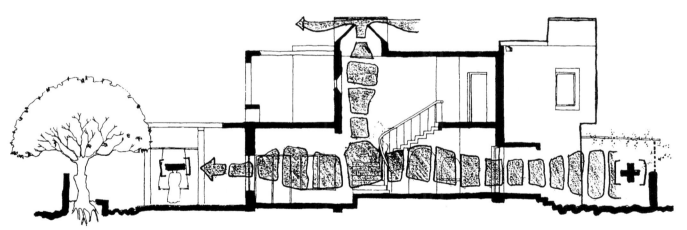

CS 5.9.
Ventilation paths through the house.

BURIED PIPES AND EVAPORATIVE COOLING

Buried pipes function by injecting into the building air that has been previously circulated underground by means of earth-to-air heat exchangers. The air is generally sucked from the ambient air by means of a fan. The temperature drop of the outlet air depends upon the inlet air temperature, the ground temperature at the depth at which the exchanger is situated, the thermal conductivity of the pipes and the thermal diffusivity of the soil, as well as the air velocity and pipe dimensions. Using Summer™ to simulate all the variables, the optimal conditions resulted in:

- length of the exchanger: 26 m
- radius of the exchanger: 0.125 m
- air velocity through the pipe: $2 \, m \, s^{-1}$
- depth of the exchanger: 2 m.

Buried pipes are being utilised for the main living areas of the house, namely the living room and the master bedroom. Since the velocity of the outlet air is low at $2 \, m \, s^{-1}$, adjustable tubes at the outlet ensure placement as the user prefers.

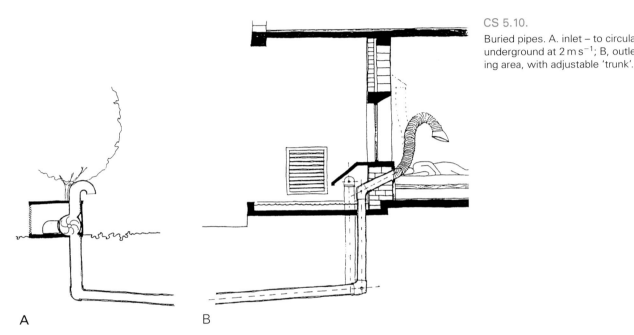

A   B

CS 5.10.
Buried pipes. A. inlet – to circulate air 2 m underground at $2 \, m \, s^{-1}$; B, outlet – for living area, with adjustable 'trunk'.

Evaporative cooling is the process that uses the effect of evaporation as a natural heat sink. Again, through simulations, results indicated that the indoor temperatures of the room fluctuate between 27.5°C and 29°C on a hot dry day. The peak humidity does not exceed 66 per cent, therefore evaporative cooling would succeed as a low-energy cooling strategy for these hot and dry months (March through June). The system used is a water pond along with an air fan. The system provides cooling by consuming just the amount of electricity necessary for the operation of the fans. Since the fans consume far less energy than air-conditioners this proves an energy-efficient design for maintaining human comfort. During the humid months evaporative coolers are rendered inefficient owing to the high humidity levels. The system allows for the ponds to be drained during these months (July through October) and window fans are used to forcefully ventilate the house.

RAINWATER HARVESTING

Hyderabed has a history of water shortages during the dry months. Receiving over 795 mm rain annually justifies storing

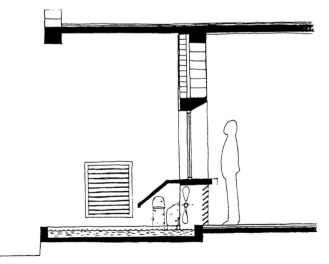

CS 5.11.
Evaporative coolling.

rainwater for inter-seasonal storage. Rainwater harvesting is a method of collecting rainwater and using precipitation from a small catchment area. The water stored will be a valuable supplement for domestic water consumption and irrigation of the garden. As soil from the site is used for building blocks, the resulting pit proves to be an optimal location for the storage tank. The storage tank is located on the northwest corner of the building under the garage for easy maintenance. The outer wall of the garage has a built-in sand filter to process incoming water, as well as temporary storage from which water can be used without the need for a pump.

RENEWABLE ENERGY

The Indian Renewable Energy Development Authority (IREDA) offers an interest-free subsidy scheme that provides soft loans for industrial and commercial projects at 8.3 per cent interest, with 5 per cent for non-profit organisations and 5 per cent for domestic applications (September 1999). This is a substantial subsidy on capital budgets, which clearly proves that as such policy decisions are taken at the level of the government, the fossil fuel situation in India is in a critical state. In Hyderabad there are four hours of power cuts each day. The client specifications were to design a system that works as a photovoltaic stand-alone system during power cuts, and as a regular grid-connected system when the grid is working. The battery chosen for this design allows for four days of autonomy, making it unlikely that the client has to use the utility power to charge the battery. The inverter is multi-functional with 24 V input, 220 V output and a rating power of 800–1000 Wp, and is readily available on the market. The array that is needed to provide the power according to user needs is 850 W. Modules with high-efficiency polycrystalline cells would need a roof area of about 7 m^2.

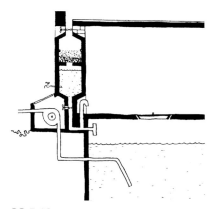

CS 5.12.
Rainwater harvesting. Section showing in situ sand filter.

SOLAR HOT WATER COLLECTOR

There are several systems available but the one chosen for Monama is a free-flow system known as a thermosiphon system. The use of the thermosiphon system is accepted worldwide owing to its simple and reliable characteristics. The system has no pump or controls and is fully automatic in operation.

In the thermosiphon system the tank is positioned above the collector. As the water in the collector is heated by the sun, it rises into the tank mounted above the collector. This causes the cold water in the tank to flow into the collector, where it is heated. In this way, flow is created and the tank is filled with hot water.

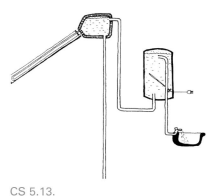

CS 5.13.
The solar water collector works by thermosiphon.

CONTACT INFORMATION

Prashant Kapoor, London, UK. E-mail: kapoor@gmail.com

6 HOUSE AT HAMAMATSU

Architect:
Touichi Akiyama, Land Architects Inc.,
OM Solar, 1991

Owner:
Syounai

Location:
Hamamatsu, Japan; 34°N, 137°E; 31.7 m
above sea level

Climate:
Tropical • 804 degree days year^{-1}

Area:
201.6 m^2

CS 6.1.
House at Hamamatsu, by OM Solar.

CS 6.2.
Nicol graph for Hamamatsu.

ECOFEATURES

• Om Solar system • Thermal insulation • Airtight • Heat chimney

DESCRIPTION/BRIEF

Typical Japanese homes have large roofs, deep eaves, wide openings, open room dividers and floors set high above the earth. These are also characteristics of tropical housing systems. These traditions are closely associated with the Japanese climate of high temperatures and high humidity. However, the winter in Japan is not necessarily warm. Even the southern parts of the main island of Japan can encounter snow and temperatures to below 0°C. The OM Solar system and the house's wooden construction allow it to regulate its indoor climate to a comfortable level between changing seasons.

ECOFEATURES EXPLAINED

OM Solar system

The OM Solar passive system collects solar energy from the roof of the house and utilises t for space and water heating. This system can provide 300 litres of water at 40–60°C. The system is an air heat collecting system that warms outside air by solar energy. Utilising air for heat collection is much safer than using water in terms of water leakage or freezing. The use of outside air is the most unique feature of this system, creating a positive room pressure and, as a result, promoting better air ventilation. The system also heats the rooms by transporting the heat collected beneath the roof to be stored under the concrete slab under the floor. At sunset when the temperature decreases, the warm air rises slowly into the room above the wood-finished floor.

Handling box

The OM handling box is the heart of the OM Solar system. The function of moving heat from the roof either to the floor (winter) or to the outside (summer) is done by this mechanical handler.

AIRTIGHT AND THERMALLY INSULATED

The heat balance in the house consists of three elements: heat collection, heat storage and airtight thermal insulation. The means of keeping wooden houses, such as the house at Hamamatsu, from losing heat after collection (wood has poor heat storage capability) is through airtightness and insulation. The house at Hamamatsu has a high degree of airtightness and thermal insulation to reduce air-conditioning loads in the summer, and winter life is made more comfortable with glass wool. Glass wool is one of the most popular thermal insulating materials and is used in the roof and walls in the house at Hamamatsu. The foundations are insulated with polystyrene foam.

ACKNOWLEDGEMENTS

He Jiang, OM Solar Association, Hamamatsu City, Japan, Website http://www.omsolar.co.jp/

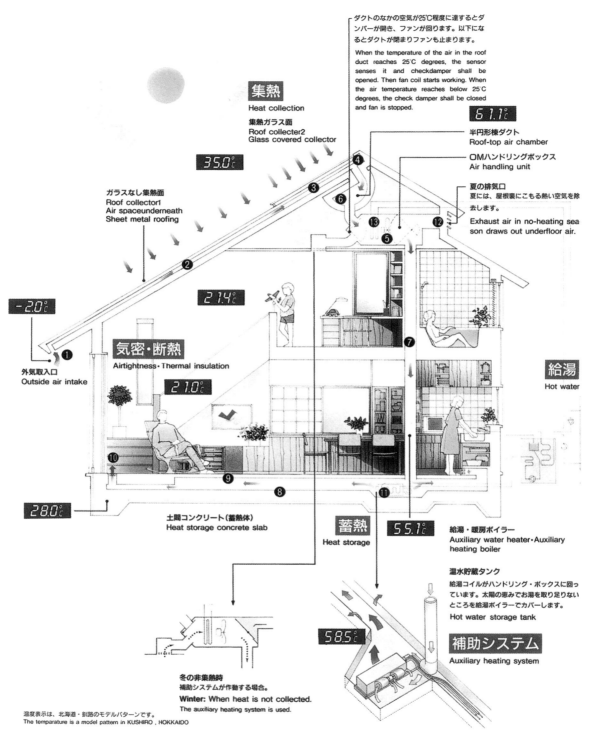

ダクトのなかの空気が25℃程度に達するとダンパーが開き、ファンが回ります。以下になるとダクトが閉まりファンも止まります。

When the temperature of the air in the roof duct reaches 25°C degrees, the sensor senses it and checkdamper shall be opened. Then fan coil starts working. When the air temperature reaches below 25°C degrees, the check damper shall be closed and fan is stopped.

6 1.1℃

集熱
Heat collection

集熱ガラス面
Roof collecter2
Glass covered collector

35.0℃

半円形棟ダクト
Roof-top air chamber

OMハンドリングボックス
Air handling unit

ガラスなし集熱面
Roof collector1
Air spaceunderneath
Sheet metal roofing

夏の排気口
夏には、屋根裏にこもる熱い空気を除去します。

Exhaust air in no-heating season draws out underfloor air.

-2.0℃

2 1.4℃

21.0℃

気密・断熱
Airtightness・Thermal insulation

外気取入口
Outside air intake

給湯
Hot water

28.0℃

土間コンクリート（蓄熱体）
Heat storage concrete slab

蓄熱
Heat storage

55.1℃

給湯・暖房ボイラー
Auxiliary water heater・Auxiliary heating boiler

温水貯蔵タンク
給湯コイルがハンドリング・ボックスに回っています。太陽の恵みでお湯を取り足りないところを給湯ボイラーでカバーします。
Hot water storage tank

補助システム
Auxiliary heating system

58.5℃

冬の非集熱時
補助システムが作動する場合。
Winter: When heat is not collected.
The auxiliary heating system is used.

温度表示は、北海道・釧路のモデルパターンです。
The temparature is a model pattern in KUSHIRO , HOKKAIDO

CS 6.3. Cross-section through Hamamatsu house.

THE MECHANISM OF OM SOLAR SYSTEM

How it works in winter

The OM Solar system uses the roof of the house itself for the purpose of heat collection. The air under the roof is heated by solar energy and used for heating water or is circulated under the floor. At the eaves:

- Fresh air from the opening is heated by the sun radiating on the roof. As it is heated, it rises.
- The glass roof surface (3) is not a special heat collection device, but a simple reinforced glass sheet placed on the metal plate to make heat collection more effective. When the air runs under this, it is heated effectively. At the top of the roof there is a thermostat (4).
- The hot air is gathered in the half cylinder duct (6).
- When the air reaches a certain temperature, a small fan (5) starts to operate.
- During the winter, with the help of this fan, this hot air is guided under the floor through the duct (7).
- The concrete slab (8) under the floor is designed to be a heat accumulation body. The heat preserved here is slowly discharged and warms the entire floor.
- The air, heated by conduction from the concrete slab, circulates in the room. The release of this fresh air also stimulates the air ventilation (10).

As the OM Solar system utilises solar energy, auxiliary heating is necessary in case of cloudy or rainy days that would not provide enough sunshine. There are many kinds of auxiliary heating devices. One such is the fan convector (11). The heat generated by the fan convector is also stored under the floor. The characteristic of the OM Solar system is that we can utilise the heating accumulation portion for both summer and winter cases.

How it works in summer

- The heated air is collected in the half cylinder duct (6).
- The air is released to the outside through the exhaust duct (12).
- At the same time, the air under the floor is vented by the air circulation.
- It is discharged outside through the downward duct (7). This can also rid the house of heat in summer.
- But, before it is discharged, it is used to heat water (13). But this means we can achieve two purposes at the same time.

Multifunctional/four seasons-solar

The OM Solar system is multifunctional, which works in all four seasons through floor heating, ventilation, heating water, eliminating heat and cooling the room in the house in summer. This system utilises the solar energy very effectively and works beneficially for energy saving and creates comfortable living conditions for people.

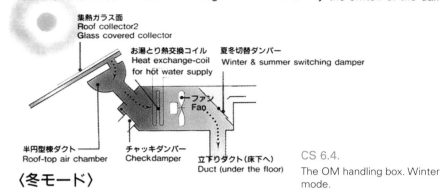

夏モードと冬モードの空気の流れを、夏・冬切換ダンパーによって、切換えます。
Summer and winter modes can be regulated on and off by the switch of the damper.

集熱ガラス面
Roof collector2
Glass covered collector

お湯とり熱交換コイル
Heat exchange-coil for hot water supply

夏冬切替ダンパー
Winter & summer switching damper

ファン
Fan

半円型棟ダクト
Roof-top air chamber

チャッキダンパー
Checkdamper

立下りダクト(床下へ)
Duct (under the floor)

〈冬モード〉

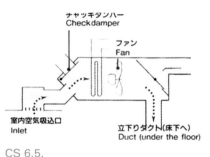

CS 6.4.
The OM handling box. Winter mode.

ナャッキダンバー
Checkdamper

ファン
Fan

室内空気吸込口
Inlet

立下りダクト(床下へ)
Duct (under the floor)

CS 6.5.
The OM handling box. Winter mode.

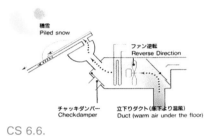

積雪
Piled snow

ファン逆転
Reverse Direction

チャッキダンパー
Checkdamper

立下りダクト(床下より温風)
Duct (warm air under the floor)

CS 6.6.
The OM handling box. Winter mode.

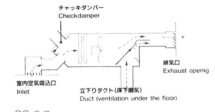

チャッキダンパー
Checkdamper

室内空気吸込口
Inlet

立下りダクト(床下排気)
Duct (ventilation under the floor)

排気口
Exhaust openig

CS 6.7.
The OM handling box. Summer mode.

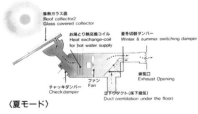

集熱ガラス面
Roof collector2
Glass covered collector

お湯とり熱交換コイル
Heat exchange-coil for hot water supply

夏冬切替ダンパー
Winter & summer switching damper

チャッキダンパー
Checkdamper

ファン
Fan

排気口
Exhaust Opening

立下りダクト(床下排気)
Duct (ventilation under the floor)

〈夏モード〉

CS 6.8.
The OM handling box. Summer mode.

7 MISAWA HOMES

Modular Home Builder:
Misawa Homes Co., Ltd.

Location:
Japan – located throughout Japan

Climate:
various – located throughout Japan

Area:
84–325 m²

CS 7.1.

ECOFEATURES

- Energy conservation, generation and fuel cell • Enhanced microclimate design
- Environmentally friendly materials • Enhanced ventilation • Earthquake resistant

DESCRIPTION/BRIEF

Misawa Homes has a long history of developing environmentally friendly products such as energy-saving housing systems. Misawa Homes has since led the industry in the field of environmental activities by developing environmentally friendly technologies and products, for example new materials and the world's first zero-energy homes. Misawa Homes adopts environmental preservation activities that produce less waste, conserve resources, develop homes requiring less energy, prolong the lifespan of homes, and build residential communities where people live in symbiosis with nature. Efforts have resulted in, among other things, the development of M-Wood which is made from recycled wood chips and recycled plastics, new ceramic material, century-long housing systems and zero-energy homes, and the building of environmentally friendly residential communities across Japan.

ENERGY-SAVING HOUSING SYSTEMS

Models 'HYBRID-Z' and 'MISAWA HOMES Z' are 100 per cent self-sufficient in terms of energy supply for daily living. They are zero-energy homes with high insulation and airtight performance, power generation by roof-type photovoltaic systems, and high-efficiency by means of complete electrification. Zero-energy homes have a noticeable merit in terms of running cost too. Take the annual total electric bill for a household living in our energy-saving home in Kanagawa prefecture for example. It showed a 'minus' figure, meaning the household sold the excess electricity to a power company because the electricity its photovoltaic system generated exceeded its needs (See

Zero-energy housing concept
※ HYBRID-Z: Living patterns are in accordance with
Architectural Institute of Japan models.
Energy consumed in conventional housing

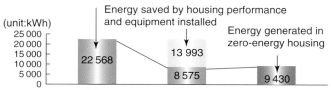

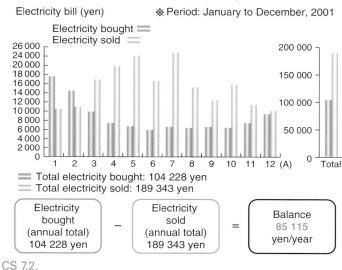

Electricity Bought and Sold in a Year; an electricity bill
balance example

- No. of family members: 2   ■ PV output: 11.3 kW
- Total floor area: 228 m^2
- Contract category: seasonal time-range usage

Electricity bill (yen)   ※ Period: January to December, 2001

Electricity bought ▬
Electricity sold ▬

▬ Total electricity bought: 104 228 yen
▬ Total electricity sold: 189 343 yen

| Electricity bought (annual total) 104 228 yen | − | Electricity sold (annual total) 189 343 yen | = | Balance 85 115 yen/year |

CS 7.2.

'Electricity bought and sold in a year' in CS 7.2). All Misawa homes are standard, with the specifications set by the government's New Energy-Saving Standards and Next Generation Energy-Saving Standards. Of all the homes sold in fiscal 2004, 78.7 per cent were those with energy-saving specifications.

ENERGY-GENERATING HOUSING SYSTEMS

Misawa Homes constructed an experimental home to conduct tests of photovoltaic generation systems in 1989. In 1994, Misawa Homes started the sale of roof-type solar panel systems. Their model 'Taiyo-no-ie,' which was placed on the market in 1997, was standard with this system. Today, they are promoting photovoltaic systems for their 'HYBRID-Z', 'MISAWA HOMES Z', 'HYBRID Chikujin-no-ie', 'HYBRID Jiyu-kukan' and other models. Misawa Homes' system has solar cell modules placed on top of the roofing bed, the first such system in the world. The roof system, composed of tempered glass that forms the surface of the modules, not only excels in design but is also impermeable and withstands strong winds. With the tempered glass curtain wall technology applied, the roof is highly durable. Because the solar panel roof weighs about only one-third the conventional tile roof, it lessens the load onto the housing structure, which is an advantage against earthquakes. A life-size experiment we conducted has proved that a home with this system withstood a seismic force of 1000 gal without developing any damage, which was much stronger than the 830 gal Great Hanshin Awaji Earthquake in 1995. In the event the solar panel roof happens to develop a problem, it is not necessary to replace the whole roof with a new one; only the relevant panels need to be replaced.

Their photovoltaic system is the first in the industry to enable the sale of 'excess' electricity to a power company ('reverse flow system'). When the electricity generated exceeds the electricity consumed, excess electricity can be sold to the power company. The annual power consumption of an average household is estimated at 4995 kWh and the average electricity generated by our standard model (Model P: 3.28 kW) is 3536 kWh per year. This means our system is capable of providing about 70 to 80 per cent of the annual electricity needs of a home subject to regional climatic conditions and the system used. (Source: 2003 Annual Residential Energy Statistics, Jukankyo Research Institute.)

CS 7.3a.
HYBRID Jiyu-Kukan.

CS 7.3b.
A residential community of PV homes.

FUEL CELL

Misawa Homes is the leader in environmental preservation activities in the industry as evidenced, for example, by the fact that they developed the world's first complete-electrification home requiring no electricity costs in 1998. However, another source of energy is also called for to further reduce CO_2 emissions. Misawa Homes has begun to supply Tokyo Gas-developed fuel cell co-generation systems to homeowners in the Tokyo metropolitan area. The system uses polymer electrolyte fuel cells (PEFCs), has heat generation and recovery capabilities, and is the first such system to be marketed. The system dispenses with the conventional water heating equipment as it generates the electricity necessary to supply hot water. It also provides electricity for use in a home. The fuel cell system can reduce CO_2 emissions by approximately 40 per cent (generating electric power 1 kWh and exhaust heat collection 1.3 kWh vs. thermal generation and conventional water heater). Tokyo Gas estimates that utility charges cost about 30 000 yen less per year.

CS 7.4.
Fuel cell (left)
Heated water storage (right).

ENHANCED MICROCLIMATE

'Microclimate' is a climatic condition to be created in the area surrounding the home. Misawa Homes designs the environment surrounding the home by taking into account various factors including local climate, wind passage patterns, sunlight characteristics, land configuration, surrounding plants, neighbouring house locations, etc. They call this microclimate design. For example, the hedge is designed to both coax a breeze and block summer sunlight into the home and allow the breeze into and out the windows, toplights and transoms to create a comfortable airflow indoors. Furthermore, heat-holding concrete floors and materials capable of absorbing and emitting humidity control the indoor air environment comfortably. Microclimate designing is a way to bring what traditional Japanese houses provided to modern days: the utilisation of natural elements for pleasant living. Its provides an ecologically sound and economical way of life. Misawa Homes promoted the development of residential communities using microclimate design. 'Mariner East 21 Midorihama' is an urban development which is designed to take in natural characteristics to the fullest extent. 'Owners' Hill Shin-Yurigaoka' is a high-end housing community development based on land planning to leave existing nature intact as much as possible. It has grown into a lovely and mature development and ten years after its birth it won a Good Design Award in 1999. Misawa Homes scientifically confirmed the effects of microclimate by conducting various tests on the effects plants, breezes and other elements provide at the residential community 'Miyazakidai-Sakurazaka'. The advantages of microclimate design can be maximised with their homes because of their high insulation and airtightness performance.

CS 7.5a.
Microclimate design.

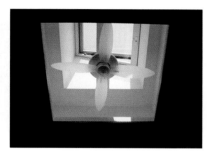

CS 7.5b.
Toplight and ceiling fan.

CS 7.5c.
Toplight open.

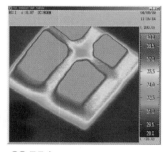

CS 7.5d.
Toplight ceiling fan on (Air volume: 250 m³ h).

ENVIRONMENTALLY FRIENDLY MATERIALS

In times of dwindling natural resources, development of products made of alternative resources is called for more than ever before. In the housing industry, it is important to use housing materials made from natural resources in sufficient supply without depending on resources in limited supply. In 1972, Misawa developed a new ceramic, an entirely new raw material. It is a high performance multifunctional material suitable for exterior walls with such characteristics as high strength, thermal insulating performance, water resistance, and sound insulation.

The production of new ceramic does not generate any waste. Powdered silica sand and limestone are made into slurry and shaped into different configurations in moulds. Any slurry waste produced during the surface treatment of moulded slurry is retrieved for reuse. The de-moulded new ceramic panels are precured and then autoclaved in a giant pressure chamber. Tobermorite crystal, a stable crystal as is found in diamonds, is created at a temperature of 180°C under high pressure (10 kg/cm²) in the autoclave. The autoclaved panels are then painted in three layers for final finish.

New ceramic panels, although they are produced in this complex process, boast high cost performance. New ceramic, featuring high strength and excellent heat and sound insulation properties, has a specific gravity of 0.54, a water content rate of 13 per cent and a dry shrinkage rate of less than 0.05 per cent. Their heat insulation excels conventional concrete by about 12 times, making it possible to build homes which provide cooler air in summer and warmer air in winter, thus contributing to energy conservation. Also, their humidity adjustment performance helps to deter water condensation, which can prolong the lifespan of houses and reduce indoor air quality problems.

Misawa Homes uses recycled boards and tiles made from waste glass and tiles as floor materials for the entrance approaches and balconies of their houses. 'RG Board' is a balcony floor material made from waste tiles and glass. It is a ceramic material cured at about 1000°C. RG boards are ideal for balconies as they have better water permeation and anti-corrosion properties. In typical glass bottle recycling, only transparent and brown glass bottles are reused and bottles in other colours are thrown out. Misawa Homes developed recycled tiles using these coloured glass bottles based on a philosophy of protection of Earth and air, resource conservation and energy-saving. Misawa Homes utilises this material for their homes and proposes that this kind of philosophy be directed toward developing a resource recycling society.

CS 7.6.
New ceramic walls.

CS 7.7.
RG board balcony.

ENHANCED VENTILATION

Volatile organic compounds (VOCs), such as formaldehyde, that are released from building materials are attributed to sick building syndrome. Japan's Building Standard Law, which was revised on July 1, 2003, sets forth the compulsory use of materials that emit less quantities of formaldehyde (Highest grade: F....) and installation of 24-hour mechanical ventilation systems.

In order to meet the highest grade specified in the Quality Assurance Law, Misawa Homes switched to the use of materials graded F.... not only for the finish materials for floors, walls, ceilings, doors, stairs and other interior items but also for those not subject to the QAL requirement for all of their houses. Also, as far as possible they make it a practice not to use building materials containing toluene or xylene.

Misawa Homes are standard with a 24-hour central ventilation system. The system helps to deter dust particles, mould and ticks, and discharges toxic substances like formaldehyde to the outside while taking in fresh air. Because the system has a heat exchange efficiency of about 70 per cent, a decrease in inside air temperature resulting from the ventilation is kept to a certain level. A germ elimination unit is also available for the system's air supply outlet installed in the living room, which is effective against germs which cannot be eliminated by air purification by means of filter filtration.

EARTHQUAKE RESISTANCE

Japan is an earthquake-prone country. Many earthquakes hit Japan every year. Given that backdrop, wooden and ceramic homes have earthquake-resistant structures. Misawa Homes wooden structures are characterised by the joining of load-bearing panels face to face each using adhesives, creating a solid 'monocoque' structure. The ceramic homes are made up of capsule units in a rigid steel-frame structure. The structure, as a single shell, supports most of a force or load applied, such as one generated by an earthquake. Full-scale seismic tests and capsule unit endurance tests have proved the strength of the structure. The earthquake-resistance capabilities of

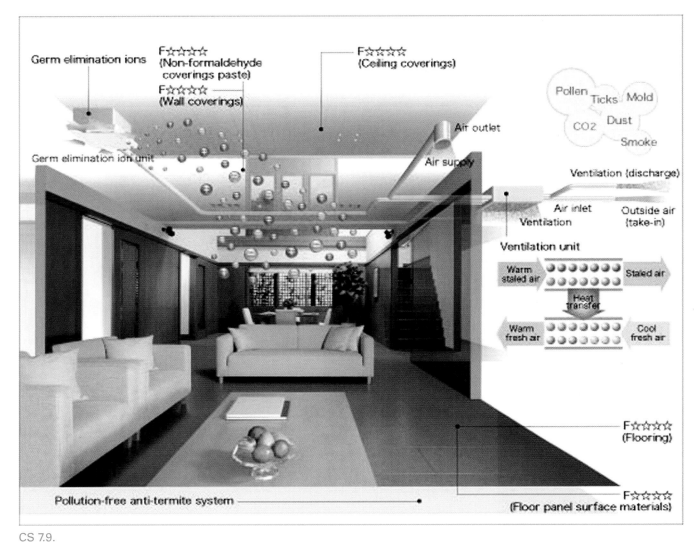

Germ elimination ions
F☆☆☆☆ (Non-formaldehyde coverings paste)
F☆☆☆☆ (Wall coverings)
F☆☆☆☆ (Ceiling coverings)
Germ elimination ion unit
Air outlet
Air supply
Pollen Ticks Mold
CO2 Dust
Smoke
Ventilation (discharge)
Air inlet
Ventilation
Outside air (take-in)
Ventilation unit
Warm staled air
Staled air
Heat transfer
Warm fresh air
Cool fresh air
F☆☆☆☆ (Flooring)
Pollution-free anti-termite system
F☆☆☆☆ (Floor panel surface materials)

CS 7.9.
24-h central ventilation system.

our wooden panel and capsule system were proved when the Great Hanshin-Awaji Earthquake occurred in 1995; all of the Misawa Homes in the affected region withstood the gigantic quake.

Misawa Homes has developed a next-generation earthquake control system called MGEO: Misawa Homes Governance System for Earthquake Oscillation Control. Coupled with the earthquake-resistance systems, this earthquake control system should provide more safety and peace of mind. Misawa Homes conducts full-scale tests using their wooden house and subjects it to 13 simulated earthquakes, including those whose seismic forces were double the Great Hanshin-Awaji Earthquake, for four days. The tests resulted in no damage to the structure or the wall coverings. They have also developed an MGEO system for their ceramic homes.

CS 7.10.
Full-scale MGEO seismic tests.

CS 7.11.
Capsule unit equipped with an MGEO unit.

8 1979 SOLAR HOUSE

CS 8.1.
1979 Solar House by Ken-ichi Kimura.

Architect:
Professor K. Kimura, Mr H. Matsuoka

Owners:
Mr and Mrs I. Sagara

Location:
Inagi, Tokyo; 35°N, 139°E; 50 m above sea level

Climate:
Composite

Area:
120 m²

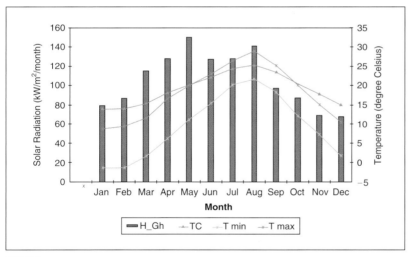

CS 8.2.
Nicol graph for Tokyo.

ECOFEATURES

• Good insulation levels in walls, roof and windows • Passive solar gain • Hybrid solar hot water system for space heating using passive and active circulation to move heat around the building • Buffer spaces • High thermal mass with external insulation • 24 m² solar hot water collector for water and space heating feeding a coil heating system embedded in the concrete slab floor • 950 litre stainless steel water tank beneath the stair in the centre of the house for the solar hot water collection system, with pumped pipe system in ground to lower tank temperatures in summer • In winter the city water was preheated through the same earth-coupled pipe system.

DESCRIPTION/BRIEF

In 1980 the house used only 5020 kWh total electricity consumption, of which 18 per cent was for the hot water supply and space heating. This is 43.5 kWh m^{-2} a^{-1}.

KEY FEATURES BRIEFLY EXPLAINED

The 1979 Solar House in Tokyo was built with good insulation levels in walls, roof and windows, even by the standards of today. This insulation, coupled with passive solar gains, allowed the house to maintain comfortable temperatures through the cold seasons. The hybrid solar hot water system for space heating uses passive and active circulation to move heat around. The roof housed 24 m^2 of solar hot water collectors for water and for space heating, feeding a coil heating system embedded in the concrete slab floor. A 950 litre stainless steel water tank beneath the stairs in the centre of the house stored the solar hot water collection system and had a pumped pipe system in the ground to lower the tank temperatures in summer. In the winter the city water was preheated through the same earth-coupled pipe system.

Type	kWh m^{-2} a^{-1}	Cost of electricity (yen)
Case study house	43	32 000
Typical house	290	210 000
Savings	257	178 000

118.15 yen = US$1.00.
The solar system had a build cost of 1 100 000 yen and a payback time of 6.2 years.

LESSONS LEARNED/PITFALLS

- Comfort was achieved in winter when the temperature in the tank sank as low as 20°C but internal temperatures were maintained between 18 and 22°C.
- Excess heat dissipation from the storage tank under the stairs in summer needed rectifying.
- The capacity of the auxiliary electric heat of 5 kW could be less.
- Cool tube system should be improved.
- Other passive cooling means should be incorporated.
- Cost reductions on solar system essential if such technologies are to be taken up.
- Heat recovery systems should be incorporated.
- Long-term heat storage system should be improved.

ACKNOWLEDGEMENTS/CONTACT INFORMATION

Mr Matsuoko, Professor Ken-ichi Kimura, Shinbo Construction Company, Chubu Create Company and Showa Aluminium Company are gratefully acknowledged.
Professor Ken-ichi Kimura, Waseda, Japan, E-mail: kimura@kimura.arch.waseda.ac.jp

9 LIM HOUSE

Architect:
Jimmy Lim, CSL Associates

Owner:
Jimmy Lim

Location:
Taman Seputeh, Kuala Lumpur, Malaysia;
3°N, 101°E; 17 m above sea level

Climate:
Hot, humid, tropical (the architect
describes the climate as having two
seasons: 'hot and wet' and 'hot and
more wet')

Area:
Site = 1415 m², house = 884 m²

CS 9.1.
Lim House, by Jimmy Lim.

CS 9.2.
Nicol graph for Kuala Lumpur.

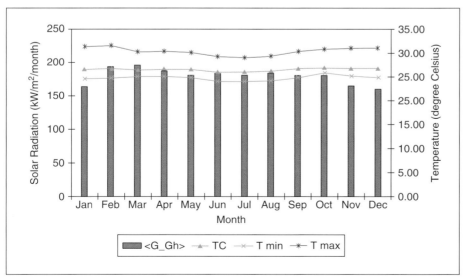

ECOFEATURES

• Material reuse • Non-insulation • Natural cross-ventilation • Adaptation • Solar shading

DESCRIPTION/BRIEF

A unique feature of the house is that additions are constantly being made experimentally and unpredictably, with gut intuition rather than proper drawing-board planning. Jimmy Lim, resident architect of this progressive hand to material, low-energy, minimum labour and cost habitat, builds for himself to obtain first-hand knowledge of construction methods and the true nature of the materials. No trees were cut down,

CS 9.3.
Interior view of living space, by Jimmy Lim.

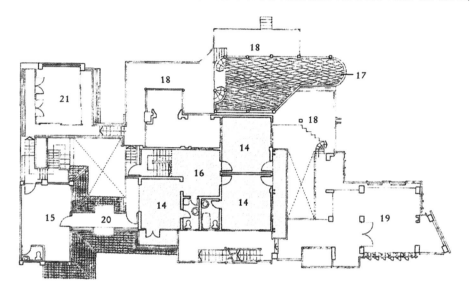

CS 9.4.
Second storey floor plan.

1 garage
2 formal entrance
3 side entrance
4 porch
5 living space
6 dining
7 breakfast area
8 entertainment area
9 kitchen
10 wet kitchen
11 maid
12 bathroom/wc
13 workshop/
   future gallery
14 bedroom
15 guest house
16 hall
17 swimming pool
18 timber deck
19 family area
20 bridge
21 music studio
22 meditation (boat
   house) area
23 fish Pond

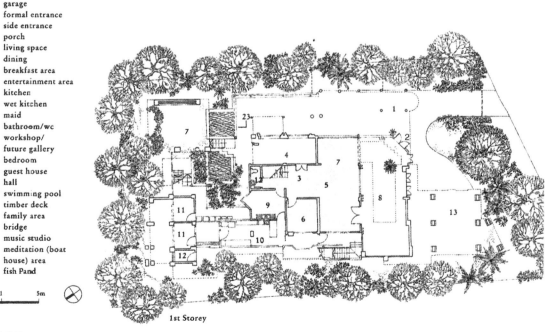

CS 9.5.
First storey floor plan.

nor was any part of the slope cut into during the constant renovations that keep this home alive. The heart of the house is the Entertainment Area, which is united with the Living Space. The perimeter spaces of the house are built of timber materials and are semi-open with large windows. Each window has wooden or canvas screens to promote cross-ventilation. All roofs are covered with unglazed tiles and there is no thermal insulation in this house. Endless flights of wooden stairs made from salvaged materials connect a rustic guest house and a music room, perched 3.5 m above the ground, to the main house. The elevated music studio for teaching sometimes doubles as a stage with openable side walls of sliding glass on two sides, a back wall made from recycled teak door panels and the bearing wall from the ground. The viewing platform for the audience is on the stage, not unlike a 'Shakespearean Globe' theatre, seating the audience on a timber deck about 5 ft lower. The arena is designed for musical concerts in the tropical heat and under the tropical stars. Jimmy Lim's home is the product of his firm belief that architecture should harmonise with nature.

CS 9.6.
The house has an adaptable envelope that can be altered to suit the time of day and year.

REUSE OF MATERIALS

The house has evolved around a pre-existing home that serves as the central core with the perimeter spaces having been built from recycled materials, such as old timber and bricks salvaged from demolished buildings. The original building form and other prime features are still intact and have been left unaltered. The main living space is about 13.5 m high and naturally lit from the apex of the roof, which is glazed. In the music room the use of old shutters and railings gives a feeling of nostalgia to the space. Jimmy Lim puts seemingly useless materials to good use in his own home as well as in his projects. Discarded Canton tiles, roofing, 80-year-old wood, broken marble and glass, grace his home. The elevated terrace balcony overlooks the garden and the house, once again putting to good use stained glass in a 'juinling' design by CSL Associates.

NON-INSULATED

Jimmy Lim's home is his personal and professional ongoing research project for understanding materials, construction jointing and connections, light penetration through the roof and ventilation. He experiments with moving wall parts and roof panels to promote ventilation while maintaining a comfortable temperature without insulation. Unlike other designers, who insist that insulation is the answer to cooling in the tropics, Jimmy Lim does not use insulation in walls or roofs in his home nor in his projects. He believes insulating a building is like putting a fur coat on a person telling them the fur is the insulation against heat getting to the skin and this will keep them cool. He asks, 'Where and how does the hot air get out?'. Although Jimmy Lim does not insulate his building he shades all windows from solar exposure.

VENTILATION

The monthly average wind velocity in Kuala Lumpur is about $1\,m\,s^{-1}$ throughout the year, except in July when it is about $2\,m\,s^{-1}$. According to Jimmy Lim, in this area the wind is caused by the heat island phenomenon of the city. The three ceiling fans in the living space and one in the entertainment area help with the cross-ventilation strategy. This atrium-like space is a central air well, inducing cross-ventilation reminiscent of the old rubber smoke houses of multi-tiered roofs, brick piers and timber trusses. However, the music house and bedroom on the first floor have an air-conditioning system chosen by Jimmy's wife, who teaches music in the adjacent music house. Teaching violin and piano for long periods in the music house, Jimmy's wife finds the air-conditioning system to be indispensable and a necessity for instruments that require a stable humidity level. This highlights the potential problem of adapting to different indoor climates in one's lifestyle.

CS 9.7.
'Sails' used for ventilation, by Robert Powell.

A number of opening devices on the roof act as 'sails' to catch the wind and assist in cooling the interior. By a strange and fortunate coincidence, Jimmy placed his apertures and openings for ventilation purposes facing west where, in this area of Kuala Lumpur, there is a cool westerly prevailing breeze in the afternoon (from about 4.40 p.m. until about 6.30–7.00 p.m.).

PROBLEMS AND RESOLUTIONS

The influence of the exhaust heat from the air-conditioning system on the naturally ventilated rooms is a problem. This problem is widely experienced in hot countries. It is considered that the exhaust heat should be directed to the top of the house rather than its current location between the veranda of the concrete house and the pool deck at the atrium. A typical problem is water discharged from the dehumidification mechanism. However, in Jimmy Lim's house he has improvised by collecting and routing the discharged water to a large basin irrigating the trees in the centre of the house. The contrast in this house between the air-conditioned and non-air-conditioned rooms highlights the importance of acclimatisation to energy consumption in buildings.

When asked about any problems with associated insects, mainly mosquitoes, Jimmy concludes that 'there are actually fewer insects in tropical Malaysia than in, say, the summers of some of the sub-tropical or temperate countries, such as Australia'. As for mosquitoes, Jimmy answers that this is dependent 'on the surrounding area that the house is in and how clean the grounds are'.

ACKNOWLEDGEMENTS/CONTACT INFORMATION

CSL Associates, Kuala Lumpur, Malaysia. E-mail: cslcyy@tm.net.my

10 SURABAYA ECOHOUSE

Architect:
Professor Silas, the Institute of Technology, Sephluh Nopember, Indonesia; Dr Y. Kodama, Kobe Design University

Owner:
Ministry of Construction, Indonesia; Infrastructure Development Institute of Japan

Location:
Surabaya, Indonesia; 7°N, 112°E

Climate:
Hot, humid

Area:
±294 m²

CS 10.1.
Surabaya Ecohouse, by Ministry of Construction.

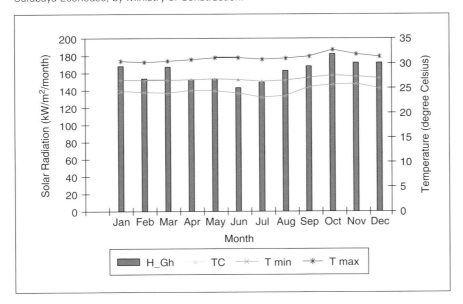

CS 10.2.
Nicol graph for Surabaya.

ECOFEATURES

• Double roof system • Deep eaves • Cross- and stack ventilation • Nocturnal cooling • Polypropylene pipe system

DESCRIPTION/BRIEF

In tropical counties, as dependence on energy-consuming cooling systems or air-conditioners increases, growing concern over future global environmental problems and a possible drain on energy resources requires important developments in passive design, especially passive cooling techniques. The Surabaya Ecohouse, with its durable concrete structure and flexible use of partitions and external walls, is an essential design in a sustainable future recycling society to improve thermal performance of buildings.

KEY FEATURES BRIEFLY EXPLAINED

The double roof system consists of a roof of tiles over a waterproof membrane with an air gap and layer of coconut fibre insulation. The roof extends with deep eaves to shade the walls and windows against heat gains. The outer wall system is made of timber to also reduce solar penetration.

CS 10.3.

Double roof, by Ministry of Construction.

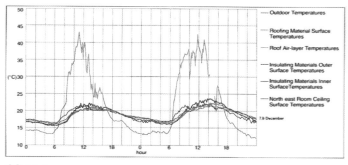

CS 10.4.

Effects of double roof.

Walls are open in communal spaces to promote cross-ventilation. Wind vents through the central roof to promote stack ventilation. Nocturnal cooling is induced by storing the lower-temperature night air in thick concrete floor slabs. A polypropylene pipe system is ducted through the floor slab that circulates water kept in an underground tank via a photovoltaic-driven pump. This water at a cooler temperature radiates through the slab keeping it cool and is then reused for flushing toilets or irrigation.

LESSONS LEARNED/PITFALLS

The double roof is extremely effective in lowering the internal temperature as shown. Night ventilation, when in use, reduces the daytime temperatures lower than the control room without it. The radiant cooling floor is very effective in lowering the daytime peak temperatures, even when the circulating temperature is 28°C.

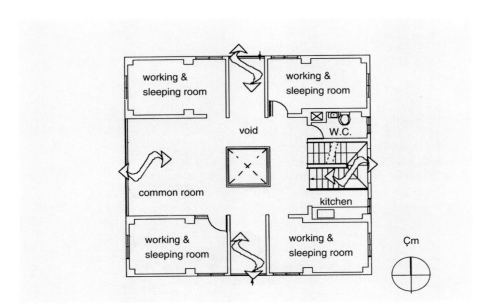

CS 10.5.
Plan.

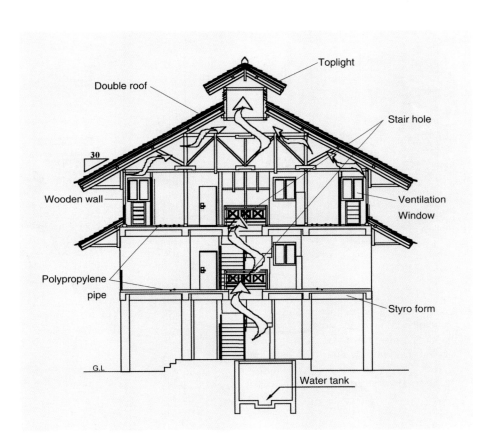

CS 10.6.
Section.

ACKNOWLEDGEMENTS/CONTACT INFORMATION

Infrastructure Development Institute, Japan, http://ww.idi.or.jp/

11 HOUSE AT YARRAWONGA

CS 11.1.
House at Yarrawonga, by Felix Riedweg.

Architect:
Felix Riedweg Architect, RAIA

Owners:
F. and F. Riedweg, 1990

Location:
Townsville, Australia; 19°S, 147°E; 300 m above sea level

Climate:
Coastal, tropical humid

Area:
450 m²

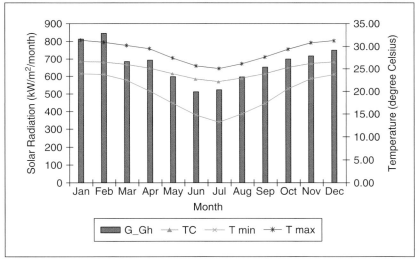

CS 11.2.
Nicol graph for House at Townsville.

ECOFEATURES

• Orientation • Shade • Cross-ventilation • Hurricane resistant

DESCRIPTION/BRIEF

The house was built in 1990 on the steep northern slopes of Castle Hill overlooking the suburb of North Ward and Cleveland Bay, with Magnetic Island in the distance. It is located about 3 km from the central business district of Townsville, the capital of North Queensland. Originally built with four bedrooms, two rooms have been converted

CS 11.3.
Section.

CS 11.4.
Upper floor plan.

into office space for the inhabitants. The upper level is open plan with living, dining, his and her studies and the master bedroom with a bath. It has a front (summer) and back (winter) veranda with views of more than 180°.

The design concept adopts the three key features: orientation, shade and cross-ventilation. The coastal area allows a pleasant outdoor living climate all year round; for comfort the client needs 'a big shading roof'. The building does not touch the ground, enabling the breezes (prevailing north/easterly summer breezes) to circulate in all directions.

ECOFEATURES EXPLAINED

Comfort is achieved by manipulating the temperature, humidity and air movement in the indoor environment. We can improve the temperature and airflow through the appropriate choice of building material (thermal mass), the right orientation, the provision of adequate shading (built or natural grown landscaping) and the selection and placement of windows for cross-ventilation.

Orientation

The house is oriented facing north with its back to the south using the embankment as its mass for keeping the lower level cool. It also orients itself to accept north/easterly prevailing winds to circulate throughout the open plan. The concept of openness and translucency is retained with well-shaded windows, and access from every internal space to outdoor areas in front and back and on both levels. The house has both internal and external stairs. The glass in the windows is largely for security purposes.

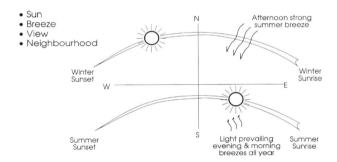

CS 11.5.
Orientation.

Shade

The native growth of the site was retained to enhance air quality as well as to assist in shading. The wide roof overhangs protect the windows and walls as, even in winter, direct sunlight is unwanted (approximate day temperature 25°C). Note that Figure 11.6 is not a direct representation of the House at Yarrawonga, but a diagram showing the strategy used.

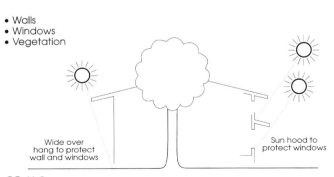

CS 11.6.
Shade.

CS 11.7.
Interior, leading outdoors, by Felix Riedweg.

Cross-ventilation

The open plan design allows optimal cross-ventilation of the north/easterly prevailing winds. The house is not air-conditioned but has some ceiling fans to assist with air movement on very still days. The inhabitants have appreciated the comfort of the house since 1990 and, comparing temperatures and airflow with the houses in the area, they have proved you can live comfortably in a tropical environment without air-conditioning. A number of energy-efficient issues are currently being addressed by the Australian Building Codes Board. It is the intention of the Code to indicate low-energy strategies for construction and equipping low-energy, cost-efficient designs. The House at Yarrawonga is truly an energy-efficient house, for its ventilation strategy utilising cool breezes uses less than one-fifth of the energy used by a five-star NatHERS (National House Energy Rating Software)-rated air-conditioned house.

- Windows (Geometry and size)
  (Location)
- Walls (With gaps)
  (Half height)

CS 11.8.
Cross-ventilation.

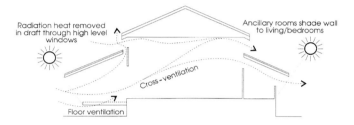

Construction

Owing to the difficult nature of the building site (steep and narrow, access between the rocks) prefabrication was an ideal option in order to retain the natural landscape without cut and fill. The steel skeleton is heavy so that it will withstand cyclonic winds of over $200\,km\,h^{-1}$. The roof uses insulated sheet metal guaranteeing shade all day throughout the year. Walls are mostly lightweight and the thermal mass is in the suspended concrete slabs of both levels.

LESSONS LEARNED/PITFALLS

Since the windows are well shaded and the house is cross-ventilated, there is no problem with overheating. However, the glare is problematic. At the time, and without the expertise and knowledge that the architect has experienced since, he felt he should have spent a little more money and installed tinted glass.

ACKNOWLEDGEMENTS/CONTACT INFORMATION

Professor Dick Aynsley, Director Australian Institute Tropical Architecture, James Cook University, Townsville, E-mail: Richard.Aynsley@jcu.edu.au. Felix Riedweg, Architect RAIA, North Ward, Qld, Australia. E-mail: Riedweg@ultra.net.au

12 DUNCAN HOUSE

Architect:
Graham Duncan, 1998

Owner:
Graham Duncan

Location:
Ostend, Waiheke Island, New Zealand;
36°S, 174°E; 10 m above sea level

Climate:
Temperate, 1100 degree-days per year

Area:
84 m²

CS 12.1.
Duncan House, by Robert Vale.

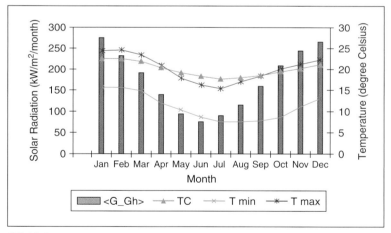

CS 12.2.
Nicol graph for Waiheke Island.

ECOFEATURES

• Solar- and wind-generated power • Solar water heating • Rainwater supplies all water needs

DESCRIPTION/BRIEF

This house is a simple two-storey home, rectangular in plan. It is located in the centre of Ostend, the administrative centre of Waiheke Island. This village also contains the island's only supermarket and building supply store. This house was designed by Graham Duncan and intended to be simple and cheap. Its pitched roofs face north and south. The north and south façades are 6 m long and the east and west façades are 7 m. The entry is from the west with the main views from the house directed towards Anzac Bay (south). The north side of the roof is uninterrupted by dormers, giving the full area for solar energy collection systems. The house is conventionally built of New Zealand timber-frame construction with R2.2 glass fibre insulation, internal linings of plasterboard on the ground floor and plywood on the first floor. External finish is plywood sheeting and the roof is a typical corrugated iron roof. Windows are locally made with single glazing in aluminium frames (with built-in draught-proofing).

ECOFEATURES EXPLAINED

Electricity

Graham's house differs substantially from a typical Waiheke house. The house is entirely self-contained for its electricity supply, although there is mains electricity available from Mercury's lines directly outside in the road. The electricity is generated from two renewable energy sources: wind and sun. The solar contribution comes from 16, 60 W Solarex polycrystalline photovoltaic panels mounted on the north-facing roof at a slope of 42° (from horizontal). The panels are placed above the roof on 50-mm-thick wooden bearers and are carried on aluminium rails fixed across the bearers. This provides spacing of about 75 mm between the panels and the roof's surface to provide an air space to cool the panels, maximising efficiency. Recently, an additional four 50 W panels were added to the north-facing wall below the roof, increasing the original 960 W capacity to 1.16 kW. In addition to the solar-generated power there are three small wind turbines. According to manufacturer's specifications these turbines have the capacity to output a total of 440 W but Graham estimates that with respect to surrounding obstructions (houses and trees), the turbines are producing about 400 W. Graham has wired his house to make the most efficient use of different sources of electricity. Since inverters tend to reduce efficiency, he uses DC lighting, through compact fluorescent lamps in special fittings; water pumps run off DC power; the refrigerator (although small) has been rebuilt with a DC compressor; and there is a DC television and radio. The 230 V inverter runs a larger television, stereo, computer, fax and washing machine.

Power generation	kWh a^{-1}
Wind power output	100
PV output	1100
Power bought (in)	0
Power sold (out)	0
Net	1200

Water heating

The water is heated by two Solarhart solar panels on the lower part of the north sloping roof and supplied through pipes to a 300 litre thermosiphon system located between the ceiling and the roof at the peak. On cloudy days, the water can be heated by a wetback on the wood burner.

Space heating

Owing to the climate, the region does not experience dramatic changes in temperature. The floor is concrete, complimenting the passive solar gains but allowing the house to maintain a comfortable temperature for most of the year. Its main source of heat is retained in the slab and supplemented by a wood burner in the centre of the house, if needed.

Cistern and sewage

Typical of island homes, Graham's house has a 25 000 litre cistern that stores rainwater for all domestic water uses. The water is pumped into the house by means of three 12 V pumps with pressure-sensing switches that activate the pumps by turning the tap. One pump is the main supply from the storage tanks and the other two serve hot and cold water supplies. These 12 V pumps are considered more efficient in terms of electric consumption. Sewage is treated by means of a conventional septic tank.

LESSONS LEARNED/PITFALLS

The total non-renewable energy consumption of the house is in the form of gas used for cooking (about 45 kg). Liquefied petroleum gas has a calorific value of $13.9\,kWh\,kg^{-1}$ for propane; this is equivalent to $626\,kWh\,years^{-1}$ or $7.4\,kWh\,m^{-2}$. Therefore the house uses much less energy than the sophisticated advanced houses of Canada and Europe, although this is achieved largely through simplicity and 'doing without' (lower internal temperatures, few appliances, smaller space and co-ordination of appliance use time).

ACKNOWLEDGEMENTS/CONTACT INFORMATION

Robert Vale, Auckland, New Zealand. E-mail: r.vale@auckland.ac.nz

13 REDEVELOPED PROPERTY AT CIVIL LINES

CS 13.1.
Façade of Courtyard House, by Ashok Lall.

Architect:
A. B. Lall Architects, 1997–1999

Client:
Ashok and Rajiv Lall, Ratiram Gupta and sons

Location:
Civil Lines, New Delhi, India; 28°N, 77°E; 220 m above sea level

Climate:
Composite

Area:
Total 1687 m²; each house 421.7 m²

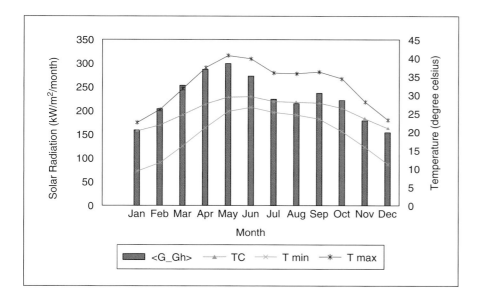

CS 13.2.
Nicol graph of New Delhi.

ECOFEATURES

• Orientation • Wind-driven evaporative cooling • Courtyard roof • Insulation materials

DESCRIPTION/BRIEF

This project explores the challenges of designing and building a house in a dense urban setting. This eco-project includes four courtyard houses built on a street. The houses on the north face of the street are courtyard houses leading towards gardens on the south side; whereas the houses on the south side of the street have their gardens on the north side and are linear. These are all large single-family houses, two to three storeys high. This enables the sections of the buildings to be designed integrally for enjoying the winter sun. The passive devices that interact with the external elements are given a central place in the architectural language of the buildings.

ECOFEATURES EXPLAINED

Orientation

The general orientation of the buildings is aligned east–west, with most window openings in the north and south faces. The courtyard houses, because of their square proportions in plan, also face towards the east and west. The windows on these faces look into narrow protected alleys or the small courtyard between the houses. The alley space on the west side is shaded by retaining the wall of the original double-storey building that had previously lined the side street.

For the linear houses on the north side, the width of the driveway that separates the two rows of houses is just sufficient to enable winter sunshine to enter the first floor windows. The sections of these houses are designed with a cutout such that the winter sun is brought into the living/dining space, the heart of the house, on the ground floor. Terraces on the second floor have skylights that again admit winter sun into the first floor rooms on the north side of the houses.

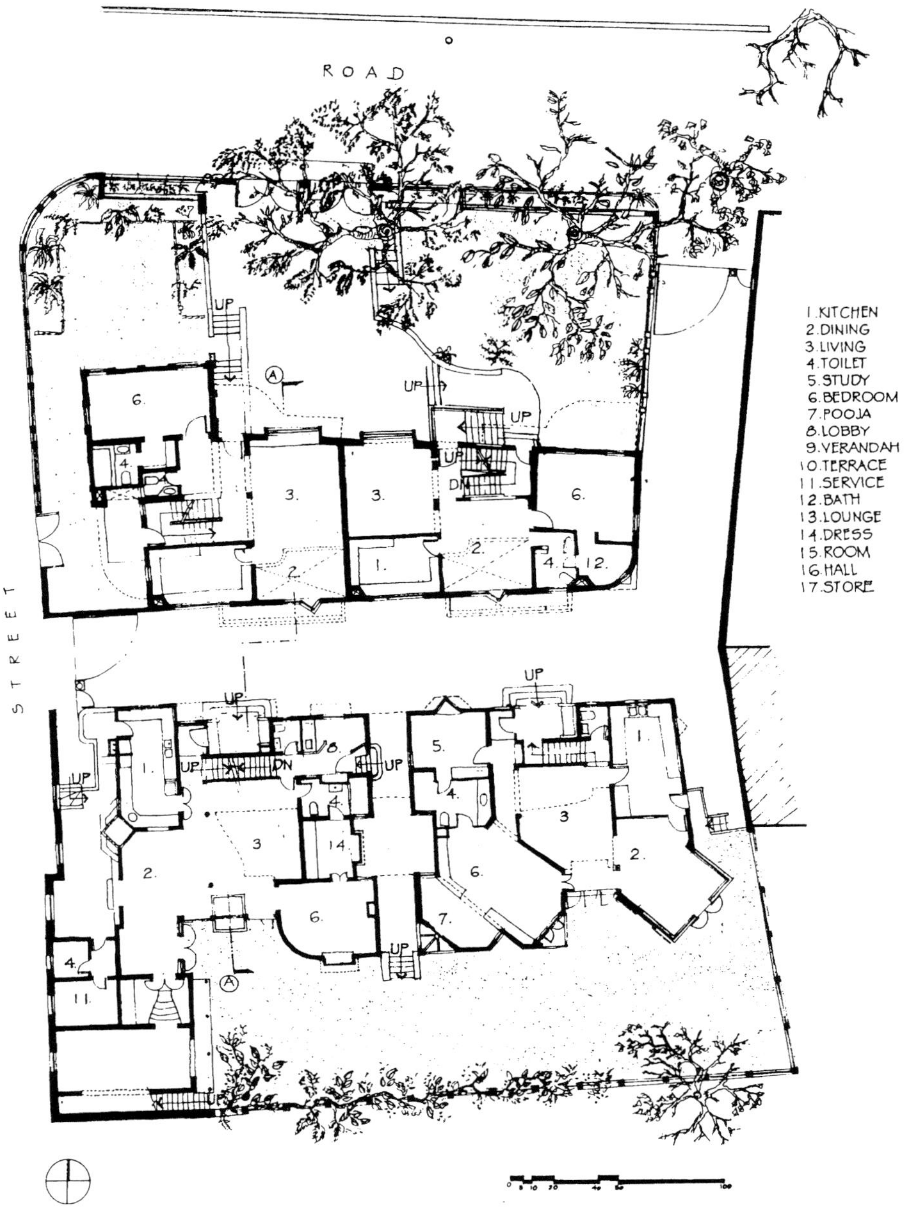

ROAD
STREET
1.KITCHEN
2.DINING
3.LIVING
4.TOILET
5.STUDY
6.BEDROOM
7.POOJA
8.LOBBY
9.VERANDAH
10.TERRACE
11.SERVICE
12.BATH
13.LOUNGE
14.DRESS
15.ROOM
16.HALL
17.STORE

CS 13.3.
Ground floor plan.

Wind-driven evaporative cooling

The West House takes advantage of the prevailing northwesterly hot winds that blow during the hot–dry seasons. A vertical screen tower is built on the west wall. This tower houses khus evaporative pads on its outer surface, fed by a water pump. The inner side has adjustable windows opening into the adjacent rooms. The natural wind pressure will drive air through the wet khus pads and will then flow into the adjacent rooms. This vertical arrangement would spread the khus fragrance across the two storeys of the house. In the summer, the combination of ceiling fans and the evaporative cooling gives a comfortable environment, except during the season of very high temperatures (38°C) and high humidity (65 per cent) before the monsoon in mid-June to mid-July. But 'if you wear skimpy cottons and drink cool sherbet – there is a refrigerator lurking somewhere – you could be comfortable enough' (Mr Lall, 19 May 2000).

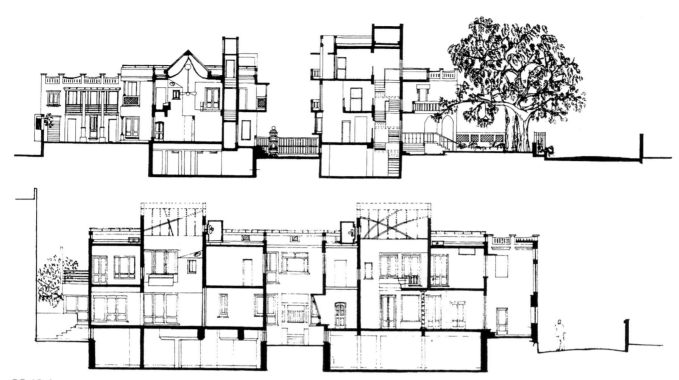

CS 13.4.
Section.

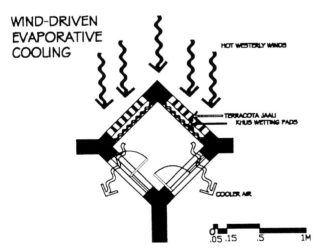

WIND-DRIVEN
EVAPORATIVE
COOLING

HOT WESTERLY WINDS

TERRACOTA JAALI
KHUS WETTING PADS

COOLER AIR

.05 .15   .5   1M

CS 13.5.
Wind-driven evaporative cooling.

CS 13.6.
The double height living room is served by a range of natural
ventilation pathways and circulation systems, by Ashok Lall.

Courtyard roof

The roofed courtyard of the two courtyard houses is intended to be the main climate response device. The hipped steel-frame roof is clad with a 20 mm glass sandwich a reflective film and frosted underside for the most part, with a panel of transparent glass on the south slope. This is under-slung by a pair of razais (quilts), which can be pulled across to cover the underside of the roof (for insulation) or allowed to hang down vertically (to allow heat transfer). Above the roof is another frame in chicks (bamboo severs), which can similarly be opened to shade the roof or rolled up to catch the sun.

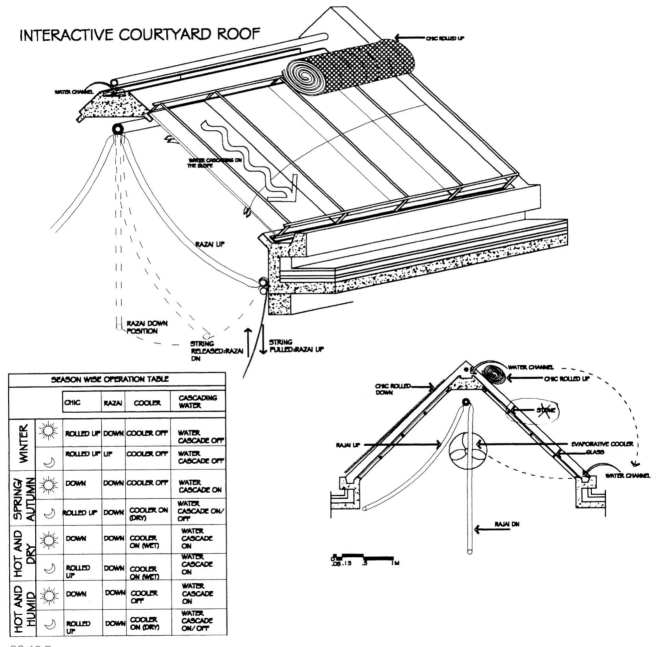

SEASON WISE OPERATION TABLE		CHIC	RAZAI	COOLER	CASCADING WATER
WINTER	☀	ROLLED UP	DOWN	COOLER OFF	WATER CASCADE OFF
	☾	ROLLED UP	UP	COOLER OFF	WATER CASCADE OFF
SPRING/ AUTUMN	☀	DOWN	DOWN	COOLER OFF	WATER CASCADE ON
	☾	ROLLED UP	DOWN	COOLER ON (DRY)	WATER CASCADE ON/ OFF
HOT AND DRY	☀	DOWN	DOWN	COOLER ON (WET)	WATER CASCADE ON
	☾	ROLLED UP	DOWN	COOLER ON (WET)	WATER CASCADE ON
HOT AND HUMID	☀	DOWN	DOWN	COOLER OFF	WATER CASCADE ON
	☾	ROLLED UP	DOWN	COOLER ON (DRY)	WATER CASCADE ON/ OFF

CS 13.7.
Interactive courtyard roof.

The ridge of the roof is a water channel from which water overflows on to the thin roofing membrane of stone and glass. Some water evaporates and excess water is collected at the roof of the slope and recirculated. This makes the roof a large evaporative cooler over the central space of the house. All rooms communicate directly with this central space. This method of evaporative cooling will supplement a conventional evaporative cooler and, in the hot–humid period of July to August, would give considerable cooling when evaporative cooling is no longer effective. The operation of the roof component: chick, water, razai, is to be adjusted from winter to summer and for day and night. The roof provides for:

1 shading from outside/insulation from inside;
2 roof evaporative cooling;
3 direct radiation.

CS 13.8.
Looking up from the Court, by Ashok Lall.

The dominant portion of the roofed courtyards with their quilts of mirrors and colourful cloth, the chicks and the possibility of visible monsoon and night sky – stars and moon – would become a strong aesthetic experience of the idea of responding to the rhythm of seasonal cycles.

Insulation/materials

The roofs are finished with broken marble mosaic, which is reflective in nature. The roof construction sandwich contains 30-mm-thick polyurethane board insulation above the concrete slab. For the courtyard houses the western wall of the upper floor, the east and west walls of the courtyard roof and the water tank walls are insulated using an innovative construction sandwich of 115 mm brick + 15 mm plaster + 30 mm polystyrene foam + 50 mm terracotta jalis, whose cavities are rendered with cement sand mortar. Their resultant construction expresses the special nature of the wall as a decorative textured surface. This strategy shifts the performance to the fabric by spending a little on insulation where it makes the most difference. The windows are single glazed (heavy curtains for summer afternoons and winter nights but tight-fitting with double rebates). This proves that an economical solution can in fact be implemented.

LESSONS LEARNED/PITFALLS

Initially the courtyard roof was to be designed with 20-mm-thick stone slab. After revisiting the idea, it was decided to replace the stone with glass sheets sandwiching a reflective film to ensure a crack-free, damp-proof cover for water to stream over.

ACKNOWLEDGEMENTS/CONTACT INFORMATION

A. B. Lall Architects, Civil Lines, Delhi. E-mail: ablarch@del13.vsnl.net.in

14 MEIR HOUSE

CS 14.1.
Meir House, by Isaac Meir.

Architect:
Isaac A. Meir, 1992–1994

Owners:
Orna and Isaac Meir with their three children

Location:
Sede Boqer Campus, Negev Desert Highlands, Israel; 30°N, 34°E; 470 m above sea level

Climate:
Arid, with hot and dry summers; cold winters; +1017 degree days per year

Area:
208 m²

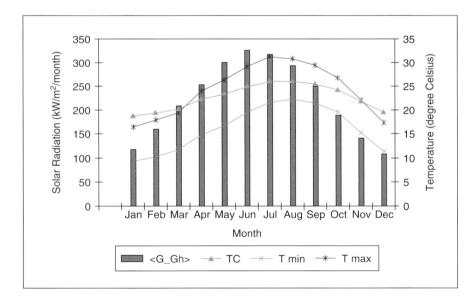

CS 14.2.
Nicol graph for Negev.

ECOFEATURES

• Orientation and plan • Thermal mass • Winter solar heating • Summer cooling • xeriscape

DESCRIPTION/BRIEF/CONCEPT

The Meir House is located in the first solar neighbourhood in Israel, Newe Zin, and was designed as a prototype towards creating an energy-conserving urban building code. It combines external insulation and internal thermal mass with open plan. Through QUICK simulation prior to construction and monitoring post-construction, the Meir House proves the success of an integrative approach to the design of a bio-climatic desert house.

ECOFEATURES EXPLAINED

Orientation and plan

Considering the site's geometry and climatic constraints, among them solar angles, air temperatures and wind directions, the log axis of the house is east–West, with four bedrooms and the living room to the south. The ground floor is exposed in all four

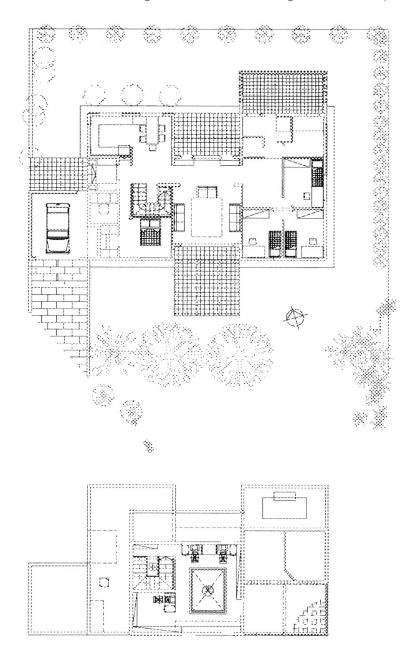

CS 14.3.

Ground floor plan (above) and first floor plan (below).

directions. The kitchen, baths and laundry room are located at the northern part of the plan and the garage serves as a western buffer. All spaces, excluding the garage, are a single thermal zone. The house also includes a number of verandas and balconies facing in different directions. Main fenestration is placed to the south, with smaller openings to the north for cross-ventilation. However, all rooms have openings in two directions to ensure appropriate ventilation. There are only a few, small, recessed openings in the west façade. The second floor is exposed in all four directions.

Winds are north and northwesterly in the early noon and evening hours, whereas at night and early morning they may turn northeast by southeast. Average maximum windspeeds range between 40 km h^{-1} in winter and 30 km h^{-1} in summer. The environmentally responsive open plan layout proved to be successful as far as heat transfer and circulation are concerned.

Another advantage that the Meir House integrates with its form is weather-protected adjacent open spaces. The south and north verandas and the southeastern balcony are protected from wind by the mass of the building to the north and west and by the garden wall to the west. These spaces are shaded partly by overhangs, partly by deciduous plants (such as vines and *Prosopis*), and partly by pergolas with agricultural shading fabric that has a 75 per cent shading coefficient.

Thermal mass

The wide diurnal temperature fluctuations characteristics of the Negev Desert climate dictate the use of thermal mass, both for internal temperature damping and for energy storage. Based on simulation results, the construction optimises thermal performance by using medium-weight exterior walls and heavy-weight interior vertical and horizontal partitions. The exterior walls are 250 mm cellular concrete (YTONG) blocks, painted with a high reflectivity ochre-coloured paint. The low conductivity (0.2 W m^{-1} C) of the YTONG blocks eliminates the need for traditional sandwich wall sections or external insulation that demands precise construction. Floors are reinforced concrete poured in place. The roof is cast reinforced concrete, covered by extruded polystyrene, aerated sloped cement and waterproofing.

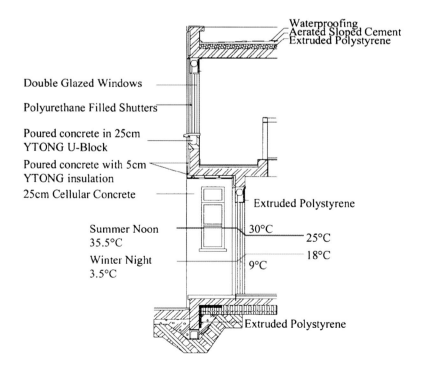

CS 14.4.
Section through wall.

Waterproofing
Aerated Sloped Cement
Extruded Polystyrene

Double Glazed Windows

Polyurethane Filled Shutters

Poured concrete in 25cm YTONG U-Block

Poured concrete with 5cm YTONG insulation

25cm Cellular Concrete

Extruded Polystyrene

Summer Noon 35.5°C

Winter Night 3.5°C

30°C

9°C

25°C

18°C

Extruded Polystyrene

Climatic conditions and termites exclude the option of wooden frames for windows and doors. Aluminium frames encase double glazing for acoustical considerations and are fitted with mosquito screens. To further reduce solar gains in the summer, external aluminium rolling shutters filled with insulation (expanded polyurethane) and interior venetian horizontal and vertical blinds are fitted.

CS 14.5.
House with shutters lowered, by Isaac Meir.

Winter solar heating and solar water heating

Approximately 24 m² (30 per cent of the south façade or approximately 14.5 per cent of the total floor area) and 8 m² of the east façada is glass, achieving a passive approach to heating the house. The addition of a collapsible greenhouse (2.25 m²) on the balcony, made of polycarbonate sheeting recovered from a dismantled agricultural greenhouse, yielded winter temperatures of 35–36°C during the afternoon (while the ambient temperature was 14–15°C) increasing the room temperatures by 1–2°C with the help of a small fan that pushes the air into the living spaces. Through passive designs, orientation, thermal mass and the collapsible greenhouse, savings of almost 90 per cent on electric back-up bought from the utility company were realised, compared with a typical electrically heated house in the Negev Desert climate. The Meir House includes solar water heating using a high-efficiency solar collector (7000 kcal for a 1.5 m² collection area) and 150 litre water heater.

Type	Heat only, excluding bathrooms (kWh m⁻² a⁻¹)	Unit cost (NIS)	Cost of electric (NIS)
Meir House	5.5	0.25 kWh	250.00
Typical house	72.2	0.25 kWh	3250.00
Savings	66.7		3000.00

Savings are US$750.

Summer cooling and stack ventilation

Although the higher windows provide solar access to the northern parts of the plan (necessary in the winter), the different height of spaces and operability enhance stack ventilation and exhaust hot air from the upper strata (during the summer). North- and south-facing windows enable cross-ventilation during summer nights, when outside temperatures are below thermal comfort. Mesh screens play a definitive role by cutting windspeed down to 20–25 per cent of external windspeeds, but these screens are a necessity, keeping out pests and insects.

Xeriscape

An intense post-occupancy project was carried out to reduce by landscaping the amount of wind-driven dust. By laying stone paving, pebble ground covering, and planting drought and salinity-resistant plants, airborne dust is trapped and kept

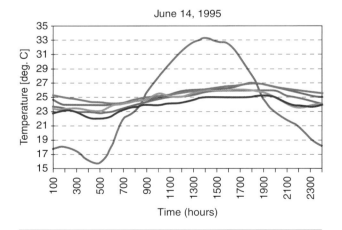

CS 14.6.
A day monitored in the summer.

CS 14.7.
Interior view of two-storey living area, by Isaac Meir.

on the ground. Plants are drip-irrigated by a computer, providing a relative humidity sensor by-pass to the automatic operation mode.

LESSONS LEARNED/PITFALLS

Initially a ceiling fan installed over the two-storey living area was thought adequate to create air movement when windows remained sealed at times when ambient temperatures were greater than interior temperatures. This proved insufficient owing to the large volume and complex geometry of the space. To correct this, a smaller fan was added on the ground floor to supplement circulation. The open plan has proved very efficient as a strategy for the creation of a thermally uniform house, but has drawbacks regarding acoustics, privacy and smells transferred from the kitchen.

ACKNOWLEDGEMENTS/INFORMATION

Center for Desert Architecture and Urban Planning. J. Blaustein Institute for Desert Research. Ben-Gurion University of the Negev, Sede Boqer Campus, Israel, 84990, Tel.: 972 7 6596880; http://www.bgu.ac.il/CDAUP; http://www.boker.org.il/davids/nvzin/sakis/housakis.htm. Issac A. Meir, Negev Desert Highlands. E-mail: sakis@bgu-mail.bgu.ac.il

15 BARILOCHE ECOHOUSE

Architect:
Research Centre Habitat and Energy
(University of Buenos Aires) with Claudio
Delbene

Owners:
Manuel Fuentes and Ana Lopez

Location:
Bariloche, Argentina; 41 °S, 71°W; 1000 m
above sea level

Climate:
Cold mountain area; 3600 heating
degree days

Area:
244 m²

CS 15.1.
Rendering of Bariloche Ecohouse, by Evans.

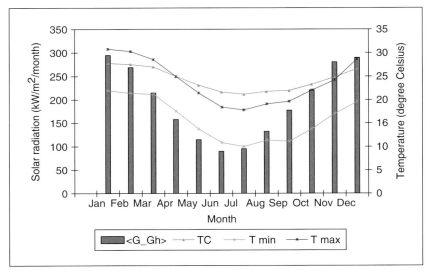

CS 15.2.
Nicol graph for Bariloche.

ECOFEATURES

• Limited site location • Thermal insulation • Greenhouse and rock store integrated into design • Roof integrated photovoltaic system • DHWS • Wastewater reuse for irrigation

DESCRIPTION/BRIEF

The Fuentes–Lopez house is located in Bariloche, an important tourist and ski centre in the cold southwest region of Argentina. The house is built in a low-density, hilly and wooded area, approximately 18 km from the town centre, with attractive views of surrounding mountains and the Nahuel Huapi National Park, Planned for convenient and flexible family living with four children, the house also provides a study and home office for the parents. the large kitchen-living-dining room forms the centre of family life. The main bedrooms are located on the ground floor. The upper floor was originally planned as a large flexible open space with possibilities for later subdivision to form additional bedrooms. The clients, with their children, were actively involved in all stages of the design process including programme formulation, location, design alternatives, detailing and construction.

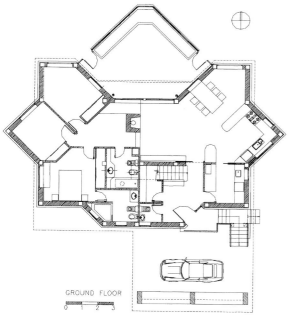

GROUND FLOOR
0 1 2 3

CS 15.3.
Ground f oor plan.

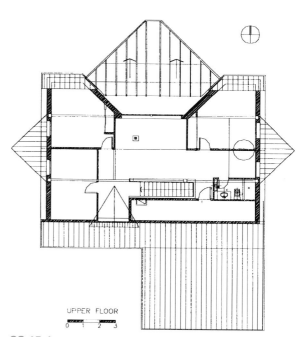

UPPER FLOOR
0 1 2 3

CS 15.4.
Upper floor plan.

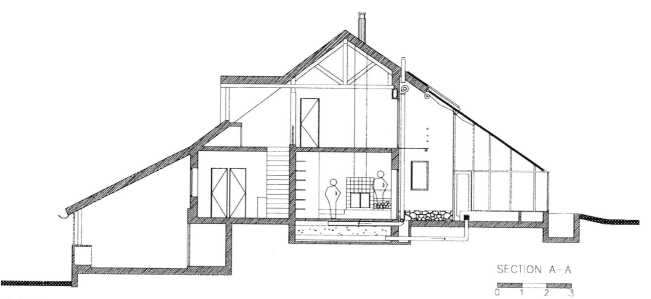

SECTION A-A
0   1   2   3

CS 15.5.
Section.

ECOFEATURES EXPLAINED

Limited site location form

Local regulations, that only allow limited tree felling impacted the design stage. Other 'setback' regulations and site characteristics limit the possibilities for locating vehicular access and siting for good solar access. The location of the house was carefully chosen to take advantage of an existing clearing in the woods and a reasonably level area, although a difference of 2 m in height within the 'footprint' of the building still exists. A heliodon (a device that simulates solar angles and measures the number of hours of potential sunshine) was used to select and define a suitable area and to detect those trees that reduced solar exposure in winter. A reasonably clear view of the sky is achieved in orientations between 45° to the east of north to 45° west of north, with maximum obstruction height of 26° to the north (note that the house is located in the southern hemisphere and receives winter sun from the north), falling to 19° to the northeast and northwest. The form combines a compact overall shape to reduce heat losses with a good exposure to the north. This is achieved by superimposing a V shape, with the principal internal sides facing northeast and northwest, on a rectangle with the longer side facing directly north.

Thermal insulation

The volumetric heat loss coefficient of the house is under $0.8\,W\,m^{-3}\,K$, considerably less than the maximum value of $1.4\,W\,m^{-3}\,K$ recommended for a house of this size in Bariloche (National Standards for Thermal Insulation). These low heat losses are a result of the compact form and very low thermal transmittance of both walls and roof. About 40 per cent of these heat losses are due to infiltration, based on a nominal one air change per hour. However, the quality of the windows will likely reduce this value to approximately 0.5 changes per hour and achieve a heat loss coefficient of less than $0.7\,W\,m^{-3}\,K$, half the recommended maximum value. A factor that increases heat loss is the north-facing glazed area. However, these losses are offset by useful heat gains on sunny days during colder periods of the year. The roof incorporates 150 mm of expanded polystyrene between the roof joists and a further 50 mm

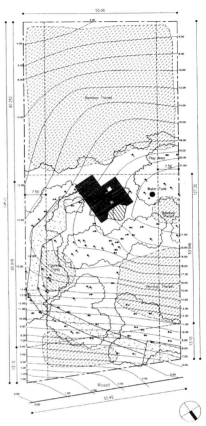

CS 15.6.

Site location and orientation.

CS 15.7.

Insulation installation, by Manuel Fuentes.

above the joists reaching $0.17\,\mathrm{W\,m^{-3}K}$. This method of incorporating a high standard of thermal insulation has the following advantages:

- no extra timber is needed to form the cavity where insulation is placed;
- the roof timbers are not exposed to indoor spaces, so rough sawn wood can be used, rather than more expensive sanded joists;
- continuous ceiling of tongue and grooved boarding, which is interrupted only by the principal roof trusses, provides an attractive and easy-to-maintain surface;
- two layers of insulation reduce the possible effect of thermal bridging.

The **walls** reach a value of $0.22\,\mathrm{W\,m^{-3}K}$. This value is achieved with a solid inner brick wall of 125 mm within an earthquake-resistant reinforced concrete structure, 150 mm of thermal insulation and an outer finish of timber boarding. This construction not only has an excellent level of thermal insulation, but also provides the following advantages:

- cold bridges are avoided, as there is negligible thermal connection between the inner brick and concrete structure and the outer finish;
- a thermal time lag of over 8 h is obtained, reducing possible overheating in summer and the cooling effect of sudden cold spells in winter;
- thermal admittance of the indoor side of the external wall is also high, $5.3\,\mathrm{W\,m^{-3}K}$, allowing effective storage of daily solar heat gains;
- as the inner brick wall, with a dense render, is less permeable than the outer finish of timber boarding, there is no risk of internal condensation, even without a vapour barrier.

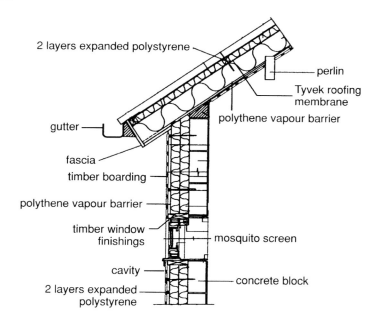

CS 15.8.
Section through wall.

PASSIVE SOLAR SYSTEMS

The northern façade incorporates four passive solar systems:

1 **The sunspace** a large glazed volume, is thermally coupled to the house by four complimentary heat flow mechanisms: forced convection to a rock bed beneath the living area, natural convection to the living areas through openable windows, radiation through the closed windows, and transmission through mass walls.
2 **Direct solar gains** are obtained through openings with favourable orientations for winter sun. These windows are in the kitchen, dining-living room and ground floor bedrooms, as well as on the upper floor.

3 **Mass storage walls** consists of two dense wall panels with exterior glazing placed on the north façade, with summer shade provided by a roof overhang.

4 **Two Trombe walls** are also placed on the north façade with a combined exposed surface area of 5.5 m^2.

Rockbed system

A rockbed system was built following the recommendations and sizing methods given by Balcomb. It consists of two 12 m^3 rockbeds with two channels each. Each channel is 6 m long and 0.8 m deep. The rocks used have an average diameter of 150 mm. The solar gains from the upper part of the greenhouse are transferred to the rockbed beneath the living area of the house using ducts with thermostatically controlled fans. After heating the rocks the air returns to the sunspace. The whole system was designed to store 21 kWh day^{-1} with a storage capacity of 1.5 days. The fans provide an airflow rate of 0.7 m^3 s^{-1}. The system is thermally coupled through the slab, acting as an under floor heating system.

The large glazed sunspace is a key feature of the house and fulfils a series of thermal and functional objectives:

- in addition to the solar gains on sunny days, the volume acts as a thermal buffer, reducing heat losses from the house on cold, cloudy and windy days;
- this intermediate buffer area can be used for family activities when the weather is unfavourable, as it is protected from rain, snow, wind and low temperatures. During sunny spells in winter the temperature increase in the sunspace will be favourable;

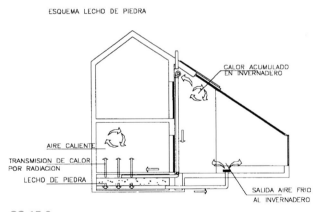

CS 15.9.

Passive solar systems.

CS 15.10.

Rockbed, by Manuel Fuentes.

- the exposure of the sunspace to summer sun may produce overheating owing to the intensity of solar radiation. Five measures were therefore adopted to control this problem:
  - upper floor balcony: provides shade, especially to windows between the sunspace and ground floor. The roof overhang serves a similar purpose on the upper floor;
  - high-level opening windows: designed to allow the exit of hot air to the exterior while allowing ingress of cooler air at a lower level. The stack effect to achieve this is reinforced by the double height;
  - thermal insulation and double-glazed windows: reduce the thermal transmission to indoor spaces in summer.

Domestic solar hot water (DSHW) system

The house has a flat plate solar collector manufactured by AES and mounted on the roof co-planar with photovoltaic panels. The solar hot water collectors are used to supplement the energy demand for domestic hot water (DHW). The 5 m² collector is considered to be cost-effective for a single family in Bariloche. The solar hot water collector was predicted to supply 76 per cent of the household requirements. The domestic hot water system was designed for the highest solar fraction. For this purpose, the roof was tilted 35°. The collector feeds directly into a preheated or 'solar' tank (250 l) that feeds into the primary tank, which is a conventional 150 litre tank heated by a high-efficiency, Peisa-manufactured gas boiler. The principle for choosing this two-tank, preheated system was to have the best technology available in Argentina that could be quickly adapted to produce a high solar fraction system with a gas boiler back-up.

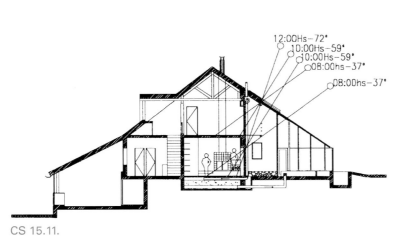

CS 15.11.
Internal morning temperatures.

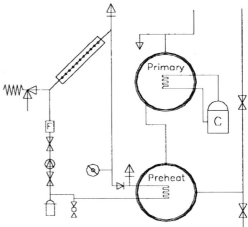

CS 15.12.
DSHW system.

PHOTOVOLTAIC SYSTEM

The house is situated in an area that receives approximately 7.8 peak sun hours in summer, but only 1.7 peak sun hours in winter. The variation in output from winter to summer is therefore significant and the array size has been specified in order to achieve a maximum level of solar input in spring and autumn. Power has to be drawn from the utility company during winter days and also at night-time. The system was sized in order to provide around one-third of the annual electricity demands for the house. It consists of 16 MST-43MV BP-Solarex thin-film modules with capacity for 700 W peak of electricity, wired to a SMA 7000 W inverter.

The PV system is connected in parallel to the electricity supply. Energy from the solar array will be consumed by the AC loads in the house with any excess energy being exported into the utility supply. Any shortfall in output from the array will be made up by importing from the supply connection. This is a fully automatic process.

The PV modules were mounted on the roof using aluminium frames designed by the architect Marshall from Marshall and Associates. These frames, designed for their simplicity, make fastening to a standard roof structure an uncomplicated procedure.

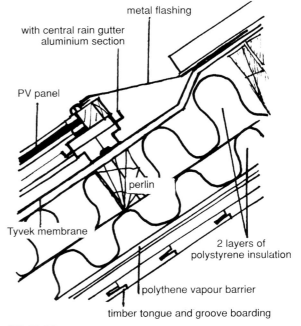

CS 15.13.
Photovoltaic system.

ENERGY BALANCE

Type	kWh m^{-2} a^{-1}	Cost of electricity (US$)	Cost of gas (US$)	Total (US$)	CO$_2$ emissions (tonnes a^{-1})	Construction cost (US$ m^{-2})
Fuentes–Lopez House	43	256	96	352	5.5	700
Typical house	235	512	575	1087	30	700
Savings	192	256	478	735	24.5	

ACKNOWLEDGEMENTS/CONTACT INFORMATION

This house was designed and built with the help of a group of people and companies that believe in the idea of sustainable architecture. The design team directed by the architects Martin Evans and Silvia de Schiller from the Research Centre Habitat and Energy, University of Buenos Aires, the architect Claudio Delbene and TEVSA SA contributed their knowledge to design and build this house. Marshall developed the structure that integrated the PV and solar collector into the roof, this being the first solar roof in Argentina. Esteban SA provided the double-glazed windows with Rehau technology and detailed the Trombe walls. Peisa provided the best heating technology available in Argentina, building a prototype for a SHW system with the goal of manufacturing and commercialising solar systems. BP Solarex provided photovoltaic modules, believing that the PVIB market is not just a dream but is the market of the future.

Dr Manuel Fuentes, Bariloche, Argentina. E-mail: mfuentes@bariloche.com.ar

16 TAMARIND HILLS NO. 15

CS 16.1.
Tamarind Hills, No. 15, by David Morrison.

Architect:
David Morrison Associates

Owners:
David Morrison and Susan Parson

Location:
Tamarind Hills, Oyster Pond Hill Road, Gibbs Land, St Maarten, Netherlands Antilles; 18°N, 63°W; 60 m above see level

Climate:
Tropical maritime, cooled by trade winds

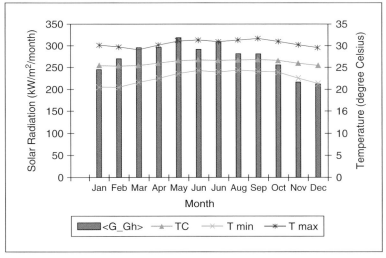

CS 16.2.
Nicol graph for St Maarten.

ECOFEATURES

• Hurricane-resistant roof appurtenances • Solar water heater • Trade wind flow optimised • Fresh and storm water cisterns • Seismic-resistant concrete-frame structure

DESCRIPTION/BRIEF

The house on Tamarind Hills cascades down a hill 60 m above the sea on an island of 37 square miles, governed by two governments. It is located 300 miles southeast of

Miami and is susceptible to hurricanes annually. With one bedroom and 1–1/2 bath on the main level, a guest bedroom and a one-bedroom apartment located below the main house, its view above Dawn Beach is spectacular, looking towards St Barts. Also at main level are a swimming pool, gazebo and deck, workshop, study and covered car port. The vegetation on the island is classified as dry scrub, acacia, and it receives an annual average rainfall of 400 mm.

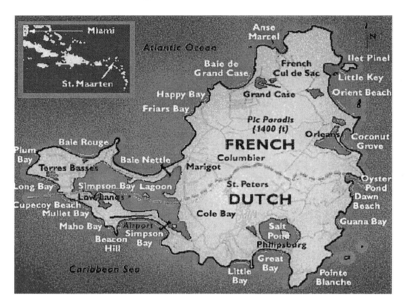

CS 16.3.

Island map, by Interknowledge © 1996.

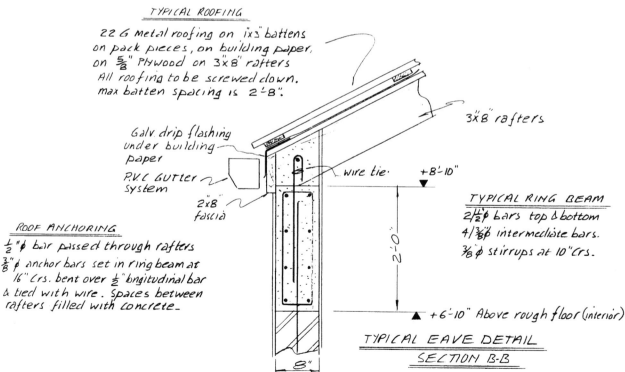

TYPICAL ROOFING

22 G metal roofing on 1"x3" battens on pack pieces, on building paper, on ⅝" plywood on 3"x8" rafters All roofing to be screwed down. max batten spacing is 2'-8".

Galv. drip flashing under building paper

P.V.C Gutter system

2"x8" fascia

ROOF ANCHORING

½"ø bar passed through rafters ⅜"ø anchor bars set in ring beam at 16" crs. bent over ½" longitudinal bar & tied with wire. Spaces between rafters filled with concrete.

3"x8" rafters

wire tie.   +8'-10"

2'-0"

8"

TYPICAL RING BEAM
2/½"ø bars top & bottom
4/⅜"ø intermediate bars.
⅜"ø stirrups at 10"crs.

+6'-10" Above rough floor (interior)

TYPICAL EAVE DETAIL
SECTION B-B

CS 16.4.
Typical hip or ridge detail.

FEATURES EXPLAINED

Hurricane-resistant structure

Built to withstand 250 kph winds this home has survived hurricanes of Category 4 and 5 more than once without structural damage. However, impact damage from flying objects is always a problem. The house has reinforced concrete tie-beams, roof rafters held down with steel anchors, floor-grade decking screwed to rafters and sealed with heat-applied asphalt (several layers); clay roof tiles are glued, screwed and cemented but are still liable to damage from wind-blown debris. Roofs are also braced internally, either by tie-rafters (exposed) or with a timber matrix and a suspended (false) ceiling. The roof pitch is important: too low a pitch increases upthrust (or uplift) owing to wind pressure and a pitch too steep is vulnerable to downward forces on the windward slope and uplift forces on the leeward slope.

Doors and windows are lagged into hardwood sub-frames and turn bolted into concrete jambs. Glass is covered by storm shutters (non-permanent) made mainly of steel or hardwood. In less exposed areas, terraces are enclosed in trampoline fabric strung tightly across openings; these allow some air-passage during a storm but protect from flying debris. The trampoline mesh protection is a less expensive and easier installation alternative than the steel and wood shutters, but has had mixed success. If not sufficiently tight, they chafe and can come apart. On the other hand, when used on covered balconies and terraces, they can allow movement to the outdoors during a storm, reducing claustrophobic effects.

Hurricane-resistant natural ventilation

Many windows are hardwood jalousie (louvre) type, promoting the flow of the trade winds through the house, eliminating the need for air-conditioning. These can survive a bad storm in themselves. The rooms are angled to increase the effects of the breeze, but only the experience of residing in the neighbourhood can perfect this orientation. These design strategies optimise the trade-winds flow and are aided by paddle fans. Artificial air-conditioning is an in-wall unit located in the study. However, the habitants never use this cooling system; it is provided in the event of a visiting guest not acclimatised to the higher temperatures on the island.

CS 16.5.
Trampoline screen in place, by David Morrison.

CS 16.6.
Bahamian style shutter, by David Morrison.

CS 16.7.
Jalousie window, by David Morrison.

Cistern

Water is at a premium with no piped water available. With only 400 mm of rain annually, as much rain as possible is collected from the roof into a fresh-water storage tank in the basement, built with gunned concrete for strength. For irrigation, deck water is also collected into a separate tank; both sources are powered by small electric shallow-well pumps.

HURRICANE EXPERIENCES AND LESSONS LEARNED

Even though hurricanes hit the Leeward Islands so frequently, sometimes more than twice a year, Hurricane Luis (August 1995) leaves behind a benchmark for constant comparison. Luis was a Category 4 Cape Verde hurricane that wreaked harm and havoc on the northeasternmost edge of the Leeward Islands, with an estimated 16 people dead and US$2.5 billion in damages, US$1.8 billion to St Maarten alone.

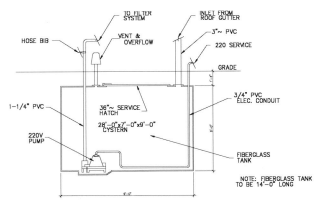

CS 16.8.
Cistern detail.

CS 16.9.
Before Hurricane Luis, protected with aluminium shutters, by David Morrison.

CS 16.10.
After Hurricane Luis (back). Winds ripped off shutters and their tracks, while flying debris shattered clay tiles. By David Morrison.

CS 16.11.
After Hurricane Luis (front). High winds and flying debris responsible for downed trees, roof tile damage and solar water heater being ripped off. By David Morrison.

CS 16.12.
Before Hurricane Lenny. Remodelled after Hurricane Luis with a new protected entry and roof tiles glued, screwed and cemented. By David Morrison.

CS 16.13.
Hurricane Lenny. Trampoline screens secure Tamarind Hills No. 15 during Hurricane Lenny.
By David Morrison.

The house on Tamarind Hills is 19 years old and, after Hurricane Luis (with winds gusting up to 325 kph), was partly rebuilt, extended and improved. Although the roof held well in this storm (other than damage caused by the neighbour's rafters) it was strengthened further, doors and windows were upgraded (including frames) and shutters improved. The house withstood Hurricane Lenny in November of 1999 very well with no damage to speak of (like Hurricane Luis, Hurricane Lenny was a Category 4 hurricane with winds gusting to 200 kph and killing three people on St Maarten).

ACKNOWLEDGEMENTS/CONTACT INFORMATION

David Morrison Associates, Philipsburg, St Maarten, D.W.I. E-mail: david@dma-architects.com

17 LINDAVISTA HOUSE

Architect:
Jose Roberto Garcia-Chavez; 1998

Owner:
Jose Roberto Garcia-Chavez

Location:
Lindavista, Mexico City, Mexico; 19°N,
99°W; 2240 m above sea level

Climate:
Temperate

Area:
300 m²

CS 17.1.
Lindavista House, by Jose Roberto Garcia-Chavez.

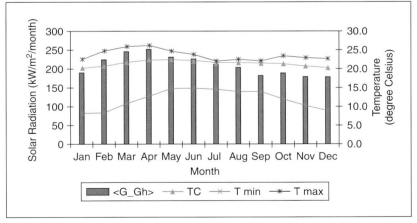

CS 17.2.
Nicol graph for Mexico City.

ECOFEATURES

• Bioclimatic design • Solar water heating and cooking • Optimised natural day lighting • Energy-efficient equipment • Low-energy materials and insulation • Rainwater collection and storage with low consumption devices • Sustainable waste treatment recycling • Healthy construction environment • Life-supporting systems: vegetable garden and orchard

DESCRIPTION/BRIEF

This house is three-storey, rectangular in plan and located in the centre of Mexico City. On the ground floor it has a car park area, studio, greenhouse, vegetable and flower garden, inorganic waste material separation, living and dining room, kitchen, studio, bathroom, rainwater collection and storage system, rainwater absorption well and garden. The second floor has three bedrooms and two bathrooms. The third floor has a studio, bedroom, bathroom, laundry room, solar photovoltaics area, terrace and flower growing area. The roof has a storage area, solar collectors area and rainwater collection area.

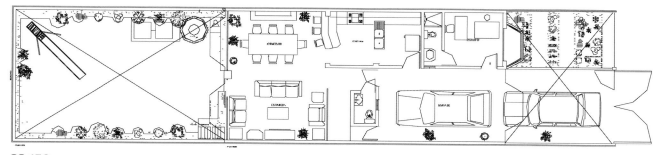

CS 17.3.
Ground floor.

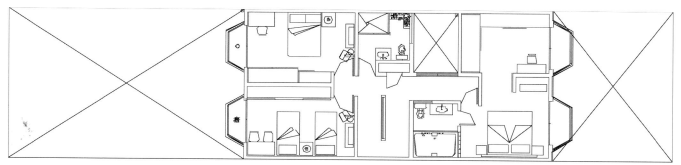

CS 17.4.
Second floor.

ECOFEATURES EXPLAINED

Bioclimatic design

Through the application of passive cooling and heating systems, good orientation, natural ventilation solutions, shading devices and evaporative cooling the entire house is naturally climatised, providing comfort conditions to occupants throughout the year.

Energy-efficient

The orientation and site placement of the house provides optimal daylight to enter the house, therefore reducing the amount of energy used for lighting. A stand-alone photo-voltaic solar system supplements artificial lighting with the use of energy-efficient fixtures and equipment. Good insulation standards for exterior walls and roof also reduce heating loads when solar heating provides space heat during underheated periods.

Materials

Regional stone, brick, concrete, earth landscaping and glass were the building materials used because they were locally available, builders were familiar with their application and because they have relatively low cost and low embodied energy. This simple and robust solution for building systems requires little user maintenance and is viable for a sustainable design.

Materials/element	U value (W m^{-2} K)	Description
Walls	1.80	Solid brick and plaster
Floor	0.54	Concrete slab and ceramic tile
Roof	1.10	Concrete and polystyrene
Windows	4.50	Glass and aluminium, solar protected

Ventilation

The house is naturally ventilated and windows have 'wing walls' to enhance air movement indoors. The windows are bay windows, with two lateral openings, and the central one is fixed. The first opening is located in a high-pressure zone (in the downwind). The wing wall is upwind of the second window, which creates suction in front of it, providing effective natural ventilation into the rooms. Openings are located 30° from prevailing winds, which has been proven to be optimum for better ventilation. The doors have manually controlled upper and lower operable louvres for promoting air movement through the house as desired. During the summer, nocturnal ventilation takes place through the louvres. The east-facing garden and vegetation act as microclimate modulators, increasing the air movement indoors. Building surfaces act as powerful 'heat sinks', providing comfortable temperatures the following day. During the winter the louvres remain closed, reducing heat losses.

	Air changes per hour
Lindavista House	Three average, and ten during overheating season for nocturnal structural cooling
Typical house	One

Water and waste

Water is conserved through rainwater collection and storage systems that supply domestic water for all uses. Devices that save water consumption in water closets, showers and taps, etc. are also used. Used water from the kitchen and bathrooms (black water) is recycled to the water closet tank. Rain water (grey) is collected and stored for gardening.

	Water consumption (m³ a⁻¹)	Water purchase price a⁻¹ (US$)
Lindavista House	42	48
Typical house	180	308
Savings		
Total	138	260
%	77	84

Food and waste

At Lindavista House there is: sorting of waste within the home for local collection sites and the possibility for some recycling, compost production used in the garden and excess organic waste for use in intensive gardening, life-supporting systems by means of organic vegetable garden and orchard, reducing solid waste. Therefore, the energy-ecological systems integrated in the house provide high levels of self-sufficiency in energy, water and food and are aimed at providing energy savings, whilst improving economy, the natural environment and the quality of life. It is expected that this design premise eventually will generate a new energy, water and food production culture and that, in turn, will promote a favourable application of sustainable development nationwide.

	Consumption (kWh a⁻¹/ kWh m⁻² a⁻¹)	Cost of electricity (US$)	Gas consumption (l a⁻¹)	Cost of gas, annual (US$)	Total cost, annual (US$)	CO_2 emissions (tonnes a⁻¹)	Construction cost (US$ m⁻²)
Lindavista House	2760/9.2	180	300	90	270	1880	315
Typical house	4500/15	300	1800	540	840	3065	300
Savings							
Total	1740	120	1500	450	570	1185	−30
%	61	60	83	83	68	61	−5

Total annual savings

- Electricity and gas   US$570
- Water   US$260
- Total   US$830
- Payback period   US$4500/US$830 a⁻¹ = 5.4 years

(Food production economic benefits from life-supporting vegetable garden and orchard not considered, but these can also contribute to reduce payback period even further.)

Healthy construction

One of the main design premises was to promote healthy building. This was accomplished by the use of healthy building materials, organic as much as possible, without inducing health hazards. Natural ventilated and moisture-open construction provided a healthy outdoor environment. The use of plant materials and vegetation forms a natural barrier against heavy local pollution and dust. This not only promotes a healthy environment for the workers but also inactive neighbours.

LESSONS LEARNED/PITFALLS

It is difficult to make clients and building occupants aware of the potential economic, health, environmental and quality-of-life benefits from implementing ecological-bioclimatic-sustainable projects.

ACKNOWLEDGEMENTS/CONTACT INFORMATION

Mr Garcia-Chavez would like to 'thank all persons involved in this project during the whole process and above all thanks to God for granting us the essential serenity and holistic understanding to overcome all difficulties'.

Jose Roberto Garcia-Chavez, Mexico City, Mexico. E-mail: jgc@correo.azc.uam.mx

18 MIDDLETON HOUSE

CS 18.1.
Middleton House in winter, by Charles Middleton.

Architect:
Charles Middleton, 1990

Client:
Charles Middleton and Peggie Beattie

Location:
Gravenhurst, Ontario, Canada; 45°N, 79°W; 270 m above sea level

Climate:
Continental; 4800 heating degree days per year

Area:
152 m²

CS 18.2.
Middleton House in summer, by Charles Middleton.

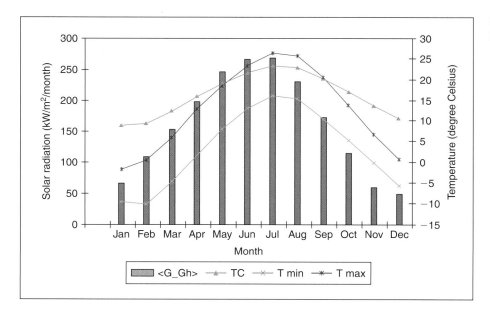

CS 18.3.
Nicol graph for Ontario.

ECOFEATURES

• Passive design • Materials, local and low embodied energy • Solar systems

DESCRIPTION/BRIEF

The main objective of this designer/occupant project, beyond the immediate issue of getting a house built, was to achieve accepted Canadian levels of comfort and amenity using only renewable-energy technologies, along with conventional, affordable construction. In other words, to show that a lifestyle based on low and renewable energy could be accessible to ordinary families, without using exotic and expensive

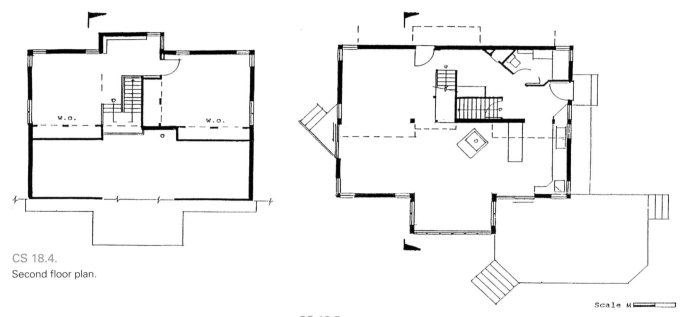

CS 18.4.
Second floor plan.

Scale M

CS 18.5.
First floor plan.

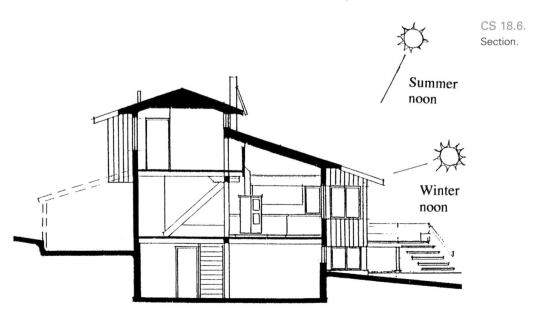

CS 18.6.
Section.

Summer
noon

Winter
noon

technologies, or having unacceptable or unreasonable expectations of the occupants. The house has been in continuous use since 1990. For minimal environmental impact, solar energy was harnessed to the maximum. This entailed design to control energy both passively and actively, winter and summer. It also required construction with low embodied energy and minimum waste. The house is the primary home for a married couple, with visits from the extended family. It is located in Muskoka in Ontario, some 150 km north of Toronto. The Muskoka region is on the Canadian Shield and is noted for landscapes of rock slabs, lakes and windblown trees. It provides outdoor recreation year-round. There are pockets of farmland, generally of marginal quality, but more than acceptable for experiments with 'sustainable' lifestyles such as this. For the idea of sustainability to become more widely accepted it has to be accessible and user friendly. The house was intended to demonstrate that this is possible using simple design techniques, showing that environmental responsibility does not mean returning to the 'horse and buggy' days, but is a step towards a more desirable and sustainable future.

PASSIVE DESIGN

The passive design strategies respond to seasonal climatic characteristics and include careful selection of site planning and orientation for good solar exposure in the winter. The house is oriented with open plan, living spaces facing south, service spaces and a garage to the north. The north wall, which has few windows, is sheltered by a sloping natural wall of rock with large coniferous trees. South-facing glazing provides solar heat gain in the winter. The eaves provide these windows with protection from the higher-altitude sun in the summer. The windows are side-hung casements. Careful choice of left- or right-hand openings in relation to the prevailing westerly winds allows ventilation without rain penetration. Roughly 30 per cent of the average annual precipitation of 993 mm falls as snow in winter when the windows are shut.

LOCAL AND LOW EMBODIED ENERGY MATERIALS

The compact design of the house was based on a 12 ft module, using standard timber sizes to minimise construction waste. Canadian wood- frame construction is well established, affordable and a means of using a renewable locally available resource efficiently. The concept of highly insulated, airtight design has been well developed through such programmes as Canada Mortgage and Housing Corporation's (CMHC) R2000 programme. With no need to reinvent the wheel, these practices were adopted for construction of the envelope.

1 Conventional wood-frame construction for low embodied energy and affordability. 5 cm × 15 cm pre-cut wood studs minimise waste, as do roof trusses pre-assembled from 5 cm × 10 cm wood.
2 Conventional fibreglass or rock-wool insulation with careful installation of vapour barrier to achieve a high level of airtightness. Wall insulation, 4.4 rsi; roof, 831 rsi.
3 Conventional concrete block basement with exterior insulation for about 1 rsi.
4 Side-hung casement windows, triple glazed.
5 Supplementary heat source: centrally located airtight wood stove using wood gathered from wood lot, eliminating need for mechanical fossil-fuelled furnace and all ductwork.

SOLAR SYSTEM

The house is powered off-grid with a range of conventional electric appliances for the kitchen, as well as computers, fax, satellite television and other conveniences. The house is fitted with a 600 W photovoltaic array for electricity and a small generator for backup. The battery stores 1800 Ah, allowing several days' use without recharge. The house has a solar hot-water system with a nominal 200-l storage tank. The system draws water from the well using a .0.5 hp (0.373 kW) pump. Rainwater is collected from the roof for use in the garden, conserving well-water and energy for pumping.

LESSONS LEARNED AND FIXES

1 Passive solar approaches work well, as do R2000 type construction, the photovoltaic and hot water systems. The latter produces more hot water than can be used at present.
2 The exterior insulating sheathing of 4 cm of dense fibreglass was found not to be vermin-proof. The problem was solved by additional sealing at the bottom of the exterior wood siding. It wood be better to use uninsulated plywood sheathing in the first place, adding further insulation if desired.
3 Photovoltaics work well but the 'learning-curve' on installation was steep. This installation seems to reflect the current state of development of this technology in North America. Components work well individually, and support is good. The problems arise with integration. Systems are not sold as complete and fully integrated packages. In that case it is all the more essential that systems should be described with clear instructions of how components contribute to a comprehensive installation. Perhaps this will improve as systems become more widely used.
4 The range of 12 V DC appliances widely available for recreational uses is welcome, but they are often expensive, e.g. water pumps or refrigerators. Careful calculation is necessary to balance capital costs versus operating costs, taking into account losses in inverting to 110 V AC. Convenience is also a factor. An increasing variety of time-dependent appliances is available. These should be avoided to eliminate stand by losses.
5 The biological toilet provided an unexpected advantage in that it drastically reduced the need for water and consequently electrical energy for pumping. However, the particular system used here was not 'user friendly'. Design was poorly developed and materials distorted in use. Manufacturer support has been virtually non-existent. The problems have been resolved by a series of fixes, but this technology cannot be considered sufficiently mature for general use. Much more committed development is needed by the manufacturers.

ACKNOWLEDGEMENTS/CONTACT INFORMATION

Charles Middleton, Gravenhurst, Canada. E-mail: mid.beat@sympatico.ca

19 PEN-Y-LLYN

CS 19.1.
The house nestles into the landscape for shelter from wind; by Christopher Day.

Architect:
Christopher Day, retrofit 1975–1977

Owners:
Christopher Day

Location:
Pembrokeshire, Wales, UK; 51°N, 4°W;
<10 m above sea level

Climate:
Temperate, coastal

Area:
103 m²

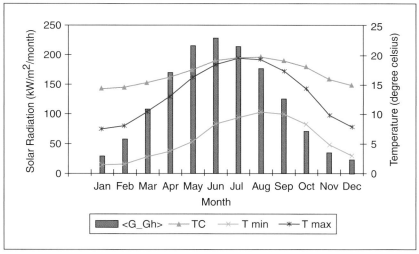

CS 19.2.
Nicol graph for Pembrokeshire.

ECOFEATURES

• Self-build • Second-hand materials • Insulation • Solar heating and wind power

DESCRIPTION/BRIEF

When the architect acquired Pen-y-Llyn in 1975, he was left with little to build from. The structure, a farmhouse occupied by caravan dwellers and vacated 20 years previously, had barely any walls with which to start, what one might call, a renovation. Today this house has been transformed to meet the changing needs of the family existence. The young children are now teenagers and the architect works from his home.

ECOFEATURES EXPLAINED

Self-build

Christopher Day has built his career promoting volunteer and self-build structures. Building with volunteers can be cheaper and, on past projects, estimates of 12–14 per cent savings on contract costs have been attributed to volunteers. In addition, there are rich cultural experiences to be gained. In one of his earlier projects, there were volunteers from over 13 nations helping to build. He found when he started rebuilding his home at Pen-y-Llyn that people were always stopping in to help, frequently without any prior warning. At the time the house did not have a phone or accommodation for volunteers. There was a chicken shed in which he and his wife lived during construction. Others had to stay in tents on the site. At times when weather was bad they would all cram into the 9 ft × 5 ft chicken shed. Some of the advantages of self-build include:

- it is economical;
- it puts the focus on activity instead of institutionalism;
- it builds communities;
- if offers the opportunity for personal growth for those involved.

Second-hand materials

Second-hand materials are not always inferior and, when you look at a raped rainforest or the hillsides raked from mining, you can begin to value the extra time it may take when using second-hand materials. Second-hand timber is frequently well studded with nails. Christopher would rarely denail the studs but would simply knock over protruding points for safety and not fully cinch them down in case they fell in the line of a saw cut. He estimates that when ordering second-hand material 20 per cent more than what is actually needed is a safe order, owing to damaged ends, rotting, etc. In Christopher's book *Building With Heart* (Day, 1990) he includes a list of those second-hand materials to look for and those to avoid.

Materials to look for	Materials to avoid
RSJs (steel beams)	Pressed steel radiators – life probably
Structural timbers	limited
Boards for	Demo hardcore
floors (time consuming to finish)	Electrical wiring (invisibly damaged
cupboard doors	Timber infected with dry rot
shelving, etc.	(or other rot, insects, etc.)
Floor tiles	Timber that has been treated with
Slates	biocides
Roof tiles	
Handmade bricks (for appearance only)	
Sinks, baths, basins	
Solid fuel heating appliances	

Insulation strategies

In the 1970s, when the Building Regulations required that a building's roof be insulated with 50 mm insulation, Christopher tripled this regulation in some rooms and doubled it in all others. Even though the regulations have changed to require

150 mm, it is apparent that his strategy paid off, although he specifies 300 mm of roof insulation in his current projects. The existing south wall of Pen-y-Llyn was approximately 600 mm thick, built of sedimentary stone that had deep capillary cracks. Owing to the climate most gales and the rain drive towards the south elevation of the house, so Christopher insulated the outside of the south wall with 75 mm insulation with 200 mm of stone-rock on top of this. The west wall was extended during reconstruction and the new construction consisted of 150 mm insulation, 50 mm rock wool insulation, a 25 mm cavity space, 100 mm concrete block and an average of 250 mm of stonework. The windows on all sides were site-built by hand and double-glazed. Owing to the amount of moisture received by the south side of the house, condensation between these window panes has required the removal of the interior pane. Also, the wooden frames around the doors and windows are constantly swelling and shrinking, causing consistent draught-proofing replacement.

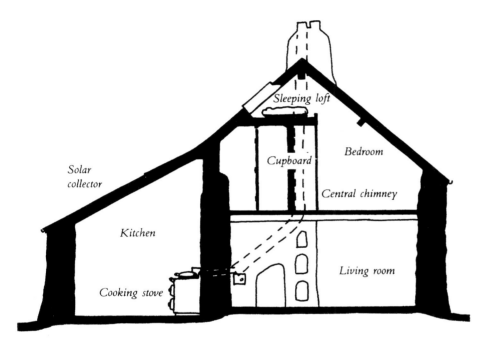

CS 19.3.
Section.

Solar heating (principal heating strategy)

A solid fuel cooking stove and central chimney provide a large area, low-temperature, radiant wall that heats the five rooms around it. South-facing windows mean that life in the house faces south and the architectural studio (converted from the hayloft) can be solar heated even on the cold winter days. A home-made solar water heater is used as a proprietary system integral to the roof; such systems were not commonly used when installed. In the summer the water is heated 100 per cent by the sun and, since there is little rain, there is a low flow setting on the hydrogenerator producing lower electricity for this cause. Between the seasons the sun is used to pre-heat the water, which is then topped up by the 1.5 kW hydrogenerator, warmed by the boiler from the stove. During the winter, the water is heated 100 per cent by the Rayburn cooking stove. The hydrogenerator diverts any power not drawn directly for use to a ballast circuit, which heats an oil-filled radiator or hot water immersion heater. In the 1980s, when Christopher monitored his electric consumption, he purchased on an average about £25 of electricity per year from the utility company. Pen-y-Llyn consumes an average of about 1.08 tons of anthracite coal per year, supplementing both heating and cooking needs. Natural gas consumption is negligible as its main use is for summer cooking.

LESSONS LEARNED

We all know family patterns change. The children grow into teenagers and technology invents new items for amusement, e.g. computers, compact disc players, etc. Since the rehabitation into Pen-y-Llyn in the 1970s, this family has also acquired new habits. It is important to build with the future in mind. Recently, Christopher has become unable to maintain the generator that was part of an ethical ritual relevant to his philosophy of building. He quotes that 'teenagers and others in the house have a different attitude to electricity and gadgeting resulting in the hydrogenerator being turned off! Hence, electric consumption has soared'.

ACKNOWLEDGEMENTS/CONTACT INFORMATION

Christopher Day, Pen-y-Llyn, Wales, UK. Tel.: +44 1239 891 399.

20 PORPOISE POINT ECOHOUSE

Architect:
Stephanie Thomas

Structural Engineer:
Dansco Engineering

Owners:
Ron and Karen Rees

Location:
Big Coppitt Key, Key West, Florida;
24°36'N, 81°39'W; <2 m above sea level

Climate:
Warm, humid

Area:
220 m²

CS 20.1.
Porpoise Point Ecohouse, by Ron Rees.

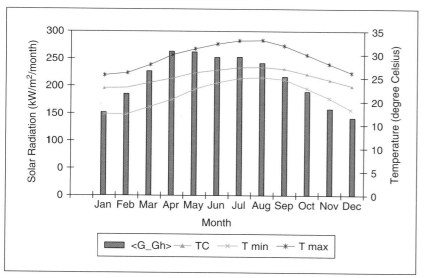

CS 20.2.
Nicol graph for Key West, Florida.

ECOFEATURES

• Energy-efficient envelope and systems • Hurricane sustainable • Rainwater reuse
and conservation • Solar thermal

DESCRIPTION/BRIEF

This project investigates strategies for reducing residential demands using computer simulated methodology, tried and tested technologies and evaluated case studies, much like the others in this book. The objective was to produce a practical design for an affordable, comfortable home. This home completed construction in June 2003. It is a ±200 m² three-bedroomed dwelling, tackling the issues of local planning restrictions, ecological sensitivity, Key West vernacular preservation, conservation, use of renewable energy sources and high performance materials.

ENERGY-EFFICIENT ENVELOPE AND SYSTEMS

The main objective of this project, beyond the immediate issue of getting a house built, was to achieve accepted levels of comfort and amenity using efficient strategies along with a conventional, affordable and hurricane-sustainable construction. The site was selected based on its proximity to the water and economical value.

The local building restrictions, and existing site conditions, which include strict setbacks, are not available to allow for ingenuitive or passive design features, i.e. overhangs, landscape, etc. Therefore, the building's envelope will perform the thermal resistance inflicted by the 200 W m² of solar radiation the site receives on average each month. The advantage of the wall composition in Figure CS 20.3 is not only the high R-value but also the provision for electrical wiring, telephone outlet and other electronic communications.

This assembly applies to all exterior walls from the ground level to the roof. Maximising floor space was a necessity for the owner, even at the expense of hindering the opportunity for overhangs. However, deep overhangs become a structural challenge due to the strong uplift forces this area experiences during the hurricane season. High performance windows are specified to complement the wall assembly. Vinyl-framed, low-e, argon-filled, double glazing allows maximum daylight with minimal heat gain. In addition to storm shutters used to protect these openings in the event of a hurricane, the shutters also work as a solar defensive mechanism during the day. The sleeping area is on the first level of the house and a control timer powers the shutters down during the day when the bedrooms are unoccupied. At dusk, they are reopened so that the bedrooms can take advantage of breezes customary to this area. The second level plan orients the terrace facing the north, not only optimising the view, but also the ventilation by providing larger glider windows on the north and northwest façade and slightly smaller openings on the east façade admitting a pressure-induced southeast prevailing wind. Figure CS 20.5 demonstrates the valuable

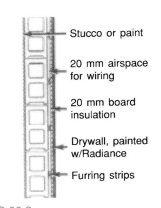

CS 20.3.

Plan view of wall construction.

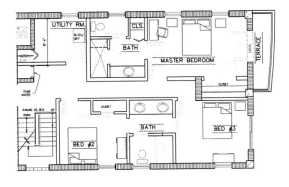
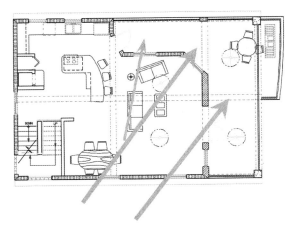

CS 20.4.

Plan of the house: first level; second level.

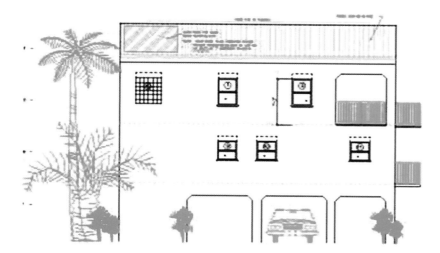

CS 20.5.
East elevation.

height that enhances ventilation to these spaces. The ground level has no habitable spaces; it only provides circulation to the first level which is 4 m above the ground plane.

There are three high-efficient HVAC systems for this house to maintain comfort temperatures where and only when comfort is needed. This may seem like an inefficient way to condition but it allows the second floor to be conditioned independently from the first floor; and the first floor has a system for each side of the house because the side of the house that has the master bedroom is typically the only side occupied. One may feel that window type units would serve this objective more efficiently but they are not aesthetically pleasing and are a bit difficult to remove and store during times when natural ventilation is sufficient for thermal comfort. Due to the occupancy schedule, improved envelope features, efficient appliances and internal finish selections, the size is adequate. The total heat gain during peak radiation of the whole house with all appliances, and equipment running is simulated at 9.4 kW. A high efficient HVAC system (SEER 12.8) is specified and the ductwork is located in a conditioned space between the first level ceiling and second level floor. The hollow core slab provides a thermal sink to keep the conditioned air at a constant temperature reducing cooling loss. Tile floors will finish all rooms and add to the thermal capacity of the floor.

Hurricane sustainability

Hurricane design and the materials best suited for resisting hurricanes are often debated by the environmentalists and structural engineers. The environmentalists want to promote the use of more renewable materials, like wood, and reduce the use of high embodied energy materials, like steel and concrete. Both sides have valid points and during the initial design phase of the Porpoise Point Ecohouse the first dilemma was whether or not to build predominantly with wood or concrete. The first requirement for the future home was to meet ROGO's code compliance of sustaining 175 mph winds. This may be the first residential structure in Key West to be built to such standards.

Contending with the lateral forces that are 4.5 times greater than gravity loads, creates the additional dead loads that are welcomed. The home's structural design must contend to height limitations (of the site) that necessitates the use of a skinny framing system. A wood system would have to be at least 60 cm deep. Taking into consideration the reduced infiltration of latent heat and the increased insulating properties that concrete possesses over wood, proves that a concrete structure can provide a more efficient envelope for an

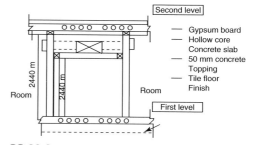

CS 20.6.
Ductwork within plenum space below second floor/above first level ceiling.

air-conditioned environment. Cement production is energy intensive and, in addition, the expended delivery and waste associated with formwork contributes to the overall embodied energy.

Calculating all factors collectively (hurricane sustainability, site location, maintenance requirements, climate characteristics, airtight capabilities, etc.) a reinforced concrete structure is the most practical, economical and energy-efficient way to construct the Porpoise Point Ecohouse. Figure CS 20.7 details the structural integrity of the home. The columns supporting the structure must create frictional forces to resist an immense amount of uplift associated with 175 mph winds. Since the site's underlayment is coral and rock, the auger piles do not have the advantage of soil to compress

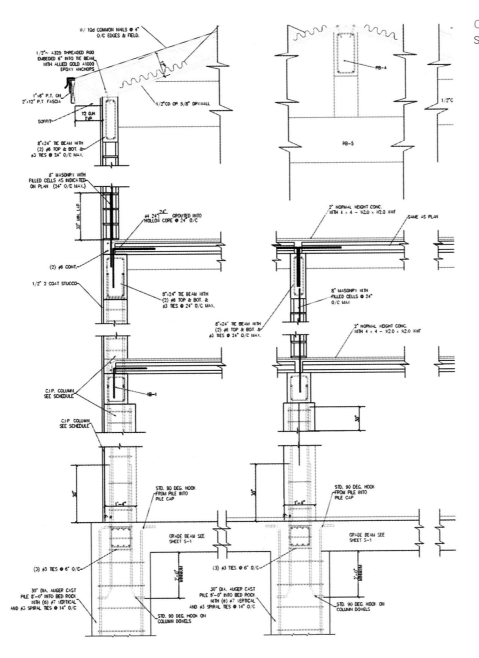

CS 20.7.
Structural plan.

against uplift. Tie beams, 610 mm in depth, 300 mm in width on the ground and first levels, 200 mm in width on the second level, wrap continuously around the structure. A 610 mm poured concrete cross beam allows the second level floor plan to be free of columns so that the vaulted roof can span across the entire width of the house without obstructions. The first and second level floors span the width of the house and shall be 150 mm thick by 1220 mm wide hollow core slabs with a 50 mm concrete topping. The external walls are concrete block with infilled cells of poured concrete, reinforced vertically every 610 mm. The ground floor level will have blow-out walls. In the event of a tidal surge, the ground level non-structural walls fail intentionally, eliminating structural failure resulting from pressure on a large surface area. The roofing consists of pre-engineered wood trusses spaced 610 mm on centre with stainless steel rods embedded 150 mm into the tie beams. Referring to the second level floor plan, the only attic space is above the stairwell, which houses the solar water system. The remaining space above the vaulted ceiling is insulated with R-20 insulation.

Cistern and fixtures

A 45 000 litre cistern is located on the North end of the house. This will supply water for flushing toilets, and an outside hose bib for car, boat and dog washing. The cistern will have a filter to strain the water, but it will not be purified for potable uses. The supply waterline for the toilets and the fixtures will be galvanised as an extra precaution against corrosion caused by saline water. The second level will be plumbed for a future combination sink/toilet. This will eliminate the need for an additional sink. Low flow taps and showerheads shall be installed and the bathrooms will have ultra-low water toilets (6.8 litres). By conserving water, sewage is curbed allowing a smaller septic system, benefiting the consumer and the environment.

CS 20.8.
Constructing the Porpoise Point Ecohouse.

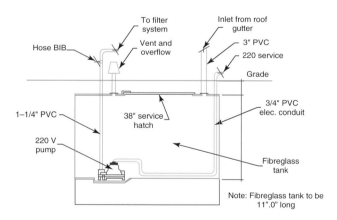

CS 20.9.
Plan of the cistern.

LESSONS LEARNED

Three years have passed since construction completion, during which time there have been eight hurricanes (in this area). While each hurricane brought rain, wind and racked nerves, the Porpoise Point Ecohouse has been left unscathed. Last year, Hurricane Wilma brought atypical floods, however the house was designed to withstand tidal surges and rising waters. CS 20.11 shows the watermark where water reached 92 cm high at the ground level floor. It was amazing how large debris like tree limbs and brush somehow 'squeezed' its way through door openings as a result of the water pressure bowing the metal door from its hinges. With regards to energy performance, we have not instrumented the house to date, however electric consumption is about 30 per cent less than the average home of the same size in

CS 20.10.
Combination sink/toilet.

this area. This efficiency has not motivated the owner to warrant instrumentation because it is performing as simulated and expected. For more information about this home or energy-efficient building in hot, humid environments, contact: sthomas@ fsec.ucf.edu

21 VANCOUVER HEALTHY HOUSING PROJECT

Architect:
Habitat Design and Consulting

Client:
Canada Mortgage and Housing Corporation

Monitoring:
SAR Engineering

Location:
Vancouver, British Columbia

Climate:
Cool temperate

Area:
137 m²

CS 21.1.
Vancouver Healthy Housing Project.

CS 21.2.
Nicol graph for Vancouver.

ECOFEATURES

• Healthy materials • Infill housing • Renewable energy • Combination water and space heating • Energy-efficient appliances

DESCRIPTION/BRIEF

This project, a winning design for a competition sponsored by the Canada Mortgage & Housing Corporation, explores the extensive use of materials which have the least impact on the environment and the occupants that they surround. The project also demonstrates a reduction of operating energy consumption to one quarter of that of conventional construction, thereby significantly reducing greenhouse gas emissions. Indoor finish materials were selected to reduce chemical emissions which, in combination with continuously operating heat recovery ventilation systems, ensures optimum indoor air quality. Wall, roof and floor assemblies were analysed for their embodied energy and embodied pollution content. As part of the competition, this infill concept increases the supply of modestly priced or rental housing stock in the city and it meets the housing needs of three growing segments of the Canadian population: single parent families, first time home buyers and retired couples. The project incorporates many technical innovations, in particular regarding the design of the building envelope and mechanical system. Although reputable researchers and practitioners support these strategies, there is considerable resistance to their implementation by Building Departments. This is often due to the hesitancy for building authorities to embrace new ideas, but also due to their lack of up-to-date technical knowledge of the inspectors, and the conservative nature of Building Codes (which are usually lagging somewhat behind state-of-the-art technology).

Materials selection

Each material used in this project was reviewed extensively for its impact on indoor air quality, operating energy, sustainability, maintainability, embodied energy and carbon dioxide content. Various wall, floor and ceiling construction options were analysed for their embodied energy and carbon dioxide emissions. The calculations of conventional wall, floor and ceiling assemblies are compared in Figure CS 21.3 to the Healthy House wall, floor and ceiling assemblies.

While the Healthy House wall assembly quantitatively has more CO_2 emissions (due to cement products) it has less embodied energy and has a higher thermal resistance due to the increased insulation values. The blown-in insulation is made from recycled newspaper and the rigid insulation allows an increased thermal barrier. These improvements outweigh the minimal increase in embodied energy.

Careful attention is necessary when looking at all aspects of a material's performance, as well as its effects. The advanced framing methods led to savings in lumber and sheathing material, and the open web joists saved a great deal of lumber in the floor and roof framing. However, due to the complex roof design, the structural requirements mandated the use of heavy laminated beams used as ridge and valley timbers. While these solutions use more steel and lumber than conventional, less complex designs, the Healthy House project proves that this compromise is acceptable to achieve the code requirements and optimise the spatial qualities and contextual character of the house.

Layout

The quality of the spaces within the Healthy House project was as viable to the success of this project as the choice of materials. Having limited space, the strategy included open plan rooms with double height ceilings to make the space feel bigger. Bringing natural light into the house was an objective that needed careful consideration so that privacy was still preserved due to the proximity of neighbouring homes. The primary living space is located above the garage. The single bedroom with a private patio, bathroom, laundry and entry is located at grade next to the garage. The loft above the main living area provides alternate possibilities, i.e. a study, office or children's room.

Embodied Energy * and CO2 Emissions From Production ** Estimate:

B: Conventional Wall Section, 2x6 framing (per M2)

Material	Energy Total (megajoules)		CO2 Emissions (grams)	
Gypsum Board	60	12%	3450	20%
Polyethy ene Sheet	4	0.8%	71	0.4%
Kiln Dried Softwood	49	10%	3314	20%
Fibreglass Batt	40	8%	1663	10%
Oriented Strand Board	135	26%	1447	9%
Asphalt Sheathing Paper	8	2%	248	1%
P.V.C. Siding	215	42%	6765	40%
TOTALS	512		16958	

* Embodied Energy is approximate energy use for production from all fuel types including enegy content of petroleum feedstocks.
** CO2 emissions indicates approximate release of CO2 incurred in production. Transportation to site not included.

D: Conventional Floor Section, 2x10 framing, G.W.B ceiling (per M2)

Material	Energy Total (megajoules)		CO2 Emissions (grams)	
Exterior Softwood Ply.	106	49%	6346	48%
Kiln Cried Softwood	52	24%	3488	26%
Gypsum Board	60	28%	3450	26%
TOTALS	218		13284	

F: Conventional Pitch Roof, joists & asphalt shingles, G.W.B. ceiling (per M2).

Material	Energy Total (megajoules)		CO2 Emissions (grams)	
Asphalt Shingles	284	41%	6468	31%
Oriented Strand Board	186	27%	1990	10%
Kiln Dried Softwood	82	12%	5486	26%
Fiberglass batt	80	11%	3328	16%
Polyethylene Sheet	4	1%	71	0.3%
Gypsum Board	60	9%	3450	17%
TOTALS	696		20793	

C: Healthy House Wall Section, advanced framing 2x6 with airtight drywall and rain screen (per M2).

Material	Energy Total (megajoules)		CO2 Emissions (grams)	
Fibre Reinf. Gypsum Bd.	40	18%	2165	10%
P.V.C. Gasket	2	1%	52	0%
Kiln Dried Softwood	44	20%	2919	14%
Cellulose Fibre (Recyc.)	5	2%	235	1%
Steel Bracing	7	3%	490	2%
Fiberglass rigid insul.	29	13%	933	4%
Polyolefin Sheet	8	4%	146	1%
Autoclaved Mineral-Cement Siding	85	39%	13999	67%
TOTALS	220		20939	

E: Healthy House Floor Section, open web joist, rim insulation and F.R.G.B. ceiling (per M2).

Material	Energy Total (megajoules)		CO2 Emissions (grams)	
Exterior Softwood Ply.	128	44%	7616	43%
Kiln Dried Softwood	30	10%	2012	11%
Galv. Steel Fasteners-(steel web)	73	25%	4826	28%
Fibre Reinf. Gypsum Bd.	40	14%	2165	12%
Al Foil Backed Ply.	15	5%	858	5%
P.V.C. Gasket	2	1%	52	0%
TOTALS	288		17529	

G: Healthy House Roof, steel web joists with fiber cement shingle F.R.G.B. ceiling (per M2).

Material	Energy Total (megajoules)		CO2 Emissions (grams)	
Fiber Reinf. Cement Shing.	170	46%	27998	71%
Kiln Dried Softwood	58	16%	3863	10%
Galv. Steel Fasteners-(steel web)	58	16%	3830	10%
Cellulose Fibre (Recyc.)	11	3%	565	1%
Fiberglass rigid insul.	29	13%	933	4%
P.V.C. Gasket	2	1%	52	0.1%
Fibre Reinf. Gypsum Bd.	40	11%	2165	5%
TOTALS	368		39406	

CS 21.3.
Comparing embodied energy and carbon dioxide emissions between conventional levels and Healthy House levels.

Ventilation, space and water heating

The domestic hot water, space heating and ventilation systems are integrated. The main heating source is a 94 per cent efficient sealed combustion condensing gas domestic water tank. Due to the low heating load of the building the gas hot water tank and solar domestic water heater and passive gains through southward facing windows will provide the total space heating requirements. A fan coil unit is used to transfer heat from the domestic hot water tank to the space. This low temperature heat exchanger prevents burning of dust as would occur in a conventional furnace heat exchanger. A low toxicity stainless steel cased heat recovery ventilator is used to provide continuous

CS 21.4.
Timber and steel structures in the roof.

ventilation. Preheated ventilation air is supplied to the continuously operating fan coil for distribution. To enhance ventilation efficiency and minimise discomfort, the air supplied by the fan coil is delivered through ceiling diffusers and return air is picked up under windows. A high arrestance bag filter and an activated carbon filter are located upstream of the air handler to remove fine particles and odours.

Energy-efficient appliances and water conserving fixtures

A house water filter was chosen to remove by-products of chlorination and to increase alkalinity to safeguard the fixtures against the acidic waters supplied in Vancouver. Off-the-shelf low flow fixtures and 7 litre low flush toilets were used. This was projected to cut consumption by 50 per cent. However, monitored studies showed that

CS 21.5.
East elevation.

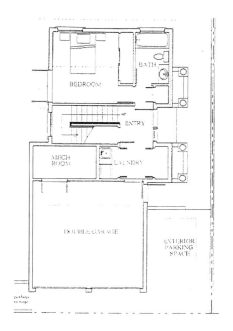

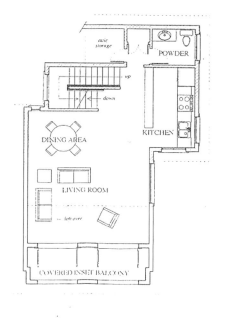

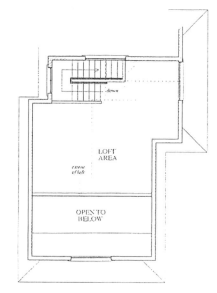

GROUND FLOOR PLAN

MAIN FLOOR PLAN

UPPER FLOOR PLAN

CS 21.6.

Plans of the house.

hot water usage varied from 87 to 116 per cent of typical usage in British Columbia, pointing to the need for more consumer education.

LESSONS LEARNED AND FIXED

1   Passive solar approaches work well, as does a R2000 type construction. The latter produces more hot water than can be used at present.
2   The exterior insulating sheathing 4 cm of dense fibreglass was found not to be vermin-proof. Additional sealing at the bottom of the exterior fibre-cement siding solved the problem.
3   The solar domestic water heating system works well but the 'learning-curve' on installation was steep. This installation seems to reflect the current state of development of this technology in North America. Components work well individually, and support is good. The problems arise with integration. Systems are not sold as complete and fully integrated packages. In this case it is all the more essential that systems should be described with clear instructions of how components contribute to a comprehensive installation. Perhaps this will improve as systems become more widely used.

CS 21.7.

Air handler coil/hot water furnace.

ACKNOWLEDGEMENTS/CONTACT INFORMATION

Chris Mattock, Vancouver, BC, Canada – e-mail: mattock@helix.net
David Rousseau, Vancouver, B.C. – e-mail: drouss@oberon.ark.com
Peter Clement, Clement Investments
Special thanks go to the following for having helped make this project a success:
Canada Mortgage & Housing Corporation, Poco Lumber, Can-Cel Industries,

Mansonville Plastics, Fiberglass Canada, Conservation Energy Systems, Nutek Plastics, Louisianna Pacific, Advanced Insulation, Dynamic Windows, ERV Parent, Glidden Paint, White Westinghouse, American Standard, Gough Electric, Int'l Waterguard Industries, Truswall Corp., Colin Campbell & Sons, Archemy Consulting Ltd, Signature Flooring, Envirosafe 2000 Cabinets, Inform, Trademark Carpets.

CS 21.8.
Stainless steel recovery ventilator.

22 TUNISIA SOLAR HOUSE/PAVILION

Designer:
National School for Engineers

Client:
Experimental

Location:
Tunis. Tunisia above sea level

Climate:
Pretty warm

Area:
66 m²

CS 22.1.
Tunisia Solar House/Pavilion.

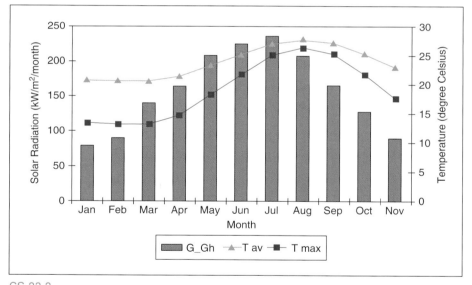

CS 22.2.
Nicol graph for Tunisia.

ECOFEATURES

• Orientation • Sloped site • Thermal mass • Trombe wall • Aerodynamic shape • Shading elements

DESCRIPTION/BRIEF

The Tunisia Solar House, built by the National School for Engineers, explores the use of a passive heating element and a Trombe wall, among other features, in identical

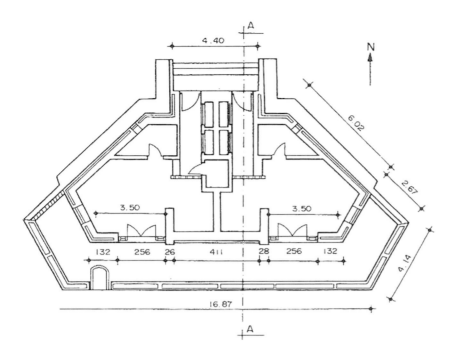

and adjacent units that total 66 m² in area. These units are monitored in side-by-side comparisons, over long periods of time with a 48-channel data logger recording outside temperatures every hour. Inside air and surface temperatures, together with temperatures at the interface of materials inside the walls, further quantify the effects that the eco-features pose on the units.

Orientation/site

The construction presents a large façade with a passive heating element and a Trombe wall facing towards the south (see Figure CS 22.3). The north façade is much smaller and degrades into the ground due to the site sloping from the north to the south (see Figure CS 22.4). The units were sited between two other buildings in order to protect them from cold north and northwest winds. The aerodynamic shape decreases the wind pressure on the sides that are potentially exposed to the prevailing winds. The shape forces windows to face 45° south of east and west.

Thermal mass

The construction materials of the west unit consist of an inner layer of 35 cm stone, an insulation of 6 cm cork and an outer layer of 6.5 cavity bricks resulting in a thermal capacity of $U = 0.51 \, W\,m^2\,C^{-1}$. The east unit has a double layer of cavity bricks separated by 6 cm of cork insulation, which provides a higher insulator but lower thermal capacity (U value = 43). The floor is a 10 cm concrete slab with 4 cm of cork insulation on 15 cm of stone. The cork is placed under the stone in the floor of south area, which is subject to direct solar radiation. This strategy helps increase thermal storage of the radiation. The roof is a 20-cm-thick concrete slab with 4 cm of cork on the outward side topped with a reflective coating for summer radiation reflectance. The high level of insulation is not customary in Tunisian dwellings. The Trombe wall for each unit is made of 35 cm stone and protected by a single glazing but without night insulation. The assembly (detail A and B in Figure CS 22.4) is indicative of the very high thermal capacity and high insulative quality in each unit's wall construction.

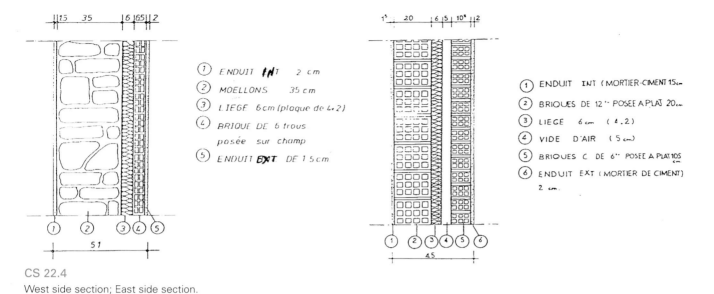

CS 22.4

West side section; East side section.

Measured performance

One of the most successful features of this experiment was the fact that the units were monitored side by side with all aspects the same except for the wall assemblies respective to each direction (see Thermal mass paragraph). The graphs in Figure CS 22.5 quantify the contribution of each component or compare different modes of operation as specified in the table.

Testing the contribution of design components

Label of test	Period of test	Direct gain shutters	Trombe wall	R
EH1	12/05–12/14	Open in daytime; closed at night	Vents open in daytime; closed at night	0
EH2	12/15–13/31	Closed day and night	Vents open in daytime; closed at night	0.340
EH3	01/01–01/14	Closed day and night	Vents closed day and night	0.408
EH4	01/15–01/31	Closed day and night	Vents closed day and night. Wall masked with a plywood panel	0.933
EH6	01/10–02/15	Open in daytime; closed at night	Vents closed day and night. Wall masked with a plywood panel	0.257

Effect of the Trombe wall

Without the direct gain element we can compare sequence EH4 in CS 22.5 with no elements functional, with sequence EH2, where only the Trombe wall is functional and notice that in both cases the room temperature is quite constant with no peaks during midday. In the presence of the direct gain element, we compare EH6 with EH1 and the average increase of temperature due to the operation of the Trombe wall is about 2.5°C.

Effect of the heating element

In the absence of the Trombe wall, comparison for EH4 and EH6 indicates that the average indoor room temperature rises from 14.3°C to 17.3°C under the effect of the direct gain element only. In the presence of the Trombe wall, results for EH2 and EH1

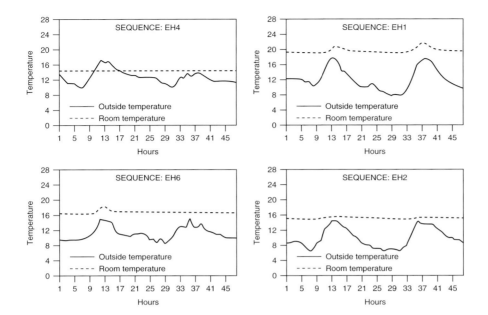

CS 22.5.
Temperature graphs.

show improvements due to a direct gain in temperature of 4.3°C. The effect of the direct gain element seems to be more substantial in the presence of the Trombe wall. However, this result should be corrected to take into account the climatic conditions for the test.

Underground duct

A cooling chimney is integrated by way of an underground duct which pulls air from a shaded area about 30 m from the pavilion. The air crosses under the garden about 80 cm below and is refreshed by the cold and humid soil above. The inlet into the pavilion on the north side and an air flue were added later to blow air near the ceiling of the sitting room, with the aid of a 30 W fan. However, operation of the underground duct when night ventilation is active has shown to be disadvantageous. This is because room air in the case of night ventilation is cooler than blown air from the underground duct.

Overheating prevention

During the first two summers after the pavilion was constructed the room air temperature exceeded the midday peak of ambient temperature. This high thermal mass is valuable in ensuring coolness but cannot be efficient alone. Some measures were apparent at the time of construction and some steps are operating modes or modifications performed only in summer time (see Lessons learned). Horizontal overhangs project over the south façade to limit direct radiation between mid-April through mid-September. The same 45° angled walls that provide aerodynamic wind protection during the winter also provide vertical projections for protecting the southeast and southwest walls in the summer. The Trombe wall is covered with white chalk or sometimes a plywood sheathing during the hot season. The Trombe wall also has an operating mode that is distinctive to each season (see CS 22.6c).

LESSONS LEARNED

The direct gain element provides more energy than the Trombe wall, but the high temperature of the inner face of the wall is an appreciable element of comfort; however,

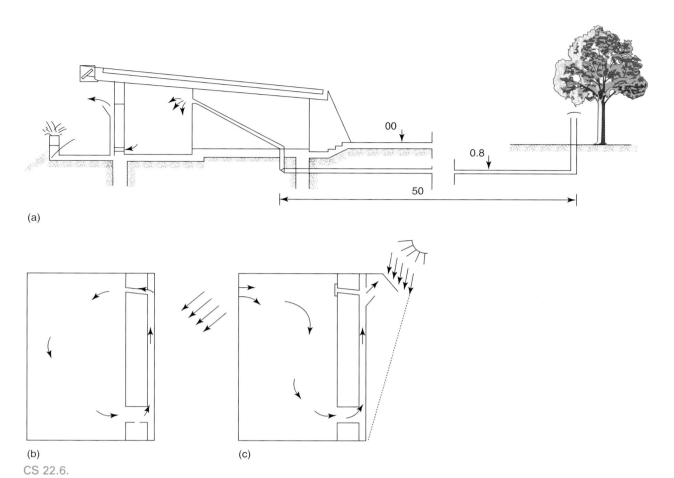

CS 22.6.
(a) Section showing underground duct and cooling chimney; (b) and (c) Ventilation is reactive to the seasons.

the thermal circulation in the Trombe wall air gap is not effective in the mild climate of Tunisia. The combined effects of the two elements are not completely additive but are complementary; those of the direct gain occurring most in the daytime, and those of the Trombe wall in the evening. The actual Trombe wall with its thickness of 35 cm of stones is a bit excessive. For this wall, double glazing is of little help and is not cost-effective. Thermal insulation is decisive for the average level of room temperature but thermal capacity allows for the temperature to remain stable, therefore this study has demonstrated that in the Tunisian climate proper design and use of passive components can guarantee a heating autonomy at a low cost.

ACKNOWLEDGEMENTS/CONTACT INFORMATION

This study would not have been successful without the help of the following:
National School of Engineers in Tunis (Tel: 216-71 87 47 00; Fax: 216-71 87 27 29);
Nadia Grahab-Morcos: nadia.ghrab@enit.rnu.tn;
Chiheb Bouden: chiheb.bouden@enit. rnu.tn;
Robert Franchisseur.

23 PRIVATE MOUNTAIN HIDEAWAY

Architect/Designer:
Johan Vorster

Owner:
Richard Bowsher and Monique Schiess

Steel Manufacturer:
Braam Mouton

Location:
Cedarberg, South Africa 32°33' S,
19°15' W 400 m above sea level

Climate:
Hot summers, wet, brief winters,
occasional snow

Area:
150 m²

CS 23.1.
West elevation.

CS 23.2.
West elevation (under construction).

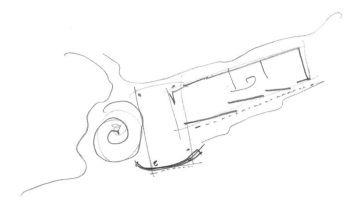

ECOFEATURES

• Climatically responsive design and materials • Adaptive roof and cross-ventilation • Compost toilets • Grey water system • Photovoltaics • Solar hot water

DESCRIPTION/BRIEF

The remote site is located in the Cedarberg Mountains (approximately 3 hours from Cape Town, South Africa). The Cedarberg is an ancient mountain range consisting of weathered Table Mountain sandstone. It lies on the cusp of the Fynbos and Karoo biomes and is extremely rich in plant diversity. The landscape is dry and rocky and the climate has long, hot summers and brief, cold, wet winters (300 mm annual rainfall).

The clients' brief was for a simple weekend 'hideaway' for small groups (up to 12 people) that they could part self-build. Spatial requirements included a two-bedroom main unit with lounge, kitchen, dining and ablutions, a large external living area, and three separate guest suites, washroom and garage outbuilding.

Of primary importance was a design that was 'thermally stable' and would be able to cope with the extreme fluctuations in temperature and season, and a structure which was easy to construct and maintain – that would be able to withstand the harsh environmental elements of the site (including baboons and veld fires).

CS 23.3.
View to the north.

SITE ANALYSIS AND DESIGN RESPONSE

A specific site was selected on a small rocky outcrop overlooking a perennial freshwater stream as it satisfied the client's 'wants' list. It had to be: accessible via a road, near the water and rock-pools, out of the floodplain, have magnificent views of the mountains and 'disappear' into the landscape. This culminated in a site selection that is predominantly west facing – a severe design challenge for the region.

With two distinct seasons the design response was to create two primary components: a large 'canopy' (primary outdoor living space), and a compact well-insulated 'house' for winter. The plan form evolved in response to the strict site constraints and to eliminate unwanted west solar gain whilst retaining views to the south.

All roofs are pre-manufactured steel structures and are set at discreetly low pitches and coloured to blend into the landscape. (Steel sheds are prevalent in this rural region.) This 'two-stage' construction process allows for precision structures to be completed prior to the 'self-build' team

CS 23.4.
View to the south.

CS 23.5.
Axonometric schematic.

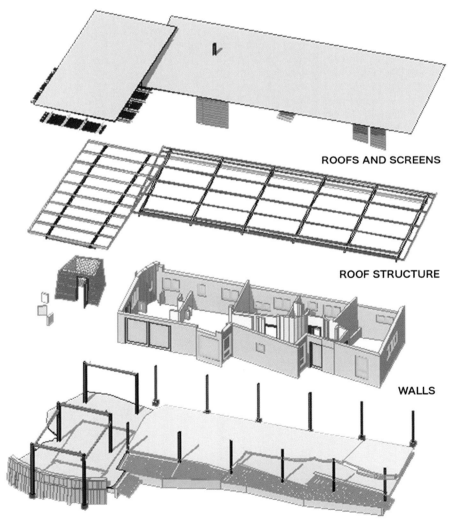

ROOFS AND SCREENS

ROOF STRUCTURE

WALLS

FLOORS AND PLINTH

moving on site. It also allows for work to be carried out in the shade during the hot summer months (and under roof in the rain).

PASSIVE DESIGN

- A heavy mass construction was selected with extensive natural (locally sourced) stone and exposed masonry to act as thermal sink and stabilise internal temperatures throughout the year.
- The roof has been double-insulated; 25 mm isoboard to the underside of the sheeting and a further 80 mm isotherm over the timber ceiling. The void has been designed to allow summer heat to ventilate at the apex during summer. (It is closable in winter to increase heat retention and improve comfort levels.)
- 'Landscaped ceiling'/section – to allow natural migration of warm air to apex vents/windows.
- Minimisation of west façade – section reduces to the west and the plan form, together with the sliding screens, eliminates west solar gain whilst allowing for free ventilation.
- Strategic placement of windows and opening configurations to maximise cross-ventilation for all anticipated wind directions.
- All openings were computer simulated to ensure maximum effect of the solar screening.

ACTIVE SYSTEMS

The entire project is off-grid:

- Solar PVs for all lighting and electrical requirements
- Solar pump from river to tanks
- Solar hot water
- Composting toilets
- Vertical grey water system
- Gas cooker
- Morso wood-burning fireplace.

CS 23.6.

ACKNOWLEDGEMENT/CONTACT INFORMATION

Johan Vorster – e-mail: arcedc@icon.co.za

24 NUEVA DEMOCRACIA, AFFORDABLE HOUSING PROJECT (SUSTAINABLE IMPROVEMENT PROSPOSAL 2006)

CS 24.1.

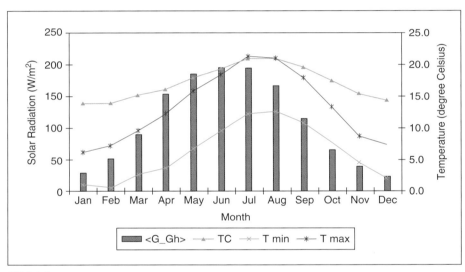

CS 24.2.

Architects:
Andres Echeverría, Pablo La Roche, Marina Gonzalez

Thermal performance improvements:
Pablo La Roche, Daniel Velazco

Location:
Maracaibo, Venezuela • 10°40'N, 71°36'W • 40 m above sea level

Climate:
Hot and humid

Area:
90–140 m²

ECOFEATURES

• Affordable and climatically adaptable • 'Growable' • Natural ventilation
• Shading • Green roof ready

DESCRIPTION/BRIEF

Nueva Democracia is a 900-unit affordable housing project in Maracaibo, Venezuela that was born as an informal settlement, initially occupied by a group of people on the 25 of January, 1994. The State Government successfully negotiated their peaceful withdrawal, promising to develop a project for the 25 hectare lot and help the '*invasores*' organise legally to buy the land. In doing this, this large extension of land began its process to become part of the formal city. To achieve this, the community, the University and the State Government worked together between 1994 and 1996 in the design and construction of this project, which was built in several phases, and promoted social orginisation of the communities at the urban, neighbourhood, and dwelling levels.

At all levels the project was designed so that it could be usable and livable with a minimum investment by the government and the people. All urban spaces and houses have been continuously developed by members of the community – the main owners of the spaces.

URBAN PROPOSAL SUSTAINABLE PRINCIPLES

- Raticnalisation of the occupation and use of the space, to optimise organisation of the infrastructure and reduce urbanism costs in a medium-density project.
- Minimisation of public and semi-public areas, which are difficult to maintain and control, whilst increasing privately-owned spaces where the owner(s) are responsible for their maintenance (61.28 per cent) private space, 11.23 per cent semi-private space, and only 14.24 per cent semi-public and 13.25 per cent public).
- Increase in the physical controls of the spaces for collective use, through the adequate definition of borders, properties and space uses.

CS 24.3.
Urban layout.

• Strengthening, through design of the space and the social organisation, of community integration so that the community supports the evolution and improvement of the housing and its urbanism.

HABITATS THAT GROW WITH THE FAMILY

The houses were designed to grow with the owner and there is no doubt that this has happened. The initial houses were 30 m² and could grow up to comfortable two-storey 140 m² dwellings. The rate of growth varied according to the families' possibilities and necessities. The minimum was a multiple-use living/sleep space with bath and laundry, which could grow to a house with five bedrooms, living room, dining room, kitchen, laundry room, backyard, front yard and internal patio, porch and car parking space. The potential owner could buy what they needed, according to their debt capacity. The house is a succession of geometrical elements, from an 'I' to an 'L' to a 'C', enclosing courtyards that provide light and ventilation to the interior spaces. Initial costs were slightly higher to permit growth, but the house had more flexibility.

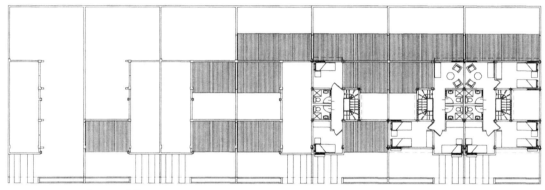

Second floor

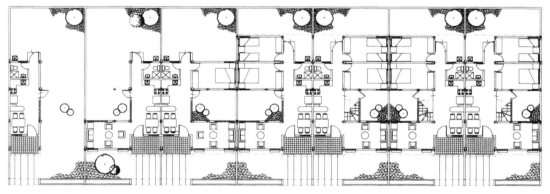

First floor

CS 24.4.
Plan showing the 'growable' scheme.

Practically all of the houses have grown way beyond their initial phases and some of them way beyond recognition. In their quest for individualisation the owners have personalised them and made them their own. This is the purpose of a project such as this – to provide a home for the family and support as the family evolves.

STRATEGIES IMPLEMENTED AND LESSONS LEARNED

Maracaibo, located at sea level and ten degrees north of the equator, has a hot and humid climate and adapting to this climate was an important project consideration. The most important strategies implemented to achieve thermal comfort were natural ventilation through windows to promote evaporative cooling from the body, and shade to reduce solar gains inside the house. Key components were the interior courtyard and the shaded 'condominium' open spaces. (The houses had some thermal capacity but no insulation. An energy code was only approved for Maracaibo in 2005 and insulation was not used in buildings before this, much less in affordable housing.)

These two strategies have worked well but unfortunately many of the owners have covered their courtyards and backyards to convert them to interior spaces, reducing air circulation inside the houses. Many of these spaces are now air-conditioned, but because they are poorly insulated they require much energy for cooling to offset solar gains, so the owner can't always afford to operate them. The increase in enclosed air-conditioned spaces also reduced airflow overall and increases air temperatures around the houses. By being flexible and permitting growth the design has been successful, but some limits should have been established for when the modifications would negatively affect the performance of the house.

CS 24.5.
Image of hallway towards courtyard.

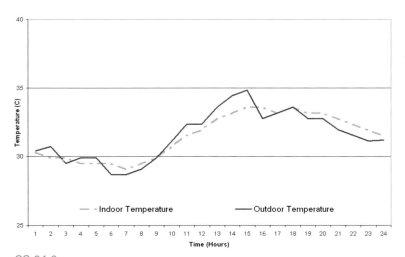

CS 24.6.
Temperature graph of temperatures in house with courtyard.

Because of some of these negative home alterations and the increase in the heat island effect, Nueva Democracia's habitants are increasingly dissatisfied with thermal conditions inside dwellings. To improve these conditions several solutions have been developed and will be presented to the community for discussion and implementation. Four strategies are proposed, the first three to be implemented in their homes and the last one in the condominium spaces:

1 Reduce solar gains through windows by shading with internal or external elements, pergolas, trees, or extending the overhang.
2 Reduce heat gains through the roof by: a) Adding internal insulation with a ceiling system that is readily available b) Installing an extensive vegetated roof in the horizontal concrete slab or in sections of this slab, which was designed to support a second storey.
3 Increase cross-ventilation in incorrectly modified and improperly ventilated spaces by adding windows so that all spaces have openings in more than one wall.
4 Increase the area of exterior green surfaces whilst reducing paved heat-absorbing areas, and promote the planting of more trees. This will also reduce the temperature of the surfaces close to the houses, whilst increasing the amount of water that goes underground.

All of these measures will contribute to the public good by reducing the heat island effect, improving thermal comfort in unconditioned houses and reducing electricity consumption in air-conditioned spaces.

This project demonstrates that it is possible for the government, the community and the designers to work as a team to generate solutions adapted to local problems.

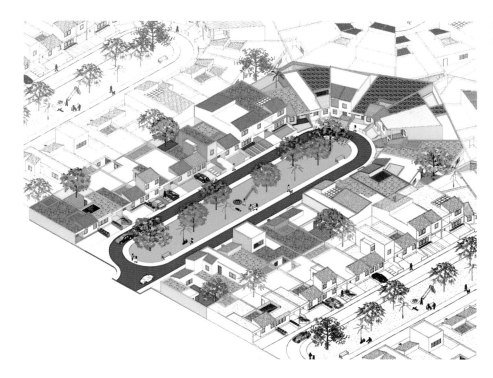

Dialogue and hard work by the community and designers permitted an area that was going to become part of the informal sector to be integrated into the city. This is a simple idea that if repeated more often could generate interesting architectural solutions in other cities of developing countries.

CONTACT

Pablo La Roche – e-mail: pmlaroche@csupomona.edu
Marina Gonzalez de Kauffman – e-mail: marinakauffman@cantr.net

25 MANUFACTURED HOUSING

CS 25.1.

Manufactured Home Builder:
Palm Harbor Homes – this example shows 'The Bellaire' model at Arietta Reserve (Mike Wnek)

Location:
Global

Climate:
All climates – built worldwide

Area:
84–325 m²

DESCRIPTION/BRIEF

Ever since the automobile industry demonstrated that mass production could be used to manufacture objects as large as a car, the same production techniques have been applied to housing. The hope was the prefabricated or manufactured homes would result in not only safe, affordable housing, but be of high quality, accessible and affordable. The prefabricated or manufactured homes were historically known as 'kit' homes and the first ones were offered in 1906 by Sears & Roebuck catalogues as a 'house by mail'. The most notable ones sold by Sears & Reobuck by mail came complete with lumber, nails, shingles and instructions (Kieran and Timberlake, 2004). Even the famous French born Le Corbusier and Walter Gropius, founder of Bauhaus, mass produced housing schemes modelled on American automotive production processes. These schemes and mail order home kits still required assembly on site. The next generation was the factory-assembled homes. General House Corporation would act as assembler in 1932, becoming the General Motors of the housing industry. Even Frank Lloyd Wright was asked to design an 'affordable home' developed not as a prefab system but rather a grid system that established modular dimensions. This timeline would establish the foundation for today's generation of manufactured housing, incorporating quality, affordable and aesthetically pleasing habitats. So will the future add eco-friendly strategies to the next era of manufactured homes? There are several companies offering 'optional' features that include energy-efficient, environmentally friendly and hurricane-resistant strategies. We have yet to find a company where all of these 'optionals' become standard. Just then they will perhaps include 'adaptable' strategies for the changing climate (i.e. increased building mass to insulate against rising and lowered ambient temperatures).

CS 25.2.
Spartan Aircraft Company built mobile trailers like this one in 1951 (Source: Spartantrailer.com and James Edwards).

CS 25.3.
Homes of Merit. This is a typical HUD-code home built today in the US market.

FROM TRAILERS TO DESIRABLE LIVING ENVIRONMENTS

There are four major segments of factory-built homes: HUD-Code homes (still often referred to as mobile homes although more often called manufactured homes); modular homes (shipped in three-dimensional sections); panelised homes (walls, floors, and roof shipped to site for construction); and production-built homes (built on-site by large-volume home builders who use factory-built components).

In the past the manufactured homes have received a bad reputation. In the 70s when the manufactured housing industry was attracting entrepreneurs, a lot of cookie cutter 'trailers' rolled out into communities worldwide. While these were 'new' and even popular they were perceived as cheap, aesthetically displeasing and even today are still energy hogs as a whole. For the purpose of this case study, manufactured housing will be discussed.

Over the past decade, the rate of growth of the manufactured housing industry has been dramatic. According to the US Census Bureau, manufactured homes accounted for nearly a quarter of all new single-family housing starts during the 1990s. Affordability is a key factor in the growth of manufactured housing, and one of the main reasons increasing numbers of consumers are choosing a manufactured home. At an average cost of $51 300 as of 2002, it is clear that a manufactured home is much more affordable than a site-built home at an average cost of $174 140 (excluding land price). With regards to the idea that manufactured homes were designed on a chassis and able to be transported or relocated, the reality is that the percentage of homes that are actually mobile remains low – only 6 per cent of those surveyed have moved the home from one location to another in the last three years (http://www.manufacturedhousing.org/understanding_today2004/cost_size.htm).

The twentieth century brought dreams of an attainable off-site architecture and many designs still transform the market into a competitive playing field against site-built construction. Manufactured housing isn't just considered 'affordable housing' anymore. The 'mobile' home has evolved into modular, quality controlled, construction governed by local jurisdictions just like site-built. Yet the industry still only produces a mere fraction of the overall housing market.

In Japan, 1.25 million homes were built in 2003. Thirteen per cent of these homes were modular or panelised. This is a declining market share for factory-built housing. Ten years ago 20 per cent of Japanese housing was factory-built. In Sweden, only 5 per cent of the housing market is made up of modulars. While the US is the largest consumer for the manufactured housing market, Japan is building the most PV integrated and self-sufficient manufactured homes with models like Misawa Home Z by

CS 25.4.
Parfait AE by Sekisui Chemical Company.

CS 25.5.
Misawa Home Z.

Misawa Holdings Company and Parfait E by Sekisui Chemical Company. These two companies are partnering with lending institutions to offer low interest rates (as low as 2.9 per cent) for units with PV power systems.

THE MANUFACTURED HOME'S ROLE FOR ADAPTING TO CLIMATE CHANGE

As our climate begins to change and we are forced to build adaptable structures of shelter, the manufactured housing industry will have the advantage and likely be a leading producer of adaptable, portable and even hurricane-resistant construction. The United States Federal Emergency Management Administration (FEMA) uses the manufactured housing industry as a solution to housing needs during natural disasters. They procure 'ruggedised' (having only the bare necessities for temporary condition) manufactured homes to provide short-term housing solutions during the repair and rebuilding phase after a natural disaster and/or acts of terrorism. These homes are currently built with minimum amenities, designed for temporary use. However, it is becoming apparent that they need to provide long-term solutions, with the increasing number of disasters and the increased intensity of those disasters' impacts. The manufactured homes built today often consume more energy than their site-built comparatives, and use materials and mechanical systems that can potentially contribute to poor indoor air quality and low durability. These manufactured homes are typically about $90\,m^2$ and are transported to large open areas in proximity to affected homeowners. As the world witnessed Hurricane Katrina's havoc on the victims of the gulf states, especially those in Louisiana where major flooding occurred, FEMA responded by ordering the construction and purchasing of over 100 000 travel trailers and 25 000 manufactured homes. However, local neighbourhoods and jurisdictions cried NIMBY (not in my backyard) and refused to give permits for locating these structures in flood-prone areas, even temporarily.

A recent task, as part of the Building America Industrialized Housing Partnership, funded by the Department of Energy, was to develop an improved specification for FEMA to use while procuring temporary homes. Starting with the specifications from the base case of typically procured ruggedised home today, two specifications were developed: the EnergyStar (*ES*) and the Building America Structural Insulated Panel (*BASIP*) manufactured home. These were evaluated using the FSEC developed EnergyGauge® USA (Version 2.5.9) software which predicts building energy consumption. The *ES* home saved 14 per cent in energy costs over the base case, which amounts to savings of $25.9 million during the first year of existence ($4.5 million in energy savings and $21.4 million in construction costs) when procuring 25 000 ruggedised manufactured homes for temporary use.

The *BASIP* home, which has a roof integrated (3.25 kWp photovoltaic [PV] array) projects energy saving of 78 per cent or $25.4 million over the base case. The *BASIP* without the PV array would be about 38 per cent more energy-efficient than the base case (analysis based on units located in New Orleans, LA and utility rates of $0.13/kWh). The annual equivalent life cycle costs for the base case and the two alternatives were calculated to be $5413 per year, $3670 per year and $3649 per year for the base, *ES* and *BASIP* respectively.

Analysis considered not only tangible benefits such as having back-up power capability for essential loads during extended power outages, but also intangible benefits like more daylit spaces and potential mating of two units. The improved specification allows for better quality control of construction and also includes renewable energy strategies that encourage occupants to take ownership if the situation warrants. The inclusion of renewable energy would create a self-powered strategy that would provide power for essential functions during power outages and interferences associated with neighbourhood reconstruction following a natural disaster. It would also ensure minimal infrastructure establishment should the home need emergency relocation.

Providing high performance features with architecturally pleasing aesthetics is the next step in the eco-manufactured housing design strategy. The best examples, or case studies, for this are displayed each year at the National Mall in Washington DC and called the Solar Decathlon. The Solar Decathlon is a competition in which 20 teams of college and university students from around the world compete to design,

CS 25.7.
University of Massachusetts Dartmouth decathlon entry.

CS 25.8.
University of Maryland decathlon entry.

build and operate the most attractive, effective and energy-efficient solar-powered house. The Solar Decathlon is also an event to which the public is invited to observe the powerful combination of solar energy, energy-efficiency and the best in home design.

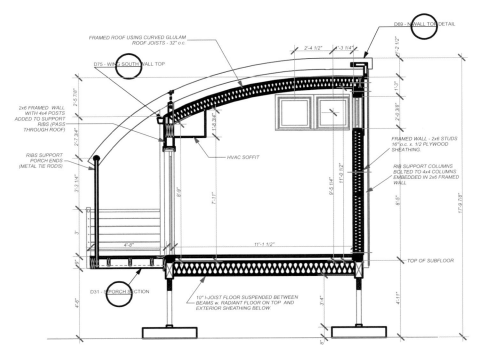

FRAMED ROOF USING CURVED GLULAM ROOF JOISTS - 32" o.c.

D75 - WING SOUTH WALL TOP

2x6 FRAMED WALL WITH 4x4 POSTS ADDED TO SUPPORT RIBS (PASS THROUGH ROOF)

RIBS SUPPORT PORCH ENDS (METAL TIE RODS)

HVAC SOFFIT

D69 - N WALL TOP DETAIL

FRAMED WALL - 2x6 STUDS 16" o.c. x. 1/2 PLYWOOD SHEATHING.

RIB SUPPORT COLUMNS BOLTED TO 4x4 COLUMNS EMBEDDED IN 2x6 FRAMED WALL

TOP OF SUBFLOOR

D31 - S PORCH SECTION

10" I-JOIST FLOOR SUSPENDED BETWEEN BEAMS w. RADIANT FLOOR ON TOP AND EXTERIOR SHEATHING BELOW.

CS 25.9.
University of Maryland decathlon entry – Section.

CS 25.10a and b.
University of Maryland decathlon entry – Interior views.

STRUCTURAL INSULATED PANELS (SIPS)

Typically, manufactured housing is stick-built in a factory with standard building materials. During the research to improve the specifications for the FEMA russedised home, the first strategy was to improve building insulation, whole building tightness and structural integrity. Pacific Northwest National Laboratory was the first to research the impacts of SIPs in a manufactured housing situation. They built and monitored the first SIPs HUD-code home and found that heating and cooling costs were 50 per cent less, the SIPs construction provided stronger and more rigid buildings and they were 50 per cent less leaky than the conventional manufactured home of the same size. With regards to costs, research by Texas A&M University for the 15th annual *Proceedings for Improving Building Systems in Hot and Humid Climates* found that of all building types SIPs were the most economical with regards to life cycle analysis and energy impact.

HIGH PERFORMANCE MECHANICAL SYSTEMS

Moving the air distribution within the thermal envelope not only improves the indoor air quality by reducing potential condensation problems but also provides zero per cent leakage within the ductwork; this further increased building tightness especially with the SIPs system as a roof/ceiling assembly. The air-conditioning system is typically ground mounted on-site once the home is located. This calls for a third party to install adding costs. The BASIP proposed to install a wall-mounted air-conditioning system that was properly sized and could be installed at the factory (and tested).

A whole house ventilation system is proposed with 40 cfm filtered outside air when the cool/heat system is operating. This keeps the house positively pressurised and eliminates the build-up of odours or other undesirable contaminants. This is needed because of the improved building tightness.

CS 25.11.

A wall section is lowered into place. Note the sealants along the base, the cutouts for the windows and the chases with the foam for wiring. (Photo: Michael Bâechler, Pacific Northwest National Laboratory.)

LESSONS LEARNED

Looking back over the years of the manufactured housing industry we have learned that thermal mass, proper sizing of the ventilation system, sealing ducts with mastic and proper location of thermal and vapour barriers have been the key strategies to eliminating building failures and improving thermal comfort. The catastrophic destruction in Figure CS 25.13 proves that minimally designed homes cannot withstand even the weak hurricanes. Decathlon entrants as well as the BASIP specification provide structural enhancement in specifying 2 × 6 construction, and/or SIPs, which allows for more thermal mass.

A lot of manufactured homes in hot and humid locations still use and install vinyl covered gypsum (vcg) and have found a lot of problems with mould and mildew as a result (vapour barrier on cool side in cooling dominated climate). Cost is the culprit

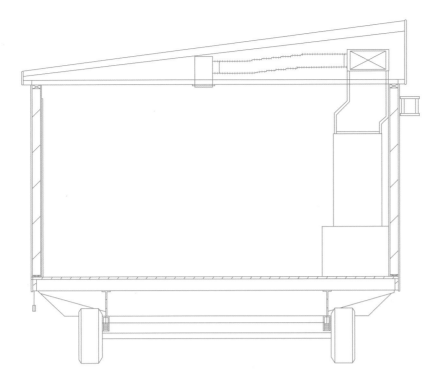

CS 25.12.
Manufactured home section showing air distribution system in 'conditioned space'.

CS 25.13.
One-quarter of a mobile home is missing, ripped up from the foundation and the entire roof is missing, yet the other three-quarters of the mobile home is still standing.

for this assembly still prevailing. The vcg eliminates a labour intensive process of mud, tape and painting and the vcg is easy to install. Providing properly sized ventilation equipment (rather than an oversized system that results in short cycling of the conditioning system hindering humidity removal), research has found that the vcg

CS 25.14.
Impermeable interior surfaces like vinyl wall coverings can result in severe mould problems in hot humid climates such as Florida's.

CS 25.15.
Mouldy ducts from duct leakage causing condensation.

can still be used with little negative effects. Some situations may call for additional humidity removal, i.e. demand dehumidifier in the winter. Properly-sealing ducts, especially those within an unconditioned attic, can not only reduce energy losses but deter condensation that could ultimately result in mould and mildew.

ACKNOWLEDGEMENTS/CONTACT INFORMATION

Palm Harbor Homes, The Bellaire, Mike Draper – e-mail: mdraper@palmharbor.com Building America Industralized Housing Partnership, Buildings Research, Subrato Chandra – e-mail: Subrato@fsec.ucf.edu

GLOSSARY

absorber
The blackened surface in a solar collector that absorbs solar radiation and converts it to heat.

absorptance
The ratio of absorbed to incident solar radiation on a surface.

aerobic
Having oxygen as a part of the environment. Growing or occurring only in the presence of oxygen.

air changes
A measure of the air exchange in a building. One air change is an exchange of a volume of air equal to the interior volume of a building.

air mass or AM
A specification for solar spectra; AM 1 is the spectrum for the shortest path through the atmosphere corresponding to the sun directly overhead (possible in the tropics); AM 1.5 is used for standard specifications because it represents the more typical condition of the sun at about 45° above the horizon.

altitude angle
The angular distance from the horizon to the sun.

amorphous silicon
A type of silicon in which the atoms have no order, as in glass, so it is not crystalline; also called thin-film silicon.

anaerobic
The absence of oxygen. Growing in the absence of oxygen.

annual specific yield
The actual electrical energy generated over 1 year divided by the peak power of the array; given in units of kWh per kWp (although a more precise notation would be $kWh\ year^{-1}\ kWp^{-1}$).

array
An assembly of several PV modules connected in series and/or parallel.

auxiliary heating
The conventional (i.e. non-solar) contribution to the total load (e.g. gas boiler, etc.).

azimuth angle
The angular distance between true south and the point on the horizon directly below the sun (negative before noon, positive after noon).

beam radiation
See 'direct solar radiation'.

berm
A man-made mound or small hill of earth, either abutting a house wall to help stabilise the internal temperature or positioned to deflect wind from the house.

biological dentrification
The biochemical reduction (conversion) of nitrate nitrogen to nitrite nitrogen and to the gaseous molecular nitrogen or an oxide of nitrogen.

black body
A perfect absorber and emitter of radiation. A cavity is a perfect black body. Lampblack is close to a black body, while aluminium (polished) is a poor absorber and emitter of radiation.

black water
Wastewater generated within a household, including toilet wastes.

calorific value
Describes the energy content of a unit mass or volume of a fuel (kWh kg^{-1}, J kg^{-1}, kWh m^{-3}, J m^{-3}).

carbon source
Carbon used as an energy source by anaerobic bacteria in the denitrification process.

casual gains
See 'internal gains'.

chimney or stack effect
The tendency of air or gas in a duct or other vertical passage to rise when heated owing to its lower density in comparison with that of the surrounding air or gas. In buildings, the tendency towards displacement (caused by the difference in temperature) of internal heated air by unheated outside air, owing to the difference in density of outside and inside air.

collector, fiat plate
An assembly containing a panel of metal or other suitable material, usually a flat black colour on its sun side, that absorbs sunlight and converts it into heat. This panel is usually in an insulated box, covered with glass or plastic on the sun side to take advantage of the greenhouse effect. In the collector, this heat transfers to a circulating fluid, such as air, water, oil or antifreeze.

collector, focusing
A collector that has a parabolic or other reflector that focuses sunlight onto a small area for collection. A reflector of this type can obtain considerably higher temperatures but will only work with direct-beam sunlight.

collector, solar
A device for capturing solar energy, ranging from ordinary windows to complex mechanical devices.

conduction
The heat moving from a warmer to a colder region in the same substance without mass transfer; this type of heat transfer depends on the thermal conductivity of the material.

convection
The mechanism of heat transfer between a surface and fluid.

creepway
Crawlspace beneath the ground floor of a house.

crystalline silicon
A type of silicon in which the atoms have a regular diamond-like structure; also called single crystal or polycrystalline.

declination of sun
The angle of the sun above or below the equatorial plane. It is positive if north of the plane and negative if below and varies day by day throughout the year from 23.47° on 3–21 June to 23.47° on 21 December.

degree days
The product of the number of degrees below a given base temperature and the number of days on which that difference occurs. The base temperature is usually defined between 15.5 and 21°C.

differential thermostat
A thermostat that operates on the basis of the temperature difference between two points. Blowers and pumps turn on or off depending on the magnitude of Δt.

diffuse solar radiation
The solar radiation as received on a surface with the exception of the solid angle subtended by the sun's disk (direct solar radiation). Solar radiation reaches the Earth indirectly through scattering in the atmosphere.

diffuse transmission
The type of solar transmission through a diffusing or translucent glazing, namely, transmission that is scattered by interaction with the glazing material. The diffuse transmitted radiation is assumed to be isotropic, that is, equally intense in all directions.

direct solar gains
Direct solar radiation passing through glass areas (mainly south-facing) that contributes to space heating (kWh).

direct solar radiation
The solar radiation from the solid angle of the sun's disk. Solar radiation reaching a surface in a straight line from the sun.

DSHW
Domestic solar hot water.

ecliptic
The great circle cut in the celestial sphere by an extension of the plane of the Earth's orbit. The great circle drawn on a terrestrial globe makes an angle of about 23°27' with the equator.

effluent
Sewage, water or other liquid, partially or completely treated or in its natural state, flowing out of any component of an ISDS or flowing beneath the ground surface in groundwater or over the ground surface.

electrical current
The rate of flow of positive charge in a circuit; units amps or A; symbol I.

emissivity
The ratio of the radiant energy emitted from a surface at a given temperature to the energy emitted by a black body at the same temperature.

extraterrestrial radiation
Solar radiation impinging on the Earth's outer atmosphere.

global irradiance
The sum of direct and diffuse irradiance. Glasshead Ltd. E-mail: tv@ glasshead.co.uk

grey water
Wastewater generated within a household consisting of sink, tub, shower and laundry wastewater, and excluding toilet wastes.

heat exchanger
A device, usually consisting of a coiled arrangement of metal tubing, used to transfer heat through the tube walls from one fluid to another.

heat load
The total energy required for space heating.

heat loss
Heat flow through building envelope components (walls, windows, roof, etc.).

heat pump
A thermodynamic device that transfers heat from one medium to another. The first medium (the source) cools while the second (the heat sink) warms up.

heating season
The period of the year during which heating the building is required to maintain comfort conditions.

heliodon
Device that simulates solar angles and measures the number of hours of potential sunshine.

hybrid solar heating system
Solar heating system that combines active and passive techniques.

I-V curve
Plot of current versus voltage for a PV cell, module or array as a load is increased from short circuit to open circuit under fixed conditions of irradiance and cell temperature.

incident angle
The angle between the sun's rays and a line perpendicular (normal) to the irradiated surface.

indirect gain
The indirect transfer of solar heat into the space to be heated from a collector that is coupled to the space by an uninsulated, conductive or convective medium (such as a thermal storage wall or roof pond).

infiltration
The uncontrolled movement of outdoor air into the interior of a building through cracks around windows and doors or in walls, roofs and floors. This may work by cold air leaking in during the winter or the reverse in the summer.

infrared radiation
Electromagnetic radiation having wave length above the range of visible light. This is the preponderant form of radiation emitted by bodies with moderate temperatures, such as the elements of a passive solar building.

insolation
A contraction of 'incoming solar radiation' meaning the amount of solar energy incident on a given area over a certain period of time; a common unit of insolation is $kW\ m^{-2}\ day^{-1}$, often referred to as peak hours per day.

internal gains
The energy dissipated inside the heated space by people (body heat) and appliances (lighting, cooker, etc.). A proportion of this energy contributes to the space heating requirements (kWh).

irradiance
Rate of incidence of solar energy on a flat surface at a particular angle of tilt (W m^{-2}).

isolated gain
The transfer of heat into the space to be heated from a collector that is thermally isolated from the space to be heated by physical separation or insulation (such as a convective loop collector or an attached sunspace with an insulated common wall).

juinling
Sun-shaped pattern at the end of a gabled roof.

kakkleoven
A traditional, European, wood-burning stove made of high-mass materials and typically covered with ceramic tiles.

khuh
Fragrant fibrous root that swells or bloats when soaked in water and can be woven into mats. Has been used traditionally as an evaporative cooling curtain, not a new technology.

kilowatt hour
Energy unit equivalent to 1000 W used for 1 hour; also referred as a unit of electricity: 1 kWh = 3.6 MJ.

latent heat of fusion
The amount of heat required to change the state of a substance from solid to liquid at constant temperature (e.g. ice to water at 0°C = 335 kJ kg^{-1}). The same amount of heat is liberated with a change of state in the reverse direction.

latitude
The angular distance north (+) or south (−) of the equator, measured in degrees of arc.

longitude
The arc of the equator between the meridian of a place and the Greenwich meridian measured in degrees east or west.

mean radiant temperature
The area weighted mean temperature of all surrounding surfaces, i.e. (s × t)/s, where t is the temperature of each surface of area, s. It is an approximate indication of the effect that the surface temperatures of surrounding objects have on human comfort.

open circuit voltage
The maximum voltage between the terminals of a PV cell or module when only connected by a voltmeter, so no current is flowing. Symbol is V_{oc}; (compare a 'macho body builder' of great strength but poor ability to move carrying a load).

orientation
The orientation of a surface is in degrees of variation away from solar south, towards either the east or west. Solar or true south should not be confused with magnetic south, which can vary owing to magnetic declination.

peak hours per day
An alternative unit to $kWh\ m^{-2}\ day^{-1}$ for daily insolation.

peak power
The maximum amount of power a PV module can generate under standard test conditions of irradiance and cell temperature; units of Wp (compare a 'wagon puller' who has both the strength to pull the load and can do so at speed).

per cent of possible sunshine
The actual number of hours of sunshine divided by the maximum possible number of hours of sunshine, expressed as a percentage for the month.

phase change material (p.c.m.)
A heat-storage medium which relies on the latent heat of phase transition for absorbing and releasing heat.

photovoltaic (PV)
The process of direct conversion of light into electricity within a material.

pyranometer
An instrument for measuring the solar irradiance on a plane surface. When the solar radiation coming from the sun's disk is obscured from the instrument, a pyranometer can be used to determine diffuse solar radiation.

radiant heat transfer
The transfer of heat by heat radiation. Heat radiation is a form of electromagnetic radiation. Radiant heating resulting from infrared radiation is very prevalent in passive systems.

RCC
Radiation control coating.

reflectance
The ratio or percentage of the amount of light reflected by a surface to the amount incident. Good light reflectors are not necessarily good heat reflectors.

relative humidity
The ratio of the amount of water vapour in the atmosphere to the maximum amount of water vapour that could be held at a given temperature.

rock bed
A container filled with rocks, pebbles or crushed stone, to store energy by raising the temperature of the rocks, etc.

selective surface (absorber)
A surface absorbing essentially all incident solar radiation (short wave – high-temperature source), while emitting a small fraction of thermal radiation (long wave – low-temperature source).

severs
Movable slats (like blinds) that can roll up or down.

short circuit current
The current between the terminals of a PV cell or module when only connected by an ammeter; symbol I_{sc} (compare a 'marathon runner' who is fast but only when not carrying any load).

solar constant
The irradiance of solar radiation beyond the Earth's atmosphere at the average Earth–sun distance on a surface perpendicular to the sun's rays. The value for the solar constant is $1.37\ kW\ m^{-2}$.

solar energy, useful
The amount of solar energy contributing to the total heat load. It is expressed in absolute figures (kWh) or per unit collector area ($kWh\ m^{-2}$).

solar fraction (or percentage solar)
The percentage of the total heat load supplied by the solar heating system, including useful losses from the storage.

solar radiation
The energy-carrying electromagnetic radiation emitted by the sun. This radiation comprises many frequencies, each relating to a particular class of radiation:

- high-frequency/short-wavelength ultraviolet;
- medium-frequency/medium-wavelength visible light;
- low-frequency/high-wavelength infrared.

This radiation is relatively unimpeded until it reaches the Earth's atmosphere. Here some of it will be reflected back out of the atmosphere, some will be absorbed. That which reaches the Earth's surface unimpeded is referred to as direct solar radiation. That which is scattered by the atmosphere is referred to as diffuse solar radiation. The combination of direct and diffuse is called global.

specific heat capacity
A measure of the amount of energy required to raise a unit mass or volume of a material through a unit temperature change ($kWh\ kg^{-1}K$, $J\ kg^{-1}K$, $kWh\ m^{-1}K$, $J\ m^{-3}K$).

specular reflectance
The proportion of incident luminous flux reflected from a polished surface.

standard test conditions
A set of accepted test conditions used by manufacturers of PV modules to specify a module's electrical output; the conditions are an irradiance of $1000\ W\ m^{-2}$ with a light spectrum of AM 1.5 and the PV cells maintained at 25°C.

storage efficiency
The percentage of solar energy input to the heat storage, subsequently used in the heat distribution system (i.e. excludes unwanted heat losses from the storage device) (%).

thermal conductance
The thermal transmittance through $1\ m^2$ of material of a given thickness for each 1 K temperature difference between its surfaces ($W\ m^{-2}K$).

thermal conductivity
The thermal transmission through a material 1-m-thick for each 1 K temperature difference ($W\ m^{-1}K$).

thermal mass
The mass of the building within the insulation, expressed per volume of heated space (kgm^{-3}). 'Primary thermal mass' receives direct sunlight; 'secondary thermal mass' is in sight of the primary thermal mass and so receives radiative and convective energy from the primary thermal mass; 'remote thermal mass' is hidden from view of both the primary and secondary thermal mass and so receives energy by convection only.

thermal resistance or R-value
The reciprocal of thermal conductance – see above ($m^2.K\ W^{-1}$).

thermal resistivity
The reciprocal of thermal conductivity ($m.K\ W^{-1}$).

thermal transmittance
The thermal transmission through $1\ m^2$ area of a given structure (e.g. a wall consisting of bricks, thermal insulation, cavities, etc.) divided by the difference between the environmental temperature on either side of the structure. Usually called 'U-value' ($W\ m^{-2}K$).

thermosiphon
The convective circulation of a fluid that occurs in a closed system where warm fluid rises and is replaced by a cooler fluid in the same system.

tilt
The angle of a plane relative to a horizontal plane.

TIM
Transparent insulation material.

thin-film silicon
A form of silicon as applied to a substrate, usually glass; atomic structure is amorphous.

tracking
The process of altering the tilt of a module throughout the day in order to face the sun and thus maximise the power output.

transmittance
The ratio of the radiant energy transmitted through a substance to the total radiant energy incident on its surface. In solar technology, it is always affected by the thickness and composition of the glass cover plates on a collector or window, and to a major extent by the angle of incidence between the sun's rays and a line normal to the surface.

ultraviolet radiation
Electromagnetic radiation having wavelengths shorter than visible light. This invisible form of radiation is found in solar radiation and plays a part in the deterioration of plastic glazings, paint and furnishing fabrics.

U-value
See 'thermal transmittance'.

vapour barrier
A component of a construction that is impervious to the flow of moisture and air and is used to prevent condensation in walls and other locations of insulation.

ventilation losses
The heat losses associated with the continuous replacement of warm, stale air by fresh cold air.

voltage
The electromotive force or electrical 'umph' that is available or being used in a circuit; units of volts or V; symbol V.

volumetric heat loss coefficient (G-value)
The total heat loss of a dwelling (through the fabric and ventilation), divided by the heated volume and the temperature differential at which the loss occurs ($W\,m^{-1}\,K$).

watershed
The land area that drains to a common outlet, such as the outflow of a lake, the mouth of a river or any point along a stream channel.

watt
Unit of power which is the rate of flow of energy, whether electrical, light or heat; definitions is $1\,W = 1\,J\,s^{-1}$; for electrical, also equals 1 VA.

watt hour
Convenient unit of energy corresponding to the use of 1 W for 1 hour; $1\,Wh = 3600\,J$, 860 calories or 3.41 Btu.

windspeed
The speed of the air measured in accordance with the recommendations of the World Meteorological Organization, normally measured 10 m above ground level.

wing wall
Vertical projection on one side of a window or wall used to increase or decrease the wind pressure or solar incidence on the wall or window.

zenith angle
The angular distance from the sun to the zenith, the point directly above the observer (at noon = latitude solar declination).

REFERENCES AND FURTHER READING

Allen, P. and Todd, B. (1995). *Off the Grid: Managing Electricity from Renewable Sources*. The Centre for Alternative Technology. E-mail: help@catinfo.demon.co.uk

Anderson, J. and Edwards, S. (2000). *Addendum to BRE methodology for environmental profiles of construction materials, components and buildings*. Building Research Establishment.

Andrews, A. (1997). *Nomad Tent Types in the Middle East*, Part 1, Vol. 2. Beihefte Zum Tubinger Atlas Des Vorderen Orients.

Anink, D., Chiel Boonstra, C. and Mak, J. (1996). *Handbook of Sustainable Building: An Environmental Preference Method for Selection of Materials for use in Construction and Refurbishment*. James and James, London.

Auliciems, A. and Szokolay, S. (1997). Thermal Comfort. University of Queensland Printery.

Bartsch, U. and Muller, B. (2000). *Fossil Fuels in a Changing Climate*. Oxford University Press.

Batey, M. and Pout, C. (2005). Delivered Energy Emission Factors for 2003. Building Establishment Note, accessed 28 August 2006 at www.bre.co.uk/ filelibrary/2003 EmissionFactorUpdate.pdf.

Beamon, S. and Roaf, S. (1990). *The Ice-houses of Britain*. Routledge, London.

Beaumont, P., Bonine, M. and McLachlan, K. (1989). *Qanat, Kariz & Khattara Traditional Water Systems in the Middle East and North Africa*. Menas Press Limited.

Berge, B (2000). *Ecology of building materials*. Architectural Press, Oxford.

Berman, A. J. (2001). *The Healthy Home Design Handbook*. Frances Lincoln, London.

Borer, P. and Harris, C. (1998). *The Whole House Book*. Cambrian Printers.

Building Research Establishment Digest (1980). Fire Hazards from Insulating Materials.

Building Research Establishment (2001). *Assessing the Effects of Thermal Bridging at Junctions and Around Openings*. IP17/01.

Carbon Vision Building Partnership (2006). Building Market Transformation First Year Report, accessed August 2006 at www.eci.ox.ac.uk/lowercf/pdfdownloads/ bmt-july06.pdf.

Carpenter, P. (1992). *Sod It*. Coventry University Press.

Centre for Alternative Technology (1995). *Save Energy, Save Money*.

Chambers, N., Simmons, C. and Wackernagel, M. (2000) *Sharing Nature's Interest: ecological footprints as an indicator of sustainability*. Earthscan Publications, London.

Chand, I. P., Bhargava, K. and Krishak, N. L. V. (1998). Effects of balconies on ventilation inducing aeromotive force on low rise buildings. *Building and Environment*, 33(6), November, 385–396.

Chartered Institution of Building Services Engineers (1998). *Energy Efficiency in Buildings*. CIBSE Guide. For more information contact CIBSE.

CIBSE (1987). Applications Manual: Window Design.

Cook, J. (1994). *Extreme climates and indigenous architecture*. Proceedings of the PLEA Conference, Dead Sea, published by Desert Architecture Unit, Ben-Gurion University of the Negev, Israel.

Cowper, A. (1998). *Lime and Lime Mortars*. Donhead.

Curtis, D. (1999). *Going with the Flow*. The Centre for Alternative Technology.

Curwell, S. and March, C. (1986). *Hazardous Building Materials*, A Guide to the Selection of Alternatives. E. & F. N. Spon, London.

Curwell, S., Fox, R. and March, C. (1988). *Use of CFCs in Buildings*. Fernsheer Limited.

Curwell, S., March, C. and Venables, R. (1990). *Buildings and Health*. The Rosehaugh Guide. RIBA Publications Limited, UK.

Day, C. (1990). *Building with Heart: A Practical Approach to Self and Community Building*. Green Books, Bideford.

Day, C. (1998). *A Haven for Childhood: The Building of a Steiner Kindergarten*. Starborn Books.

Day, C. (2003). *Places of the Soul: Architecture and Environmental Design as a Healing Art*. Architectural Press.

Day, C. (2004). Spirit and Place: *Healing our Environment*. Architectural Press.

Department of Civil and Systems Engineering (1978). *Design for Tropical Cyclones*, Volumes 1 and 2. James Cook University of North Queensland.

Dichler, A. (1994). *A review of the Technical merits of a proposed PV house in Oxfordshire*. ETSU S/02/00128/24. Energy Technology Support Unit, Harwell.

Diprose, P. (1999). *Architectural Implications of Sustainability on Built Form*. Ph.D. Thesis, Department of Architecture, University of Auckland, New Zealand.

Docherty, M. and Szokolay, S. (1999). Climate Analysis. PLEA Note 5. University of Queensland Printery.

Dommin, S. (1999). *A Hurricane Hunter's Photo Album*. http://www.members.aol.com/hotelq/page10.html

Dunn, G. E. and Miller, B. I. (1964). *Atlantic Hurricanes*. Louisiana State University Press, Baton Rouge, LA, 326 pp.

ECI (2000). *Lower Carbon Futures*. Environmental Change Institute, Oxford.

Energy Research Group (1999). *A Green Vitruvius*: Principles and Practice of Sustainable Architecture. James and James, London.

Energy Technology Support Unit (1996). S/P2/00240/REP. *A study into lifecycle environmental aspects of photovoltaics*.

Energy Technology Support Unit (2000). *Photovoltaics in Buildings Safety and the CDM Regulations*. ETSU Report No. S/P2/00313/REP. For more information contact BSRIA or e-mail: electrics@bsria.co.uk

Erell, E. and Tsoar, H. (1997). An experimental evaulation of strategies for reducing airborne dust in desert cities. *Building and Environment* 32(3), May, 225–236.

Farmer, J. (1999). *Green Shift*. Architectural Press.

Fawcett, T., Lane, K. and Boardman, B. (2000). *Lower Carbon Futures for European Households*. Environmental Change Institute, University of Oxford.

Galambos, T. V. (1990). *Making buildings safer for people: during hurricanes, earthquakes and fire*. van Nostrand Reinhold, New York.

Gipe, P. (1999). *Wind Energy Basics*. Chelsea Green Publishers.

Givoni, B. (1994). *Passive and Low Energy Cooling of Buildings*. Van Nostrand, New York.

Gleick, P. (1993). *Water in Crisis*. Oxford University Press, USA.

Hall, K. (ed.). (2006). *The Green Building Bible*, 3rd edition. Green Building Press.

Halliday, S. (2000). *Green Guide to the Architect's Job Book*. RIBA Publications, London.

Harris, R. (1995). The Thermal Performance of Timber Window Frames. *21AD: Offices*. Oxford Brookes University, School of Architecture Publication.

Headley, O. (2000). Renewable energy and the Small Island Developing States (SIDS): a case study of the Caribbean. *Proceedings of the TIA Conference*, Oxford. TIA, Oxford Brookes University.

Herschong, L. (1979). *Thermal delight in Architecture*. The MIT Press, Cambridge, Mass.

Hestnes, A., Hastings, R. and Saxhof, B. (1997). *Solar Energy Houses, Strategies, Technologies, Examples*. James and James, London, pp. 31–34.

Holland, G. J. (1993): 'Ready reckoner'. Chapter 9, *Global Guide to Tropical Cyclone Forecasting*. WMO/TC-No. 560, Report No. TCP-31. World Meteorological Organization; Geneva, Switzerland.

Houghton, J., Jenkins, G. and Ephraums, J. (eds) (1990). *Climate Change: The Intergovernmental Panel on Climate Change Assessment*. Cambridge University Press, Cambridge.

Howard, N., Edwards, S. and Anderson, J. (1991). *BRE methodology for environmental profiles of construction materials, components and buildings*. Building Research Establishment, ISBN 1860812945.

Howe, J. and Viljoen (2005). *Continuous Productive Urban Landscapes: Designing Urban Agriculture for Sustainable Cities*. Architectural Press.

Humphreys, M. (1995). Thermal Comfort and the Habits of Hobbits, in Nicol et al., *Standards for Thermal Comfort*, Spin, London.

Humphreys, M. A. (1978). Field studies of thermal comfort compared and applied. *J. Inst. Heat. & Vent. Eng.* 44, 5–27.

Humpreys, M. A. and Nicol, J. F. (2000) Outdoor temperature and indoor thermal comfort: raising the precision of the relationship for the 1998 ASHRAE database of field studies *ASHRAE Transactions* 206(2), 485–492.

Hyde, R. (2007). *Bioclimatic Housing: Innovative Designs for Warm Climates*. Earthscan Publications.

Jonsson, A. (2000). Tools and methods for environmental assessment of building products. *Building and Environment*, 35(3), 223–238.

Kachadorian, J. (1997). *The Passive Solar House*. Chelsea Green Publishers.

Kieran, S. and Timberlake, J. (2004). *Refabricating Architecture: How Manufacturing Methodologies are Poised to Transform Building Construction*. McGraw-Hill Companies Inc.

Kindangen, J., Krauss, G. and Depecker, P. (1997). Effects of windshapes on wind-induced air motion inside buildings. *Building and Environment* 32(1), Jan., 1–14.

King, S., Rudder, D., Prasad, D. and Ballinger, J. (1996). *Site Planning in Australia*. Australian Government Publishing Service, Sydney.

Kirbay, T. and Piggot, H. (2000). *Windpower Workshop*. Centre for Alternative Technology Publications.

Krishan, A. (1995). *Climatically Responsive Energy Efficient Architecture – a Design Handbook*. 1. Department of Planning at Delhi University, Delhi.

Krishan, A., Yannas, S., Baker, N. and Szokolay, S. (2001). *Climate Responsive Architecture*, McGraw-Hill Publishing Co., Delhi.

Kruse, C. (2004). *Climate change and the construction sector*. International Investors Group on Climate Change (IIGCC) briefing note.

Kukadia, V. (1997). *Ventilation and Air Pollution: Buildings Located in Urban and City Centres*. Building Research Establishment Limited.

Kwok, A. and Grondzik, W. (2006). *The Green Studio Handbook*. Architectural Press.

Langley and Curtis (2004). *Going with the Flow: Small Scale water power*, CAT Publications (available mail order: 01654 705959 or via www.ecobooks.co.uk).

Laughton, C. (2006). *Tapping the Sun: A Solar Water Heating Guide*, 5th edition. Centre for Alternative Technology Publications.

Law, B. (2005). *The Woodland House*, Permanent Publications.

Lawson, B. (1996). Building Materials, Energy and the Environment. Royal Australian Institute of Architects, Canberra, Australia.

Le Corbusier (1924). *Une Petite Maison*. Le Corbusier Aux Editions d'Architecture, Zurich.

Lechner, N. (2001). Heating, Cooling, Lighting: Design, Methods for Architects. John Wiley and Sons.

Lee, K., Han, D. and Lim, H. (1994). Evaluation of the thermal performance of traditional house in Ullungdo, Korea. *Proceedings of the PLEA Conference*, Dead Sea, Israel.

Lippsmeier, G. (1980). *Tropenbau, Building in the Tropics*. Verlag Callwey, Munich.

Lynes, J. (1992). Daylight and energy. In *Energy Efficient Building: A Design Guide*. Eds S. Roaf and M. Hancock. Blackwells Scientific Publications Ltd.

Macher, J. (ed.) (1999). *Bioaerosols: Assessment and Control*. American Conference of Governmental Industrial Hygienists (ACGIH), Cincinnati, Ohio.

Macks, (1978). *Design for Tropical Cyclones*.

Majoros, A. (1998). *Daylighting. PLEA Note 4*. The University of Queensland Printery.

Markham, S. F. (1982). *Climate and the Energy of Nations*. AMS Press, New York. First published in c. 1947.

Mathews, E. (1997). *Building and Environment*, 32(1).

Matthews, J. (2000). The Havelis of Jaiselmer. Ph.D. Thesis. East London University.

Mazria, E. (1979). *The Passive Solar Energy Book*. Rodale Press, Emmaus, PA, USA.

McCann, J. (2004). *Clay and Cob Building*. Shire Publications.

McHarg, I. (1971). *Design With Nature*. Doubleday & Company Inc.

Mould, A. (1992). 'Designing effective insulation'. In Roaf, S. and Hancock, M. (eds), *Energy Efficient Building: A Design Guide*. Blackwell Scientific Publications, pp. 145–174.

National Asthma Campaign, UK (1997). *Asthma in Daily Life*. Website: http://www.asthma.org.uk

National House Building Council (1998). *Sustainable Housing – Meeting the Challenge*. NHBC Annual Conference. For more information contact the HSBC or see: http://www.nhbc.co.uk

Neumann, C. J. (1993). Global Overview. *Global Guide to Tropical Cyclone Forecasting*. WMO/TC-No. 560, Report No. TCP-31. World Meteorological Organization, Geneva, Switzerland.

Nicol, J. F., Jamy, G. N., Sykes, O. et al. (1994). *A Survey of Thermal Comfort in Pakistan toward New Indoor Temperature Standards*. Oxford Brookes University, Oxford, UK.

Nowak, A. S. and Galambos, T. V. (eds) (1990). *Making Buildings Safer for People*. Van Norstrand, New York.

Oliver, P. (1997). *Encyclopedia of Vernacular Architecture of the World*. Cambridge University Press, Cambridge.

Olivier, D. (1992). *Energy Efficiency and Renewables: Recent Experience on Mainland Europe*. ISBN 0-9518791-0-3. Energy Advisory Associates.

Olivier, D. (2000). Plugging the air leaks. *Building for a Future*, Journal of the Association for Environment Conscious Builders, 9(4), 16–17. AECB.

Oreszczyn, T. (1992). Insulating the existing housing stock: mould growth and cold bridging. In Roaf, S. and Hancock, M. (eds), *Energy Efficient Building: A Design Guide*. Blackwell Scientific Publications, pp. 174–189.

Oreszczyn, T. (2000). Mould index. In, Rudge, J. and Nicol, F. (eds), *Cutting the Cost of Cold*. E. & F. N. Spon, London, pp. 122–133.

Oreszczyn, T. and Littler, J. (1989). *Cold Bridging and Mould Growth*. Final Report to the Science and Engineering Research Council by the Research in Buildings Group at Westminster University, London.

Pearson, S., Wheldon, A., Hadley, P., Awabi, N. and Parker, A. (1994). The Effects of Plants on the Environment in Non-Domestic Buildings. Report for the Building Research Establishment, Reading University, UK.

Piani, C. B. (1998). *Novel, Easy to Use Energy Saving Guidelines for South Africa*. Ph.D. Thesis, Department of Mechanical Engineering, University of Pretoria, South Africa.

Pitts, G. (1989). *Energy Efficient Housing – A Timber Frame Approach*. TRADA, ISBN, 0-901348-79-1.

Pitts, G. (2000). *Timber Frame: Re-engineering for Affordable Housing*. TRADA Technology Report 2/2000. ISBN 1900510251.

Pullen, S. F. Energy used in construction and operation of houses. *Architectural Science Review*, Vol. **43**, No. 2, June 2000, 87–94.

Quirouette, R. L. and Warnock, A. C. C. *Basics of Noise*. Building science Insight website by the National Research Council of Canada. www.nrc.ca/irc/bsi/85.1_E.html

Rappaport, E. (1993). Preliminary Report 10 December 1993. National Hurricane Centre.

Rawlings, R. H. D. (1999). Ground Source Heat Pumps (TN 18/99). BSRIA.

Reinberg, G. W. (1996). About the language of solar architecture. *Proceedings of 4th International Conference on Solar Energy in Architecture and Urban Design*. Berlin, pp. 108–111.

Ricklefs, R. E. and Miller, G. L. (1999). *Ecology*. 4th Edition, W. H. Freeman and Co., New York.

Roaf, S. (1979). *A Study of the Architecture of the Black Tents of the Lurs*. Diploma Thesis at the Architectural Association, London.

Roaf, S. and Hancock, M. (1992). *Energy Efficient Building*. Blackwell Scientific Publications.

Roaf, S , Horsley, A. and Guptal, R. (2004). *Closing the Loop: Benchmarking for Sustainable Buildings*, London, RIBA Publications.

Roaf, S. Crichton, D. and Nicol, F. (2005). Adapting Buildings, and Cities for Climate Change. Architectural Press.

Rose, J., Sun, G., Gerba, C. and Sinclair, N. (1991). 'Microbial quality and persistence of enteric pathogens in greywater from various household sources'. *Water Research*, 25 (1), 37–42.

Rudge, J. and Nicol, F. (2000). *Cutting the Cost of Cold*. E. & F. N. Spon.

Sandifer S. (2000). Thermal effects of vines on wall surfaces. *Proceedings of the TIA Conference*, Oxford. Contact e-mail: sandifer@ucla.edu

Santamouris, M. and Asimakopoulos, D. (eds) (1996). *Passive Cooling of Buildings*. James & James Ltd, London.

Schaeffer, J. et al. (1994). *Solar Living Source Book*. Chelsea Green Publishing Company, White River Junction, VT.

Seymour, J. and Girardet, H. (1987). *Blueprint for a Green Planet*. Dorling Kindersley Limited.

Snell, C. and Callahan, T. (2005). *Building Green: a complete how-to guide to alternative building methods*. Chelsea Green Publishers.

Stephens, H. (1996). *Solar Energy in Architecture and Urban Planning*. H. S. Stephens and Associates.

Strong, S. and Scheller, W. (1993). *The Solar Electric House*. Sustainability Press.

Szokolay, S. (2003). *Introduction to Architectural Science*. Architectural Press.

Talbott, J. (1993). *Simply Build Green*. Findhorn Press, Scotland.

Thomas, H. R. and Rees, S. W. (1999). The thermal performance of ground floor slabs – a full-scale in-situ experiment. *Building and Environment* 34(2), 139–164.

Trimby, P. (1999). *Solar Water Heating a D-I-Y Guide*. The Centre for Alternative Technology.

U.S. Protection Agency. *A Citizen's Guide to Radon*. OPA-86-004.

Vale, B. and Vale, R. (2000). *The New Autonomous House*. Thames and Hudson Limited.

Viljoen, A. (1997). *The Environmental Impact of Energy Efficient Dwellings, Taking into Account Embodied Energy and Energy in Use*. European Directory of Sustainable and Energy Efficient Building 1997; James and James, London, pp. 47–52.

Warm, P. (1997). Optimum thickness of insulation. In *Building for a Future*, Journal of the Association for Energy Conscious Builders, 7(3), 11. Tel. and Fax: +44 1559 370908, e-mail: admin@aecb.net, http://www.aecb.net

Warm, P. (1998). 'Reflective, thin insulations'. In *Building for a Future*, Journal of the Association for Energy Conscious Builders, 8(2), 48–49.

Wells, M. (1982). *Gentle Architecture*. McGraw-Hill, New York.

Were, J. (1992). Air is stupid (it can't follow the arrows). *Proceedings of the PLEA Conference*, Auckland, 1992 (in press with Steven Szokolay).

Williamson, A. G. (1997). *Energy Efficiency in Domestic Buildings, a Literature Review and Commentary*. Ministry of Commerce, New Zealand.

Woolley, T., Kimmins, S., Harrison, P. and Harrison, R. (1997). *Green Building Handbook*. E & F N Spon, London ISBN 0 419 22690 7.

WWF (2002) Living Planet Report, 2002. http://www.panda.org/living-planet/lpr02/

Yannas, S. (1994). *Solar Energy and Housing Design*, Volume 1. E. G. Bond Limited.

Yannas, S. (1994). *Solar Energy and Housing Design*, Volume 2. E. G. Bond Limited.

Yates, A., Brownhill, D. and Howard, N. (2000). *EcoHomes The Environmental Rating for Homes*. Construction Research Communications Limited. A BRE Publication.

Zold, A. and Szokolay, S. (1997). *Thermal Insulation*. PLAE Note 2. University of Queensland Printery (for a copy, contact: s.szokolay@mailbox.uq.edu.au).

USEFUL WEB ADDRESSES

Ecohousing

www.bioregional.co.uk – developments like Bedzed and more on 'one-planet living'.

www.brithdirmawr.com – a collective ecovillage in Wales.

www.cat.org.uk – Centre for Alternative Technology site.

www.dwellwell.org – lots on affordable homes and communities.

www.ecovillagefindhorn.org – Findhorn centre with courses and publications.

www.hockerton.demon.co.uk – lots on ecovillages and courses to take.

www.permaculture.co.uk/ – permaculture magazine and related publications.

www.theyellowhouse.org.uk – eco-refurbishment of a terraced house.

Climate change

http://climatechange.unep.net/

http://www.aip.org/history/sloan/gcm/1965_75.html

http://www.ukcip.org.uk

http://www.ipcc.ch/

https://www.nas.nasa.gov/About/Education/Ozone/history.html

http://www.theozonehole.com

http://unfccc.int/index.html

http://www.gci.org.uk

CONVERSION FACTORS by Andrew Bairstow

$1\,m^2 = 11\,feet^2$

$1\,cm = 0.39\,inches$

$1\,m^3 = 35\,feet^3$

$1\,km\,h^{-1} = 0.62\,miles\,h^{-1}$

$1°C$ change $= 1.8°F$ change

$0°C = 32°F$

$1\,l = 0\,22\,gal$

INDEX